D1000767

THE AGED
IN
AMERICAN SOCIETY

JOSEPH T. DRAKE

PROFESSOR OF SOCIOLOGY

DAVIDSON COLLEGE

THE RONALD PRESS COMPANY > NEW YORK

Copyright, ©, 1958, by

THE RONALD PRESS COMPANY

All Rights Reserved

The text of this publication or any part
thereof may not be reproduced in any
manner whatsoever without permission in
writing from the publisher.

HQ
1064
.U5
D7

Library of Congress Catalog Card Number: 58–5642

PRINTED IN THE UNITED STATES OF AMERICA

Preface

This book is designed as a college text book for courses in gerontology and geriatrics, as a supplementary textbook for courses on population, social problems, and social legislation, and as an up-to-date survey for all who are concerned with the problems of the aged. As such, an effort has been made to place the material in a sociological framework without making it unintelligible to the student not versed in sociology. An even more rigorous effort was made to select and interpret the data and information in an objective, scientific manner.

The increase in both number and proportion of the population sixty-five years of age and over during the past half century has not been matched by the growth of scientific knowledge of this segment of society. Although some studies pertaining to gerontology were made prior to World War II, most of the scientifically oriented research has been conducted only since that time. And, as in any emergent science, much of this scientific study of the phenomena of old age has been concentrated on limited aspects of the topic. Thus while our knowledge of the subject has been expanded, it has become increasingly difficult to select for study material that provides an adequate coverage of the entire subject. The purpose of this book is to bring together under one cover information and data from many sources on all the pertinent aspects of gerontology.

The book is divided into five major parts. Part I analyzes the sociocultural environment in which the aged in modern America live. This analysis helps to explain some of the current attitudes held by society about older people in terms of our cultural heritage. Part II views the older worker and job seeker in terms of potentialities for continuing employ-

iii

Alma College Library
Alma, Michigan

ment or re-employment against the background of belief and practices formulated in an era when this country had a younger population. Part III investigates the various sources of income which have been provided by the federal government, local governments, and private industry for retired workers and their dependents. Part IV seeks to understand the older person as a physical, psychological, and social entity rather than a social statistic. Part V discusses some of the efforts being made by society to help older people continue as functioning individuals—to add life to their years rather than only years to their lives. This part serves as an indication of society's increasing awareness that money alone will not solve the problems pertaining to the aged population.

While this book provides a general, comprehensive coverage of the aged in society, it is often necessary to emphasize the importance of economic factors. It is not the author's belief, of course, that adequate income is the solution to all the problems of the aged population. Obviously, money will not buy happiness or contentment. But it will help pay for proper food, medical care, housing, and other material comforts which are necessary for an adequate standard of living. Those who are not able to buy the necessities of life, or those who fear that they will not be able to, are more often unhappy than are those who have few financial worries.

The author is grateful to the many writers and their publishers for ideas and data which were used. Footnotes assign credit insofar as it is possible to do so. The rather extensive, but by no means complete, bibliography lists most of the materials which were read before and during the preparation of the manuscript.

Grateful acknowledgment is given to my wife, Grace, who bore with me during the seemingly unending days of work on the manuscript; to the Library Staff at the University of Tennessee, especially to Miss Eleanor Goehring, Miss Helen M. Hier, and Mrs. Jo Ann Headrick; to students in the course on "The Aged" who offered suggestions and criticisms of mimeographed sections of the manuscript while it was being used in class; to Mrs. Jeanne Martin who read the manuscript and offered constructive criticisms; and finally, but not least, to Dr. William E. Cole for his continued interest and encouragement.

Joseph T. Drake

Davidson, North Carolina
    January, 1958

Contents

Part I
Adjustment of the Aged to Societies

Part II
Labor Force Status of the Aged

Part III
Meeting Economic Needs

Part IV
Characteristics of the Aging

Part V
Society and Its Aging Population

Tables

Part I

ADJUSTMENT OF THE AGED TO SOCIETIES

1

Introduction

This book is devoted to a study of the aged in American society. Until recent years this portion of our population has been neglected as a topic of study, even though other segments have been the center of exhaustive surveys and have received much attention from social workers, socially conscious individuals in many walks of life, as well as scientists and lawmakers. Children and young people, the working population, married couples, members of racial or ethnic minorities, and many other groups have been carefully studied. Not so the aged.

The aged in American society

From the point of view of the sociologist, whose concern is the study of human society, there are some possible explanations for the neglect of the aged as a special topic of study. First, it has been only recently that this category of people has composed an appreciable percentage of the total population of this country. Even now, in the total world population, the aged are of little statistical importance. Second, it will be noted that the categories which have come into the public eye for study are primarily those which seem to constitute problems in American society. They are considered social problems because of their status positions. Children and young people, women, and members of social minority or ethnic groups have been stereotyped by the dominant members of society. They are believed to possess certain unalterable characteristics by reason of their status position which render them incapable of changing their positions in society. This categorization has put these groups at a social disadvantage in comparison to others. There

3

has been the feeling that society should do something to help these "unfortunate" or "underprivileged" people. At least it is felt that something should be done to ameliorate some of the less desirable conditions under which these people live and through which they compete for their share of the good things of life.

It follows then that social categories of people who apparently get along well in society and do not present a problem to society are neglected as subjects of study. There seems to be no value in studying people or groups of people who are not problems. Until the years immediately prior to the Great Depression in this country, the aged were not considered a problem sufficient in extent to merit much study. They were relatively few in number. They constituted less than 4 per cent of the total population. Traditionally, each family was responsible for its own indigent aged. At the same time, it was believed there should be no indigent aged because everyone was supposed to be able to prepare for his own old age while he was still in the productive years of life. This idea has been one of the strongest social myths built up regarding our economic order. Any exception to the idea that adults could provide their own economic security could be explained in terms of lack of diligence, lack of will power to work or save, or just plain improvidence or laziness. The implication of these explanations was that if a person reached old age and was not in a position to take care of himself it was his own fault. Some people with a more generous turn of mind blamed this inability on bad luck or God's will, depending upon their social-religious orientation.

With the coming of the Depression a change began to take place in the thinking of those who were interested in social problems. They noted the rapid increase in the number of the aged in the population as well as the relative growth of the percentage of the aged. Note was also made of the fact that many of these older people were not provided for economically by their own savings or by relatives or charitable organizations which previously had been able to take care of the indigent aged. Many of the aged could not find work, and it was believed those who did were keeping younger adults out of work. Adult children could not support their parents because they had their own children to support. Finally, public and private charitable organizations were unprepared to meet the heavy demands placed upon them for the support of people who were in financial distress.

During the Depression the first concern for the older people was their financial standing. This was met on the state-federal level by old-age assistance and on the federal level by the old-age and survivors insurance program. The old-age and survivors insurance program (OASI), as will be indicated in a later chapter, was designed as a long-term program partially to meet the needs of the older workers who retired. In studying the financial needs of the aged, it was necessary to study the population distribution of the aged. Demographers became more interested in the aged as a population category. Old people, like any other segment of the population, are not merely statistics, so the social studies became interested in the aged as individuals. Questions were asked, some of which still need to be answered. When is a person old? What makes a person old? Is a person old at 65? What are some of the physical, mental, social, economic, and employment characteristics of old people which distinguish them from people of younger years?

From the point of view of the sociologist one fact began to emerge from these studies. This was that many older people are in effect "men without a country." In other words, there is a sparsity of socially necessary and socially meaningful status positions and roles for older people to occupy and play. True, there have always been some old people in every society with a number of jobs or status positions for them to occupy. The number of such socially defined and meaningful status positions in our society, however, began to be exceeded by the number of older people who were capable of filling these positions. As a consequence there is an ever-increasing number of statusless and roleless older people. The implication is that there is no place in our society for as many old people as the society contains or that our society has not been able to or has merely failed to provide adequately for a meaningful life for perhaps the majority of people after they have reached chronological old age. Hence, one of the questions which is now being raised is this: Can society create status positions for its older members? Can society find something for the aged to do which will provide them with a life which is meaningful, so that their later years will bring them rewards just as their earlier years are supposed to have done?

The status position of the aged

Over the years since society first became established, most social groupings have decreed that individuals should be prepared by society and should prepare themselves in the early years of life for the status positions which they will assume in young adulthood, middle age, and the older adult years. Almost if not all of the productive work necessary for the continuity of society has been the function of people occupying these three subdivisions of the adult years. As a matter of simple expediency nothing of great social importance has been relegated to the aged. This has been true because in early society, as well as in most pre-industrial societies existing today, there have been few people who, according to chronological measurements, have lived to old age. If societies had left certain important jobs to be done or socially meaningful status positions to be filled only by old people, and if there had been no old people or too few to do this work, the work would not have been done. Consequently the society so organized would not have functioned properly.

This hypothesis then raises an interesting question. If there are old people in such a society, in what way will the society give them a meaningful part to play or a meaningful packet of status positions? Or, failing this, will society simply relegate them to a "statusless" status and "roleless" role, allowing them to be shelved to live out their lives as extra, nonuseful members of society, being mistreated, ignored, or to be gotten rid of at the earliest possible time?

An alternate solution to this problem is an outgrowth of preliterate society; that is, people are not considered old merely because of an excessive number of years. People in some societies of this type gradually moved from one status position to another, much as they had moved from one to a succeeding status position in youth, adulthood, and older adulthood. If an individual was underfunctioning in one position he would be promoted to a more demanding position where his talents could be put to better use. For instance, if a person at the age of twelve was a good shepherd he would not necessarily be a good warrior. At the age of twenty this same person would presumably be a good warrior but a waste to society if he were retained in a status position which could be filled adequately by a lad in his early teens. At the other end of the scale of years a person forty-five years of age might not function adequately as a warrior but might fill the position of organizer or general or member of a war council, drawing upon his previous experiences and knowledge of warfare so as to direct the active fighting of the younger men. When his mind became less alert or in the event that he became too cautious to direct others in warfare, his position would be changed from member of the war council to that of a person who repaired the implements of war or manufactured them.

Our modern armed forces reflect somewhat this same assignment of status positions. As the physical demands of a person's military status position becomes less exacting, the age limits for entrance into or retention in these positions is extended. Officers are accepted as general officers at a later period in life than are field officers. Company officers, while younger than field officers, can be much older than enlisted men or draftees. After retirement, the more prominent officers, especially those of general grades, have been employed by industry, government, or educational institutions where presumably their active military service, or the knowledge which they have acquired, serves them in the nonmilitary status position.

Other societies such as China put much value on the status of old age. This was accomplished by arbitrarily attributing to old people, as such, the most important position in society. This was a socially contrived trick which in effect said that a position occupied by an older person was of great social importance merely because the person occupying it was old. Positions occupied by younger persons were important only as they contributed to the adequacy of the person to function in the position he would occupy when he became old. As a consequence, in Chinese society, old age was the most important part of life and everyone aspired to it. Conversely, old age in other societies was less attractive because the status positions left open to be occupied solely by old persons became less socially significant and less meaningful.

Roughly classified then, modern society has three broadly defined choices in dealing with its older citizens. First, they can be retired, put on the shelf, put out to pasture, or deprived of any meaningful role after they reach chronological old age. Second, progressively they can occupy less demanding status positions as their faculties begin to be exhausted, albeit these successive positions need not necessarily be occupied only by old people. If younger people also occupy these positions, they will not be classified as status positions for the aged. When this occurs, theoretically there will be no stigma attached to any status position as being an old man's job, or a job fit only for those unfitted by age to perform elsewhere. Third, the values of society can be manipulated by society so that any position occupied by old people will come to be of social significance. As a matter of fact, the now relatively "statusless" position of retiree could attain such importance and prestige by manipulation that it might replace employment in the minds of individuals as being the ultimate to be desired in life. By taking on added functions the status position of grandparent, which is now relatively meaningless, could completely replace the social role of parent and consequently leave the biological function as the only role of the status position of parent. If this were done the grandparent status would be more socially meaningful than it is now and at least as meaningful as social parenthood is at present.

There is no law of nature and no universal social law which demands that old people receive the same treatment in different times and places. The kind of treatment they do receive is determined largely by the values of the society at any particular time and to some extent by the condition of the old people. The values which society holds toward its old people are partially the result (or it might be argued the other way) of the stereotypes society has of old people. More correctly perhaps it may be that the values and stereotypes tend to reinforce each other. Together these two factors set up what has been called the "self-fulfilling prophecy." Society pictures old people as being unable to do productive work. It then refuses to hire them after they reach the age of 65. After this is done, younger members of the society look around them and find that only a small proportion of people over 65 are employed. It is then concluded that people over 65 are unemployable or else there would not be so many unemployed people over that age.

The years beyond the age of 65 could be just as important and meaningful as those prior to 65 generally are. People past 65 are similar to those under 65 in one important way. Everyone, regardless of his age, is a product of his heredity and his physical, cultural, and social environment. Personality is the product of interaction in group life and the personality an individual takes with him into old age is the product of this interaction, as much as was his personality prior to that age. Where there is a difference in the characteristics of the persons in this age category it does not lie with the age of the person alone. It lies also in the way in which society views these people. If society treats people 55–64 years of age differently from the way it treats people 65–69, then those in the older level will begin to react in a different way than those in the younger level. True, the mere physical difference between people in these two levels may be the grounds for some of the differential treatment, but by no means all of it. If the reaction to differential treatment results, then the older age group will act in a different way which will further tend to mark them as being different. In this manner the attitude of society will have been reinforced in regard to the older people.

What is old age?

It is becoming increasingly important for society to recognize that old age can be measured by norms other than the number of birthdays. This is the easiest way of measuring old age, but for some purposes it is the least satisfactory way. Closely related in the minds of many people to chronological age is physiological age. This age, instead of being measured by the calendar, is measured by the rate of physical development, maturation, and subsequent decay of the organs of the body. It is a truism that no two people age at the same rate, and it is questionable whether any two organs within the same body age at the same rate. A person's age can be measured intellectually by noting the decline in the ability to learn new ideas or to retain those which he has learned. Intellectual age can also be measured by the ability to grasp new thoughts and assimilate new ideas.

Finally, a person's age can be measured sociologically. This is perhaps the most subjective of all the measures of age. Social old age begins at some time during the later life of the individual. When he is sociologically old, there are certain physical, mental, and psychological characteristics manifest in his behavior pattern. These behavior patterns are largely determined by his prior interactions and the way he thinks other people think about him. It should be noted, however, that these ways of measuring old age do not exhaust all of the possible ways in which it can be measured.

Recent research shows rather conclusively that people beyond the age of 65 rarely think of themselves as old or so classify themselves. This is a characteristic which is also associated with other age categories. It is only when people in their later years have their chronological age forcefully brought to their attention that they begin to think of themselves as being old. This can occur if they hear others call them old and treat them as though they were infirm. It may occur when they are retired and cannot find further employment, or it may occur when their health becomes impaired by any of the infirmities generally associated with old age, such as loss of hearing or sight, heart attacks, high blood pressure, and similar disabilities.

Summary

The extent to which our older citizens are a "problem" segment of the total population depends upon the values which society holds in regard to these people. Insofar as they do constitute a problem, it can be "solved" or ameliorative action can be taken by both the total society and the individuals who are classified as being old. Society's first step is to revise its stereotyped ideas to conform more closely to reality. The individuals involved can do much to help revise some of the false ideas held toward them. This can be done on the individual level by each person preparing for his own old age economically, socially, physically, and psychologically. To be successful, this process of preparation must start in early life. When it is carried out systematically and with the help of experts, the older individual continues to function as a normal part of society and is not a problem to himself nor to society. With a changed and realistic attitude toward people who are chronologically old, society accepts these people as an integral and important segment of the total population.

2

Status of the Aged
in Agrarian-Oriented Societies

A great deal of what we have and what we are is determined by what our human ancestors had and were. It is therefore fitting that this study of the aged in American society in the mid-twentieth century begin with a glance backward to see how the aged have fared in other societies and other times. Immediately the thought arises that human relationships are governed by folkways and mores which have been developed by individuals living in societies. The way in which the members of a society treat the aged is governed by the folkways and mores or customs of the society. Folkways and mores governing human relationships vary from time to time and place to place. They differ because of different historical origins, different geographical environments, different types of family organization, religion, and economic and political organizations. The aged, as the conservers of tradition, have encouraged the belief that a person should honor his father and mother, and that in so doing he in turn would be blessed. Being old, the parents were in a position to exercise power over their children. Obviously the aged would soon die, but it was believed that after death they might return to punish their children or the entire society for having been insubordinate.

In nonliterate and rural-agrarian societies life generally has been hazardous. Some nonliterate peoples believe there is no such thing as a "natural" death from old age. If children and adults escape violent death and live to old age they die or are killed by evil spirits or because magic is practiced upon them by their enemies, not because of old age per se.

12

In societies where the life expectancy is 30 years or less, there are few old people. This is true even if the chronological aspect of age is discounted. In nonliterate societies exact ages are not known; hence, people are classified as old when they are unable to function as younger adults do. Even if chronological age is disregarded it seems probable that the percentage of functionally (or organically) aged in nonliterate and rural-agrarian societies would constitute from 1 to 3 per cent of the population. When birthdays and not the ability to function are used as a measure of old age, there are relatively few chronologically old people in nonliterate societies.

As late as 1948 in India only 2.2 per cent of the population was 65 years of age and over, in Mexico only 2.9 per cent, and in Brazil 2.5 per cent. At the turn of the century in the United States only 4.1 per cent of the population was in the aged category.[1] The aged are not a problem in most nonindustrial societies because there are so few of them. Further, they would not be a problem precisely because the societies are nonindustrial. Little in the culture of nonindustrial societies tends to increase the percentage of the aged. When the percentage does increase, as it usually does when modern medical practices are introduced, the aged may then become a problem.

The aged in nonliterate societies

The role of the aged in nonliterate societies is the function of four variables: [2] (1) the individual who is involved, or the personal characteristics of the old person; (2) the kinship relations of the society or tribe in which he lives; (3) the economic or other contributions the aged make to the welfare of the society; and (4) the total configuration or pattern of culture of the society. There is nothing in old age alone which demands respectful and kind treatment on

[1] T. Lynn Smith, "The Aged in Rural Society," in Milton Derber (ed.), *The Aged and Society* (Champaign: Industrial Relations Research Society, 1950), p. 41.

[2] Leo Simmons, *The Role of the Aged in Primitive Societies* (New Haven: Yale University Press, 1945), pp. 205–10.

the part of the young toward the aged. Old people in seventy-one tribes which were studied could enhance their own status within the framework of the social order. In so doing they were often taking out for themselves the primitive equivalents of social security: health, life, old age, and burial insurance. The techniques old people used to obtain security were numerous. These methods varied among individuals, along sex lines, and from tribe to tribe. These methods can be classified as follows.

First, the older members repeated folklore and mythology to the younger members of the tribe. The heroes of these stories were often old as were the storytellers themselves. The heroes were represented as having invented and introduced new and useful traits into the culture. These traits included dances, songs, hunting techniques or religious rituals. The themes of some of the stories centered around ill fortune brought upon the tribe or individuals as a result of unkind or unsympathetic treatment of the aged. These stories were intended to elevate the prestige of the teller because of the telling itself and because of the moral involved in the story. Storytelling was also a form of entertainment just as was singing or dancing. Besides telling stories for tribal entertainment, the elders taught songs, stories, and dances to selected members of the tribe so that tribal lore would not be lost.

The acquisition of property or capital was another way to insure security in old age. The amount and kind of property to be acquired depended upon the nature of the tribal economy. As a general rule, women in the hunting, gathering, and fishing societies could acquire property. Women were not so successful in the patriarchal tribes which were largely agricultural or herding in nature. Land, flocks and herds, boats, homes, and family treasures were among the items which the aged could own. Where the older people owned property they would not make the mistake of disposing of it until the last possible minute. Too early disposal of property would surely have left some of them at a disadvantage.

A third and related way of maintaining economic and social security was by marrying a much younger person who could work for the older person. Where this was the practice older men often selected their wives from the younger age groups, leaving only widows for the younger men to marry. A circumstance such as this, occurring more frequently in established patriarchal societies, would indicate the strong position of the elderly males in the cultural framework. It was a frequent occurrence for older women in the matri-archal societies to marry younger men, thus maintaining for themselves security in old age. First wives would encourage their husbands to marry again so that some of the burden of housekeeping and other tasks could be passed on to the younger second or third wives. The practice of taking younger mates might also serve a secondary purpose. The aged would be related to the younger generation both by lines of descent and by the bonds of matrimony. This dual tie would bind the two generations together more securely, thus giving the aged more assurance of care and respect in their later years.

A fourth method used by the aged to gain security was to contribute to the economic and social welfare of the tribe. In any society there are tasks which have to be done. Some of these tasks can just as well be done by the aged as by the younger adults. Depending upon the economic organization, old people can fish, clean game, make items for household use, tend garden plots, or herd animals in pasture. Such activities release younger adults for more strenuous work. Old women can baby-sit, attend women at the birth of children, and otherwise make themselves useful in the life processes.

Fifth, the aged maintained their status in the community by making civic and political contributions. It is important to note that the status of the aged in this area of life depended upon their position before attaining old age. Men were more often found in positions of political authority than were women. Older people in positions of authority were allowed to keep their place in the social order as long as they functioned to the satisfaction of the tribal members. If the person could not demonstrate an ability to serve, he would no longer keep his position. Old age by itself, with no other qualifications, was not enough to guarantee individuals positions of importance in any society. They had to continue to function satisfactorily.

Among the Balinese there was a specific formula which had to be applied before an older person could become a member of the council or executive committee.[3] Selection of the council was more on the basis of ascribed than achieved status. Hard work, capital goods, religious interest or administrative ability, bravery, hunting prowess or "push" were not taken into consideration. Potentially every male could become head man, but he ascended the ladder only as those ahead of him were disqualified. Disqualification occurred, for instance, if a person did not have both a son and a daughter. If a man's wife died, or if the person became diseased or permanently injured he lost his position. However, if a person did manage to become one of the head men, he was considered somewhat sacred presumably because he was able to overcome the odds against becoming head man. Head men enjoyed high prestige in the society, but they had to perform their executive activities in such a way as to maintain good public relations.

In a New Guinea tribe an old person was given prestige not because of age but because he had occupied an outstanding position while he was young. Old men in this tribe had authority because they had had authority when they were young. The aged had no rank or title to attend their age. When they were no longer capable of maintaining their authority they lost it and became relatively insignificant in the life of the tribe.

It might be asked what the aged accomplish by all this manipulation. What was the point of it all? The answer was the same for them as it is in our society. It was by

[3] Gregory Bateson, "Cultural Ideas About Aging," in Harold E. Jones (ed.), *Research on Aging* (New York: Social Science Research Council, 1950), pp. 49–54.

these means that they achieved economic and social security, for they wanted to be a part of society as long as they were members of it. Where they were shown deference because of age they were also allowed certain liberties not allowed others. Choice foods, often taboo to others, were reserved for the aged. Among the Aztec it was against the mores to drink intoxicants and anyone who drank was severely punished. This taboo did not apply, however, to the aged. Old women in some societies were allowed to become "shamen" and touch sacred objects which they could not touch when they were younger. The primitive aged probably enjoyed honor and deference just as modern man does. Obviously, there were distinct advantages to owning property which would assure a home and food for the old person. Or again, the kind of death or last days might be determined by the status the person had enjoyed in younger life.

In certain societies it was the custom to kill or to abandon the aged, especially during periods of unfavorable economic conditions. An early missionary recounts how he watched members of a Northwest Indian tribe descend an embankment as they prepared to cross an ice-covered river in pursuit of game. One of the young men of the tribe was pulling a sleigh on which his old mother was lying. For some reason he was unable to take her down the path to the river, so he let her roll down a steep place to the bottom of the embankment. After this procedure the son walked down the pathway to the river. The feeling on the part of the other members of the party was that the son was doing the mother a favor: he was hastening her death. For they knew that the old woman was going to die soon anyway, and since the son could not cure her or drag her along indefinitely unless food was found, this procedure was considered an act of compassion as were other instances wherein the aged or sick were killed in order to get them out of their misery.[4]

[4] Margaret Mead and Nicholas Calas (eds.), *Primitive Heritage* (New York: Random House, Inc., 1953), pp. 536–37.

Evidence indicates that the aged often requested to be killed when they were no longer able to keep their status positions in the society. In some instances when the older person recognized that he was a hindrance to rapid movement when game was being pursued, he would request to be left alone to die. In certain Eskimo tribes the eldest son would make a snow house for the old person to retire to, and after farewells had been taken the aged person would select a robe and move to the hut. The son at some opportune moment would seal the opening in the burial house, enclosing the aged person in it. After a few days had elapsed the adults of the family would go to the burial house, remove the body, and bury it. No mention was made of the deceased person and no emotions were displayed.[5] Often death was preferred to being cast out of the tribe, living by door-to-door begging, or sleeping out of doors.

Finally and probably not the least important reason for trying to maintain status was that many primitives believe that in death they will occupy the same position they did in life, both socially and economically.

The large-family system of rural-agrarian societies

The great family of China has often been used to illustrate the status of the aged in rural-agrarian societies. In rural China one finds that the aged are generally held in high esteem. The aged patriarch is the executive and financial head of the family. He has the authority to compel all of the family members to turn over to him all their income.[6] It then becomes his task to redistribute the family income in an equitable manner for the benefit of the entire family. In some instances the head of the Chinese family may be forced to give up his authoritative status.[7] If the eldest son has attained adulthood and is economically capable he may replace his father as functioning head of the family.

[5] *Ibid.*, pp. 537 ff.

[6] Bernard J. Stern, *The Family, Past and Present* (New York: Appleton-Century-Crofts, Inc., 1938), p. 141.

[7] Ernest W. Burgess and Harvey J. Locke, *The Family, from Institution to Companionship* (New York: American Book Co., 1945), p. 44.

This occurs more frequently if the father is very old, economically or physically disabled, or generally incompetent to make the required adjustments to the larger community. Transfer of economic functions does not mean that the father loses the respect of the eldest son or of the family. The same conditions obtain here as in some of the non-literate societies. The status position of the aged is neutralized by such factors as personality, ability to function, and actual achievement. Elderly Chinese women in the agrarian setting rule the household activities. It is their task to direct the rearing of each succeeding generation of children. They also teach the daughters-in-law the traditions of the family, assign household tasks to them, and see to it that the family remains a functioning whole.

Such extended kinship groups are also found in other countries where they are closely associated with rural life. They are rarely found in the urban environment.[8] All the members of the family are subordinate to the group; that is, individuals of all ages function primarily as members of the family, secondarily as individuals. The aged are also a vital part of this type of family. Indeed, they are the directors and controllers of this collectivity of families. In these familistic societies one finds that the head of the family also acts as its religious leader. Even where the religious functions have been taken over by the church the head of the family still performs the functions of religious instruction. As long as the aged head is active there is no chance that he will be regarded as unimportant in the family unit.

In India the joint family is composed of several generations also. The father and mother both enjoy places of honor in the system. The father controls and directs the whole family. If the father becomes too old or too sick to function, his place is taken by the eldest capable son. The sons and their wives show great respect for both the mother and father. It is the mother who often instigates and must always approve any action of concern to the household. Both the artisan and agricultural joint or great families

---

[8] T. Lynn Smith, *op. cit.*, pp. 46–47.

provide the aged of the family, regardless of the degree of relationship, with a kind of old-age insurance which cannot be found in any other kind of family organization.[9] There is evidence that the elderly parents may take advantage of their positions of authority in the joint family system. The elders tend to become authoritative and set up a "dictatorship of love." They are exalted by the family regardless of their ability or merit. This pattern can be discovered in the treatment of new daughters-in-law by the elderly mothers who are inclined to "lord it over" the newly arrived wives.

The joint family system is closely integrated with the over-all culture of the Hindus. Veneration of the aged is not far removed from ancestor worship. If one's ancestors are responsible for all good things, they will be remembered and honored. The joint family system, its roots lost in ancient history, fosters such attitudes. Under the impact of urbanism, westernization, and industrialization the joint family system is being weakened both in China and in India.

In connection with the above discussion, two things should be kept in mind. First, the joint family in one form or another has been a widespread phenomenon. Large farms lend themselves to this type of family organization, particularly when there are few laborers to be hired. Second, the joint family was not the only form of family organization to be found in these societies. The aged in smaller families probably suffered hardship to a degree, depending upon the economic standing of their families. Insofar as the efficient functioning of the joint family is correlated with the size of the estates, a majority of the people are laborers, not landowners. The aged of the laboring class probably occupied an unenviable position, only the aged of the landowning class being counted among the blessed. Certainly it would be an error to think that in all times and places the aged have been honored, revered, and surrounded by the good things of life during their last years on earth. It might be more correct to say that in different times, places, and

[9] S. Chandrasekhar, "The Hindu Joint Family," *Social Forces,* XXI (March, 1943), 327–33.

circumstances treatment of the aged has ranged all the way from worship to murder.

The aged in urban-influenced rural settings

An outgrowth or perhaps a Western variation of the large or joint family has been called the stem-family. This type of family is found where the peasant class of farmers is well established on the land. The estate is held from generation to generation by one landlord family and worked from generation to generation by one family of peasants. It might also be found in the landowning class where holdings are relatively small. In either case, limited farm size limits the size of the family which depends upon the land for a living.

One of the central characteristics of the stem-family is that there must be a love of the farm and of farming as an occupation. The first generation starting with a young married couple works the farm. As the children become old enough they work with their parents, learning farming methods, and help to increase the family income. As the children mature, all but the eldest son leave the farm and are given a start in life away from the home farm. The eldest son marries and so the cycle begins again. As the eldest son learns the farm methods he assumes an ever-increasing amount of work and responsibility. As the father becomes older he ceases to work so hard and begins to relegate responsibility to his son. Both father and mother continue to live on the farm and enjoy a living from it. They contribute some labor, direction, and advice to the son. The son in turn furnishes them with board and bed. The other brothers and sisters have no ownership or tenantship interest in the farm because they have been given a start in life away from the farm.

Some indication of the transition from a rural-peasant to an urban-nonpeasant economy can be seen in a study of a French rural commune.[10] The French Civil Code states that

[10] Adapted from O. R. Gallagher, "Looseness and Rigidity in Family Structure," *Social Forces*, XXXI (May, 1953), 332–39.

property of the parents shall be divided equally among all the children. Obviously small landholdings of the peasants would soon be reduced to acreages too small to be farmed economically. As soon as children are born to peasant families the parents begin to plan for their future. As a general practice the eldest son is selected to continue on the farm, gradually replacing the father in the capacity of farm manager. When the father dies the son who has been selected becomes the owner. In order to satisfy the legal obligations to the other children, both the eldest son (or the son selected to keep the farm) and the father provide for their education, establish the boys in business, and arrange a "good" marriage for the girls. Many of the peasant girls marry the sons of neighbors and begin the peasant family cycle again. Under this arrangement the elderly peasant parents remain on the farm and enjoy their last years in relative security on the land.

The nonpeasant inhabitants of the commune are, in many cases, descended from the peasant class. As a consequence of insufficient land these people have become the artisans, domestics, and tradespeople or have gone into other similar work. If their children cannot obtain work in the commune as they grow to maturity they migrate to the large cities or to neighboring communes. There is some indication that nonfarm jobs are inherited, but the system of job inheritance is not as workable as that of land inheritance.

One of the consequences of the migration of nonpeasant children is that the parents become isolated from their children and remain alone without adult children in the commune. Since these people are oriented to peasant values, they complain about the fact that their children have deserted them and that the younger generation does not respect the older one as was the case when they were young. Upon reflection, however, some of them see that the system practiced by the peasants, although still an ideal for the nonpeasants, is not practical or workable under the nonpeasant organization.

In addition to the aged peasants who remain on the land and the older nonpeasants who move to and work in the neighborhood, there is a third source of old people in the commune. This category consists primarily of the nonpeasants who, as young people, have gone to the urban area and worked for many years. Upon reaching retirement they receive their old-age pensions and return to the commune. Two reasons are given for their return: first, it is more economical for them to live in the rural area on their pensions, and second, they are frequently drawn back by emotional ties with their remaining relatives. Occasionally an isolated older person of the nonpeasant category is forced by economic pressure to leave the commune and go to the urban area to live with adult children who have moved there to find work.

It is under the peasant system that a greater family solidarity is found and where people enjoy greater social security as they grow older. The system of land inheritance and manipulation of land inheritance is inflexible enough to insure security for the members of the family who remain peasants. At the same time it can be modified to the extent that it does not detract too drastically from the status of the individual. The system is defined well enough so that there are not as many insecurities as there are in the nonpeasant families. The flexibilities which are found are still within areas of relationships which the peasants understand. They tend to fit both individual and family needs.

Under Hitler the National Socialist Party of Germany, drawing from the German custom of land inheritance, formulated a policy similar to and based upon the philosophy of the stem-family. The Inherited Freehold Act instituted by Hitler covered all German farms over 20 and under 310 acres. Families with farms in this category held inalienable rights to the land. Only one son could inherit the land. He was required to help his brothers obtain an industrial education and to give his sisters dowries when they married. Those who left the farm had the right to return if they were unsuccessful in nonfarm life. The farm policy of the Nazi government was an attempt to root the farm family in the soil and at the same time to try to endow it with a feeling of moral responsibility as being the food, blood, and cultural source of the German people.[11]

This pattern is of interest primarily because of its variation found in this country. Descendants of German immigrants, particularly in Wisconsin, have a stem-family organization of a similar type. In this country there is no interference on the part of the government. The eldest son or the son who wants the farm enters into an agreement with his parents. This agreement is called either "Bonds of Support" or "Bonds of Maintenance." These bonds vary from family to family but can be made legally binding on both parties. The real value of these agreements is that the aged parents are cared for and the land is kept in the family.

Under these bonds the son who is to inherit the farm agrees to support and care for the parents as long as they live. Some bonds designate which rooms and what yard and garden space is to be used by the parents. Sons agree to furnish specified quantities of food, fuel, and sometimes cash to the parents. When the families of the two generations cannot live together in harmony, provision is made for another home on the farm. Sometimes the son pays rent for his parents in an off-the-farm home. The parents may help the young couple by working on the farm or around the house. They may merely offer advice or suggestions, or they may devote their time to activities of their own such as raising vegetables, fruit, or chickens as a supplement to diet or income. In return for money, housing, and food, the son receives the farm and all farm property from his parents, the allotment of goods which the son furnishes being a sort of payment for the farm. Often the elderly parents retain ownership of the farm, and the son receives it by will after the death of both parents. This technique is one of the best forms of insurance available to the parents since

[11] John B. Holt, *Under the Swastika* (Chapel Hill: University of North Carolina Press, 1936), pp. 99–100.

they can always change the will if the son does not live up to the letter and spirit of his contract with them.

There is some evidence that these bonds of support are not as widely used now as they have been in the past. Part of the difficulty can be traced to the inability of two families to get along together under the same roof, especially if the second family is large and the roof small. It has been said that it is less expensive to heat two houses with fuel than one home with family friction. Another difficulty among the German-American citizens of Sheboygan and Monitowoc counties in Wisconsin has been that the sons do not want to stay on the farms.[12]

Variations in this form of family organization are to be found in other areas of the United States. Where the aged farmers are able to retain control of property and continue to be a dominant force in directing the economic activities of the farm their position in society is superior to that of the aged in urban settings. Even though the aged farmers may not do all their own work, they have a directing influence over those who do. It should be noted in this connection that "improper" farming techniques may be passed down from father to son.

Inheritance of farm land in the United States

Much modern farming in this country is carried on with mechanized equipment, and modern urban conveniences are thought of as being a necessary part of a large number of farms today. Farm parents often feel that they should be paid for the farm even if the purchaser is a close relative. It has been estimated that if a son is to obtain a fairly high level of living from a farm he should buy one worth at least $10,000 and stock and equip it with at least $3,000 worth of property. If the parents are unable to sell their farms for a reasonable price, they retain an equity in them. The farm thus becomes an investment for them, from which interest,

[12] Oscar F. Hoffman, "Culture of the Centerville-Mosel Germans in Monitowoc and Sheboygan Counties, Wisconsin" (Doctoral Dissertation, University of North Carolina, 1942), pp. 104–9.

in the form of rent, can be used for support in old age. This often means that when the parents die they have not yet disposed of their capital investment. They have not and never will be able to realize a return on the original investment. As a consequence of this practice many farms are being split up into uneconomic units by the laws of descent or inheritance and by wills. Although there are more equitable ways for the aged to dispose of their property to their own and to their heirs' advantage, these methods are not yet in general use.

These and other factors have the combined effect of defeating the traditional place of the farm as a form of social security in old age. The aged farm owners are often forced to stay on the farm as operators of smaller and smaller plots of land, receiving smaller and smaller incomes. In the meanwhile the untilled parts of the farm lose their value as farm land. The sale of farms to nonrelatives offers disadvantages also. When this occurs the farm home is usually sold and the retiring farmer and his wife have to move to a nonfarm residence. The old couple begins using up their capital, and in this day of higher prices and longer life expectancy there is always a question as to whether the money in the bank will last as long as the life of the couple lasts. When the farm is sold to a nonrelative, the farm children will not be able to rely on it if they are unable to get along well in the urban setting. As long as farm parents do nothing positive to keep their sons on the farms the sons will not be able to fulfill the traditional rural obligation to look after the welfare of their aging parents.

Summary

It is difficult to generalize about the status of the aged either in nonliterate or rural-agrarian societies. As with other aspects of life and social relations their status is not constant in time or place, nor is it constant from individual to individual. Regardless of other conditions, it can be said that if the aged person is still active and well, still has a contribution to make, and has some capital in one form or another, he will retain a safe place in society. If, on the other hand, he has reached the latter part of old age, is chronically ill, can make no contribution and has no capital, he will have a rather unpleasant time. As a rule it seems that nonliterate tribes have status positions which can be achieved by the few aged they have. In general these positions are so constituted that a person may not aspire to them until he is old and until he has shown that he is an apt candidate for the position in question.

The extended family has been found in one form or another in almost all rural-agrarian societies. As a rule the families occupying large farms were well able to carry on farm life with this family arrangement. Under this system the whole family, including several generations, lived and worked together under the supervision and leadership of the senior male head. As head of the family he had a high degree of prestige and occupied a position of responsibility. As he became older he began to lose his authority to his eldest son. As long as he lived he was still honored, as his position was buttressed by the religious order. The elder women in the family occupied a position of authority within the household which was comparable to the father's position on the farm. Considering the over-all culture of these societies, it is probable that the aged enjoyed as much security as anyone did. The position of aged peasants was probably very inferior to that of the aged landowners.

Family farm life in the United States has some elements in common with rural-agrarian societies of other times and places. Several instances can be found which reflect a modified form of the large family organization, although rural life is being modified and urbanized to such an extent that one rarely finds a true large family organization in this country. Where the modified rural-agrarian family is found, one of the sons usually takes the farm at the death of the parents. Usually he has worked with the father and understands that he will receive the farm eventually. In return for the farm he supports his parents until they die. Where there is no such arrangement, farm children move to an urban or nonfarm job. The farm parents stay on the farm and try to carry on as they can, either by doing the work themselves or by renting land. Upon their death the farm is often divided into small, economically unproductive plots. These plots are willed to the children. Thus it is that the farm ceases to be a source of security for either generation.

3

Status of the Aged in
Urban-Industrial Societies

The major emphasis of this chapter will be on the aged in the urban-industrial United States. It should be remembered that the status of the aged in urban-industrial societies, as in the rural-agrarian societies, is a function of the total cultural configuration, varying from time to time, place to place, and from individual to individual. It is a function of several variables. First, it is a function of the personal attributes of the individual himself. One would hardly expect a chronically ill person to enjoy the same status as a healthy, active person. Usually persons in the latter years of old age or senility are regarded differently from those in the early years. Second, the more heterogeneous the population and the more diverse the subcultures, the less able is one to generalize accurately about old age and the aged. In the modern United States it is probable that the aged constitute one of the most heterogeneous of all the social categories. Third, the rapid rate of social mobility and the high degree of social stratification tend to multiply the variations in the status position of the aged.

Modern industrial societies pose certain problems for the aged which generally are not found in primitive or agrarian societies.[1] In the first place the aged are a problem because of the type of society in which they live. There could not be such a high proportion of the aged in any

[1] Kingsley Davis and J. W. Combs, Jr., "The Sociology of an Aging Population," in Donald B. Armstrong (chm.), *The Social and Biological Challenge of Our Aging Population* (New York: Columbia University Press, 1950), pp. 150–51.

society but modern industrial society. This type of society is the very one in which there is a premium on youth and a liability on old age. The status of the aged is altered, they are made to feel useless and so experience a feeling of insecurity ordinarily not encountered in rural societies. Second, the aged are a problem because there are so many of them. In nonliterate societies the actual number is small and so also the proportion of the aged to the total population is small. This is another way of saying that modern civilizations have few status positions for the aged to occupy and that there are too many aged for those positions which are available.

Old age as a product of urban-industrial society

The ways in which old age is a product of urban-industrial society can be shown in two ways: first, by comparing the proportion of the population aged 65 and over through a period of time as various countries have become industrialized.

TABLE 1

Proportion of the Population Aged 65 and Over
(Selected countries, 1880–1901 and 1930–1947)

Country	Date	Per Cent	Date	Per Cent
Australia	1901	4.0	1947	8.0
Austria	1880	4.4	1934	7.9
Belgium	1900	6.1	1930	7.6
France	1891	8.3	1936	9.8
Switzerland	1900	5.8	1941	8.6
U.S.	1890	3.9	1940	6.8

SOURCE: Wilbert E. Moore, "The Aged in Industrial Societies," in Milton Derber (ed.), *The Aged and Society* (Champaign: Industrial Relations Research Association, 1950), p. 27. Based on official national statistical sources.

The second way to show that old age is a product of urbanization and industrialization is to compare the proportion of the aged population in industrial countries with that of less industrialized ones. For instance, compare the percentages given in the last column of Table 1 with the following: the proportion of the population aged 65 and over was 2.2 per cent in India and Burma in 1931; 2.4 per cent in Brazil in 1940; 2.9 per cent in Colombia in 1938; 3.0 per cent in Mexico in 1940 and 3.5 per cent in Chile in 1940.

Briefly stated, the proportion of the aged in a population increases as fertility and birth rates are reduced. In order for people to live to old age, mortality must be reduced also. The size of a given population is maintained or grows by saving lives rather than by merely allowing many infants to be born. The reduction of infant, child, youth, and adult mortality rates means that there will be an increased number of people living to advanced ages. If the fertility rate is reduced there will be a corresponding increase in the proportion of older people. In nonliterate societies with high birth rates and high death rates the proportion of the aged to the total population is kept low. Because of high death rates in the younger age levels few people live to become old.

What are some of the socioeconomic characteristics of societies with reduced mortality and fertility rates? These are countries with a high standard of living, high level of education, a highly developed scientific body of knowledge, which includes medical science and sanitary engineering, and a well-developed social consciousness as well as other related factors. Countries which have highly developed material culture and scientific knowledge have low fertility and mortality rates. Without an urban-industrial culture few nations will attain the demographic goals of low fertility and mortality and, concurrently, a high proportion of aged. Rural-agrarian countries have a small proportion of aged precisely because they are rural and agrarian.

One of the values of Western societies is that of preserving the lives of the members of their populations. Because of the nature of modern industry, value is also attached to speed, stamina, and dexterity, characteristics which are usually associated with youth, not old age. The very culture which makes it possible for people to live long also decrees that they shall not work during their later years.

Contrasts in the small and large family form and function

The family as one of the major social institutions has undergone remarkable changes in urban-industrial societies. There arises a serious question as to whether an industrial society could have developed as it has in Western countries if the extended family system had been practiced. The continuation of the extended family in India and China can be considered one factor in the industrial "backwardness" of these countries. Individuals in the large family system are assigned to status positions on the basis of their birth order regardless of their individual capacities. In the small, two-generation family as it is found in Western societies, ascribed statuses of age, sex, and family are important but they are often overruled by individual ability and training. The function of the large family is to fit the child for his role in the family organization. The function of the small family is to prepare the child for participation in the larger society.

In this country the ideal goal of the family is to send the child to school so he will be able to go to work when he becomes old enough to leave home. It is expected that the young man will establish his own household when he reaches social maturity and economic independence. These expectations carry with them the idea of both social and spatial mobility. Middle-class parents traditionally try to give their children a "good start" in life so that they may have a better life than their parents had. This frequently means that the parents expect their children to lead their lives away from the parental home. This expectation on the part of the parents carries with it the implication that the parents "write off" any claim on their adult children to support them when they reach old age. They also disclaim any continued social relationships with the new family which is set up by their children. It is not the function of children of small families to support the older members of the families in which they were reared. That the parent and child families are related by blood and bound together by one common member is more or less immaterial.

It should not be assumed that the small family is the only type to be found in modern societies. Even in industrial centers there can be found traces of the stem-family or large family. Remnants of these families still exist to some extent in the upper socioeconomic classes where social status is bound up with ancestry. It is most evident where large amounts of family property are involved. There is a tendency in these families for the eldest son to receive the family name and property so that the family line will be carried on. Another variation of the family type is to be found in the lower class, especially among Southern-reared Negro families. These families are "mother-centered" and so favor a different kind of family organization. Even in white middle-class urban society there are found wide variations in the small family system.

In any society where spatial mobility is easy and extensive the large family has tended to disappear.[2] Individual, unmarried family members break away from the stem-family if they are not satisfied with their lot. Employment opportunity and the belief that economic security is attainable outside the confines of the family attract these individuals. Generally the same may be said for young married couples. If young couples believe their economic advancement is being hindered rather than aided by the large family organization, they leave. Apparently they see little advantage in staying in the old home to inherit an undivided share of the property when they can acquire property for themselves with relative ease.

Essentially, the conflict between the large and small family can be traced to a conflict between custom on the one hand and utility on the other. In a rapidly changing social order, where these two types have appeared, the small family "wins out." The familial folkways and mores of the large family tend to be weakened with the removal of religious and other institutional patterns which have given it sanction over the years. Neither the large nor

[2] Harvey J. Locke, "Mobility and Family Disorganization," *American Sociological Review*, V (August, 1940), 493–94.

small family could continue to exist without change because each must fit into the total institutional framework. The small family comes much nearer coinciding with the patterns of the educational, economic, religious, and political institutions of the Western world than does the large family.

The significance of this shift from large to small family lies in the fact that the life span of the family is essentially shortened. The large family is a continuous, on-going association. The death of a member, or the death, in series, of several members, does not appreciably alter either its function or structure. Policies, practices, and activities remain essentially the same in spite of a continuous change in the personnel of the family. This cannot be said of the small family. Each family is formed at the marriage of a couple. Each family ceases to exist at the dissolution of the marriage. The family lasts only as long as the couple remains a unit, not as long as the relatives continue to live. As a consequence the small family ceases to be of great social significance after it has performed its basic function of reproduction and socialization of the offspring. The large family is continuously performing these basic social functions as each succeeding generation replaces the outgoing generation.

Temporal duration of the small family

For what length of time can the average couple expect to live together after they form their family of reproduction? Table 2 gives a comprehensive picture of the major events in the life of the small family in this country in 1890 and 1950. For the purpose of this analysis four points will be noted. First, the age at which the couple established their families has been reduced. At both dates the median age of first marriage for men was higher than it was for women. In 1950 there was not as much difference between the ages of the mates as there was in 1890. Second, the interval between marriage and the birth of the last child has been reduced by three and nine-tenths years. The average number of children born per woman in 1950 was about 2.35. Thus, the median age of mothers at the birth of their last child was approximately 26 years. Conversely, in 1890 with the average of 5.4 children, the average mother was about 32 years old when her last child was born. With a later marriage and more children to bear, the average wife of 1890 was

TABLE 2

Median Age of Husband and Wife at Selected Stages of the Life Cycle of the Family
(United States: 1950 and 1890)

Stage of the Life Cycle of the Family	Median Age of Husband		Median Age of Wife	
	1950	1890	1950	1890
First marriage	22.8	26.1	20.1	22.0
Birth of last child	28.8	36.0	26.1	31.9
Marriage of last child	50.3	59.4	47.6	55.3
Death of one spouse *	64.1	57.4	61.4	53.3
Death of other spouse †	71.6	66.4	77.2	67.7

SOURCE: Paul C. Glick, "The Life Cycle of the Family," reprinted from *Marriage and Family Living*, XVII (February, 1955), 4. By permission.

  * Husband and wife survive jointly from marriage to specified age.
  † Husband (wife) survives separately from marriage to specified age.

5.8 years older at the birth of the last child than her granddaughter was in 1950. The average father of 1890 was 7.2 years older at the birth of his last child than his grandson was in 1950.

Third, in addition to "saving time" by earlier marriage and fewer children, parents of 1950 save time because their children marry at younger ages than they themselves did. The father in 1950 was 9.1 years younger at the marriage of his last child than his grandfather was. The mother in 1950 was 7.7 years younger at the occurrence of this event than her grandmother was. Finally, the extension of the length of life between the two dates should be noted. This can be illustrated by the fact that the average couple who married in 1950 can expect to live together for 41.3 years with 13.9 years being spent together after the last child has married. In 1890 couples could look forward to only 31 years together.

They could not look forward to any time alone, for the marriage would have been dissolved by the death of one or the other on the average of two years before the marriage of the last child. Thus, several factors have converged to extend appreciably the length of life of men and women beyond the marriage of the last child. Continued early marriages, fewer children, and extension of life expectancy will accentuate this trend in the future.

The aged in an urban setting

The significance of the extension of life is that there is a longer period in which the father and mother have no positive functions to perform. Their primary objectives have been fulfilled. They are too old to have more children, and their adult children have been socialized to the limits of the ability of the parents to socialize them. Sociologically speaking this means that even though they are occupying ascribed positions, the role expectations associated with these positions have been reduced in number. It also means that whereas these older people have retained their ascribed status positions, there is no universally defined status position left open for all of them to achieve. The family role expectations of aged adult parents with married adult children are those of husband and wife, father and mother, and of grandparents. To varying degrees they carry out the role expectations of husband and wife, but to almost no degree do they carry out the expectations of the role of parents. The status of grandparent as a rule has few if any role expectations which are socially significant. Grandparents who attempt to carry on the role expectation of parents toward their adult children often find that their efforts are not appreciated. When grandparents attempt to carry out parental roles in relation to their grandchildren the same thing may occur. With the shift from the large to the small family there has come a shift in the status position of the aged parents. The position of family head used to involve the functional role of directing the entire family and controlling its destinies. The position of family head for the aged without a family is an empty phrase as well as an empty status position.

With the de-emphasis of the family status position of the aged there has come a corresponding de-emphasis of the status position of the aged in the framework of the other social institutions. An increasing number and proportion of the aged find that there are no status positions that are left open to be achieved solely by old people. There are no achieved positions open to older adults which cannot be filled by younger adults. In nonliterate and rural-agrarian societies this condition did not obtain. The sage, counselor, religious leader, and skilled artisan among others were status positions generally left open to older adults only. The relatively few old people had status positions in all the major social institutions which could not be filled by anyone except older adults. Aged people in urban-industrial societies hold achieved status positions in the various social institutions also. These are usually status positions which they achieve as younger adults, not as old people. The primary difference between positions achieved by younger adults and those held by older adults lies in the terminology which is used. There are parents and *grand*parents, statesmen and *elder* statesmen, preachers and *superannuated* preachers, professors and professors *emeriti*. In each case the prefix or suffix tends to emphasize the fact that the person has served in the capacity faithfully for many years, not that society expects him to continue to serve much longer.

Folkways and mores pertaining to the aged

It is well known that the folkways and mores change slowly even in modern industrialized societies. It was seen in Chapter 2 that the body of mores concerning the aged was well established in both nonliterate and rural-agrarian societies. Everyone knew what the status positions of the aged were and what their role expectations, rights, and duties were. Any unexpected event or circumstance involving the aged could be and was settled within the broad pattern of culture, and the solution was generally to the satisfaction of all concerned. In urban-industrial societies the same conditions do not apply. The old, long-established mores are not the controlling forces they once were. This is not to say that the mores involving relations with the aged have been completely swept aside. Some of the values still are held very firmly, but with qualifications. For example, it is a value to honor one's father and mother, but what, precisely, does "honor" mean? Should the "honor" be extended to all older persons in the society, whether relatives or not? Does this commandment apply equally to all children or to some all of the time and to others not at all? Does it apply when one's parents are healthy, active, and easy to live with as well as when they are poor, chronically ill, and continually difficult to live with? The mores today are not tailor-made to fit circumstances that vary widely. It is within the broad generalities that each person finds his own "best" way or within which a new set of generally accepted and acceptable folkways evolve.

There are several factors involved in the shift of family folkways and mores. The shifting or changing in mores has been interpreted as a clash in values between two generations or as a clash between persons reared under two sets of mores. People who have or will become old during the decade beginning in 1950 were born between 1880 and 1890. During the early years of their lives the United States was vastly different in many respects from what it is now. Rural life and rural living was the norm. Families were larger then than now. Urbanization and industrialization on a large scale were influences just beginning to be felt. Although there was a public educational system it was not as well developed as it is now. For these and other reasons education was not as highly valued then as now. Religion and the church probably were more dominant factors in family life during the earlier era. Most old people of today can be characterized as having had a rural oriented youth. Their educational level was relatively low. Many of them were reared on the Bible in families where the father was the undisputed leader. As children they probably had well fixed and relatively uniform ideas about filial responsibilities and regard for older people.

Parents of those who are currently in the category of the aged did not, on the average, live together as a couple without children in the home. The parent who outlived the other had only a short life expectancy after the death of the mate. This is one reason the aged were not a social problem before the turn of the century. There were fewer parents to be cared for, they did not live as long after the death of the spouse, and there were more children to care for the parent than is the case today. As a matter of fact, the adult children did not have much choice as to whether they would care for the remaining parent since few provisions were made outside the home for the care of the indigent aged. It was rather firmly established in the mores that children were responsible for the care of their indigent parents. The aged were a family responsibility, not a social problem.

Traditionally there has always been a gulf between the generations. The saying that the younger generation is "going to the dogs" probably originated with Adam and Eve. This idea is reflected in other phases of life also. Each college generation feels that the old college will "go down hill" when they leave. When people leave positions in political, economic, or religious organizations they often leave with the idea that their replacements will not be able to carry on as well as they did. So it is with each succeeding generation. Young people, it is felt, do not have the experience and other necessary attributes to insure social and cultural continuity. It is with fear that the aged relinquish their leadership to the young. There is a clash between the generations as older people attempt to retain the status positions and the prestige they once held. This situation is probably present to some extent in all societies, but it is accentuated in urban-industrial ones.

The clash between generations is especially noticeable when an older person goes to live with married adult children. How well the old and young get along under the same roof depends upon several factors, all of which may be summed up under the head of personality. The following are some of the conditions which accentuate conflict between the generations.[3] If the two generations have lived apart for many years, adjustments are harder to make. Both have lived independent lives and must again learn how to accommodate themselves to each other. If the younger couple has lived in an urban environment and the older person in a rural area, the least flexible of the two will be expected to make the most change.

To differences in education and religious orientation must be added a possible difference in socioeconomic class. Social mobility is prevalent enough in this country to make it possible for the second generation to climb above the level of the parent generation. Some people would not welcome an old uneducated snuff-dipping or tobacco-chewing man or woman into their urban homes even if the person were their father or mother. Old people who go to live with their young relatives have to give up the emotional security of their old homes. They have to give up personal freedom when they move in with the younger generation. On the other hand, the young couple has to give up freedom also. Where there are children of the third generation, the middle generation may feel uncomfortable in the role of parents. Real or imagined criticism by the grandparents is not welcomed.

Reactions to changing conditions

How have older people reacted to loss of status in the urban-industrial society? It is interesting to note that their action roughly parallels that of the aged in nonliterate societies. First, the aged seek to retain the highest status which they have held. They usually refer to themselves as retired businessmen, farmers, or the like. Rarely are they referred to merely as retired men, and when that does occur, it is

[3] Adapted from Ruth S. Cavan, *The Family* (New York: Thomas Crowell Co., 1942), pp. 247–59.

said in a rather apologetic manner. This may be an indication that the status of retirement does not yet carry much prestige. After retirement some people attempt to create a new prestige-bearing status position by opening up a new enterprise or trying to make a positive contribution in one way or another. "Grandma" Moses has been cited as an illustration of how an older person has created a status position and incidentally both fame and fortune for herself.

Generally there has been a de-emphasis on the role of the aged as teachers of the young. With the growth of culture the aged no longer serve a function as reservoirs of knowledge. However, there is evidence that supervision by the aged is used during apprenticeship terms in some industries. In addition to transmitting some technical knowledge the aged can pass on other kinds of knowledge. There is still some unwritten wisdom, or "intellectual and moral capital," which is valuable to young people taking over jobs or professions from their parents. It is in good will, good public relations, or in how to win and keep friends for the business that the knowledge of the aged can be of great help. This is called the folk wisdom of human relations. Because of the discontinuity of urban-industrial society there are many young people today who start business without this moral or intellectual capital.[4] If they have no guidance from the older generation they must rely on their own judgment or the judgment of friends. Even when such advice is available young people often consider it as criticism. If it is not so considered, they may agree with the older person but shrug off the advice by convincing themselves that it is old-fashioned or not applicable to present-day life.

The aged who are self-supporting retain their status and prestige by methods often used by nonliterate people. They are not financially dependent upon others, and they can maintain a position in the family although it might be given grudgingly. They have property which will be disposed of.

[4] Robert E. L. Faris, "Interaction of Generations and Family Stability," *American Sociological Review,* XII (April, 1947), 160–61.

In this manner they can exert some influence over the younger generation. Few old people dispose of all their property before they die. The majority dispose of property either by will or by the laws of inheritance which are effective after death. In this manner they also have a degree of control even after death. Some older people make contributions to their families by making themselves useful doing little tasks around the home. Modern electrical equipment and paid baby-sitters have almost eliminated any real need for this function, however. In the role of storytellers the aged have been replaced by radio, television, and other forms of entertainment. The aged in modern society have not been able to retain any status or prestige through the religio-ancestral system as is the case in some nonliterate societies. Although some sanctions still remain, they are of such a minor and unimportant nature that they carry little weight. The religious and other institutional patterns have been removed, and the familial folkways and mores once buttressed by these institutional patterns have been weakened.[5]

Adult children of aged parents face a dilemma. They are faced on one hand by the values which they were taught as children. On the other hand they are faced with a very practical situation. If parents are financially unable to care for themselves, children have to choose between looking after the parents in accord with the old set of mores or giving themselves and their children a higher level of living. In former times and in a different institutional framework there would have been no choice. Many of these adult children today are in the unenviable position of being "damned if they do and damned if they don't." They are the objects of criticism if they appear to neglect their needy parents. They are the objects of pity if they have to care for the parents. This is particularly true of some unmarried adult children who devote their lives to serving their aged parents.

The extent to which children believe they should support their aged parents seems to vary according to the religious

[5] Locke, *loc. cit.*, p. 492.

affiliations of the children and according to their place of residence.[6] Catholics more often than Protestants believe that they should support their aged parents. Rural residents more often than urban residents believe in this obligation. Forty-nine per cent of urban and 53 per cent of rural Protestants and 74 per cent of rural and 71 per cent of urban Catholics agreed to the statement that children should be looked to for the support of aged parents. To the statement that aged parents should understand they have to get along without aid from children, 20 per cent of urban and 13 per cent of rural Protestants agreed, while only 9 per cent of urban and 4 per cent of rural Catholics agreed.

Children now also consider personal relations before deciding to accept support responsibility. A series of questions was devised with statements ranging from favorable to unfavorable conditions. Unfavorable conditions depicted the parents as being sick and unpleasant to live with. The more unfavorable the hypothetical conditions became the smaller was the percentage of children willing to take care of their parents. In each of the circumstances presented, the Catholic children were more willing than Protestants and rural residents more willing than urban residents to take responsibility in caring for their aged parents.[7]

There are some cases on record where children absolutely have refused to support their parents. It is probably more often the case that children will not support their parents if some agency or institution will. The experience of the state of Maine in 1948 illustrates this. In 1947, as a consequence of the increasing old-age assistance load, the state legislature passed a law which disqualified any recipient of assistance unless he filed written proof with the commission that he could not support himself. Each adult child or spouse of the recipient had to file a statement of inability to support the recipient, giving income, assets, and liabilities. The commission set up a formula based upon the

[6] Robert M. Dinkel, "Attitudes of Children Toward Supporting Aged Parents," *American Sociological Review*, IX (August, 1944), 375 ff.
[7] *Ibid.*

amount of income and the number of dependents other than the aged person seeking assistance. This law closed 2,150 cases. Three-fifths of the cases were closed because the statements showed ability of relatives to support; the remaining two-fifths were closed because no statement was filed. Later about 8 per cent of the cases were reinstated. There were then about 2,080 cases closed under the new law. In December, 1947, there were 14,618 old-age assistance cases on the roll in Maine. The cases closed because ability to support was established amounted to about 14 per cent of the total number.[8] Allowing for errors, it is safe to assume that at least 10 per cent of the aged receiving public assistance in Maine in 1947 had relatives who could but would not support them as long as the state would. It must be assumed that the responsible relatives in these cases preferred to have their indigent aged kin supported by the state rather than to suffer the financial disabilities of supporting them.

Summary

The family in urban-industrial society is in a transitional state. It is changing from the extended type to the small type, which consists of a couple with offspring—only two generations. Each child, as he attains adulthood, is expected to and usually does establish his own family. This process leaves aged parents on their own after children leave the parental home. Each new family has to look after its own welfare. Parents are expected to look after their own welfare after the children have gone. Frequently unable to do so, they are having to rely more on other sources for financial support. They have no status position in the new family and no status position which is universally reserved for older persons in society. As a consequence, each older individual, if he is to achieve a status position in the institutional framework, must do so as he has achieved other

[8] David H. Stevens and Vance G. Springer, "Maine Reviews Responsibility of Relatives," *Public Welfare*, VI (July, 1947), 122 ff.

status positions throughout his life. This is done by his own effort apart from the fact that he has attained old age.

The high degree of urbanization and industrialization found in this country could not have been developed without the small family, and the small family, as we know it, could not have developed in any other type of society. The principle involved here is that when a change occurs in one part of culture, changes are brought about, often simultaneously, in other parts of culture. The folkways and mores involved in the family relationships of past centuries and in other societies are no longer applicable today. Some of the older values remain, but it appears that a new set of folkways applicable to the family has not been formulated. In America both generations often find themselves in a dilemma regarding their relationship to each other. None of the other institutions has, to this time, formed an answer to the questions left unanswered by the shift from the large to the small family.

4

Demographic Characteristics
of the Aging Population

In societies where people know their exact age the chronological aspect of age tends to be stressed. In nonliterate societies the emphasis is more on organic age. The social implication of this tendency is that in civilized societies the trend is toward correlating chronological age with other aspects of life. The assumption is that if a person is classified as being old in years he must be old in every other way. In nonliterate societies if a person can play his social roles he is not classified as being old regardless of how many birthdays he has celebrated.

Some of the following chapters will indicate that one of the major difficulties in age relations is found in the often untenable belief that a chronologically old person cannot function in any capacity. It is a matter of common knowledge that there is a negative relation between age and some occupations, a positive relation in others. Young athletes, actresses, waitresses, or receptionists are more in demand than are older ones. An athlete is old in his 30's, some women who are in contact with the public may be considered too old at 25. Older lawyers, doctors, and scientists are more in demand than those who are just beginning their careers. There is a widely held belief that workers in certain occupations begin to become less efficient as they grow older. For this reason the older workers often have difficulty obtaining jobs if they lose the ones they have. The same is often true of professional people unless they have attained a high degree of esteem in their field.

Some classification of age other than a chronological one might be of great social value. However, any other way of determining age would be much more difficult to arrive at in an objective manner. It is more socially expedient but less valuable to use chronological age as the way to designate the dividing line between mature adulthood and old age. The age of 65 is generally used as the lower limit of old age. It will be used in this way in this book. Briefly, this age is used because it is generally accepted as the age at which people enter retirement. Both the old-age and survivors insurance and the old-age assistance programs set 65 as the lower limit to old age. Many industrial and private pension plans do also. Some effort is being made to lower the retirement age to 60 years, or at least to make 60 an optional retirement age. On the other hand there is an indication that some firms want to postpone the time of retirement to 68 or 70 years. If the expectancy of life and the span of life are extended appreciably in the future with a corresponding increase in activity and better health, the age of 70 may come to be designated as the official lower limit of old age.

Growth of the aging population

There are two ways in which growth of a segment of the population may be shown; first in absolute numbers, second in percentage increase. Table 3 shows growth of the aged population of this country in both of these ways.

There are several reasons why the actual number of the aged in this country has increased from 1.7 million in 1880 to more than 12 million in 1950, and to an estimated 14,404,000 in 1956. First and most important, this increase is due to the saving of the lives of infants. Most of the people in our population who have passed their 65th birthday were born after 1860. Prior to 1860 the birth and death rates in this country were relatively high. As the country began shifting from the rural-agrarian to the urban-industrial way of life, the death rate was reduced. Important changes were taking place in science, medical knowledge, sanitation, and modes of living. From 1860 until the turn of the century, the birth rate remained between 30 and 40 births per 1,000 population. At the same time the death rate declined. A high birth rate and a low death rate means a rapid growth of population.

TABLE 3

Number and Proportion of the Population 65 Years of Age and Over
(United States, 1880–1956 and estimates to 1975 *)

Year	Number of Aged	Per Cent of Aged to Total
1880	1,723,459	3.4
1890	2,417,288	3.9
1900	3,080,498	4.1
1910	3,949,524	4.3
1920	4,933,197	4.7
1930	6,633,805	5.4
1940	9,019,314	6.9
1950	12,322,000	8.2
1956	14,404,000	8.8
1960	15,800,000	8.8
1965	17,371,000	8.9
1970	18,879,000	9.0
1975	20,655,000	9.1

SOURCES: Adapted from United States Bureau of the Census, *1950 Census, Characteristics of the Population,* II, Part I (Washington, D.C.: 1953), Table 39, pp. 1–93; U.S. Bureau of the Census, *Current Population Reports,* Series P-20, No. 73 (March 12, 1957), p. 11; and U.S. Bureau of the Census, *Current Population Reports,* Series P-25, No. 123 (October 20, 1955), p. 8.

* Estimates used for the total population are those based upon the assumption of most rapid population growth, i.e., that the 1954–1955 level of population growth will continue to 1975.

More babies were born and lived beyond infancy, childhood, and young adulthood into old age. Prior to this time there had been relatively few old people because of the high rates of death in earlier years of life.

In addition to the above mentioned factors, the years between 1890 and 1914 witnessed a mass emigration movement from Europe. Most of the immigrants who entered the United States were young adults. During the first decade of the present century upward of one million immigrants found their way here each year. The vast majority of these people have already celebrated their sixty-fifth birthdays or will do so in the not too distant future. These two forces have had the combined effect of making the aged population grow at a more rapid rate than the total population of this country has grown. Table 4 gives the com-

TABLE 4

Rates of Growth for the General Population and the Aged Population
by Decades
(United States, 1870–1880 to 1950–1956)

Decades	Per Cent Growth of Total Population	Per Cent Growth of Aged Population
1870–1880	30.1	49.4
1880–1890	24.9	40.5
1890–1900	21.4	27.1
1900–1910	21.0	28.2
1910–1920	14.9	24.9
1920–1930	16.1	34.5
1930–1940	7.2	36.0
1940–1950	14.5	36.6
1950–1956	7.0	16.9

SOURCES: Adapted from United States Bureau of the Census, *1950 Census, Characteristics of the Population*, II, Part I (Washington, D.C.: 1953), Table 39, pp. 1–93; and U.S. Bureau of the Census, 1957, *Current Population Reports*, Series P-20, No. 73 (March 12, 1957), p. 11.

parable rates of growth for the aged and the general population for the past eight decades. While the percentage growth in the general population has been almost consistently decreasing from decade to decade, that of the aged population has been increasing since 1920. At no time since 1870 has the rate of growth of the aged population been as low as that of the population as a whole.

A different situation presents itself when a segment of the population is studied in its percentage relationship to the total. Table 3 shows that the per cent of aged has increased steadily from 3.4 in 1880 to 8.2 in 1950, and 8.8 in 1956. In connection with Table 4, this indicates that the aged segment is growing more rapidly than the general population. In each succeeding decade the total population is equal to 100 per cent. If one segment constitutes an increased proportion of the total, other segments are losing ground and are constituting a smaller proportion of the total. In this country the proportion of the aged has increased because some other segments have decreased. The most striking instance of this has occurred with the shift of percentages from the segment under the age of 5 years to the segment over the age of 65 years. Table 5 illustrates the

TABLE 5

Per Cent of Population 65 and Under 5 Years of Age
(United States, 1880–1956)

| Year | Per Cent of Total | |
	65 and Over	Under 5
1880	3.4	13.8
1890	3.9	12.2
1900	4.1	12.1
1910	4.3	11.6
1920	4.7	10.9
1930	5.4	9.3
1940	6.8	8.0
1950	8.2	10.8
1956	8.8	11.4

SOURCES: Adapted from United States Bureau of the Census, *1950 Census, Characteristics of the Population*, II, Part I (Washington, D.C.: 1953), Table 39, pp. 1–93; and U.S. Bureau of the Census, 1957, *Current Population Reports*, Series P-20, No. 73 (March 12, 1957), p. 11.

percentage loss for the level under 5 years and the corresponding gain for the level above 65 years. As a matter of fact this same general loss can be detected for all ages under 30, with a gain for all ages 45 and over. Essentially the reasons for this phenomenon are the same which have caused an increase in the growth of absolute numbers of the aged population, that is, a decrease in the mortality rate and a declining birth rate.

In the decades between 1880 and 1950 the aged have gained 4.8 percentage points, and until the upsurge in births in the 1940 decade the under 5 age group had lost 6.3 percentage points. Between 1950 and 1956 both these categories gained 0.6 per cent. Part of the decline in births is traceable to the fact that the immigrant groups are moving out of the reproductive period of life. Traditionally the reproductive rate of immigrants to this country has been very high. The birth rate which remained high during the 1910 and 1920 decades has fallen partially because the second generation immigrants have not followed in the reproductive footsteps of their immigrant parents.

It is a relatively easy matter to predict the future numerical growth of the aged population.[1] This category of the population can grow when those who are now young move from the younger levels into old age. It is unlikely that the number of people over 40 years of age will increase appreciably because of immigration. Life table calculations can be used to estimate the number of deaths in each age level for each succeeding year and decade. Applying such a device, estimates of the future size of the aged population are reasonably accurate. It should be understood that the accuracy of any such calculations depends upon a continuation of present death rates. Any catastrophe which would increase the death rate appreciably would make population estimates relatively worthless. On the basis outlined above, Table 3 gives estimates of the future aged population up to 1975. Such an estimate sets the number of people over 65 to be about 20.6 million in 1975.

It is more difficult to calculate the percentage of aged to the total population. It can be inferred from the foregoing discussion of percentages that the rate of births in the future will play a decisive role in determining what percentage the aged will be of the total population. Table 5 shows that

[1] Warren Thompson, "Our Older People," in T. Lynn Smith (ed.), *Problems of America's Aging Population* (Gainesville: University of Florida Press, 1951), p. 8.

the percentage of children under the age of 5 decreased each census year between 1890 and 1940. There was an increase in this percentage in the 1950 census due to the increased birth rate and the number of births between 1945 and 1950. No one can be sure what will happen during the next 30 years as far as the birth rate is concerned, so it is possible to find wide variation in estimates as to what the percentage of the aged will be in the future.

One of the social implications of an increase in both size and number of the aged population is that there will be fewer adults in the productive years to carry the nonproducers who are either too young or too old to work. The ratio of nonproducers to producers is increased by artificially postponing the time of entrance of the young into the labor force. It is further increased by the establishment and enforcement of compulsory retirement. An extension of life expectancy has the effect of increasing the number of people in retirement so that the aged live longer as nonproductive dependents.

Life expectancy of the aged

Most census classifications divide the aged into three age levels: 65–69; 70–74; and 75 and over. The statistics on employment indicate that almost half of the males in the first level are still in the labor force. After the age of 70, retirement is a common practice. An age distribution also gives a broad indication of the degree of physical dependency of the aged population and some indication of marital status. Physical incapacity is much more widespread among those 75 years of age and over than among the other two old-age levels.

In both of the last two census years those 65 to 69 have made up 40 per cent or more of the total number of aged. It can be expected that in the future those 70 to 74 and those 75 and over will constitute a larger share of the total number of aged. As the absolute number and percentage of those over 70 increase, there will be a proportionate decrease in the backlog of potential workers over the age of 65. Correspondingly there will be an increase in the percentage of aged who are economically, socially, and physically dependent upon the remaining part of the population for care and support.

Most of the spectacular progress in the extension of life expectancy has affected the early years of life. However, some progress has been made in extending the life expectancy of those past the age of 65. It should be remembered that two conditions result when the death rates of younger people are reduced. First, more of them live into old age. Second, the morbidity or rate of sickness, as well as the degree of severity of diseases, is reduced. The net effect is to insure that very few who do survive to old age are semi-invalids who die later as an indirect result of the diseases of childhood or young adulthood.[2] Even if there had been no direct effort made to prolong the length of life of the aged, progress has been made toward keeping them freer from impairments contracted in youth. As a result of these efforts the life expectancy of those at 65 has been increased from 11.9 years in 1900–02 to 14.2 in 1951, and 14.4 in 1954. The population projection of the Bureau of the Census indicates that with a low mortality rate life expectancy at the age of 65 will be increased even more during the period between 1955 and 1965.[3]

Mortality from all causes has declined for those 65 to 74 as well as for those 75 and over during the decades since 1900. However, mortality from degenerative diseases has increased for both these age levels since 1900. This has been true in spite of the amount of study and research on heart diseases, cancer, diabetes, and nephritis. Basically there seems to be one reason that death rates for the aged cannot be reduced much further. This reason is that people are going to die sooner or later and if they are saved from death by one disease they will die from some other disease. It would seem

[2] Henry S. Shryock, Jr., "The Changing Age Profile of the Population," in Milton Derber (ed.), *The Aged and Society* (Champaign, Ill.: Industrial Relations Research Association, 1950), pp. 3 ff.

[3] "*Ibid.*, p. 12.

probable that the answer to an extension of life and a declining mortality rate among the elders may not lie in some secret drug or fountain of youth. Rather it may be found in improving the health of people all during their lives so they will be less susceptible to the diseases which are now associated with old age.

Sex and marital distribution of the aged

In 1956 there were 6,670,000 aged males and 7,734,000 aged females in the population. Thus the females exceeded the males by more than one million.[4] Women at almost all ages have a lower mortality rate than men; consequently their life expectancy is greater than that of men. The difference between the life expectancy for men and women has increased each decade since 1900. In 1900 the average length of life of white males in this country was 46.6, for white females it was 48.7; in 1951, 66.4 for white males and 72.4 for white females. Comparable figures for 1954 were 67.4 and 73.6 years respectively.[5] In 1950 the death rates per 1,000 white males 65 to 74 years of age was 52.9 but only 36.1 for white females at this age level. With these differences in mortality rates and life expectancy it becomes clear that the sex ratio for the aged population would be below 100. Just how much the sex ratio varies in any locality depends upon several factors. Rural areas usually have a higher sex ratio than urban areas have. The sex ratio of a locality in earlier decades might be a factor of importance in determining the sex ratio of the aged in that locality at the present time. Urban areas which attracted younger women to work in light industry or commerce at an earlier period would probably have more older women than men. Conversely, sections of the country such as the West which attracted large numbers of unmarried men would probably have a low sex ratio among the aged at this time.

---

[4] United States Census, *Current Population Reports*, Series P-20, No. 73 (March 12, 1957), p. 11.

[5] United States Department of Health, Education and Welfare, *Abridged Life Tables United States, 1954*, LXIV, No. 2 (Washington, D.C.: 1956), 44.

By examining the data concerning the marital status of the aged one is able to draw some conclusions concerning their residential habits. Most old people who are married live with their spouses. Nonmarried elders live alone, with relatives, or as unrelated individuals in boarding houses, hotels, or institutions. Table 6 shows the distribution of the

TABLE 6

Marital Status of the Aged, by Sex
(United States, 1956)

Marital Status	Males		Females	
	Number	Per Cent	Number	Per Cent
Total	6,670,000	100.0	7,734,000	100.0
Single	468,000	7.0	602,000	7.7
Married	4,616,000	69.2	2,798,000	36.2
Widowed	1,500,000	22.5	4,259,000	55.1
Divorced	86,000	1.3	75,000	1.0

SOURCE: United States Bureau of the Census, *Current Population Reports,* Series P-20, No. 72 (December 21, 1956), p. 9.

aged by sex and marital status. There is practically no difference in the percentage of aged men and women who were never married. There is little difference in the percentage of each sex who are divorced. There is, however, a marked difference in the percentage of those who are currently married and of those who are widowed. More than two-thirds of the aged men are married while only 36.2 per cent of the aged women are. In contrast, more than half of the women and slightly less than one-fourth of the men are widowed. As a rule men marry wives who are younger than themselves, and since the life expectancy of men is shorter than that of women there are more widows than widowers. It is also true that widowed men remarry more frequently than widows do. Since older men who remarry usually marry women younger than themselves, older widows have less opportunity to remarry. Besides observing the general custom that women do not marry men younger than themselves, many older women refrain from remarriage because they might lose their pension rights by remarrying.

The significance of the above information is that a larger proportion of the aged men have homes in which to live. Fewer of them are dependent upon relatives other than spouses for family living, and fewer of them have to spend their later years in boarding houses, homes for the aged, and similar places.

Migration of the aged

Information concerning the mortality rates of the population is adequate to serve all necessary purposes for estimating the number of the aged in future years. It is possible that in the future the regional and state distribution of the aged will present more problems for some places than for others. Migration of the aged or migrations of young people which occurred during earlier decades will influence the state and regional distribution of the aged population. The different age levels in the population are not equally mobile. Young adults in their 20's are the most mobile of all the age categories: about 37 per cent of all these people changed their residences between March of 1955 and March of 1956. Among adults 30 years of age and over mobility tends to decrease with increasing age; among those 65 years and over only 10 per cent changed residences during this period. This pattern of decreasing mobility for each successive age class is generally characteristic for each type of mobility.[6]

Table 7 illustrates several points. First, the aged population is relatively immobile, as is to be expected. Homeowners do not leave their homes unless there is good reason to do so. Old people generally seem to prefer to remain in their own communities during the later years of life. Second, the vast majority of those who move do so from one residence to another within the same county. Of those who move from county to county, most stay within the same state. Of the aged who moved, only 29.5 per cent of the men and

[6] United States Bureau of the Census, *Current Population Reports*, Series P-20, No. 72 (December 21, 1956), p. 11.

26.5 per cent of the women moved into other counties. Of all the moves made by the aged, 87.7 per cent were moves within the same state. Third, men and women in the older age levels are about equally mobile, with women being slightly more mobile. This difference is more apparent when it is seen that 39 per cent of the women who leave the county

TABLE 7

Migration of the Aged Population by Number, Per Cent and Sex
(United States, 1955–1956)

Type of Move	Total Aged		Males		Females	
	Number	Per Cent	Number	Per Cent	Number	Per Cent
Nonmovers	12,961,000	90.0	6,020,000	90.3	6,941,000	89.7
Movers	1,441,000	10.0	650,000	9.7	791,000	10.3
Same County ..	1,039,000	7.2	458,000	6.9	581,000	7.5
Different County	402,000	2.8	192,000	2.9	210,000	2.7
Within State .	225,000	1.8	127,000	1.9	128,000	1.7
Between States	147,000	1.0	65,000	1.0	82,000	1.1

SOURCE: United States Bureau of the Census, *Current Population Reports,* Series P-20, No. 73 (March 12, 1957), p. 11.

of origin move to other states, whereas only 33.9 per cent of the older men who leave their county migrate to other states.

There is one other consideration to be taken into account when discussing migration. It has been seen that only 10 per cent of the aged are movers and that of those who move only slightly more than one-third move into different states. When considered in terms of absolute numbers the aged migrants could change the characteristics of any local population appreciably. Everything considered, they would be much more inclined to migrate in large numbers to a few localities than they would be to move from a few localities in large numbers. Both California and Florida are coming to be considered Meccas for old people. Some counties and cities in these states receive a concentration of old people while others receive virtually none. If one takes the hypothetical figure of 10 per cent of all aged interstate migrants and puts them in two or three communities in either of these two states the problem of the aged in those communities would be greatly multiplied. Using the hypothetical 10 per cent, the number of aged migrants would be more than 1,000. If that number of aged moved into one or two counties in a short period of time the percentage of aged in those counties might be increased by as much as 50 to 100 per cent, depending upon the number of aged already there. Such a mass movement would increase the proportion of the aged to the total population also. Any marked increase in the proportion of the aged would be particularly noticeable and significant if there were simultaneously an outward movement of the younger adults. This is said to be the case in some communities in Florida. California on the other hand is the destination of migrants of all ages. The proportion of elders to the total population in California would remain more constant or "normal" than it would in Florida.[7]

In spite of the fact that older people do migrate, it seems that the present distribution of the aged is more a function of the prior distribution of people in the younger ages.[8] If an area has a disproportionate number of old people, it may be due to the fact that in prior years there had been an immigration of young people. For instance, the growing number of old people in Northern industrial centers can be traced to the fact that in prior years expanding industry attracted large numbers of young people who since migrating have remained in these centers and grown old. The large number of old people in Oklahoma at the present time reflects the fact that when that state was opened for homesteaders in 1912 it was settled by young people who have since become old. States which are attracting large numbers of young people today will have large populations of older people in due time.

There are two possible by-products of the migration of young people. First, their outmigration may change the age

[7] R. P. Wolff, "Comments," in *Problems of America's Aging Population*, p. 31.

[8] Rupert B. Vance, "The Ecology of Our Aging Population," *Social Forces*, XXXII (May, 1954), 330–35; and T. Lynn Smith, "The Migration of the Aged," in *Problems of America's Aging Population*, pp. 15 ff.

composition of the population which they leave as well as that of the area to which they move. Second, as they become established they may be joined by their widowed mothers. Older nonmarried women who migrate tend to do so to join their children who have left home. More generally older men, regardless of their marital status, do not move to be with their children. They migrate to more economically attractive places. If they are seeking work, they move to places where they believe older people are being employed. If they have already retired and are living on pensions, they seek new homes where they believe the cost of living is low and the climate is comfortable.

A great deal of the migration of the aged both in the recent past and in the future is a function of the total economic structure of the nation. The shift from rural to urban living and the general decline in self-employment, both farm and nonfarm, has meant that employees are capable of being more mobile now than ever before. They are not tied down by ownership of capital goods. On the contrary, large numbers of people are employed by firms with more or less adequate pension systems which are related to old-age and survivors insurance. This "economic independence" enables them to move more readily than if there was no income in retirement. The possibility of being able to migrate becomes a reality because of other cultural factors. Being migrants when they were young means that older persons today may not have established firm primary group relationships where they have settled; hence one move tends to beget another. Better communication means that old people have an opportunity to hear, in detail, about new places in which to live. Lack of primary group ties and responsibility makes it unnecessary to break ties, and economic independence makes it financially possible and attractive to carry out the inclination to move.

Summary

The aged population in this country is increasing both in number and percentage. The high birth rate of the late

1880's, declining mortality, and a large number of immigrants coming to this country between 1875 and 1914 are factors responsible for the increase in numbers of the aged. The percentage increase has been due to a decrease in the percentage of those in the other age levels, particularly those under five years of age. It is relatively easy to forecast the number of people in the aged population in the future but a much more difficult task to estimate their percentage to the total population. Since the mortality rate of women is lower than that of men there are nearly a million more older women than men in this country. There is a larger proportion of aged men who are married than of aged women.

Between March, 1955, and March, 1956, only about 10 per cent of those over 65 years of age changed their residences. A majority of those who moved did not cross state lines. Of those who did cross state lines, a majority migrated to noncontiguous states. While the percentage of interstate aged migrants is small, the absolute numbers migrating may change the population composition of the communities to which they move. Migration of the aged to Florida, the Gulf Coast states, and California is especially high. The area receiving aged migrants is affected where the migrants tend to congregate in a few localities. The aged population of these places may be increased by several times or at least experience a rapid proportionate growth in the aged population. The age composition of the county or state of destination is changed from the national average if there is also an outmigration of those in the younger age levels. The age composition of the states from which the aged migrate is not changed as much as is that of the state of destination.

Part II

LABOR FORCE STATUS
OF THE AGED

5

The Aged in the Labor Force

The primary emphasis of this chapter will be on the aged workers, that is, those 65 and over who are in the labor force. It should be understood that almost all workers over the age of 45 meet the same kind of problems that confront those over 65. What differences in problems there are tend to be of degree, not of kind.

Basically problems of retention of, or entrance into, jobs at the older ages results from factors which have been examined in preceding chapters. Briefly these factors are as follows. First, there has been the shift from the agrarian to the industrial economy, with a resulting decline in self-employment. Employed persons have become dependent upon employers, not themselves, for their jobs. A second factor is the ability acquired by citizens of civilized societies to count and to determine age in terms of years rather than in terms of function. Third, there is the ability acquired by civilized societies to prolong the lives of their citizens, and conversely, consciously to cut down on the rate of fertility. These factors have increased the absolute number of the aged and have, at the same time, increased the proportion of the aged in the total population. Fourth, the "deification" of youth, speed, dexterity, physical strength, and endurance often has made it difficult for those without these characteristics to retain their employed status in the American industrial organization.

It would be well to bear in mind that the question of employment of the aged is receiving a great deal of serious consideration at the present time. As the population continues to grow older it will be given even more consideration. It was indicated earlier that the folkways and mores governing age relations are in a process of change. Those which evolve within the next few years will influence the society for years to come. While it is obvious that this society cannot and will not adopt a national policy of genocide to rid itself of the "problem" of the aged, it is equally clear that its present lack of policy cannot continue indefinitely.

Why men work

One of the deeply embedded folkways of the American culture is that of working for a living. The idea of working is a part of our personalities. From early childhood one learns that when he becomes older he will work. It is no wonder that work is the tie that binds the individual to society. Ordinarily the status position of the worker and his family, as well as his place in society, is determined by the kind of work he does. Related to this fact is the economic necessity of working. Society has not devised any way which will allow the majority of the population to remain idle while only a few work. When a person is idle for any length of time others begin to wonder if something is wrong with him, or they begin to wonder where the money comes from. It has been noted in fiction that when a person has no obvious means of support he is suspected of being a part of some illegal organization from which he derives his income. The personal factor should also be considered as a reason why men work. Over a period of several decades one becomes accustomed to the daily routine associated with working. The habit of working and the personal relationships formed at work are strong forces which hold men to their jobs.

For these and related reasons it is not surprising to find that men start working at relatively young ages, are employed through middle life, and stay on their jobs as long as they are allowed to. In general older people work for the same reasons younger ones do, but there may be more pressure on older than on younger people. For instance, work patterns are more firmly established in older persons, and daily routine built up over a long work life is very difficult to lay aside. The relationship among workers is also strengthened by years of daily contact on the job. Further, the social pressure on individuals to retain their status positions may be greater on the aged than on the young. Older persons may fear a loss of their jobs because they have seen their contemporaries lose their status positions as functioning adults in the economic environment. They do not want this to happen to themselves. It is also possible that this social pressure to conform and to maintain a social position is quite as powerful as is the economic necessity of continuing to earn money. When one retires he runs the risk of losing social status by being unemployed as much as he runs the risk of having to lose economic status by adjusting his level of living to a curtailed income.

Complementing this desire on the part of the older employee to remain at work is the social pressure, which may be either direct or indirect, upon the employer to retain the older worker on the payroll as long as it is feasible to do so. This situation is particularly applicable to employers of relatively few people when a personal relationship has been retained between employee and employer. A feeling of loyalty between the two which has been built up and maintained over the years presents a situation wherein the employer hesitates to retire older workers. This hesitancy would be more apparent where there is no pension plan in force. Impersonal relationships and pension plans are responsible for a weakening of the sense of personal responsibility on the part of employers toward older employees. In any event, the employer must be conscious of his employee relations. No employer can lightly disregard either employee or community opinions and attitudes when dealing with his "hands." More and more the question of worker morale is being considered. Few employers are completely inured to the influences which "bad" labor relations might have upon their workers and the general public.

Age and occupational distribution of the labor force

As the population of this country becomes older more of the labor force will be composed of older persons. This trend has been evident here for several decades. The significance of it can be seen from the figures presented in Table 8. The proportion of elders in the labor force increased from 4.3 per cent in 1890 to 4.8 in 1950 and to 5.1 in 1956. The total number of older persons in the labor force increased from less than one million in 1890 to nearly three million in 1950 and to 3.4 million in 1956. As the population of the country has grown and shifted from rural to urban residence the number of people required to manufacture and distribute goods and services has increased. The higher level of living enjoyed now than at the end of the last century is both partial cause and effect of a continued high employment rate. It is not surprising to discover that in each of the four age levels given in this table the actual number of persons in the labor force has increased appreciably. It is in keeping with the shift from agricultural to industrial employment and from a lower to a higher level of living that the following changes in composition of the labor force are to be noted. First, the percentage of youths in the labor force has been reduced from almost one-third of the total in 1890 to less than one-fifth in 1950 and slightly more than one-sixth in 1956. Pressure has been exerted during the decades under consideration to encourage younger people to remain in school longer. This has been done by making school attendance compulsory up to certain ages and by passing child-labor legislation which indirectly encourages further education by discouraging or forbidding younger people to enter the labor force. Union practices have encouraged both of these actions by supporting legislation pertaining to these things. Higher levels of living encourage higher educational attainment which in turn makes a higher level of living more of a possibility. Any nation in which people have to leave school and start working at relatively young ages is generally one with a low

TABLE 8

Age Distribution of the Labor Force in Number and Per Cent, by Sex; United States, for Selected Years
(In thousands)

Ages	1890 Number	Per Cent	1920 Number	Per Cent	1950 Number	Per Cent	1956 Number	Per Cent
Total	21,833	100.0	40,282	100.0	59,857	100.0	66,785	100.0
14–24	6,755	30.9	10,452	25.9	11,107	18.6	10,387	15.1
25–44	9,729	44.6	18,667	46.3	28,154	47.0	30,967	46.4
45–64	4,413	20.2	9,600	23.8	17,714	29.6	22,041	33.0
65 and over	936	4.3	1,563	3.9	2,882	4.8	3,390	5.1
Male	18,129	100.0	32,053	100.0	43,533	100.0	45,933	100.0
14–24	4,833	26.7	7,027	21.9	7,157	16.4	6,296	13.3
25–44	8,513	47.0	15,353	47.9	20,644	47.4	21,910	47.7
45–64	3,937	21.7	8,290	25.9	13,353	30.7	15,149	33.0
65 and over	864	4.7	1,383	4.3	2,379	5.5	2,578	5.6
Female	3,704	100.0	8,229	100.0	16,323	100.0	20,852	100.0
14–24	1,922	51.9	3,425	41.6	3,950	24.2	4,091	19.6
25–44	1,216	32.8	3,314	40.3	7,510	46.0	9,057	43.4
45–64	476	12.9	1,310	15.9	4,361	26.7	6,892	33.1
65 and over	90	2.4	180	2.2	503	3.1	812	3.9

SOURCES: Bureau of Labor Statistics, *Employment and Economic Status of Older Men and Women,* Bulletin 1092 (May, 1952), p. 15; and United States Bureau of the Census, *Current Population Reports,* Series P-20, No. 73 (March 12, 1957), pp. 12–13.

level of living based upon agriculture as a primary source of income.

Second, the process of shifting to a higher level of living by higher educational attainment has resulted in a lower birth rate. Under these conditions the proportion of youths in relation to both young adults and older adults has been decreased. As the society has shifted from the patterns generally prevalent in 1890 to those of 1950, there are proportionately more potential workers in the two adult age levels. A larger proportion of the adult population finds jobs available due to the reduction of participation of youth in the labor force. From Table 8 it can be seen that in 1890 the two adult levels (ages 25–64) constituted 64.6 per cent of the total labor force; in 1920, 70.1 per cent; in 1950, 76.6 per cent; and in 1956, 79.4 per cent. It is to be noted that it is in the older adult level, 45–64 years of age, that most of this increase has occurred.

It can be seen from the data presented that the people 65 years of age and over constitute a much larger part of our population than they did in 1890. In spite of this, they have contributed only a small proportionate increase to the total labor force and proportionately fewer of them are to be found in the labor force. Why is it true that a smaller proportion of those over 65 are employed now than in 1890? Again it becomes necessary to examine the sociocultural environmental changes which have occurred in this country during the past several decades. It is important to remember that the older workers of today began entering the labor force as early as 1890 or 1900. There are several related factors which are responsible for the decreased activity of the aged in the labor force. Accompanying the shift in residence has been a shift in the amount of self-employment opportunities for the entire population. In both the past and the present there has been a larger proportion of aged males from rural areas in the labor force than from either rural-nonfarm or urban areas. The significance is that as the population has moved urbanward during the past half-century fewer and fewer of the aged have remained in the rural areas, thus cutting down the total number and percentage of the aged who are in the labor force.

Some of the major occupational changes which have occurred in this country since 1910 are shown in Table 9. Ex-

TABLE 9

Percentage Distribution of the Labor Force
(United States, for selected years)

	Per Cent		
Group	1910	1930	1950
Professional persons	4.4	6.1	7.5
Proprietors, managers, and officials	23.0	19.9	16.3
Clerks and kindred	10.2	16.3	20.2
Skilled workers/foremen	11.7	12.9	13.8
Semiskilled workers	14.7	16.4	22.4
Unskilled workers	36.0	28.4	19.8

SOURCE: Bureau of Labor Statistics, *Employment and Economic Status of Older Men and Women,* Bulletin 1092 (May, 1952), p. 19.

amining this table with the aged in mind, it should be noted that the broad occupational classifications, where one would expect an older working force, have declined in relative importance. The first of these two categories is that of proprietors, managers, and officials. The American ideal is that of climbing the occupational ladder to managerial positions. If this ideal were based on reality, one could expect a large number of older persons to be employed as managers. Reinforcing this social myth is the tradition of acquiring capital and skill during the early years of life, then launching into business for oneself. It is noted that in 1910, 23 per cent of the labor force was engaged in these activities as contrasted with only 16 per cent in 1950. Opportunities for openings in these jobs are not proportionately as numerous as they were in the past. Unskilled labor has also become less important in the total employment picture. Possibly the proportion of unskilled workers has been reduced as that of semiskilled workers has increased. The second category of jobs in which one might expect to find older workers employed is that of skilled labor and foremen. It should be noted that although this category constitutes a greater portion of the labor force in 1950 than it did in 1910, the increase is almost negligible in the total picture. Of the two categories in which one would look for a higher employment rate of older workers, one has decreased and the other increased in importance but little since 1910. Thus it appears that the largest proportion of those 65 years of age and over are generally to be found in the occupations which have been decreasing in relative importance during the decades since 1910. As the number and percentage of older men have increased, the occupations which have attracted a higher proportion of these people have been declining in importance in the overall labor picture.

Some further factors should be investigated as to why older people are found in the labor force to a lesser extent than they are found in the general population. First is the fact that in the past and in rural areas at the present time older people prefer to remain at work. When they own or operate family-sized farms they can continue work at a reduced speed. They move from active work to active supervision or else engage in activities demanding less physical vigor. A similar technique is often resorted to by the self-employed, both in business and in the "free" professions. Proprietors of stores may limit their activities to supervision or may be present in the store for only a limited time each day. Doctors may take office calls only or refuse to take any new patients. At the present time there are fewer opportunities for the aged to engage in the type of work in which they have an opportunity to "taper off." Generally they are expected to work full time until the day of retirement. The shift in emphasis from skilled to semiskilled operations has worked an employment hardship on the older workers also. In skilled trades the older person had the advantages of experience and patience over younger people. Semiskilled machine tending today is considered an occupation more suitable for younger people. Because of technological innovations new machines have to be mastered on the same job from time to time. There is the general belief that younger persons learn to tend new machines more rapidly than older ones do, and as a result, older people lose out.[1]

A final factor to be considered is that older workers are often overrepresented in the older occupations, whereas younger men are overrepresented in the newer industries. For instance, the proportion of older men in railroading is generally high, while in air transportation there are relatively few older workers except perhaps on the managerial levels. A similar case could be made for the difference in average age between employees in the wagon and self-propelled missile industries. Older workers are found more often in the tobacco, woolen, and worsted industries than in the rayon or synthetic fabrics industries. Older workers may hesitate to leave steady employment in an established industry to enter employment in a new industry even if the pay is higher. If foremen and managers are young, they may resist hiring older men whom they will have to supervise.

The unemployed aged

Most older people who have been in the labor force while young will continue working if they can do so. Work habits and social and economic pressures tend to make this true. If they are physically able to continue work and have the opportunity to work, few of them will retire voluntarily. Of those who do retire many later seek full- or part-time re-employment. Data show that, from 1940 to 1946, of all the men and women who could have drawn old-age and survivors insurance 30 per cent or less did so.[2] Only comparatively few of those who left their jobs did so voluntarily. Of those who did leave work, whatever the reason, from 60 to 90 per cent later sought re-employment. Among other things, this study shows that the participation of the aged in the labor force fluctuates seasonally and from year to year de-

[1] W. H. Stead, "Trends of Employment in Relation to the Problem of Aging," *Journal of Gerontology*, IV (October, 1949), 290 ff.

[2] Margaret L. Stecker, "Beneficiaries Prefer to Work," *Social Security Bulletin*, XIV (January, 1951), 15–17.

pending upon economic and other circumstances. If jobs are available for them, older people are usually willing to keep on working or to return to work after a period of unemployment.

Work opportunities for older people increase in times of labor shortages and decrease again in so-called "normal" times. This is another way of saying that our economy is not providing job opportunities for all those who are capable of working and want to work. Some of the older people who cannot find work remain in the labor force for as long as a year or more looking for work. As long as they are seeking work and are able to work, they are counted as part of the labor force.

In March, 1940, following the depression decade, there were nearly eight million unemployed persons in this country. Data for that year and month show the duration of the period of unemployment, by ages, and the length of time these people had been looking for work. Those 65 years of age and over who were unemployed constituted 13 per cent of all the unemployed experienced wage and salary workers. Half of the unemployed aged had been looking for work for a year or more. One-third had been seeking work for less than six months. The data show that in the ages 55 to 64 the unemployment experience was very similar to that of the aged. Youth under 24 years of age were unemployed in slightly higher proportions and had less difficulty in securing new jobs. Those in the ages 25 to 44 generally were unemployed to a lesser degree than either the young or the old. The duration of unemployment for this age level was shorter than for either the young or the old.[3] This pattern of fluctuations in rates of unemployment from year to year and the higher degree of unemployment for youth and the aged can also be seen in similar unemployment data for the period 1948 to 1956, as given in Table 10. The year 1948 was one of near minimum unemployment, and the rate declined even more with the expansion of employment in 1950 following

[3] Bureau of Labor Statistics, *Employment and Economic Status of Older Men and Women*, Bulletin 1092 (May, 1952), p. 30.

the outbreak of the war in Korea. The increased rates of unemployment for older workers in 1949, 1950, and 1951 can be attributed in part to the fact that industries which began to curtail some of their activities were those which had

TABLE 10

Unemployment Rates for American Wage and Salary Workers, by Age Groups

First quarter, 1948–1956

Age Groups	Year					
	1948	1949	1950	1951	1952	1956
14–24	8.8	10.0	13.5	6.5	6.7	8.0
25–44	3.6	4.9	7.0	3.8	3.1	3.4
45–64	4.0	5.5	8.3	4.4	3.4	3.8
65 and over	6.0	7.9	9.8	8.1	5.0	2.9

SOURCES: Adapted from Bureau of Labor Statistics, *Employment and Economic Status of Older Men and Women*, Bulletin 1092 (May, 1952), p. 31; and United States Bureau of the Census, *Current Population Reports*, Series P-20, No. 73 (March 12, 1957), pp. 13–14.

a large proportion of older male workers.[4] The decreased rate of unemployment for older workers in 1956 may be accounted for partially in terms of an increased rate of retirement encouraged by higher retirement benefits. After having lost their jobs, older persons were more inclined to withdraw from the labor force than to remain in the labor force as unemployed persons.

The aged have benefited by increased employment, but they have not benefited proportionately as much as have the younger adults. It is interesting to note that even though the unemployment rate for the aged is relatively high and the duration of the unemployment is usually long, those who are employed stay on the same job longer than those in the other age levels do. Part of this is due to age itself; that is, those workers between the ages of 14 and 24 could not be expected to have been at work on one job very long. Older people may be assumed to have "settled down" and either to

[4] *Ibid.*, p. 30.

have found jobs they want or to have given up hope of ever finding the type of jobs they want.

The labor reserve

In addition to the unemployed there are others in the population who are not at work. Some of those in this group may have had recent work experience, others not. These people are in the labor reserve. They are not classified as unemployed, for they are not actively engaged in seeking work. They are not classified as unemployable, for they are considered capable of working. It is assumed that they are physically capable of working and would re-enter the active labor force during periods of full employment or as work opportunities presented themselves. Such a situation existed during the period of the Second World War. People who had been out of the labor force for many years, as well as some who had never worked for wages, found employment. Any future emergency situation or any condition which calls for a more thorough utilization of manpower would call many of these people into active employment.

For the purpose of this book the labor reserve is of special interest since a sizable part of the reserve is composed of older persons. It can be assumed that the aged flow into the labor reserve in relatively large numbers and rather steadily as well. When older persons lose their jobs, they begin to lose their skills as anyone else does. After continued failure to obtain employment, they finally withdraw from the labor force; that is, they stop looking for work.

In 1951 there were slightly more than 13 million people in the labor reserve who had had some work experience (90 days or more) since the beginning of the Second World War. The aged constituted 12.8 per cent of the total, or 1,706,000 persons. These figures indicate that there are large numbers of older persons who are capable of productive work. They also show that older people were employed in large numbers during the period of so-called labor shortage during the 1940 decade. The data indicate in another way that with a return to times of less than full employment the aged move into the labor reserve rather rapidly. It should be remembered that some of these older people may have started work during the war when they were not 65 years of age. Many of those who worked during the war but not afterward may have reached older age levels where their rate of employability began to decline. If a man in the labor reserve resumed active work in 1941 at the age of 65, worked during the war years, and lost his job after the war, he would have been 75 in 1951 when the census was taken. Everything else considered, he would not remain available for full-time work for many years after 1951. Many of those over 65 in 1951 are leaving the labor reserve by virtue of the fact that they are no longer able to work.

Part-time work

Some of the older people who seek re-entrance into the labor force look for full-time work, while others seek part-time employment. Some of these do not feel capable of doing full-time work; some seek part-time work as a means of supplementing their retirement income or want to work some of the time so they can have something to keep them busy. In May, 1951, the Bureau of the Census made a survey to determine reasons why people work part time.[5] During the survey week those over 65 constituted 4.9 per cent of the total population in the labor force. The aged constituted 4.3 per cent of all who worked full time and 8.5 per cent of those who worked part time during the survey week. Those 65 years and over are overrepresented in the categories of workers who gave as their reasons for part-time work that they usually did work part time, preferred to work part time, and would accept only part-time work. Among beneficiaries of old-age and survivors insurance residing in several cities during different employment periods it was found that from 40 to 60 per cent of the retired workers were willing to take either light work or any employment they could find. From one-fourth to one-third specified they would take light work

[5] United States Bureau of the Census, *Current Population Reports,* Series P-50, No. 34 (September 20, 1951), pp. 6–7.

and from 15 to 37 per cent believed they were able to do any type of work.[6]

In 1954, 75.5 per cent of these 65–69 years of age who worked were employed full time, and 24.5 per cent part time. Of those 70 years of age and over who were employed, 62.5 per cent worked full time, and 37.5 part time. In the younger adult ages a much smaller proportion of those who were employed chose part-time work. In the ages 45–54 only 11.7 per cent were engaged in part-time work; those 55–59, 12.7 per cent; and those 60–64 only 15.8 per cent. Thus, either from necessity or choice, as workers become older an increasingly larger percentage are engaged in part-time work activities.[7]

It is apparent from the foregoing that older people who are classified as being unemployed or in the labor reserve are willing and able to work either full or part time. Evidence shows that opportunities for employment do not exhaust the potential supply of these older people except possibly in crisis situations. It should be kept in mind that regardless of what is done there will seldom be full employment for all the aged who are capable of working and want to work. During periods of high employment the aged will have to take their place with other social minorities who usually encounter difficulties in employment. Concerted efforts have been made over long periods of time to break down employer resistance to hiring women, members of racial and ethnic minorities, and handicapped persons. As a general rule employers seem to prefer young, native-born white males as employees.

It is possible that the aged meet with more discrimination than members of the other minorities mentioned above. If this is true, then they would be the last group in the labor reserve to be employed and the first to be fired when conditions returned to "normal." The primary concern of those who suggest special training and placement services for the

[6] Margaret L. Stecker, "Beneficiaries Prefer to Work," p. 16.

[7] United States Bureau of the Census, *Current Population Reports*, Series P-50, No. 59 (April, 1954), p. 35.

aged is the chronic shortage of laborers in the younger ages. They believe that if the demand for laborers cannot be filled by the younger people and employers are persistent in refusing to hire older people, the economy of this country will face a serious crisis. Meanwhile there is a feeling that the attitude of the employers toward the aged may be "softened up" with an eye to what may occur later.

Summary

In spite of the fact that it is part of our way of life to work and that the aged in the population are increasing in both number and percentage, only four out of every ten elders are in the labor force in this country today. These older people are employed in occupations of declining significance in the over-all labor picture. These are the occupations generally associated with a rural economy. This helps explain why a larger proportion of the aged were employed in 1890 than in 1950 and why the employment rate of older men is higher in rural than in urban areas.

The number of unemployed aged fluctuates seasonally as well as from year to year. The years of World War II marked a sharp increase in employment of the aged. A decrease in participation of the aged in the labor force followed the war, but the expansion of industrial activity since 1951 has furthered employment of this category of people.

The aged contribute more than their proportionate share to the labor reserve. This reserve is composed of people who worked during and since the war but are no longer in the labor force. Evidence points to the fact that if the aged are employed they keep their jobs longer, on the average, than those in other age levels. If older people lose their jobs they have more difficulty in re-entering the labor force than people of younger ages. In an effort to retain their position in society, to keep occupied, and to supplement their incomes, older people often seek to re-enter the labor force. They try to become self-employed or seek full- or part-time work, depending upon their financial need and their physical capacity to work.

6

Barriers to Employment of the Aged

Information has been presented in Chapters 4 and 5 to show that the labor force is becoming older as the population of the country ages. More people are living to reach old age now than ever before. At the same time there is a trend toward establishing a fixed retirement age of 65 years. This means that the length of time between retirement and death is greater now than it has been before. In addition to the extended length of life after retirement, another factor, which will be examined in this chapter, is that as people reach the older age levels and lose their jobs they encounter barriers to re-employment. Barriers are erected at different ages for different people depending upon the type of employment which is being sought. These barriers under discussion are based upon chronological age, not upon the individual's ability to function as an employee. Age barriers are erected by society, the prospective employee himself, unions, and employers. It is the decision of the employer which is final in determining whether a person will or will not be accepted for employment. It is apparent that many of the objections attributed to employers for failing to hire older workers are based upon ideas which do not necessarily coincide with facts. These ideas may be valid when applied to some individuals, but they are too often enlarged into inflexible generalizations. In effect they become stereotypes of older workers, which like other stereotypes are easy to pass along and easy to believe, but difficult to dispel.

Characteristics of the unemployed aged

Reference has been made to the fact that it is comparatively easy for older workers to retain the jobs in which they have been employed. It is not possible for all older workers to keep their jobs for an indefinite period of time, however. Some lose their jobs in slack periods or periods of more pronounced depression. Other older persons are fired for one reason or another. Some are forced to drop out of the labor force because of illness, forced moves, or their employer's retirement policy.

The number of older persons in the labor force who are unemployed varies from time to time but generally the number of unemployed aged is proportionately larger than the number of unemployed of other age levels. It has been pointed out that generally an unemployed person still feels he is a member of the labor force.[1] He is still oriented to work and assumes he will be rehired shortly. He has not begun to lose his skill and believes he is capable of many more years of employment. After unsuccessfully seeking work for a period his skills begin to decline. Probably as important, he begins to lose his work orientation and tends to accept unemployment as a permanent condition. He thus becomes psychologically unemployable. In the course of time after many unsuccessful attempts to find work he may withdraw from the labor force. He may give up further attempts to find work and may resign himself to the fact that he cannot find further employment. Some workers give up more easily than others. The ease with which they resign themselves to unemployment varies with several factors. Past work history is important but the company they keep and the kind of rumors they listen to are important also. If they frequent places where those who are psychologically unemployable "hang out," they may soon become convinced that no jobs are available for themselves or anyone else.

Not all categories of the aged are affected in the same way. In general it is the industrial employees who encounter the most difficulty in finding re-employment. It was found by the New York State Employment Service that age barriers were evident proportionately more frequently in

[1] Arthur Naftalin, *et al.*, *An Introduction to Social Science* (Philadelphia: J. B. Lippincott Co., 1953), Vol. II, pp. 162 ff.

entry jobs, unskilled work, and in sales and clerical occupations.[2] Practically no resistance was found for highly skilled and technically trained personnel as far as age was concerned. Generally, older women seemed to encounter greater age restrictions than men did.

It is interesting to note that the United States is not the only country where difficulties are encountered by older people. The problem does differ somewhat from one country to another as well as from time to time. Problems are roughly similar in countries which have attained similar levels of industrialization. It seems valid to conclude that discrimination against the older worker is common throughout the world.[3] It apparently makes little difference whether pension plans, workmen's compensation systems, or state social security programs are in operation. Discrimination exists regardless of these things.

Extent of age discrimination

There is some reason to believe that age as a barrier to employment is more real than apparent. In all probability there are instances where employers when asked whether they discriminate in hiring older workers deny doing so for the same reason people deny being in favor of sin. Some firms feel strongly enough about the matter to admit an age-hiring policy. These firms seem able to justify or rationalize their policy to their own satisfaction. Numerous studies have been made on the subject of discriminatory hiring for different purposes by different organizations using various techniques. Although these studies may not be sufficiently valid in the strictest sense, at least they do not gener-

[2] New York State Employment Service, "The Public Employment Service Views the Older Worker," in Thomas C. Desmond (chm.), *No Time to Grow Old* (Albany: New York State Joint Legislative Committee on Problems of the Aging, 1951), p. 114.

[3] Albert J. Abrams, "Discrimination in Employment of Older Workers in Various Countries of the World," in Thomas C. Desmond (chm.), *Age Is No Barrier* (Albany: New York State Joint Legislative Committee on Problems of the Aging, 1952), pp. 69 ff.

alize from "hunches" or wild, uninformed guesses on the subject. In the study made by the New York State Employment Service, there were approximately 3,500 job openings. Only one-fourth of this number specified age restrictions.

Similar studies in Columbus, Ohio; Lancaster, Pennsylvania; Birmingham, Alabama; and Dallas, Texas present a different picture. In these cities the percentage of openings which had specified age restrictions varied between a high of 90 per cent in Birmingham to a low of 50 per cent in Dallas.[4] In an analysis of "help wanted" advertisements appearing in the New York Times 38 per cent of the 3,474 job opportunities included a limitation on age. Three studies made in firms in New York State, two of which were state-wide, reveal that from 29 to 40 per cent of the firms responding either did not make it a practice to hire older workers or actually imposed an age limit above which they would not hire new employees. Two nationwide surveys with a time interval of twenty years reveal that 26 per cent and 28 per cent of the respondents erected age barriers of one kind or another in hiring employees.[5]

During a three-month period in 1956 an analysis was made of 21,386 job openings listed with state employment offices of seven cities (Detroit, Miami, Minneapolis–St. Paul, Philadelphia, Seattle, Los Angeles, and Worcester). This survey revealed that more than 50 per cent of the jobs listed in five of the seven cities contained maximum hiring ages. In the seven cities combined, 58 per cent of the job openings listed during the survey months had some upper age limitation. More than one-half of the job orders specified upper ages of under 55 years, 41 per cent under 45, and 25 per cent under 35. In general the larger industrial concerns specified upper age limits most frequently and the smaller ones specified limits least often. However, where age limits were

[4] Albert J. Abrams, "Barriers to Employment of Older Workers," The Annals of The American Academy of Political and Social Science, CCLXXIX (January, 1952), 62.
[5] Ibid., pp. 62–63.

given, the age specified was more liberal for both large and small firms than that specified by firms of intermediate size.[6]

The occupational groups with the most restrictive limits were clerical, unskilled, professional and managerial, and sales, in that order. Services and semiskilled and skilled occupations had the most liberal age requirements. Of the industrial divisions finance, insurance, real estate, transportation, and communication were the most restrictive; service, construction and governmental services the least restrictive.

State employment office staff personnel indicated in this study that many employers set up too rigid physical requirements which many older people could not meet even if there was no age limit set. Where rather rigid educational levels are specified older persons find it more difficult to qualify for job openings than do younger job-seekers.[7] It may also be the case that less formal but just as effective barriers are erected though not through the official policy of the firm. Young hiring agents or personnel managers might have a conscious or unconscious prejudice against older job-seekers, or it may be known that in general the management would prefer younger to older employees.

The foregoing analysis should be interpreted with care because the barriers to employment based on age vary from occupation to occupation. There is also evidence to show that the age barrier is not the only reason some older persons encounter difficulty in finding employment. Even where discrimination based on age or on related factors is found, it may either be laid aside in times of labor shortage or permanently laid aside because of a change in attitude on the part of the employer.

Basically there seem to be two primary reasons accounting for the difficulties of the older worker finding employment. The most obvious of these is a scarcity of jobs. This is borne out by the fact that in times of high employment older job-seekers, like those of any other age or classification,

---

[6] Abraham Stahler, "Job Problems and Their Solution," *Monthly Labor Review*, LXXX (January, 1957), 21 ff.

[7] *Ibid.*, p. 25.

remain unemployed for shorter periods than in times of lower demand for workers. Discrimination may be latent at all times and employer preferences still may be for younger employees who at the moment are not available to the individual employer. This conclusion leads us to look further into the causal factor for this phenomenon. It seems that the prejudice against older workers reflects the inability of industrial thinking to gear itself to the mid-twentieth-century life expectancy of the average worker. This fact is the second basic reason for the difficulties encountered by older job-seekers. The tacit refusal of employers to hire women, members of ethnic minority groups, and physically disabled persons on the same basis with young, white, native-born males reflects a similar lag in their sociological thinking.

Classes of barriers

The barriers to employment of the aged can be broken down on four levels for further analysis: first, the cultural or social; second, the personal; third, barriers erected by unions; and finally, industrial barriers. Some of these barriers do not lend themselves to being compartmentalized into neat cubbyholes in everyday practice. It has been mentioned that employers do not function in a vacuum. They are influenced by the broader culture in many different ways. Our society until relatively recently has been a young one and it glorifies youth and the attributes of youth. Youth is set as the norm and everyone is measured by this norm. More often than not the measurements are stated in chronological terms. There has as yet been no widely accepted criterion introduced to measure age in any other way. In many areas of activity a person is judged by his age rather than by his performance. Our society has failed to adjust its thinking in terms of longer life expectancy and better health of its older citizens.

A by-product of this line of thinking is the idea often expressed by employers and others that industry and business need youthful enthusiasm, restlessness, adaptability, and other such attributes. Industry and business are supposed to

thrive on change.[8] The assumption is that these characteristics are found in almost all young people, but rarely if ever
in old people. An implication growing out of this idea is
that other social institutions do not live by change. The
truth of the matter is that all social institutions are constantly
changing even though the change may not be as spectacular
in some of them as it appears to be in business and industry.
The relatively slower rate of change in the other institutions
is a cultural phenomenon not dependent solely upon the age
of the institutional personnel. American society glories in
technological and economic change and progress but only
as long as it is within a relatively conservative frame of
reference. As long as progress is in accord with our value
system we accept it. If it threatens to upset one or more of
our dearly held values, we reject it. It would not be
particularly difficult to show that the desired attributes
mentioned above are not positively correlated with chronological age unless a person with these qualities is defined as
being young. Even though the age distribution may vary
from institution to institution, all the adult ages are represented in each of these institutional areas. The amount of
change a society wants and the definition of desirability of
change and dynamic growth are matters which are culturally
defined and not determined solely by the age of the personnel employed in any given institution.

The aging job-seeker reacts in different ways within the
cultural environment. All too many erect barriers to their
own re-employment.[9] Long periods of unemployment may
have an adverse influence on the elderly who are retired or
lose their jobs and later seek re-employment. They may
have a great deal of technical knowledge in their areas of
employment, so they seek new jobs in similar fields. They
may find themselves unable to think in terms of other occupations because of long years of employment in one area.

[8] J. Douglas Brown, "The Role of Industry in Relation to the Older
Worker," in Milton Derber (ed.), *The Aged and Society* (Champaign, Ill.:
Industrial Relations Research Association, 1950), p. 67.

[9] Cf. Abrams, "Barriers to Employment of Older Workers," pp. 65–66
and Stahler, "Job Problems and Their Solution," p. 26.

Personal habits also become geared to the job. A person may look for work in the same section of the city where he has worked formerly because of familiarity with transportation facilities or for other similar reasons. The person may be unwilling to make a drastic break with habit and routine in order to obtain work. Some older job-seekers refuse to take jobs which pay less than their former ones or which carry less prestige. Any of these factors mean that the unemployed person is limiting his chance of being re-employed.

Older people sometimes fail to recognize the fact that they are old and that some of their faculties are failing. They cling to the idea that to wear glasses or hearing aids is to reveal one's age. Some resent the idea that they need a period of apprenticeship or retraining before entering new employment. Then too, having been employed regularly for a long period of time, older job-seekers often do not know how to sell themselves as potential employees. They do not know how to go about looking for work in the most effective and efficient manner. Sometimes after fruitlessly searching for a specific job they become discouraged. Their job approach then is that they are "willing to do anything." The difficulty in this is that few employers want people who can do anything. They look for employees who can do specific jobs. And yet almost all of these self-erected barriers to re-employment can be overcome provided the older worker is given adequate aids in seeking re-entry into employment. There is evidence to show that some employers are willing to hire older workers if they have the skills which are required of individuals to fill jobs for which there are openings.

It might be supposed that unions would do nothing to bar older workers from obtaining employment. The worker is the very life of the union. Usually unions have policies and practices such as seniority regulations which are designed specifically to benefit older workers, but as a rule most of the union practices and regulations benefit those who are already employed, not those seeking work. These regulations sometimes work to the detriment of older persons who are looking for work.

Briefly there are four ways in which unions indirectly hinder re-employment of older workers.[10] First, by the enforcement of seniority rules, preference is given to those who have been employed but later are "laid off" in periods of industrial inactivity. According to union rules, this means that all who have at one time been employed by the firm will have an option in re-employment before any nonunion person is hired. Second, many unions will not downgrade older workers in either pay or job. Some unions insist that so long as an older worker remains in the same position he will draw the same pay. Strict adherence to seniority rules works to prohibit downgrading in the type of job held. Third, unions that control hiring sometimes require a period of apprenticeship for new employees. In such cases older workers find that in order to be approved for work they must serve as apprentices. Thus, if there is an age limit on apprentices, they are not able to qualify for opening jobs. Finally, some unions will not allow older workers part-time employment. If an older worker desires to do part-time work or home work he is prohibited from doing so even though such work is available without detracting from the work available for regular full-time employees. Presumably here the principle is the same one that governs downgrading in work and pay. Breaking such rules would constitute an exception to union policies of uniform pay for similar work.

The rationale of age prejudice

Employers have erected the most formidable barriers to the employment of older job-seekers. This section will explore some of the reasons given by employers for their lack of enthusiasm in hiring older people.[11] The validity of these reasons will not be examined here. The basic assumption

[10] Cf. Albert J. Abrams, "Unions and the Older Worker," in *No Time to Grow Old*, pp. 119 ff.; and Samuel Barkin, "Union Policies and the Older Worker," in *The Aged and Society*, p. 75.

[11] Cf. Federal Security Agency, "Employment, Employability and Rehabilitation," in *Man and His Years* (Raleigh, N.C.: Health Publications

relative to these reasons either given by or attributed to management is that subjective reality is as strong a force in determining policy as objective reality is. If the employers or their agents define a situation as real, it *is* real in its consequences. There is, of course, no indication that all employers are always governed by all of the reasons given here; still, if an employer believes any one of these reasons with enough assurance then this one reason will suffice to determine his attitude and action toward hiring new employees who have reached advanced ages.

Reasons given for not hiring older people may be classified as follows: (1) those presumed to be inherent in the personality of the older person, (2) those due to the social relationship of the older worker with his fellow-employees or the public, and (3) those due to the impersonal forces of industry and the economic system. Ultimately all the reasons given under each of these headings hark back to the question of the value of the older individual as a contributor to the economic welfare of the firm for which he works.

Personal factors which are assumed to be inherent in old age are both psychologically and physiologically oriented. It seems to be the common belief that older workers are slower performers than younger ones are. From this it is reasoned that if they are hired there has to be some preference given them on the job; but any special consideration or below-average performance on the job reduces the total productivity of the firm. Hence, according to this logic, the older worker's services would cost as much or more than the value of the goods which he produced. The conclusion of such thinking is obvious.

It is further argued that the sickness and accident rates of the aged are higher than those of younger workers, that they lose more time from work and have a shorter work-life expectancy. This also ties in with the general idea that if an older worker has to be trained on the job he is slower to

Institute, 1951), p. 83; and Elizabeth Breckinridge, *Community Services for Older People* (Chicago: Follett Publishing Co., 1952), p. 45.

learn than younger people are. All of these factors combine to give the idea that he will not work efficiently at his job long enough to justify the cost of special concessions and training. Then, too, there is the generally accepted idea that older workers will not accept or be content with jobs carrying less prestige or lower wages than those formerly held. Finally if an older worker is hired at one level he will refuse to be downgraded in job or salary if it is found he cannot perform at his originally assigned task.

Under the second classification of *interpersonal relationships* is the idea that employees who come in contact with the public should be young and physically attractive. This is especially applicable to women who are waitresses, receptionists, or clerks and those who have similar jobs. Although a person may retain such a position after many years of service older persons would not be hired. A second general type of interpersonal relationships involves "friction in the family." Theoretically, most firms work on the basis of promotion from within. There seems to be some hesitancy to go outside and hire a person "over the head" of someone who has had several years' service. It is agreed that this policy of promoting from within is good for the morale of the workers, its opposite bad. Employers also like to maintain a semblance of an age balance in their plants. This desire may be explained partially on the grounds that they therefore never have more than a small number of replacements to hire and break in at any given time. Should a company hire a larger proportion of older men, in addition to those already at work, they would find dissatisfaction in the ranks of the younger employees and perhaps later be faced with the problem of a disproportionately large number of employees reaching retirement age at the same time. Related to this is the idea that older people do not like to be "bossed" by younger foremen and conversely that younger men feel ill at ease when they direct the activities of people who are older than themselves. This is to say that the unity or morale of the firm is disrupted by introducing older people into a plant where harmony has been maintained through the proper functioning of promotions and the chronologically based hierarchal system of authority.

The third classification consists of the *impersonal factors* which are given as reasons for hesitating to hire older workers. These factors may be lumped under the heading of increased cost of welfare programs. The argument used is that if there is a balanced work force, costs of these programs can be carried by the employer. On the other hand, a work force overweighted with older employees will be more expensive. It is said that workmen's compensation will be more expensive because older employees, if not more prone to accidents, require longer periods of time to recover than younger ones do. In effect, accidents suffered by older workers are more serious and hence more expensive than those of younger men. If men hired at older years are to benefit by group insurance or pension plans to the same extent as others, the rate of premium payment or payment into the pension fund will be out of proportion to that of workers who have been employed over a long period of years. It is said that either the employer or the worker himself would object to a lesser degree of insurance coverage or a smaller pension than other workers have. This would be true especially since the periodic premium payments would be at the same rate as those paid by younger men. Thus, in order to preclude inadequate coverage or no coverage at all and the possible resulting ill-feeling on the part of the employees, it is thought better not to hire a person after he has reached a specified age where premiums increase. This should not be taken to mean that regular employees will be fired when they attain a certain age for the sake of maintaining a low welfare program cost. The crux of the matter lies in the length of service rather than chronological age per se.

The whole area of discussion, as well as that concerning special work privileges or concessions made to older workers, can be examined under the heading of cost to the employer. The idea of considering the employee as a nonhuman element in the chain of production had a wide following in past times and still does in some circles today. This reasoning is rooted in the so-called classical school of economists. The greater profit falls to the firm which hires the most productive workers. Workers are hired in relation to the supply of labor and are paid in accordance with the market price, that is, the amount that they can obtain, which, in the final analysis, is determined by the amount of competition for the position. Profits which accrue to the firm are determined by the difference between the cost of raw materials and processing and the selling price of the finished products. It follows then that if an employee with a high record of production can be hired for a low wage his value to the company is great. Conversely, his value deteriorates as his productive abilities wane, unless his wages are reduced correspondingly. When social or union pressure forbid the reduction of wages, the gap between the cost of the employee and his value to the employer is narrowed. At some point the employee becomes a liability rather than an asset: it no longer benefits the employer to retain him.

If one follows this line of reasoning it becomes obvious that any special concessions in the way of physical material reduce the value of the worker to the employer. Longer periods required for training or retraining with a correspondingly shorter work life of older, re-employed persons put the employer of older persons in an unfavorable competitive position with those who have a young, alert, well-trained, stable work force. Obviously, some re-evaluation of this economic orientation will be necessary as the population becomes older. There is already some indication that the general stability of older workers, their sense of responsibility, the greater care that they take in producing, and the safety-consciousness they display may offset whatever reduced production of units per hour there is. There is also reason to doubt whether—at least up to certain rather advanced ages—production per worker is as low as it is generally assumed to be.

Some objective considerations of age prejudice

Some of the so-called self-erected barriers to employment are all too real. Yet were older job seekers to become more realistic or objective some of them would encounter less difficulty in finding re-employment. Older people seem to feel an inordinate amount of pride when told that they look or act 20 or 30 years younger than they actually are. Conversely, older people often try to hide their age or are ashamed of it if they cannot hide it. This state of affairs may call for a redefinition of the value of age. Perhaps the most realistic approach to the matter would be to make old age worthwhile or to create status positions, with social prestige, for older people. One way in which this can be accomplished is by making old age a useful, productive period of life. After all, it seems possible that time may be a friend of older people. When there are as many as 20 million people 65 and over in our population and many more than that in the older adult ages, emphasis may shift from the ideal of staying young to that of growing old. When this occurs, age in itself will be no barrier to re-employment.

As a rebuttal to the objections raised by employers to hiring older workers, consider the following points. First, the aged are a heterogeneous category. There is an undetermined amount of difference between individuals in their physical abilities. There is a wide range in the jobs which older people can perform. One man at the age of 70 may be perfectly capable of doing a job that another man at the age of 50 cannot do. It is a case of fitting the right person to the right job under the right circumstances. Second, the amount of research carried out in this field appears to be of such nature that so far it would be dangerous to formulate any general principles concerning the matter. It might be wise to indicate the strong possibility of bias on the part of some who have carried out studies of older workers. Suffice it to say that if there is no definite proof that employers are influenced by false assumptions regarding the aged employees, it is equally true that there is no definite proof that they are correct in the assumptions attributed to them.

One of the objections mentioned in the preceding section alleges that older workers are slower to learn new skills and in general are slower producers than young workers are, so that the cost of employment outweighs their value to the company. These criticisms will be dealt with here on the level of psychological-physiological inability or inaptitude to adapt to the job. Contrary to general belief, experiments show that where speed is not a factor the ability of older persons to learn is high. There is no conclusive evidence to indicate that the ability to learn is reduced significantly in middle age or later. Nevertheless most of the tests on learning and motor reaction show that as individuals become older there is a reduced capacity to function. It is necessary, however, to bear in mind several factors relating to such studies. First, few if any studies have taken a given group of people and studied comparatively their functioning at older and younger age levels. In other words, studies generally compare or contrast a group of older workers with a group of younger ones. Obviously there are individual differences present which influence the test results. Second, most test results are given in terms of averages. Such tests show that there is an overlapping of scores. Some old people perform at higher levels of efficiency than some young ones do, although the averages are generally lower as the age of the subjects advances. Third, in relation to employability, few of the tests so far devised are designed for specific jobs. They are rather general tests that do not apply specifically to specific tasks of employment. Finally, many of the tests are of short duration. These may indicate a high level of performance for older people which would be impossible for them to maintain over an extended period of time.[12]

An analysis of the length of time workers retain their jobs indicates that the labor turnover for older workers is not as great as for younger ones. Older people have more socio-economic reasons for wanting stable occupations. As compared to workers in their teens there is little occupational shifting after the age of 40 is reached. Once employed, older workers are less likely to be separated from employ-

[12] A. T. Welford and D. Speakman, "The Employability of Older People," in *The Aged and Society*, pp. 187–89.

ment than are younger workers. Workers 45 and over in the seven-city survey cited above represented 34 per cent of all workers employed at the end of the survey period but they experienced less than 25 per cent of the annual separations.[13] At the ages of 65 and over, workers voluntarily left their jobs less than half as often as those under 45 years of age. Workers 45 and over were less likely to be discharged than were those under this age. The rate of discharge was just half that of the younger age levels. The greater job stability of men over 45 is demonstrated in that those who have been employed for a year or more on one job have a lower separation rate than younger workers have. However, the separation rate for older men is high if they have been employed for less than one year. These men are the ones who are employed either on seasonal or temporary jobs.[14]

The accident rate for younger workers has been shown to be higher than it is for older workers. The average number of disabling injuries for those under 21 years of age is about one-third higher than for workers between the ages of 40 and 54. For workers 60 and over the rate is lower than for those under 21 years of age.[15] In a survey of 109 companies it was found that the peak of disabling injuries was reached at about the age of 41 and that of nondisabling injuries at about the age of 26. Both types of injuries declined until the age of 75 was reached (there was a slight rise in disabling injuries between the ages of 50 and 55, however). The number of nondisabling injuries at the age of 75 amounted to one-third of the peak number.[16]

It is true that the average length of time required for healing is greater as age increases. In a specific study, the

[13] John I. Saks, "Status in the Labor Market," *Monthly Labor Review*, LXXX (January, 1957), 18.

[14] *Ibid.*, pp. 19–20.

[15] Cf. Nathan Shock, "Older People and Their Potentialities for Gainful Employment," *Journal of Gerontology*, II (April, 1947), 97–99; and Welford and Speakman, "The Employability of Older People," in *The Aged and Society*, pp. 186–87.

[16] Mary E. Switzer and Howard A. Rusk, "Keeping Older People Fit for Participation," *The Annals of the American Academy of Political and Social Science*, CCLXXIX (January, 1952), 151.

average healing period for workers 55 years and over was thirty-four days while that for workers between the ages of 21 and 24 was twenty-three days. The greater length of the healing period is more than offset by the diminished accident rate for older workers. Indications are that older workers tend to lose more time from work because of illness than younger ones do, that is, it takes the older ones longer to recover, but there is some indication that the frequency of illness decreases up to a certain age.[17]

The arguments pertaining to the older person not wanting to be downgraded or being unwilling to accept lower paying jobs are probably true in some instances. It is true that the more desperately a job is sought the less demanding the job-seeker is that the job meet all of his requirements. One possible consequence of accepting a lower level of work is that potential employers might hesitate to employ a person who has been employed in a lower grade of work. Temporary self-imposed downgrading would tend to become permanent downgrading. So long as an older worker hopes or believes he is still employable, he might display a hesitancy to take a lower grade job.

Whether older workers fit in with other employees is another matter that depends primarily upon the personality of the individuals involved. There is said to be a certain amount of natural antagonism between the generations. This may be true in some settings but it is probably not true in a firm where the range of employee age is not only wide but where representatives of all ages are present. It is also contended that hiring older workers disrupts the orderly promotion of younger employees. Apparently this objection is based on the false assumption that all employees are always promoted and promoted in the same order in which they are hired. If there is anything approaching a time schedule of promotions within firms and businesses based on age and time with the company it is probably derived from the old life-tables and old work-life expectancy tables. In the light of

[17] Nathan Shock, "Older People and Their Potentialities for Gainful Employment," p. 100.

current life expectancy it would seem that whatever system of promotions now exists will have to be changed. Promotions still will be possible but they will not be as frequent as they now are. If promotions are now based on a 25-year work life they will later be based on a 30-year work life.

The question of additional costs of group insurance, workman's compensation, and pension plans apparently needs some clarification. The argument states that group life insurance programs offer no reason for discrimination against older workers.[18] Evidence indicates that the percentage of employees in various age levels does not differ much between the total working force and some nearly nine million group-insured employees. It is stated that employers who adopt group life insurance on their own initiative do not dismiss workers solely because of advancing age. To fire employees because of age would be to defeat the very purpose of insurance. Insurance premiums are based on the attained age of the employees, not on the length of service with the employer. There is then no reason to justify not hiring an older person any more than there is to fire an older employee.

On the other hand, to the layman who is not well versed in the intricacies of insurance, it might appear that some of the arguments could be used to discourage employers with group life insurance plans from hiring older workers. The standard monthly gross premium rates per $1,000 of group life insurance are $.48 at the age of 30, $.72 at 40, $1.28 at the age of 50 and $2.59 at the age of 60. "The employer would have paid for $2,000 of group insurance, on a gross basis, approximately five cents a day more for an employee at age 50 than for an employee at age 30."[19] It may be true that the difference between premium costs is more apparent than real, but it is a very apparent difference. The argument is that the insurance companies would not do anything to discourage the employment of older workers because it

---

[18] Reinhard A. Hohaus, "Group Life Insurance and the Employment of Older Workers," in *No Time to Grow Old*, pp. 193 ff.

[19] *Ibid.*, p. 193.

would adversely affect the ability of the employees to pay premiums on their other insurance policies.

There are ways of minimizing the differences between age groups so far as group life insurance is concerned. One such way is to reduce the amount of insurance at older ages. This plan has been tried on a limited scale primarily to insure persons over 65 with a differentiation between active and retired employees. It appears that the premium rate is reducible only by reducing the amount of insurance. Pension plans can be devised to exclude those who are hired after they have attained a certain age. There might be serious objections from the employee relations point of view ". . . not to mention State insurance laws prohibiting such practices—against adopting the same procedure in the case of a Group Life plan where the reduction in cost would be negligible." [20] It would appear from the foregoing that virtually everything in the argument presented could be taken as rather concrete reason for employers with group life insurance plans to refuse to hire older employees although there might be no incentive to fire older ones.

There seems to be little doubt that pension costs increase when older men are hired. The cost varies with the type of plan in force. It would not apply to systems which disregard age and are operating on a cents-an-hour basis.[21] Several observations seem to be in order here. First, not all employers have private pension plans. Even though pensions for older workers are more expensive than for younger ones they are not expensive for firms which have no plan. Second, if private plans were universal and uniform and were transferable no problem would be involved. Third, where plans are in force, one or more solutions seem possible. The older worker could be hired with the understanding that pensions are based on years of service (where they are) and therefore some benefits would not be as great as others. Although employers may argue that they do not like to hire older people and then fail to place them on their pension

[20] *Ibid.*, p. 194.
[21] Albert J. Abrams, "Barriers to Employment of Older Workers," p. 67.

rolls, this is not so serious a deprivation as it would have been prior to old-age and survivors insurance when there were few pension plans in force. It is self-evident that unemployed persons in the later middle age levels would rather have a job and no pension than no job and no pension. It might appear that a person who refused a job because there were no pension provisions was not very interested in a job under any circumstances.

Evidence gathered by the Bureau of Employment Security in the seven-city survey referred to above indicates that employers frequently use pension costs as an excuse for not hiring older people. Firms without pension plans, in six of the seven cities surveyed, hired from one and one-half to two times as many persons over 45 years of age as did firms with pension plans. The difference in the proportion of older workers hired by firms with and without plans widened as the age of the workers increased.[22]

Apparently employers are not clear as to the reasons they believe pension costs increase with increased age. It is reasonable that paying pension costs for younger workers is more expensive than for older ones; however, the greater expense is spread out over a much longer period of time. Where pension plans call for a maximum number of years' service, newly hired older workers are automatically excluded from coverage, so they would not cost the employer anything. In the final analysis, the real pension expense is determined by the number of years a pensioner lives in retirement, not by the age at which he is employed.[23]

Although indirectly unions may hinder the re-employment of older people, their programs of seniority are designed specifically to aid the older employee. So far as union members are concerned union activity actually may reduce the number of older job-seekers. In an analysis of 1,687 major contracts in operation in 1955 and 1956 covering nearly 7.5 million workers, it was found that seventy-six of the contracts had

[22] Bureau of Employment Security, *Pension Costs in Relation to the Hiring of Older Workers*, No. E150 (September, 1956), p. 2.

[23] *Ibid.*, p. 23.

provisions which required or encouraged hiring of older workers. Some of these contracts required one older person to be hired for every five younger people. Eighteen contracts contained a ban on maximum hiring ages. More than two hundred of the contracts made some kind of provision for transferring older workers who were already employed to less exacting or more suitable jobs. Some of the contracts made provision for pay adjustment in the new assignment, whereas some others made provision for pay adjustment as the worker became older with no mention of job transfer.[24]

Steps toward training older workers to learn the intricacies of automation are being taken by both unions and management. Training classes originally organized only for younger workers, in some instances, now are enrolling older men in the ratio of one to every two younger ones.

In the final analysis, three things apparently remain to be done in this area. First, a series of realistic, scientifically conducted studies could be made to determine the employability of every individual who is interviewed for a job. Second, social attitudes could be re-evaluated in the light of findings of these tests. Third, a device other than chronological age could be established upon which to make objective decisions concerning the employability of any given individual for any given job. Whether or not these three steps will ever be carried out, the fact remains that in the future if the production capacity of this country is to be maintained, the labor force will consist of an increasingly large proportion of older workers. They can be assigned to jobs on an arbitrary, hit-or-miss basis as has obtained in the past or they can be placed in jobs where they would be more productive and of greater benefit to themselves, their employers, and the over-all economy of the country.

Summary

As individuals approach later middle age or old age, they begin to find it more difficult to obtain employment than it

[24] Harry P. Cohany, "Employment and Age in Union Contracts," *Monthly Labor Review*, LXXIX (December, 1956), 1404–7.

was earlier in life. Studies made on this subject reveal that approximately one-fifth of the employers questioned state that they have set age limits beyond which they will not employ people. The age specified varies from occupation to occupation. In all probability age discrimination in hiring practices is not limited to formal regulations but finds expression in the personal attitudes and prejudices of the hiring agent or the personnel manager. It seems that this prejudice against hiring older workers is more prevalent among employers of large numbers of workers than in small firms. There is evidence that where age is the only negative factor it is sometimes overlooked in hiring practices. If older persons have desirable personal qualities and good records in certain classes of occupations, the age barrier may be set aside for them or originally may not have been set very low in that particular occupation. Temporarily setting aside age barriers does not necessarily mean that prejudice against hiring older workers no longer exists.

Advancing chronological age is assumed to bring with it certain physical, psychological, and personality characteristics that do not meet with the approval of potential employers. Whether or not the various prejudices held against older job seekers are based in fact, employers often react subjectively and refuse to employ older people. Claims are made that older people are more accident-prone than younger ones are and the incidence of sickness is greater, or that they do not fit in well with other employees and disrupt the system of promotions. Further, it is alleged that the various welfare programs are more costly when the age hierarchy is disrupted by a disproportionate number of older workers. Finally, employers hesitate to hire older workers because it is believed that they are not as productive as younger ones and thus cost the firm more than they produce.

7

Re-employment of the Aged

The preceding chapter inquired into some of the barriers which have been erected in various sectors of society to the hiring of persons on the basis of their attained chronological age. While this practice has been occurring there have been some countertrends also. That is, steps have been and are being taken to assure the employment of older job-seekers. It is well to recall that all unemployed older people have only two characteristics in common: they are unemployed and they are chronologically old enough to encounter difficulties in finding re-employment. There is an indication that age of itself is not a sufficiently valid reason for refusing a person employment. It was indicated in the preceding chapter that other reasons are often given by employers. However, the general inference is that age is correlated positively with these other so-called valid reasons. It is erroneously assumed that if a person has reached a particular age he must have certain undesirable characteristics which are presumed to be absent in younger people.

This chapter will explore some of the devices which have been and may possibly be used in reducing the amount of unemployment in the older age categories. Is there anything that can be done to help the older job-seekers find and retain their new jobs? Finding jobs for older workers is rather difficult. Very often it involves re-education of the job-seeker, the employer, and the agent whose task it is to find employment for the unemployed. The primary problem of older people is that they encounter difficulty if they are retired or fired from their jobs before they are willing, either economically or psychologically, to stop work. But it may be asked: What prevents older people from re-entering the list of active employees? Part of the answer has been presented above—there are resistances to the employment of older people. The simplest way to meet the problem involved here is to state that a social situation should be created whereby the aged unemployed could regain employment. This would, for the purpose of this discussion, involve three interrelated activities: first, aid to the job-seeker in the form of counseling, retraining, and hints to help him find a job; second, an educational program directed toward employers; third, the establishment of agencies, both public and private, to facilitate the programs necessary to carry out both the first and second propositions. In addition to re-employment these three activities could be applied to part-time employment, hobby-income activities, or self-employment of the aged. In short, this chapter will inquire into the possibilities of improving the earned income of persons 65 years of age and over who are capable of earning money and want to spend full or part time doing so.

Aid to job-seekers

One of the cherished traditions in this country has been that every person worth his salt is capable of standing alone and competing for employment in what has been called the "open market." The theory behind this is that of supply and demand. If a labor shortage occurs in one industry or geographic area, wages will consequently increase and surplus labor will be drawn in from areas where there are too many workers or where the wages are low.

A large number of the working population depends on the seek-and-find method of obtaining employment. The establishment of both public and private employment services was a step away from this hit-and-miss type of job-seeking. These services have tried to bring employees and employers together with a minimum of waste in time, money, and effort on the part of both. Certain categories of job-seekers may resort more frequently to employment services than others do. This would be especially true for those who had unsuccessfully sought jobs for any length of time. These

people in all probability are workers who have characteristics that operate to make it difficult for them to obtain work.
These categories include members of minority racial and
ethnic groups, unskilled workers, women, the handicapped,
and older people.

In addition to both public and private employment agencies, older job-seekers can refer to help-wanted advertisements in the newspapers. They can follow news stories
concerning expansion of plants or the establishment of new
plants or businesses in the community in which they live.
They can also keep in touch with former employers and
friends who are in a position to know about vacancies. Various interested agencies have compiled "helpful hints" for
elderly job-seekers which are designed to assist them in writing letters of application for jobs and in "selling" themselves
to prospective employers.

Self-employment

As many people become older they either elect or are
forced into self-employment as a means of supplementing
their incomes. Traditionally one of the primary sources of
self-employment has been the occupation of farming. Statistics indicate that this is still a popular area for self-
employment of the aged, attracting people from all walks
of life, especially people from the industrial centers.

Some of the implications of retirement farming are indicated in a survey which was made in Duval County, Florida,
in 1951.[1] Of the 307 family heads included in the study, 25
per cent were operating retirement farms. A variety of reasons were given by the respondents for choosing a farm on
which to retire. Nearly 40 per cent preferred rural life, 15
per cent had always lived on farms, 13 per cent wanted to
retire on a farm, 12 per cent believed they could reduce the
cost of living, and 10 per cent chose a farm because of
chronic illness of the head of the family. In all, 42 per cent

[1] D. E. Alleger, "Retirement Farming in Duval County, Florida," in T.
Lynn Smith (ed.), *Living in the Later Years* (Gainesville: University of
Florida Press, 1952), pp. 87–89.

of the family heads were permanently disabled and 46 per cent were having serious financial difficulties and hoped that retirement farming would solve some of their problems. About 70 per cent of the farms had an acreage of five acres or less. Half of the operators cultivated less than one-half acre of land. Livestock and poultry were relatively unimportant sources of food or cash income. About 19 per cent of the operators had neither livestock nor poultry, and less than 4 per cent owned two kinds of meat animals. The study concluded that, in terms of dollars alone, more retirement farmers failed than succeeded. The farmers are handicapped by lack of capital as well as by lack of work power. Farming in Duval County, as elsewhere, is beset by many hazards which retired people are ill-prepared to meet.

Retirement farming measured in monetary terms seems to be a failure rather than a source of security for older people. It would appear that if the study reviewed here is indicative of some of the difficulties encountered by those who enter retirement farming, some extensive educational work with older people, relative to retirement farming, falls in the classification of a "must."

Older people are faced with at least two difficulties in the area of self-employment. First, they are handicapped by a lack of knowledge. Many have little information about farming or business. While many of them may be physically able to work hard, hard work is not the sole prerequisite to success. The lure of a little farm of one's own, especially to those reared in rural areas, may be great. The idea of buying a corner grocery store may be equally attractive. Perhaps the psychology behind both sorts of enterprise may be summed up in the idea that "Well, we can always raise enough to supply our own table" or "As long as we sell groceries we can buy our own at wholesale prices." Even if these statements were true, it should be kept in mind that more than food is needed by an aged couple today. Also, the original outlay for the business or farm may take all of the cash and yet require monthly payments. Second, older people are handicapped by a lack of sufficient capital for an investment which would yield large enough returns on which to live. This is not to say that people who take financial risks do not succeed. However, if a 6 per cent return from a business or farm investment can be expected as "normal," it should be rather clear that $6,000 invested would not be as profitable as $60,000 would be. It would be unsound financial thinking to expect enough yearly return from the lesser amount to justify going into business as the sole source of future income. With no detailed inquiry into the subject, a person might imagine that all corner grocery stores or drugstores and all family-sized farms constitute sources of sure, steady, and high incomes. Such a picture is sometimes alluring for the younger population. At first guess, it would seem that little work is involved and good income is assured. Closer inquiry into the situation would reveal a different picture.

Besides re-employment and self-employment there remains the possibility of older persons turning a hobby into a source of supplementary income. Either alone or in organized groups many older people are seeking income from the sale of hobby products. No doubt much more will be done as the science of gerontology progresses. There are many people who reach the later years with no hobby which can be made to yield an income. However, as will be pointed out later, there is apparently no law of man or of nature which forbids older people to learn a hobby. If hobbies can be learned early in life they can be learned late in life. The lack of a hobby is no proof that there is an inability to learn one. There is no indication that useful, productive hobbies cannot be turned into money yielding hobbies with the proper study and direction.

Educating employers

At first glance it would seem that employers would have no more than a passing interest in the problem of the employment or re-employment of older persons. But when employers are unconcerned, it indicates rather that the task of education of employers is just as necessary as that of educating the employee and the public as a whole. The following is a list of eight factors with which management should be concerned in dealing with the problem of the employment of older workers.[2] First, as more older people are excluded from private employment, more of them will turn to the government for aid. Second, as the number of nonproductive old people grows, private and public pension funds will have to grow. Third, this growing program of pensions will increase the rate of corporate taxation for their support. Fourth, it is doubtful that the growing number of nonproductive old people can be supported without endangering the level of living of everyone. Fifth, negotiations with unions over pension plans and welfare funds will probably become more complex. Sixth, the community suffers from a decrease in productivity as well as a decrease in purchasing power when large numbers of the population are nonproducers. Seventh, ill-will toward management is engendered when the cost of living increases with no provision being made for an increase in pension payments. A fixed dollar value pension plan set up years before retirement may prove wholly inadequate upon retirement. The employer is in no position to remedy the situation and the employee becomes bitter. Finally, the employer should be as concerned with his older workers as he is with all employees; study and analysis of performance, health, and happiness of employees in general relate better adjustment in retirement.

One means to educate employers is to publicize comments made by employers who have favorable attitudes toward older workers. As reported by staff members of state employment offices, some of the employers of older workers favor their retention for the following reasons. Older workers are more mature in their work habits and thus add stability to the work force. Older workers waste less time on the job than do younger workers. Older employees have steady work habits and a more serious attitude toward work. They are not absent as frequently as younger people are. They

[2] Adapted from Elizabeth Breckinridge, *Community Services for Older People* (Chicago: Follett Publishing Co., 1952), pp. 37–38.

have a well-developed sense of responsibility and are more loyal to the job and to their employer. After the worker has become oriented to his job, older men require less supervision than do younger ones. Older workers are not as easily distracted by outside interests and are more capable of greater concentration on the job.[3]

Employment services

The existing employment services were evolved in an era in the history of this country when there was no problem of aging. These agencies were concerned primarily with getting new workers started in the labor market, with finding jobs for the "average" workers who were temporarily unemployed, and with finding employees for jobs which were available. There were certain categories of jobs into which people with the necessary qualifications could fit. Little if any adjustments had to be made. If a person had the qualifications to fill a job vacancy he was assumed to be able to do the work. If he could not qualify for this job, then he would have to wait for an opening for which he possessed the necessary qualifications. It was a relatively simple assignment to fill out the blanks in the personnel data form and file the card under the appropriate heading. Interviews could be completed in a relatively short time and then the next person in line could be taken care of.

Due to heavy work loads and lack of time, and in many cases lack of skilled personnel, many employment bureaus are in no position to spend long hours consulting with, counseling, and guiding the job-seeker with special problems. Employment services on an assembly-line basis will not satisfy the needs of older workers or the handicapped. With the ever-increasing number of aged, some readjustment is called for in the placement of older workers in jobs where they will be of social and economic usefulness to themselves and to society. This rethinking entails re-education of employment agency personnel and a re-formation of attitudes

[3] Abraham Stahler, "Job Problems and Their Solution," *Monthly Labor Review*, LXXX (January, 1957), 25.

in the prospective employee and employer. Evidence indicates that where re-education is attempted and where more time, effort, and patience are exerted, the seemingly unemployable elderly person can find employment with an employer who may have seemed unwilling to hire any but younger people.

Some short-range experiments have been carried out by various agencies. These experiments have been designed to see what has to be done and to ascertain the results of a concerted, well-devised plan to attempt to place older workers. As a guide to possible action, the Community Project for the Aged, of the Welfare Council of Metropolitan Chicago, makes the following observations and suggestions.[4] It is clear that during times of labor shortages, employers are often forced to hire older people when ordinarily they would not do so. Furthermore, during such periods technological changes are made and laborsaving devices are installed. Often during emergency periods when older people are employed, employers have some unpleasant experiences with them. These unpleasant experiences probably lead to a hardening of the preconceived stereotypes already held by the employer. Adverse occurrences confirm existing prejudices, whereas pleasant relationships dispel these stereotyped ideas rather slowly. As a consequence of the above conditions, the Project believes that the time for action is the present, for it cannot be assumed that an increase in the employment of the aged now will automatically remain high in the future when demand is not so great. This means that if anything is to be done it should be done while older people are employed, not when the market is filled with great numbers of older people seeking work.

The Project recommended the establishment of a Senior Employment Division in the Illinois State Employment Service. The following eight functions of this proposed division were suggested: (1) to analyze and classify jobs which can be filled by older workers, (2) to "promote work opportunities" for older people, (3) to provide skilled counseling

[4] Breckinridge, *Community Services for Older People*, pp. 39–41.

about work opportunities, and retraining programs, as well as to determine the work abilities of the applicants, (4) to find jobs for the workers, (5) to encourage the development of a secondary occupation for those who can no longer pursue their primary job activities, (6) to introduce retraining programs along lines designed to meet future employment needs, (7) to plan with both public and private agencies in a vocational rehabilitation program for older people, and (8) to help promote part-time employment opportunities for older people in their own local communities.

The Project foresaw three possible objections to the establishment of such a division.[5] These were, first, that there was a scarcity of available money; second, that such a program would be relatively useless until employers removed restrictions on hiring older people; and third, that the existing Employment Service staff could deal with the problem adequately. The answers to these three objections were stated as follows. First, it is better to spend money to save money than merely to spend it. Second, the Senior Employment Division would do much to eliminate employer barriers. Third, past experience demonstrates the necessity of a specialized program. It is misleading to older people to accept their registrations for jobs without providing an adequate follow-up program. In other words, it is a waste of the time and money of both the Employment Service personnel and the applicant.

In New York a study was made by the State Employment Service as part of a survey initiated by the United States Bureau of Employment Security.[6] This study included 3,688 men and women aged 45 years and older. This number was about equally divided between the control group which received the same treatment normally given older people and the experimental group which received concerted attention from the placement staff and counselors. Five different em-

[5] *Ibid.*, p. 41.
[6] New York State Employment Service, "The Public Employment Service Views the Older Job Seeker," in Thomas C. Desmond (chm.), *No Time to Grow Old* (Albany: New York State Joint Legislative Committee on Problems of the Aging, 1951), pp. 97 ff.

ployment branches participated in this activity. Included were the Commercial and Professional Office, Needle Trades Office, Queens Industrial Office, Service Trades Office, and Sales Office. Counselors and placement staff members were instructed to give as much aid to the older job-seekers as they could without interfering with their other activities. In addition to the regular placement interview counseling was used where necessary. Only a fraction more than 25 per cent of the experimental group received counseling service. The control group was given no more consideration than older workers were usually given and little if any more than the younger workers were given. In the experimental group 522 persons were counseled.

At the beginning of the study twelve major problems were encountered with older applicants. Table 11 gives some indication of the various types of problems involved

TABLE 11

Employment Problems of the Aged

Kind of Problem *	Per Cent of Group Affected
Physical handicap or loss of strength	15
Too specialized experience or overqualification for job	14
Unrealistic or too rigid demands	14
Recently unemployed with good work record; need help	13
Spotty work record or inadequate training	9
Loss of speed or need to shift to new field	9
Low morale due to rebuff	8
Personality and emotional problems	5
Lack of insight into own limitations	4
Poor personal appearance, grooming, etc.	3
Entering or re-entering with no skill or rusty skill	3
Lack of knowledge of English language (Refugee or D.P. group)	2
Unclassified	1

SOURCE: New York State Employment Service, "The Public Employment Service Views the Older Job Seeker," in Thomas C. Desmond (chm.), *No Time to Grow Old* (Albany: New York State Joint Legislative Committee on Problems of the Aging, 1951), p. 99.

* Some of the applicants fall into two or more of the classifications as these categories are not mutually exclusive.

and the distribution of persons interviewed in the experimental group.

It was found that some of the applicants needed little or no aid in obtaining employment. Persons possessing skills which were in demand, those who had only recently become unemployed, and those with a steady work record needed little if any aid. On the other hand, there were some persons to whom the employment service could give little help. Primary among these were the unemployables or borderline unemployables, those with serious personality problems, those who did not want to be downgraded, and those who, for any reason, had to change to a new field of employment.

However, for those who needed help and could be helped, the following techniques were put to good use. The most effective single technique used was that of individual job solicitation. This included four types: field visits to employers, telephone solicitations, special letters, and the sending out of profiles for individuals. The Commercial-Professional office found that telephone solicitation was the most effective of these types. Either this or letter writing or profiles were advantageous because the interest of the potential employer could be aroused before he had a chance to be prejudiced by the person's age. In solicitation by telephone the employment office staff stressed good qualities first and only if pushed by the employer would state the applicant's age. Counseling was of importance, and where necessary, much time had to be spent on this process. This was necessary so that job-seekers would be referred to jobs where their skills could be used and where they would fit into the job well.

Another very important factor which helped in the referral and placement of the older job-seeker was that the employment service personnel knew where to look for openings for the applicant and where it would be a waste of time to look. Smaller concerns with no age restrictions, the non-glamour jobs, and employers who had records of hiring older people were usually the ones approached. One instance is given where the employer specified an age limit of 30 years for a stenographer. The interviewer "sold" him on a 47-

year-old woman who not only got the job but was promoted very shortly. Later the same employer, in looking for other stenographers, specified that he wanted older persons.

There was no doubt in the minds of the people who participated in this experiment that it was a successful one. It must be pointed out, however, that as far as job quality is concerned there is insufficient evidence to conclude whether the control or experimental group fared better. The bulk of placements of the applicants were in their usual occupations. Due to the relatively small numbers involved as well as to the difference in composition of the two groups, no unqualified conclusion seems justifiable as to the amount of wages received after placement in jobs. In the experimental group all of the applicants received service beyond the reception point. Counseling service was given to 27 per cent, jobs were solicited for 16 per cent, 36 per cent were referred to jobs, and 19 per cent were placed. In the control group only 3 per cent were given counseling service. There is no way of knowing how many had jobs solicited, 16 per cent were referred to jobs, and 8 per cent were placed.

It should be noted that the persons in the control group represented the most placeable of the job applicants over the age of 45. Among persons 45 and over, only about one-third pass the reception desk, as a rule. This fraction is selected on the basis of placeability on the current market. In other words, the two-thirds who do not get beyond the "sift" desk fail to do so because there appears to be no job for them. The one-third who do are the most placeable of the applicants. On the contrary the experimental group was not selected on this basis but was composed of unselected individuals who included marginal and unplaceable individuals. In view of this qualification the success of the venture might be considered to be more marked than the bare statistics indicate.

Due to several factors it is possible to draw only tentative conclusions concerning the characteristics of the members of the experimental group who were placed. Those beyond the age of 65 with only grade school education or those with a college education did not fare very well. Fewer women than men were placed and fewer nonunion than union members found jobs. Skilled and semiskilled workers had better luck than the unskilled or professionals. There appears to be a clear-cut negative relation between length of time of unemployment and ease in becoming re-employed. This does not rule out the fact that many persons unemployed for one or two months could not be placed nor that some who had been without work for as long as a year were placed.

Early in 1956 a program similar to the one outlined above was begun in the seven major cities referred to earlier. This was a demonstration counseling and placement program arranged by the Department of Labor in cooperation with national, state, and local employment services to help develop methods of assisting older workers obtain employment.[7] The technique for this pilot project was similar to the one carried out in New York. A total of 7,400 persons 45 years and over was selected at random from workers seeking employment through local offices in the seven cities. These job-seekers were divided about equally between an experimental group and a control group. Persons in the experimental group were given intensive counseling and placement services whereas the members of the control group were given only normal placement services.[8] The special services included intensive interviewing, employment counseling, group guidance, use of aptitude and proficiency tests, referral to training facilities for new skills, solicitation for jobs, and an effort to eliminate age specifications in job orders.

An analysis of the results of this program demonstrates that job-seekers who received intensive service were more successful than were members of the control group in obtaining employment. In each successively older group over the age of 45 a higher percentage of job-seekers in the experi-

[7] James P. Mitchell, "An Introductory Note," *Monthly Labor Review,* LXXIX (December, 1956), 1402.

[8] Abraham Stahler, "Job Problems and Their Solution," pp. 26 ff.

mental group succeeded in obtaining employment than of those in the control group.[9] The conclusion reached was that as many as four times more older job-seekers could be placed if given the benefit of such services.[10] Growing out of the success of this experiment all state employment offices were asked to extend and improve the services to older job applicants. Special funds were allocated by the Department of Labor for specialized personnel in each state office and in seventy local offices. These special funds were used to augment existing services to older workers.[11]

From the foregoing analysis it seems safe to conclude that such projects are worthwhile. Although the experiments in placing older people were not 100 per cent successful, they were appreciably more successful than normal placement services are. Since it appears that there is more difficulty in placing people who have reached their sixty-fifth year, the value of programs of this nature might lie in placing people before they reach this age.

Job-making for the aged

Some clubs and organizations have been established in this country for the purpose of giving employment to their own members and to other retired people. In some instances these clubs, composed of retired financial or business executives or lawyers, are organized solely as advice-giving agencies. They offer their services either free or at a nominal cost to young men who are beginning business careers. Others are organized by older people who start into business for themselves. They make it a practice to hire only people who have reached retirement age and have been retired from their regular employment. In addition to these clubs some long-established enterprises make it a practice to hire, in certain branches of their firms, only older people. Privately owned and operated concerns, such as "Sunset Incorporated,"

[9] *Ibid.*, p. 26.
[10] Mitchell, "An Introductory Note," p. 1402.
[11] *Ibid.*, p. 1402.

have been organized by individuals or groups for the specific purpose of hiring older people who want to re-enter the labor market.

Progress in this area of activity seems to be expanding to some extent within recent years and might be classed as "remarkable." However, it appears that only certain categories of skills or professions can be utilized in these enterprises. So far many semiskilled or unskilled older people have not been able to participate to any appreciable extent in these organizations, and there are professional groups which may not have been reached. In the academic world many smaller colleges and universities are following the practice of appointing teachers who have been retired from larger schools. Frequently colleges with lower than average salary scales can attract high-caliber professors to their staffs who would rather be employed at a reduced salary than not at all. The benefits are mutual. The Ford Foundation has endowed a project for the employment of a limited number of retired college teachers. The Foundation helps selected institutions pay the salary of the retired professor as he assumes his duties in "retirement" teaching.[12]

An organization known as Senior Achievement, Incorporated, has been set up in Chicago by industrialists of that city to provide useful part-time work for retired people. This project also has as one of its aims increasing the income of older people who have inadequate retirement incomes. After careful study and planning, the program was announced in December of 1955. Financial assistance was obtained from leaders in business and industry as was cooperation in organizing the program. The money which was donated was used to obtain suitable space and to equip a fairly complete woodworking shop, metal shop, soft goods department as well as drafting and engineering departments. Already this program has enough diversity to make use of professional people, engineers, skilled craftsmen, stenographers, semiskilled and unskilled people. As it develops and more peo-

[12] Ronald I. Robinson, "Beyond Retirement," *American Association of University Professors Bulletin*, XLI (Summer, 1955), 328 ff.

ple are employed, use can be made of human abilities in almost all areas of economic activity.

Corporations in the Chicago area subcontract work to Senior Achievement, Incorporated which pays the people who are employed. The "out-service" department has placed more than two hundred older people in various types of office work and in other services. Employers hire the service and Senior Achievement, Incorporated, acts as a go-between by hiring the employees who are then sent out to various jobs. This procedure makes it unnecessary for the cooperating business to deal directly with the older person as employee. The program has obtained subcontracts of numerous kinds from both small and large manufacturing concerns. It is anticipated that the program will be expanded appreciably so that more retired persons will be able to find part-time employment and thus be able to supplement their incomes.[13]

In some areas both public and private agencies have organized sheltered workshops in which they employ older and handicapped workers who cannot adjust to usual or normal factory situations. Where necessary, arrangements are made so that all work can be done while the operator is seated. Hours of work are shorter with more frequent and longer rest intervals. It is highly debatable whether such enterprises are economically worthwhile from the entrepreneur's point of view. From the social point of view, however, it seems that they are worthwhile. In the first place, work is given to people who want to work. They are gainfully employed, they are helping to support themselves and at the same time are contributing a share to the total national income. Although such an enterprise would probably show no profit in operation it is reasonable to assume that publicly owned workshops of this nature could save money in the long run. The more money earned by the employees the less public money would have to be spent in supporting them. From the economic view they are producers as well as consumers. Even

---

[13] David E. Sonquist, "The Effect of Work Activities on Health," an address before the Ninth Annual Conference on Aging, Ann Arbor: 1955; and David E. Sonquist, *Senior Achievements, Inc.* (Chicago, Ill.)

if such projects were to spend a dollar to save 95 cents, it would be worth something to the older persons to be kept busy, within the limits of their abilities, at some productive job. How long it will be before such workshops are widespread remains to be seen. The movement, like many others, seems to be off to a slow start. There appears little reason to believe that there will be a great demand for such enterprises even if there were proof that, in the long run, the taxpayer would save money.

Summary

There are four possible steps to be taken toward the solution of the problem involved in finding re-employment for the unemployed aged. First, there is the problem of research to determine objectively whether older workers are as productive as younger ones, or in which areas they are or are not as productive. After this is done, there is the problem of publicizing the results so as to attempt to change the attitudes of employers toward hiring and retaining older persons. Second, federal and state governments could be encouraged to follow the lead of such states as New York and Wisconsin in revising their retirement laws to make retirement voluntary at a late date. These states have removed the mandatory retirement laws from their books as long as the employee can function properly. So long as federal and state governments refuse to hire older persons or force relatively early retirement of those who work for them, there is little reason to believe that private industry will change its course of action. Third, a general widespread organization of sheltered workshops or supervised piecework in the homes could be set up. This program could be carried on either by private concerns subsidized by public funds or by local governmental welfare agencies. Money used could be drawn from the source now used to support the aged who are able to work under favorable conditions but who can find no work. Maximum standards of safety and comfort should be a matter of public policy. Fourth, antidiscrimination laws could be passed making discrimination against workers, because of age, punishable by law. Massachusetts' law of 1937 was largely inoperative because there were no penalty provisions attached. Later, in 1950, the Fair Employment Practices Law was revised to include the aged; in addition penalty provisions were added. As it now stands, the Massachusetts law makes it illegal to discriminate against a person because of race, religion, age, and so forth. As with other similar laws, this one tries to work on the basis of persuasion, not force. If persuasion fails to get the desired results, a penalty can be imposed.

There is no reason to believe that legislation can solve all the problems in the area of gerontology. There is some reason to believe, nonetheless, that a legislative program, along with the other three proposals made above, might go a long way toward solving the problem. As a matter of fact, if the first three points were to become action programs, the laws might not be needed except as a prod to laggards. Without the first three points, the law would probably be obeyed only by those employers who would not discriminate anyway. It would be evaded or broken by others who might be convinced that it would be more economical for them to pay the fines than to run an economic risk by hiring older employees.

8

Preparation for Retirement

It has been the concern of the preceding chapters to inquire into the extent of employment of older workers, barriers to re-employment, and the possibility of eradicating some of these barriers so that the worker might again become gainfully employed. This chapter will deal with retirement. Save for its practice by the privileged few, retirement is a relatively recent phenomenon in this country. The idea runs counter to the Protestant-capitalistic philosophy in which voluntary idleness had no place. Idleness was looked upon as something to be shunned because "an idle brain is the devil's workshop." Laziness, slothfulness, and idleness were all considered to be vices differing only in degree from some of the grosser sins. The idea seems to have been that there was a cause-and-effect relationship between idleness and the more serious immoralities. However, there was a concurrent idea that the very wealthy could retire without suffering any loss in status or reduction in prestige. This may have been the case because obviously wealth could come only as the result and reward of hard work. Those who had worked hard and had acquired enough money for a comfortable retirement would have earned the additional reward of being able to spend the remainder of their lives in idleness, living on the fruits of past labor. It should be noted that even the "idle" rich were not supposed to be idle in the sense that they could spend the rest of their lives doing nothing. They maintained an office to which they could go, if only to study the stock market. They were often engaged in activities associated with the wealthy such as horse racing and horse raising, yachting, hunting both at home and abroad, and giv-

118

ing and attending social functions, or otherwise keeping busy in their idleness.

Members of the less favored classes could not afford this variety of leisure that engaged the time of the rich. Workers who lost their jobs or were forced to leave their employment were ordinarily in no financial position to keep busy in conspicuous ways of time-killing. Since the coming of full industrialization, the Depression of the thirties, and the New Deal, the ideas surrounding labor and retirement have also undergone something of a change. There was and is a great deal said on the subject of the dignity of work. This is contrary to the implication that work is a punishment for the sin committed by Adam. Besides being supposed to receive a fair day's pay for a good day's work, the laboring man is increasingly asking, expecting, and being expected to receive a certain amount of sick leave with pay, paid vacations, and a financed retirement. So far there is little evidence that our values have undergone such a change that it is expected a person can retire without making some monetary contribution to his retirement income. The federal old-age and survivors insurance program, for instance, is not considered to furnish sufficient income for a comfortable retirement. Rather it is thought of as being a cushion, or a supplement to money saved during a lifetime of work. A person is still supposed to make at least part of his own way to a comfortable retirement by saving his money and investing it wisely in stocks and bonds. The money thus saved is to be supplemented by savings which he is forced to make through payroll deductions matched by contributions from the employer. Even forced savings added to employer contributions are not supposed to supplant voluntary savings.

In addition to the way in which their retirement income is theoretically derived, the new leisure class, composed of retired workers, follows in the footsteps of the original leisure class in another way. This second parallel is that of migrating to more comfortable geographic and climatic environments. Their idle hours are supposed to be occupied in some active or passive pursuit. The retired person is supposed to be doing something even if it is only watching television, reading, or attending sports events. If he is able, it is thought he should be engaged in some activity such as club work, community activities, playing games, dancing, making things, and so forth. If one cannot raise and race horses he can at least go to the races. If he cannot own a baseball team, he can watch the team play. If he cannot engage in the activities of the original idle rich, he can at least participate vicariously by seeing movies or television. The attitude that one must do something in retirement is reflected in questionnaires given to retired persons and in programs designed to save them from spending their remaining years in idleness. Idleness is supposed to lead to boredom, to unhappiness, and ultimately to an untimely and premature death.

It is the purpose of this chapter to inquire into some of the questions surrounding retirement. These questions have to do with the concept of a fixed, arbitrarily selected retirement age versus that of a flexible retirement age, preparation for retirement on the part of the employee and employer, as well as some of the facts of retirement.

What is retirement?

As discussed previously in this chapter and preceding chapters, retirement involves several factors. First, the implication is that a person must have been gainfully employed during some period in his life. He must have stopped work and changed his status from one of worker to one of nonworker. This concept carries with it at least an implication that it is no longer necessary for the person to work; he is presumably able to live on past savings or pensions. Retirement ordinarily occurs late in life. In theory it occurs when the worker is too old to work or when he no longer feels it is necessary for him to do so. In common parlance if a retired person seeks and finds another job he is said to have reentered employment. Stopping work at a relatively young age with no intention of returning to work and being able to live on one's income or savings is retirement, but this condition should be qualified as "early" retirement.

There are degrees of retirement as was indicated in an earlier chapter. "Tapering off" from active to supervisory work is an example. A person may retire or be retired from his regular field of activity and be employed later in another field. When this occurs he is classified as a retired preacher, for instance, who is now selling religious pamphlets. To be completely retired a person must cease being employed or cease working for money except incidentally. Re-employment or death are the only two ways a person may lose the status position of retirement.

Retirement may be classified as either voluntary or involuntary.[1] *Voluntary retirement* occurs when an individual of his own free will decides to and actually stops work. He believes he has enough money, insurance, or other assets to support himself and his dependents for the remaining years of his life. It is probable that a great many of the aged in this category look forward to and make plans for retirement, and that they enjoy retirement. They have what is known as a positive attitude toward retirement and have little if any difficulty in adjusting to it.[2] They have an adequate or nearly adequate income and can continue to live in dignity and comfort.

Involuntary retirement is brought on by circumstances beyond the control of the individual. Included under this heading are the following factors. First, being "laid off" or discharged for such reasons as disability through old age, inability to adapt to new employment conditions, or irregularity of attendance at work due to chronic ill-health. Second, leaving the job because of the realization or subjective belief that one is about to be discharged. Third, leaving to attend to family affairs which necessitate the presence of the worker in the home rather than at work. Any one of these types of involuntary retirement might be considered temporary by an employee who had the idea of going back to the

---

[1] Edna C. Wentworth, "Why Beneficiaries Retire," *Social Security Bulletin,* VIII (January, 1945), 16.

[2] Otto Pollak, *Social Adjustment in Old Age* (New York: Social Science Research Council, 1948), pp. 117 ff.

old job or finding a new one when health or other conditions allowed. Whether the involuntarily retired workers are financially able to retire is of little consequence in early adjustment to retirement. In most cases their attitude toward retirement is negative.[3] However, the aged who are financially able to retire do not feel a compelling necessity to re-enter employment. They acquire a positive attitude toward retirement more quickly than those who have to seek ways to support themselves. It is possible that many workers who voluntarily retire and have a positive attitude toward retirement may later realize that they cannot live on their retirement income. Others may become unhappy in retirement and so develop a negative orientation toward retirement.

Should there be a fixed retirement age?

The arguments for and against a fixed chronological age for retirement are similar to the arguments used for and against retirement itself. Due to the Social Security Act the "normal" age of retirement is usually considered to be 65 years or the first of the month in which one reaches his 65th birthday. The following are given as reasons for having a fixed chronological age for retirement.[4] First, all employees are treated alike. Both workers and managers are retired at the same age. Under any other method besides arbitrary fixed retirement for all, the system would be criticized and doubts would be raised as to the fairness of the program. Second, effective plans for retirement can be made. Plans can be made by employers for replacements; a schedule can be set up so that it will be known how many employees will be retiring at different times. On the basis of this information new personnel can be hired and trained to replace those who retire. The employee knows exactly when he will retire. He can prepare for retirement both psychologically and fi-

[3] *Ibid.,* p. 117.
[4] Stanley C. Hope, "Some Managements Say Yes," *The Annals of the American Academy of Political and Social Science,* CCLXXIX (January, 1952), 72–74.

nancially over a period of years. Third, it provides incentives for capable younger employees. The lack of a mandatory retirement system may destroy the morale of younger workers, especially in the managerial classes. If older men are retained indefinitely the company will become top-heavy with old conservative executives who resist innovations and progressive change. Younger employees will not know what to expect in the way of advancement and so will be lost to the company. Fourth, it is desirable from the employee's personal standpoint. Employees can retire without having to make excuses. There is no implication that the retired worker is either mentally or physically incapable of working, merely that he has reached an age at which all workers are retired. Fifth, it provides the most practical solution. A method based on anything other than an arbitrarily chosen chronological age lends itself to human judgment, which is subject to error. This is especially true in borderline cases. There appears to be no satisfactory answer to the question as to whom the final say should be given if some other criterion for retirement is chosen. Human judgment does not enter when age alone is used. Sixth, it is desirable from the general economic and social standpoint. It is possible that the mandatory retirement age should be changed from time to time in order to meet changing economic, social and demographic conditions. This does not detract from the fact that there are distinct advantages inherent in the mandatory system. There are positions and activities in many areas of activity which are now only partially fulfilled or completely neglected. People who are retired at a given age before they lose their abilities can fulfill these needed activities. If they do not retire until they have lost their capabilities, these services to the economic, political, religious, and business community will have to go unfinished. There are vital status positions which remain to be filled by retired workers. It only remains for society to discover what these are and to fill them with physically and mentally capable retired workers. If retirement comes only with deterioration, these status positions will not be filled and society will be penalized.

There are others who seek more flexibility in determining the retirement age.[5] Their arguments are that retirement is, or should be, a time during which older people can achieve the goals which they cannot attain while they are regularly employed. Just as a shorter work-week is important, so a shorter work-life should be. Both these show that technological advancement is of great importance in making life more worthwhile. A certain amount of rigidity should be adhered to in retirement. This will help management plan for replacements and help laborers plan for retirement. Replacement of the old by the young is important especially in the executive branches of business. However, the age of retirement should not be so inflexible that it would not take account of the broader social and economic conditions of the country. Provision should be made to make full use of the skills of the older workers in times of labor shortages. One would not support a program wherein an older worker, eligible for a retirement income, would be retained as an employee while a younger worker, dependent upon current income, would be without work. The goal of society should be to provide economic security for people in their later years and to try to set up new and worthy goals for them. Such goals are those which can be attained only during the time in a person's life when he is capable of working, is economically secure, yet is not employed full time.

Some equally convincing statements have been formulated by those who oppose an arbitrarily determined mandatory retirement plan.[6] Four arguments are given against the policy of compulsory fixed retirement ages for industrial workers. (These arguments, however, do not necessarily apply to executive personnel.) First, the worker is not anxious to retire. He becomes used to employment over a long period of time. He is used to supporting himself and be-

[5] Craig P. Cochrane, "Some Managements Prefer Flexibility," *The Annals of the American Academy of Political and Social Science*, CCLXXIX (January, 1952), 74–77.

[6] Solomon Barkin, "Organized Labor Says No," *The Annals of the American Academy of Political and Social Science*, CCLXXIX (January, 1952), 77–80.

comes habituated to the independence which is associated with self-support. His life is adjusted to work and his relationship with the community is work-oriented. The fact that so many retired people seek re-employment after a short period of retirement indicates that they prefer to work. Second, most workers cannot afford to retire. The combination of old-age and survivors insurance and industrial pensions seldom constitutes an adequate retirement income. Third, there are many jobs in industry for older people, and many other jobs can be made available to older workers. Times of high employment indicate that there are steps which may be taken to adjust older workers to employment. Better and more careful placement techniques can be put to use. Jobs can be redesigned to fit the needs of older people. Instead of trying to change the man to fit the job, the job can be redesigned to fit the man. Fourth, the social and economic costs of retirement are so huge that means must be considered to extend employment opportunities. The more workers there are who are actively producing goods and services, the fewer people there are to be supported by the producers. A high level of living demands a high productive level and high income which in turn can be obtained best by a high rate of employment.

In any discussion of this problem of compulsory retirement age, several things should be kept in mind. From the sociological point of view there is here a good illustration of the fact that the folkways or technicways have not been formulated in this area. Society has not had enough time to "make up its mind" on the subject. This whole area of retirement is such a relatively new thing that it has not been possible yet for industry, labor, and the public to reach any substantial agreement concerning it. There appears to be a wide diversity of opinion on the part of management and labor as to the economic and social aspects of a fixed retirement age. Each of these groups presents its side of the picture, and these two groups do not always see eye-to-eye on every issue. Neither of the two groups is speaking for older people. It is doubtful that any person could speak with authority for all older people. There is some indication, too, that a misunderstanding has been created on this subject. For example, those who advocate company pension plans do not at the same time advocate a fixed retirement age. Yet it seems to be true that some types of pensions are more easily administered if the age of retirement is fixed. At the present time it is clear that there is not enough factual knowledge on the subject to warrant more than broad generalizations.

The strongest argument in favor of a mandatory retirement age is that the employee knows that he will be retired and that he also knows the approximate date of retirement. The advantage in this is that he will be given ample time to prepare for the event. The truth, however, seems to be that many persons believe until the last day that the rule will be waived for them. And there is evidence to indicate that even those who believe they will be retired on schedule make few if any plans. Plan or no plan, there is almost inevitably a psychological shock when one realizes that his life work is done.

It should be remembered that the age of 65, while considered the normal retirement age, is not universally adhered to as the mandatory age of retirement. Nothing in the Social Security Act makes it compulsory that retirement take place at that age. If one elects to and is allowed to do so, he is at liberty to continue working beyond that age. The principal organizations with a compulsory retirement age are industrial and governmental concerns which have pension plans. It seems quite possible that only a minority of the people approaching the age of 65 are actually affected by the compulsory retirement practices which take effect at the age of 65.

The crux of the matter is the total question of retirement rather than retirement at an arbitrarily established age. Basically the question is whether or not people want to retire while they are still capable of working at regular full-time employment.

Workers' attitudes toward retirement

There are two relatively accurate ways of determining the attitude of workers toward retirement. The first is to ask them, and the second is to find out how many actually retire when they become eligible for retirement. Unfortunately data upon which to base conclusions are not abundant. This is especially true in regard to the stated attitudes of workers toward retirement. As a general principle it can be said that workers like the idea of retirement. Most of them like to know that if they are not able to continue working or if they want to stop working they will be able to stop and that they will have some kind of income after they do.

The majority of the workers in one survey did not as a rule favor 65 as the retirement age.[7] There was a wide difference of opinion among these workers as to the exact age at which retirement should come. This study, conducted by Jacob Tuckman and Irving Lorge, found that as workers approach the age of 65 they have a less favorable attitude toward retirement than younger workers have. Perhaps there is a psychological explanation to be found in the fact that some situations appear less appealing as the time for fulfillment approaches. This would be especially applicable when the individual involved views retirement as an almost complete change in daily activities, a recasting of the economic aspects of life, and a breaking away from association with fellow-workers. No doubt at younger ages some people view retirement merely as a time when they can "thumb their noses at the clock" and nothing more.

The sample in the Tuckman-Lorge study consisted of three categories of industrial workers who were members of the International Ladies Garment Workers Union. These categories consisted of 204 workers still on the job, 216 who had applied for retirement, and 240 who had already retired. About half of the number in each of the three classes either

[7] Jacob Tuckman and Irving Lorge, *Retirement and the Industrial Worker* (New York: Columbia University Press, 1953), pp. 28 ff.

looked forward to retirement or said they liked it. However, 35 per cent of the men still working and 58 per cent of those who had applied for retirement gave poor health, inability to do the job, or old age as reasons they were looking forward to retirement.[8] Forty-two per cent of those who had retired said they liked retirement because they had not been able to keep up with their jobs before retirement. Of the men in all three categories, 60 per cent of those working, 32 per cent of those who had applied, and 47 per cent of those already retired, who were looking forward to or liked retirement, gave as their reason that they wanted to rest and that they believed they had worked long enough. Among those who did not look forward to retirement or did not like it, reasons given were that they were still able to work, they were concerned with finances, or they would not know what to do with their spare time. A majority of those who said they were looking forward to retirement did so because they viewed retirement as an escape from an unpleasant situation, not as an escape to a pleasant one. Those who did not like or were not anticipating retirement took this negative attitude because they viewed retirement as forcing them into a situation less pleasant than their working life had been.

Periodically since 1940, the Social Security Administration has conducted a series of studies to determine why those who were entitled to receive old-age insurance had left their jobs and were receiving benefits.[9] Table 12 indicates that from 25.5 to 55.7 per cent of the 3,506 beneficiaries interviewed left their jobs at the instigation of their employers. Of those who quit their jobs voluntarily, from 35 to 65 per cent did so because of ill-health. Only about 5 per cent in all four samples quit because they wanted to retire. About 6 per cent of those who quit did so because of "other reasons" (including such things as family pressure to quit, quitting to look after an ill person in the home, and similar reasons). It should be noted that the percentages of workers leaving

[8] *Ibid.*, p. 22.
[9] Margaret L. Stecker, "Beneficiaries Prefer to Work," *Social Security Bulletin*, XIV (January, 1951), 15–17.

work varied according to conditions of the general economy. Before and after the war dismissals were proportionately greater than were voluntary movements out of the labor force. During the war the majority of those who left their work did so because of ill-health.

TABLE 12

Reasons for Termination of Last Covered Employment Before Entitlement (Male Old-Age Insurance Beneficiaries, in 20 Cities, 1940–47)

Reason	Place and Year of Entitlement			
	1944 7 Large Cities	1941–42 12 Mid-sized Cities in Ohio	1944 Boston	1946–47 Philadelphia and Baltimore
Number of beneficiaries ..	2,380	567	341	218
Lost jobs	55.7%	46.2%	25.5%	53.2%
Quit jobs	44.3%	53.8%	74.5%	46.8%
Health	33.8%	41.1%	64.8%	34.9%
Wished to retire	4.7%	5.6%	4.1%	5.5%
Others	5.8%	7.1%	5.6%	6.4%

SOURCE: Margaret L. Stecker, "Beneficiaries Prefer to Work," *Social Security Bulletin*, XIV (January, 1951), 16.

There are several differences between this study made by Margaret Stecker and the Tuckman-Lorge study. The primary difference is that in the Tuckman-Lorge study ill-health is included under the heading of reasons given for wanting to retire. When the Tuckman-Lorge figures given for wanting to retire because workers desired rest and felt they had worked long enough are compared to the Stecker results, no marked difference appears. The figures are 14 per cent applying for retirement and 10 per cent retired in the Tuckman-Lorge study as compared to 5 per cent in the Stecker study who wished to retire. Part of this difference can be explained on the grounds that retirees in the Tuckman-Lorge study were going to receive income from the union retirement fund. It cannot be determined how many of the respondents in the Stecker study had any income beyond old-age insurance benefits. It is safe to say that relatively few of those interviewed in the Tuckman-Lorge study actually lost their jobs through the direct intervention of the employer or union. The only information which may have a bearing on this is that approximately 5 per cent of those applying or retired did so because they had no job.

Another series of studies available gives figures as to the number of employees in various industries who had reached retirement age and the percentage of those eligible who had actually retired. These studies do not indicate why those who retired did so. The fact remains that all of these people were eligible for pensions and the nonrailroad employees were eligible for old-age insurance also.

None of the companies listed in Table 13 insisted, in 1950, on retirement at specific ages although employees became

TABLE 13

Number and Per Cent of Employees in Selected Occupations Eligible for Retirement, 1949–1950

Industry	Number Eligible	Per Cent Retired
Railroad	92,000	23.9
U.S. Steel Corporation	Not Given	40.0
Allegheny-Ludlen	450	27.6
General Motors	7,400	9.8
Ford Motors	5,000	36.9
Chrysler Corporation	1,700	11.0

SOURCES: Railroad Retirement Board, *Annual Report, 1950* (Washington, D.C.: 1950), p. 113; and "Old Hands Snub Pensions," *Business Week* (November 18, 1950), pp. 124–25.

eligible for retirement at the age of 65. In the number "retiring" under the Railroad Retirement Act are also included those over 65 in 1950 who were separated from their jobs and those who died during the year as well as those who retired. The consensus is that many who retired did so because of ill-health. In the three automobile companies, many of those who retired were on sick leave and retired officially in order to be able to collect pensions. The primary reasons given for a relatively low retirement rate during this period were as follows. Both pay rates and prices were rising and there was little pressure brought on employees to retire. Some of those who had expected to retire in 1950 may have postponed retirement because expected amendments to the Railroad Retirement and Social Security Acts would provide higher retirement annuities. When pensions are set up on the basis of years of service the longer the employee stays on the job the higher will be the pension payment when he elects to retire.

There are also other important data available on the operation of the federal old-age insurance program. The average of retirement of old-age insurance beneficiaries is between 68 and 69 years. Unless forced to quit prior to this age because of a fixed retirement age or loss of job as a result of company action, most employees who leave voluntarily do so because of ill-health. Many people at 65 feel perfectly capable of continuing work for several more years. The majority of people who are working when they reach 65 continue doing so for about three more years largely for financial reasons. These facts seem to add up to the conclusion that most older workers would continue working well beyond the age of 65 if given absolute control over themselves and their employment situation.

Individual preparation for retirement

Retirement from active employment brings a shift in activity which is roughly comparable to that of shifting from nonemployment to employment at a younger age. As it is now, approximately twenty years of a person's life are spent preparing for employment. Education and social as well as economic pressure is brought to bear on the individual to help him prepare himself for employment. There are odd jobs, summer jobs, holiday jobs, and after-school jobs for younger people as well as training periods or periods of apprenticeship. These things help the potential worker get used to work in more or less easy stages. It would be equally desirable that individuals approach retirement in easy stages so that there would be no shock at retirement.

There are two fundamental reasons why society has not established schools for preparation for retirement or at the least, why there is no widely available "training period" for retiring workers. First, retirement as a general goal or as a real possibility is for most people a relatively new phenomenon. Second, society feels more responsibility for preparing immature youth to assume the work of the world than in preparing mature adults to stop work. It is assumed that adults are responsible free agents and, since they are aware of the fact that they will retire, they should do something about it. But it is felt that society cannot afford to make any such assumption regarding the preparation of youth for work.

Prevailing opinion on the subject is to the effect that preparation for retirement should be made by the individual. Most studies show that a larger proportion of those who plan for retirement are happier than those who do not plan for this event. A larger proportion of the planners are happy in retirement, a larger proportion of nonplanners are unhappy. Yet in a survey of retired men in Cleveland made by Stanley Payne, it is pointed out that planning is no guarantee of happiness in retirement.[10] There is a difference between merely planning for retirement and being able to implement the plans when retirement finally comes.

Some distinction should be made between types of planning. On the one hand there is a superficial type of planning that is nothing more or less than haphazard "thinking" about retiring, or simply becoming aware that one is going to retire at some future date. Further along this line would be talking over plans with relatives and other retired persons, finding out what others do to fill their days in retirement, and making tentative plans to travel. Daydreaming about such things as fishing, traveling, or going to ball games would come under this head. At the other pole would be a well-formed plan which would include all the facets of life in retirement, a blueprint for action in retirement. This type of

[10] Stanley L. Payne, "The Cleveland Survey of Retired Men," *Personnel Psychology*, VI (Spring, 1953), 81 ff.

planning could begin as long as ten years before the actual time of retirement. The kind of plan made under this second heading would depend upon several variables such as health, interests, and financial, mental, and social resources of the individual. If one wished to travel it could include the securing of travel folders and magazines which described various places of interest. If one wished to begin a small business or to farm in retirement it might mean obtaining information on the subject from various governmental bureaus. The spare time of ten years could be spent profitably in acquainting oneself with the various aspects of a little business or farm before any money was invested in the project. If a person decided to stay at home and engage in no financially remunerative job, he should first work out a tentative budget on the basis of what he thinks his income in retirement would be. He could begin by clearing up debts and paying for his home, or by buying stocks and bonds which would yield a steady income.

To occupy one's time in retirement, there is always volunteer work within the community or church. It should not be expected that all old people want to do this type of work, nor are they all temperamentally suited for it. Those who are could get a good start many years before retirement by gradually breaking themselves into these activities. If an older person wants to continue working after retirement, he could learn a secondary occupation during his preparation for retirement. This could take the form of the development of a hobby which could be turned into a money-making project or a skill which could be used in regular part-time employment. Under the heading of "just puttering around" would be such things as doing odd jobs in the community either for pay or as favors. Writing to or visiting "shut-ins" of all ages or similar activities could be engaged in by many people.

It would be a mistake to assume that people who are inactive or not busy all the time are invariably unhappy. This idea probably stems from what may be a national belief that one should be "busy." Some people actually prefer merely to sit rather than to sit and think, or to sit and read or listen to the radio rather than to be engaged in some physical activity. This variation in the desire to be doing something reflects the fact that the aged population is a heterogeneous one.

The truth of the matter is that, since wholesale retirement is a relatively recent thing, few people go all-out to plan for it. Basically, if a person is happy before retirement he is likely to be happy in retirement. Life before 65 will largely determine life after 65. The best way to avoid a shock seems to be to make some positive plan for retirement long before the time of retirement. The basic characteristics of personality change or can be changed over periods of time, so the best way to be happy in retirement is to start early rather than to try to make all the adjustment when retirement age is reached. There is little to indicate, for instance, that a person with no interests beyond his work will be able to develop interests the day after he has retired.

One final point is the matter of health. A healthy youth and middle age does not guarantee a healthy old age, but it helps. Doctors recommend physical examinations twice each year for people beyond the age of 40 years so they will be able to detect and possibly to correct any physical disability before it is too late. To maintain good health in old age and retirement, the same general rules apply which have applied during a person's younger days. It is much less expensive in time and money as well as in suffering to prevent than to cure illness in old age.

There is a widely held belief that retirement almost invariably brings about a breakdown in the health of the individual. There is some truth in this contention for two reasons. First, a large number of older workers retire or do not object to retirement because of ill-health or because they do not feel as well as they have previously. Second, people reaching the retirement age have, on the average, only about twelve more years of life. This means many of them actually die before the end of the twelfth year. The studies cited above, however, indicate that retirement in itself is not a cause of ill-health.[11]

There is also a relation between health after retirement, attitude toward retirement, and attitude of a person's family toward the retirement of the individual involved. In the Tuckman-Lorge study it was found that of the respondents in the retired group 34 per cent reported their health was the same, 48 per cent said their health was better, but only 18 per cent reported that their health was worse than before retirement.[12] In the Payne survey 21 per cent said they felt better, 45 per cent the same, and 34 per cent worse than they had prior to retirement.[13] Tuckman and Lorge conclude that those reporting poorer health may do so as a psychological reaction to loss of jobs and that there is reason to believe the health situation after retirement is related to the type of work they were doing. In other words, the more personal satisfaction derived from the job, the more likely that health would be worse upon retirement. In both of these studies the health of those who wanted to retire was generally better than the health of those who had a negative attitude toward retirement. Tuckman and Lorge found that the health of those whose families wanted them to retire was better than the health of those whose families did not want them to. The same conclusion can be inferred from Payne's survey in which he found that about 25 per cent of his sample had families which had not wanted them to retire. He reported this was one of the most dissatisfied groups in the survey.

What some organizations are doing

Many old people do not have the personal resources which enable them to prepare for retirement without outside aid. It would be just as unreasonable to expect our youth to

[11] Tuckman and Lorge, *Retirement and the Industrial Worker*, p. 34; Payne, "The Cleveland Survey," pp. 89–90.

[12] Tuckman and Lorge, *Retirement and the Industrial Worker*, p. 34.

[13] Payne, "The Cleveland Survey," p. 89.

prepare for a work life alone as it is to expect the aged to prepare for a retirement life without aid. No doubt some could and do find it possible to do so, but proper counseling, supervision, and direction by experts make the process easier and more successful. The three groups that seem most vitally concerned with retirement at the present are industry, unions, and public educational institutions. The part these organizations play covers a span of activity ranging from no action at all on the one hand to well-developed programs on the other.

From the information available, only relatively few industries now have any program of preparation for retirement. In some very superficial programs the prospective retiree is called in one month before his retirement becomes effective. He is told that he will be retired and is advised to make some plans for the event. He is then supposed to come back during the month and confer with the personnel director on the subject. An indirect method is used by some other concerns. A free subscription to the magazine *Life-Time Living* is sent to all employees who are approaching retirement. It is hoped that this magazine, designed for retired persons, will help the individual prepare for retirement and will open up for him some of the possibilities for activity during retirement.

Another method is used by Wrigley Chewing Gum Company.[14] The plan is to have each employee, during his sixty-fifth year, take one month of leave without pay. The following year he takes two months' leave, and so on. Each succeeding year he draws more money from his company pension and old-age insurance and less from regular employment. The principle behind this program is that the person adjusts his level of living to what his retirement income will be. In addition, during the period of forced vacations, he adjusts himself psychologically and socially to retirement. Vacations which increase in length each succeeding year are a good way to make the transition from work to retirement.

[14] Katherine Close, *Getting Ready to Retire*, Public Affairs Series, No. 182 (New York: Public Affairs Committee, Inc., 1952), 1–23.

Esso Standard Oil Company has published a pamphlet which outlines its program for retirement.[15] The idea behind this program is that industry has a responsibility in the social as well as in the financial adjustment of the employee in retirement. The company hopes its program will be participated in voluntarily by the employees, but believes individual counseling and help are needed. In order to bring in those people who possibly need help the most and to discount the feeling of resentment which might arise if such a program were forced on the employees, a plan has been devised whereby small groups of employees are encouraged to participate in a seminar or discussion period on the problems of retirement and the ways in which successful adjustment can be made. Personnel are free to attend or not, and the discussion takes place on company time. These group discussions are open to employees whose retirement is about a year off. The sessions last for about an hour and occur at intervals of about four days. There are three principal objectives which the program is designed to achieve: first, to give the prospective retiree a picture of the problems he will probably face; second, to stimulate thinking toward suitable interests and activities; and third, to generate action or plans before the person actually becomes retired.

A program which promises much in assisting older persons to make good adjustments in retirement has been designed and "field-tested" by the Industrial Relations Center of the University of Chicago.[16] The personnel at this center felt that even though management was spending considerable sums of money to ease the financial burdens of retirement something more was needed. In their view a formal preparation for retirement would be beneficial to the retired person in helping to prepare him for the problems which arise in retirement. It was also believed such a program would benefit employers in that employee morale would im-

---

[15] Esso Standard Oil Company, *Preparation for Retirement: A Study of Post-Employment Adjustment.*

[16] Industrial Relations Center, *Making the Most of Maturity* (Chicago: The University of Chicago).

prove, employer-employee relations would become better, and better public relations would follow because of better morale of both workers and retired persons.

After four years of research and planning, the Industrial Relations Center set up a retirement planning and preparation program which was tried out in several large companies in the Chicago area. The procedure followed is first to contact company officials and then to assist representatives from the company in organizing the program around certain major objectives. The program consists of eleven sessions. Prior to each session the "class" is given a booklet outlining the topic to be pursued during the following session. Topics for the conference sessions include a study of physical and mental health, financial planning, use of leisure time, possible ways of increasing retirement income, family, friends, and living arrangements in retirement.

Participants in the program have reacted favorably to it. The program is designed so it may be given from time to time in the same company, using the same trained company conference leaders. The Industrial Relations Center has follow-up training conferences for leaders and keeps them up to date on the latest available materials which come from a continuing program of research and study. As this program receives favorable reaction in the Chicago area its influence may spread and stimulate the establishment of similar programs in other sections of the country.

Esso Standard Oil Company has sought to avoid a situation which calls for compulsory attendance at such meetings. On the other hand, the company has taken positive action and opened a program for attendance by individuals who wish to be present. Payne found that about half of his respondents were opposed to compulsory attendance at company sponsored counseling programs on the subject of retirement.[17] Only about 20 per cent of the respondents in his survey had received any help from the company in the way of advice and counsel in planning for retirement. The very least a company could be prepared to do would be to notify

[17] Payne, "The Cleveland Survey," p. 103.

the worker of the approximate date of retirement well before the time comes and, at the same time, give him specific information as to the amount of money he could expect monthly from company pension and/or old-age insurance benefits. No doubt individual employees could calculate, within a reasonable limit, the amount of their retirement income, but it is probably a mistaken assumption that more than a small minority know that they can do so or take the trouble to figure it out for themselves.

Although some unions may be actively engaged in programs of preparation for retirement, no information on the subject is immediately available. Since both unions and industry are concerned with the subject, they could work with one another to develop a worthwhile program for employees approaching the retirement age. There is no doubt that unions can render a service to retired workers by establishing a union center for retired members. The center need not necessarily be an elaborate affair, but merely a place for the retirees to gather for sedentary activities of various kinds. The primary purpose and justification for such centers would be to serve as a social center where the retired members would be able to visit each other, talk, play games, and maintain their relationship with the past and with each other. Tuckman and Lorge found that an overwhelming majority of their respondents favored such a center.[18] Furthermore, a majority of the workers interviewed said they would attend such a center if one were available. The replies of women were somewhat less favorable to such a project than those of men. Those still working were more favorable to the project than those who had applied for retirement or had already retired. In the combined groups, 89 per cent of those working, 82 per cent of those who had applied for retirement, and 83 per cent of those retired favored a union center. In the same sequence, 88, 77, and 72 per cent said they would attend such a center. From the statements of a number of retired United Auto Workers union members in Detroit who spoke on the subject in Ann Arbor at the Sixth Annual Con-

[18] Tuckman and Lorge, *Retirement and the Industrial Worker,* p. 56.

ference on Aging, it appears that the union center which has been established in Detroit is a very satisfying project as far as the retired automobile workers are concerned.

Finally, adult education programs have been established for the purpose of acquainting older people with some of the situations which they may face in retirement. These classes are conducted by the public school systems in some communities and by university extension services in others. Attendance at these classes is usually good and is usually sustained throughout the series. This indicates that older people are interested in such courses. The courses are generally similar in content to the series of five classes conducted by Esso Standard Oil Company although they may meet for more sessions and a larger proportion of the time may be utilized in discussion periods. A later chapter will deal more fully with the adult educational program of which preparation for retirement is only a part.

Summary

Full retirement is a more or less sharp break in activity from a condition of employment to one of not being employed. Retirement usually is thought of as occurring at about the age of 65 years after a lifetime of work. Arguments have arisen about the desirability of an arbitrary, compulsory retirement age based on chronological age alone as opposed to retirement based on other criteria. Evidence indicates that of those who are employed at the age of 65, only a small proportion leave work because they want to. A great many more leave because of ill-health or because they feel they are not physically able to keep up with their jobs. The largest portion of those who retire at the age of 65 do so because they lose their jobs. The average age at which beneficiaries of old-age insurance retire is about 69 years. Most of the workers remain at work as long as they do because of the financial necessity of continuing work, although, no doubt, many want to keep on working because work is a lifelong habit.

Relatively few workers seriously plan for retirement. Part of this may be due to the fact that they do not have the necessary information or incentive to do so, and part may stem from the fact that large-scale retirement is relatively new and that this generation of senior citizens is pioneering in the field. Some industries thus feel a responsibility for helping employees plan for retirement. Such assistance varies from a mere notification of the impending retirement to well-planned courses for retirement. Quite possibly the action taken by industry has been limited for the same reason individuals do not do more for themselves; that is, retirement is a relatively new thing and society has not yet fixed any responsibility for preparation to meet it. Moreover, industry feels that retiring employees do not appreciate or want any compulsory lectures on the subject.

The condition of happiness or unhappiness or a positive or negative attitude toward retirement is related to several variables. These are the preretirement attitude toward retirement, the extent of planning for the event, the attitude of the family toward the individual's retirement, the health of the individual, and his financial condition. There is no indication that all retired persons either want to or have to engage in some active pastime in order to become adjusted to retirement. There is no evidence that retirement, as such, inevitably brings about a rapid deterioration in the physical condition of the retiree. Two available studies on the subject indicate that a majority of the retirees interviewed believed their health to be either better than or as good as it was prior to retiring. Certainly this should be the case where people retire because of ill-health and are freed from the pressure of work.

In the final analysis a person takes with him into retirement the personal characteristics and resources which he has acquired during his life of work. Adjustments have to be made, but retirement need not be a period in a person's life used solely as a preparation for death.

Part III

MEETING ECONOMIC NEEDS

9

Income Needs and Sources
of Income

As already noted in an earlier chapter, it has been considered traditional in this country for each family unit to be self-supporting. In addition to the ability to earn enough income to meet current expenses, each earning unit has been expected to earn enough to save for the traditional "rainy day." Even though such a "rainy day" might come in the form of periods of unemployment of either long or short duration, or of illness or disability of the wage earner or other members of his family, there has always been the idea that wage earners could save for old age as well. It is a general belief on the part of those who have sufficient income from which savings can be set aside, that others also could and should set aside a certain amount of income for future use. Failure to make provision for "hard times" has been counted as unwillingness to discount the present for the future, or as natural improvidence.

This view is still rather widely held by some of the people in this country. It is generally these people who look with disfavor on old-age and survivors insurance, old-age assistance, or any form of pensions which make compulsory savings a part of their plan. They reason that if people are assured, by compulsory programs, of having an adequate income in old age, their natural improvidence will be aggravated. One or more of several unfortunate practices will result from such forced savings. Those forced to save will be less anxious to obtain work; they will spend more money for nonessentials; they will be less inclined to save on their own initiative. An assured, even though low income in old age will virtually destroy almost everything which is held to be worthwhile in relation to our system of capitalistic private enterprise. This attitude gives rise to questions such as: "Are you in favor of compulsory old-age insurance?" This question is asked in the same tone of horror used in asking if one is in favor of sin, communism, or incest.

For the most part, there has been a shift from the earlier idea that all individuals can be self-sufficient under all circumstances to a realization that there are many people in the older age levels who have not been able to save enough for their own comfort or even for bare necessities during the later years of their lives. Part of this change in attitude is a result of the following factors: the findings of recent studies on the subject of cost of living as related to income; the growth in the number and percentage of the aged in the population; the knowledge that older people are more frequently unemployed than younger ones; and the feeling that young married adults are no longer morally responsible for looking after the financial and economic needs of their aged relatives. It is also true that interest in these topics has been stirred up by more interest in pensions and old-age insurance in general. Consequently advocates of pensions have discovered means to justify doing something about the needs.

There is a growing acknowledgement that on their own initiative older people are not able to accumulate enough savings to tide them over in comfort until they die. The assumption is that these people, with the help of private and public pension plans, income from current employment, or gifts from relatives and friends, are able to live on a level of comfort and decency in old age. This chapter will inquire into the validity of such conclusions. It should be noted that there is disagreement among the experts in this area of income needs and income distribution. Often even when statistics are available, they are slanted to prove or disprove a point. There is often a difference in definition of key terms used. Furthermore, it should be kept in mind constantly that these statistics are usually in terms of the median or average. While the statistics may be valid for the sample represented at the time of the sampling, conditions change. Although averages are used, the concern is not with numbers and figures as much as with individual men and women who have reached the age of 65. Although an aged couple might be comfortably situated one day, the next day might find them in financial difficulties. This change might be due to loss of their home by fire, illness of one of the couple, a marked increase in the cost of living, partial loss of income, or a reduction in old-age assistance due to an effort on the part of the state government to curtail expenses. Any number of other circumstances might completely alter a situation which today seems to offer cheer and hope to one of fear and foreboding.

Estimated living costs

It is generally conceded that it does not cost an aged couple as much to live as it does a younger couple. In the normal course of events, people accumulate furniture, china, cooking utensils and electrical appliances of various kinds over the period of their early years of marriage. The result is that even though new items may be bought or old ones replaced, expenditures for these items are not as great as they are during the years when couples are starting life together. In addition to decreased expenditures for such items, as people grow older a higher proportion of them own their homes, mortgage free. Where this is the case, the item of rent or monthly payments on the home would not enter into the budget. On the other hand, however, property taxes, hazard insurance, utilities, and painting and repair bills might add up to a considerable amount each month. Home ownership does not mean that no money has to be expended for a place in which to live. Probably these expense items are not as large as rent or monthly purchase payments are. In general, it may be assumed that older people spend less on entertaining, both in and out of the home, than younger ones do. It is also possible that young couples spend more on food than older ones do although there is no evidence that older people need less nourishing food. General expenses are not so great for older people either. And the expenses of younger family units are greater than those of older units because it is relatively rare that dependent children are found in the households of couples over the age of 65 years. It is a relatively rare occurrence that such children's expenses as those relating to education, clothing, toys, and so forth, have to be met in full by the breadwinner and spouse who have reached old age.

On the other side of the picture, it is well known that medical expenses for older people exceed those for younger people. Individuals in the lower income brackets are sick more frequently and for longer periods than are those with higher incomes. It should be kept in mind that even though the assets of the aged, on the average, may be greater than those of younger people, one cannot live on assets alone. Cash or assets which can be converted easily and quickly into cash are necessary to maintain a decent level of living.

The Bureau of Labor Statistics estimated the cost of living for family units of various ages and sizes for both the years 1947 and 1950. Samples were taken in thirty-four cities in the United States as the basis of these estimates. The budget was designed to provide an elderly couple with the goods and services which are considered necessary to maintain a decent, healthy level of living. The budget included items which would allow the couple to continue a normal participation in community life. It was figured on the assumption that the couple would rent a two- or three-room dwelling; that they were able to get about and look after themselves; and that the husband was either retired or only occasionally employed. No item was included for purchase or maintenance of an automobile. The cost of living for elderly couples was estimated at between $1,700 and $1,800 per year for the thirty-four cities, with a low of $1,602 for New Orleans and a high of $1,908 for Milwaukee. The estimated average for elderly couples in these thirty-four cities was approximately half of the estimated cost of the city workers's family budget for four persons for the same year. The most important single item accounting for differences among the various cities in size of the budget for elderly couples was the cost of housing.[1] In the detailed, itemized budget published for 1947, housing for couples was the largest single item. In the selected cities in 1947 this amounted to approximately one-third of the total estimated budget. Housing, as defined in the itemized budget, included rent, heat, and utilities, as well as household operations and furnishings.[2]

The following information is presented to test the validity of the sample budget as far as housing costs for the aged are concerned. In 1950 approximately 94 per cent of the aged lived in households, with 69 per cent of them in their own homes. Additional information indicates that of the nonfarm dwelling units occupied by heads of 65 years of age and over, 68.2 per cent were owner-occupied in 1950.[3] In 1952, 80 per cent of the homeowners in the aged category had no mortgage on their homes. Only 28 per cent of the nonfarm dwelling units with head of household over 65 were rented in 1952. In 1950 of nonfarm housing units with head of household over 65, more than two-thirds were occupied by only one or two persons and approximately 38 per cent of such units had six or more rooms. Of the elderly heads of households who paid rent in 1950, 40 per cent were in housing units which rented for less than $30 per month as contrasted with 24 per cent of all nonfarm dwelling units renting for this amount. Only 14 per cent of the elderly heads of households paid rents of $60 or more as contrasted with nearly 20 per cent of all nonfarm renters paying this amount. In 1950 most of the older persons lived in their own or rented households with either spouses, relatives, or nonrelatives. The homes owned by most older people were older and were located in the older neighborhoods than was true for the

[1] Sixth Annual Conference on Aging, *Pertinent Facts on "Earning Opportunities for Mature Workers"* (Ann Arbor: The University of Michigan, 1953), p. 10.

[2] Joint Committee on Railroad Retirement Legislation, *Retirement Policies and the Railroad Retirement System* (Washington, D.C.: 1953), Part II, 27–28.

[3] *Ibid.*, p. 32.

general population. An estimate of the value of nonfarm dwellings in 1950 showed the median value of units occupied by older people to be $6,000. The median value of housing units for the general nonfarm population was $7,400. Part of the difference in value may be due to lack of sanitary facilities and poorer maintenance of the units occupied by this category of people.

Medical care for the aged usually costs a good deal more than it does for younger people. The estimated budgets for the thirty-four cities mentioned above allowed approximately $100 per year to the aged for medical care. Although this sum may be adequate to meet medical needs of healthy couples it would be inadequate for many other older people. This is particularly true of the older people who are least able to afford medical care. Older people are sick more often and for periods of longer duration than are younger ones. These periods of sickness range from temporary disability lasting one week or longer to chronic illnesses.

Older people suffer major impairments much more frequently than younger ones do. Elderly persons spend almost twice as many days in hospitals in the course of a year's time as the average person does. In addition to this they use private and visting nurses more frequently and receive more doctors' home calls and visit doctors' offices more frequently than the general population. In 1951 the number of hospital days per person of all ages was 10.1, but the number of hospital days per person 65 and over was 22.5.[4] Although there are some exceptions, the averages indicate that older people with hospital insurance are admitted more frequently to hospitals than are those without insurance and usually spend less time in hospitals than those without insurance. In the three categories, nonwhite, farm, and those in the labor force, there was an appreciably greater number of hospital days per 1,000 persons among those who had some insurance than among those who did not have. The logical conclusion to be drawn from these data is that the noninsured categories, especially nonwhites and farm

[4] *Ibid.*, pp. 32 ff.

aged, were forced by lack of money to leave the hospital before they were completely recovered. The aged who are better off financially can afford hospital insurance and their health is generally better than that of the aged who have no insurance. This is borne out by the inverse relation between income level and amount and duration of illness.

A contributing factor is that it is difficult for older people to buy health and hospital insurance. In the year ending June, 1953, only 26.3 per cent of the people 65 and over were covered by hospital insurance. After retirement and as these people grow older insurance coverage falls off rapidly. It is virtually impossible for a chronically ill person of any age to buy such insurance. In addition to the age factor many of the aged are not able to afford health and hospital insurance. There is information to indicate that many aged persons who need hospitalization do without it and others have to have relatives or friends pay their bills, or else they are classified as "charity" cases.[5]

Distribution of income

A good deal of difficulty and confusion arises when one attempts to analyze the income of persons aged 65 and over. Part of the difficulty derives from confusion of terms, part from inadequate data, and part from over- or understatement to census interviewers. Much of the difficulty is found also in the attempt to distinguish between income as earned wages and unearned income, between the income of income recipients who are 65 and over and the income of spending units (roughly families) whose head is 65 and over. In reading tables and text, care must be exercised in interpreting the data which are presented.

In the United States, as elsewhere, income fluctuates from year to year, depending upon economic conditions. With some major exceptions, such as prolonged periods of depression, median income generally shows an upward trend. For instance, in 1947, 1951, and 1955 the median income of all males 14 years of age and over was $2,230, $2,952, and

[5] *Ibid.*, p. 37.

$3,354 respectively. For the years 1950, 1951, and 1955 the median income of all females 14 years of age and over was $935, $1,045, and $1,116. (The figure for 1950 is used as it is the lowest for the period between 1947 and 1955.) The median income of males 65 years of age and over during this eight-year period was well under half of the income for all males. In 1947, 1951, and 1955 the income for males aged 65 and over was $956, $1,008, and $1,337 respectively. The median income for older women fluctuated from $551 in 1947 to $536 in 1951 but reached $700 during 1955.

It is clear from the foregoing that the annual median income of both males and females aged 65 and over is considerably lower than it is for the total working population. In 1955 only 12.8 per cent of the males 65 years of age and over had incomes above $3,999, whereas nearly 40 per cent of all males 14 years of age and over had incomes above that figure. At the other extreme, only 18.2 per cent of the labor force males had $1,000 or less per year, but 38 per cent of the aged males were in this income bracket.[6]

Comparing incomes for the aged with the Bureau of Labor Statistics budget presented earlier in this chapter, or assuming that the cost of living has increased at least 12 per cent since 1950, it is apparent that the older person still is having a difficult time living on a level of decency and comfort. There is reason to believe that older people in general are somewhat better off financially than they were before benefit payments from the various social security programs were increased. That is, on the average, income appears to have increased somewhat faster than the cost of living has.

Another approach to the problem on a different level is to consider the income of family units with heads who are aged 65 or over. The statistics presented in Table 14 do not indicate whether the aged head is working or even whether he has any income. The data do not indicate how many other

---

[6] United States Bureau of the Census, *Current Population Reports, Consumer Income,* Series P-60, No. 11 (May, 1953), p. 8, and United States Bureau of the Census, *Current Population Reports,* Series P-60, No. 23 (November, 1956), p. 13.

members of the spending unit, household or family, are earners, or what part each plays in contributing to the total income of such units. While there is no doubt that there is a relation between the preceding figures and those in Table

TABLE 14

Distribution of Families and Unrelated Individuals by Total Money Income and Age of Head, United States, 1954

	Families		Unrelated Individuals	
Total Money Income Total Number (in thousands)	Total 41,934	65 and Over 5,402	Total 9,623	65 and Over 3,117
Under $500	4.6%	9.1%	21.7%	27.7%
$500 to 999	4.2%	11.8%	23.5%	37.7%
$1,000 to 1,999	11.0%	24.4%	19.3%	19.6%
$2,000 to 2,999	11.9%	15.2%	14.3%	7.6%
$3,000 to 3,999	15.4%	11.2%	10.7%	3.4%
$4,000 to 4,999	15.6%	9.0%	4.8%	1.3%
$5,000 and over	37.3%	19.2%	5.6%	2.8%
Median Income	$4,173	$2,294	$1,224	$796

SOURCE: United States Bureau of the Census, *Current Population Reports, Consumer Income,* Series P-60, No. 20 (December, 1955), p. 13.

14, they are not absolutely comparable. There are numerous families in this country which contain one or more than one person over the age of 65 who cannot be classified as the head of the family. Furthermore, there are many persons over the age of 65 who are "unrelated" individuals, being neither the head of a family nor a member of a family with a younger person as head. Statistics on unrelated individuals are also presented in Table 14. The median income for families with aged heads is well above that for people over the age of 65, but only 54 per cent as great as the median income for all families in 1954. It is possible to explain part of the very low income of unrelated individuals by the fact that the income of unrelated females would tend to lower the average for the group as a whole. It would be a safe assumption that there are more unrelated female than un-related male income earners. The conclusion can be drawn that the amount of income of unrelated individuals, es-pecially the aged, would not in itself be sufficient to insure a level of living that would comply with health and decency requirements.

Family income tends to reach a peak at about the same time the head of the family is receiving his highest income, that is when he is between 45 and 50 years of age. In ad-dition to the greater earning capacity of the head of the fam-ily at this age, there are more income earners in the family. As the head becomes older and his earning power and his in-come are reduced, total family income becomes less as the younger members reach majority and establish families of their own. In addition to this the proportion of family heads in the labor force reaches a peak by the age of 55. These three factors—reduced earning ability, loss of supplementary family income, or actual loss of job—are explanations for the rapid drop in income of family heads as they approach and enter old age. Younger people with low incomes can look forward to receiving more income as they grow older, whereas elders with low incomes can look forward only to ever-increasing economic distress.

Savings, assets, and net worth

It is not surprising to find that few older people are able to save. Their expenditures are more likely to be equal to their income or to exceed it than is the case with earning-spending units whose head is neither retired nor 65 years of age. Counting homes, real estate, and other assets, the units with heads 65 and over were in better financial con-dition than other units. There is evidence to indicate that the assets owned by the older people are less readily con-verted into cash to be used in meeting current expenses. In-debtedness is found less frequently in spending units with aged heads. More frequently there are no debts on the home and fewer payments on furniture and other items which are usually bought before old age sets in. There is therefore less need for saving and less money to save as well as less indebtedness to consume the money which is available. A larger proportion of the money that is avilable can be allocated to current needs such as food, clothing, and medical care.

As a rule in this country cash income, not assets, determines economic status and if assets are devoured income from assets will accordingly cease.[7] In 1949 a survey made by the Federal Reserve Board found that asset holdings, other than real estate, were largest in late middle age prior to retirement.[8] This same survey found that one-third of the unit heads 65 years and over had no assets if real estate holdings were excluded. One-half of the unit heads in this age category had asset holdings of less than $500 and seven out of ten had assets valued at less than $2,000. A more recent survey made by the Social Security Administration indicates that somewhat more than half of the commercial and industrial workers who had retired in recent years had some assets other than real estate. However, these assets were typically small. Another survey in 1951 indicates that only 13 per cent of old-age beneficiaries had as much as $5,000 in savings (not including real estate). One-fourth of the beneficiaries had no assets at all, and two-thirds had no assets other than real estate or had cash assets of less than $1,000. The conclusion may be drawn that most people do manage to save something for old age, but that savings are small. Very infrequently would savings be sufficient to provide an adequate income for old age, even if pension payments are considered. If a person were to buy an annuity of $75 per month beginning at age 65, he would have to save nearly $12,000 during his work life. For an annuity of this size, a woman would have to accumulate almost $14,000. Few industrial or commercial workers would be able to accumulate such sums.

[7] Federal Security Agency, *Fact Book on Aging* (Washington, D.C.: 1953), p. 52.

[8] National Planning Association, *Pensions in the United States* (Washington, D.C.: 1952), pp. 7–8.

Sources of receipts

Data presented both in this and in earlier chapters indicate that (1) the employment rates of older men are only about half the rates of younger men; (2) the rate of retirement increases rapidly after the age of 69 so that employment after the age of 75 is practically zero; (3) the employment rate of older women is very low so they, with unemployed men, must rely on other sources of income for support in old age. Data reproduced below show that approximately 29 per cent of the aged derive their income from employment either as wage earners, are self-employed, or are the wives of wage earners. Somewhat more than half of those 65 years of age and over derive their income from social insurance and related programs. Public assistance, in the form of old-age assistance and other aid to those aged 65 and over, was received by 18 per cent of the aged. As many as 1.2 million aged received income from more than one source. Eleven per cent, or more than 1.5 million older people, in 1955 either had no money income or received income from sources other than those given in Table 15. Most of the aged who were receiving retirement payments under private pension plans were also receiving old-age and survivors insurance benefits. It has been estimated that there were about 950,000 retired persons and their aged wives with private retirement benefits at the end of 1954. There is no doubt that this number has increased since that time.[9]

The number of beneficiaries of social insurance and related programs has increased over the years since 1940. This trend is due to two major factors. First, it reflects the relative decrease in the number of the aged who derive their income from employment. This is a reflection of declining opportunities for older persons to participate in the labor force. Second, it indicates the rapid growth in the number of retirement programs and the increased number of people

[9] Lenore A. Epstein, "Money Income Position of the Aged, 1948 to 1955," *Social Security Bulletin*, XIX (April, 1956), 8.

eligible for participation in these programs. An increase in the number of aged with relatively less opportunity for work, plus an increase in the availability of pension plans and an increased participation in these plans, are factors which are

TABLE 15

Estimated Number of Persons Aged 65 and Over Receiving Income from Specified Sources, June 1955
(in millions)

Source of Income of Population aged 65 and over	Total	Men	Women
Employment	4.0	2.4	1.6
Earners	3.1	2.4	.7
Wives of earners	.9	—	.9
Social Insurance and related programs	7.2	3.8	3.5
Old-age and survivors insurance	5.9	3.1	2.8
Railroad retirement	.5	.3	.2
Government employee retirement programs ...	.4	.3	.2
Veterans compensation and pensions	.6	.4	.2
Beneficiaries' wives not in direct receipt	.2	—	.2
Public assistance	2.5	1.0	1.5
No money income or income from other sources	1.6	.2	1.4
Income from more than one of the above sources	1.2	.8	.4
	14.1	6.6	7.6

SOURCE: "Money Income for Persons Aged 65 and Over, June 1955," *Social Security Bulletin*, XVIII (December, 1955), 22.

responsible for the continued growth of the number of persons who are eligible for retirement benefits. The growth in the gross amount of annual benefits paid to the beneficiaries is due to the increased number of beneficiaries as well as to the increase in the average annual payments to individuals. The gross payments would have increased even had there been no increase in the amount of benefits to each individual. With an increase in payments to each individual, the total gross amount has been increased even more. Payments under old-age and survivors insurance (OASI) have increased more than those under other plans, although the increased payments under other plans have not been inconsiderable.

Approximately 7.2 million aged in this country were dependent to some extent on the money received from retirement programs. In 1952 the programs with the lowest average payments were the programs with the largest number of beneficiaries or recipients. The programs with the highest average payments had the smallest number of beneficiaries. In June of 1955 the average monthly payment under OASI was $61.03; for Railroad Retirement, $100.97; for Federal Civil Service, $118.00; and for old-age assistance, $52.30. This increase in average payments under these programs is reflected in a deceasing percentage of persons aged 65 and over receiving less than $1,000 per year and conversely in an increasingly larger percentage receiving more than that amount. For instance, between 1948 and 1954 there were 7 per cent fewer persons in this age category with less than $1,000 per year. In 1948 only 13.3 per cent of the aged population received more than $2,000 per year whereas in 1954 as many as 18.2 per cent received this amount or more.[10]

Although some of the technical details of these retirement programs will be examined more closely in succeeding chapters, it is well to indicate one or two points here. First, probably a majority of beneficiaries of private industrial pensions (listed in Table 16 as group and individual annuities and trusteed pension plan benefits) are also beneficiaries of OASI payments. Second, in considering that the sums given here are in terms of averages, it is well to know that most programs have fixed minimum payments. If a person is eligible for any payments whatsoever, he receives the specified minimum regardless of the fact that the amount, as calculated by the pension formula, might have been less than the minimum. Although there may be different formulas for each program, many of them are stated in terms of a certain percentage of average annual salary multiplied by the number of years served. In the programs

[10] Epstein, "Money Income Position of the Aged," p. 9.

which have been in operation for longer periods of time, such as the Railroad Retirement System, the Civil Service Retirement System, and some local and state government plans, more employees are likely to have completed the maximum number of years' service under the program. Where this is the case, they are eligible for payments which are nearer the maximum than the minimum amounts allowable.

TABLE 16

Average Annual Payments Under Selected Programs: June 1952 *

Program	Average Annual Payment
Railroad retirement:	
Retired beneficiaries	$1,144
Couples benefit	1,588
Old-age and survivors insurance:	
Retired workers only	480
Retired worker and eligible wife	840
Federal Civil Service Retirement System:	
Employee annuitants	1,188
State and local government retirement systems:	
Employee annuitants	1,100
Veterans' compensation and pensions: payable to	
Spanish American war veterans	1,117
Group and individual annuities	692 †
Trusteed pension plan benefits	900 †
Old-age assistance	516

SOURCE: Joint Committee on Railroad Retirement Legislation, *Retirement Policies and the Railroad Retirement System* (Washington, D.C.: 1953), Part II, 25.

* These average monthly benefits include benefits paid as a result of early retirement, disability retirements, and short service, but exclude survivors benefits.

† Estimated by the Twentieth Century Fund for 1951.

On the other hand, certain of the private industrial pension plans have been in operation for only a few years. There are relatively few of the retiring persons who have accumulated enough wage credits to be drawing anywhere near the allowable maximum. Even where such programs allow for prior service, the number of individuals who are eligible for the full amount is still small due to the rapid labor turnover in industry. This condition also holds true for the old-age and survivors insurance program. As a consequence of these factors the average annual benefits payable under the older retirement programs are more probably weighted nearer the maximum than the minimum amounts. The opposite, or weighting nearer the minimum, would be the case with programs which have been in operation only a few years. The passage of time will do a great deal to remedy this situation.

Summary

From the evidence presented it is clear that lack of money is an acute problem of aging people in this country. A majority of them have some assets consisting primarily of real estate and some cash income. Cash income is derived mainly from current earnings and pensions in one form or another. The earned income of the aging is generally less than it is for younger people. The unearned income from pensions alone is inadequate in amount to assure them of a decent level of living. Standard budgets of 1947 and 1950 set $1,800 as the minimum budgetary requirements for an aging couple. Information gathered by the Bureau of the Census in 1950 showed that there were 5,600,000 nonfarm households maintained by persons over 65. Forty-six per cent of this number received less than $1,000 per year and less than 15 per cent had incomes over $4,000, while approximately 77 per cent received less than $3,000 per year. The number of pension plans has increased rapidly within the past fifteen years as has the number of pension payments. In spite of this fact it is clear that a majority of the aged couples fall short of having enough assets and income to maintain themselves on a desirable level of decency and health.

10

Old-Age Assistance

Title I of the Social Security Act of 1935, with subsequent amendments and changes, deals with public assistance to the needy aged. Prior to the passage of this act many of the states had old-age pension laws in operation. In spite of, or perhaps because of this, interested people both in and outside the federal government wanted to include old-age pensions under a state-federal system. These observers thought it necessary to have a public assistance program to take care of the aged who would not qualify under the old-age survivors insurance (OASI) program which was being considered at the same time. It was felt to be necessary, or at least desirable, to have uniform requirements which would be conformed to by the several states. Since the average state pension allowances were low, there was need to increase the amount of assistance to those who were receiving it. Some of the states had no provision for assistance and some of the counties within states which did have such provisions were not making payments to the needy aged.

The desired end was to make adequate amounts of assistance available to all the needy aged, regardless of their place of residence. To accomplish this end, use was made of the device of federal grants-in-aid to the states. Under this expedient the federal government shares with the states the financial burden of the program. In order to qualify for the federal grants, individual states would be required to meet certain minimum administrative and legal standards set forth by the federal bureau which was to administer the program. States were allowed sufficient time to pass the necessary legislation. Early in 1938 these minimum, uniform laws were operating in all forty-eight states as well as in Alaska and Hawaii. It was the expressed hope of Congress as well as other interested parties that the necessity for an old-age assistance (OAA) program would diminish in the years following the enactment of the law to the point where OAA would no longer be necessary.

The number of OAA recipients has varied appreciably from time to time. Both the relatively large number of recipients and the variation in numbers of recipients are due, primarily, to the following factors. The number of recipients has shown a tendency to increase because of (1) the increasing number of aged in the population; (2) more lenient laws passed by the individual states regarding eligibility for assistance and more lenient state administrative policies; (3) increased amount of federal moneys available to the states for use in the assistance program; and (4) a decline in the opportunity for employment of older people. In times of relative economic distress more people remain on the rolls to be joined by more newcomers to the program. The number of individual recipients on the assistance rolls tends to decrease under the following conditions: (1) stricter state laws in determining need, eligibility, and responsibility of relatives to support; (2) state drives to economize on money spent for public relief, resulting either in a decrease in the number of recipients (through stricter enforcement of the law) or in a reduced amount of assistance to individual recipients; (3) improved economic conditions, which mean more jobs available for recipients or higher wages for relatives of recipients, thus enabling relatives to support their indigent aged; and (4) an increase or broadening of the OASI program to include more people and to increase the amount of payments to those already drawing OASI. If OASI coverage is broadened it means that later there will be more old people with OASI coverage. Increasing OASI payments goes a long way in reducing the number of people on OAA rolls who are unable to live on OASI alone.

There are said to be several disadvantages to a noncontributory system such as the OAA program.[1] First, either new taxes must be introduced or old taxes must be increased to meet the cost of the program, and since appropriations must be made yearly, there is always the question whether Congress will appropriate sufficient funds from year to year to meet the cost of the program. Second, despite whatever financial problems may attend such a program, there is always lesser or greater pressure to increase the benefits and to lower the eligibility requirements in one way or another. Third, such assistance programs, unless universal, convey the idea of charity. Fourth, a means test must be applied; that is, the would-be recipient has to undergo inquiry into his financial condition, the amount of property he owns, and the ability of his responsible relatives to support him.

On the other side of the picture, a noncontributory system such as this has several advantages. Such a system can be made effective at once in meeting the financial problems of the aged. All classes can be included in the system. Taxes to finance a noncontributory system are equitable, in that the money can be derived from taxes imposed upon those who would benefit. "Straight pensions" are more socially just since old people have, by their services to society, earned these pensions. Assistance is much easier to administer than insurance is since separate accounts do not have to be maintained for each person during his work life by both government and employer. In the case of assistance records, all that need be kept is a record of applicants, pensioners, and the number and amount of the payments made.

The subject of this chapter, old-age assistance, is but one phase of the state-federal assistance program. In practice and in legislation, this program is closely related to the other

[1] Harry A. Millis and Royal E. Montgomery, *Labor's Risks and Social Insurance* (New York: McGraw-Hill Book Co., Inc., 1938), p. 395. By permission of McGraw-Hill Book Company.

phases of the assistance program. However, insofar as possible, because the other phases are of no direct concern in this book, the discussion here will be confined to this one aspect of the program.

Background of assistance legislation

Prior to the passage of the Social Security Act, the problem of supporting the indigent aged in this country was one of local concern. Estimates as to the number of persons 65 years of age and older who were dependent upon public charity in 1930 vary between 1.2 and 1.5 million. The number of indigent aged at that date amounted to about one-third of the total of 6.5 million people 65 years of age and older in this country. A survey of four large eastern cities in 1927 indicated that for the country as a whole there were some 1.9 million older people who had no property; over 2.4 million had no earnings, and nearly 1.2 million had neither property nor earnings. In 1935 the Committee on Economic Security estimated that at least half of the approximately 7.5 million people in this country 65 years of age and over were dependent upon others for their support. Of this number about 850,000 were on federal and local relief rolls and an additional 180,000 were receiving pensions from various state systems.[2]

In attempting to meet the ever-increasing problem of old age dependency, various devices were employed by the states, counties, and municipalities. First, by laws, some states sought to decrease the number of indigent aged by placing more legal responsibility on relatives to support their aged kin. Second, the amount of "outdoor relief," or giving aid to the needy in their homes, was increased. This aid was often in the form not of money but of necessity items such as food and clothing. Usually there was inadequate investigation of cases and where need was determined, an inadequate amount of aid given. The critics of both public and private outdoor relief have emphasized that disbursements are haphazard, inadequate, and wasteful; the

[2] *Ibid.*, pp. 361–62.

amounts either inadequate or uncertain; and the circumstances under which relief is given are degrading to the recipient. Third, care in almshouses or poorhouses in the 1920 decade as well as in preceding decades was a favorite form of care for the aged. Administration of these "homes" amounted to a large part of the total spent and the expenditures per inmate were consequently low. All classes of indigent persons were housed together indiscriminately. With few exceptions the physical conditions in almshouses were uniformly substandard; overcrowding and unsanitary conditions prevailed. As a rule the staff of these institutions was inadequate, untrained, and unsympathetic. Fourth, in addition to public almshouses there were numerous private homes for the aged. In general, conditions in these "homes" were little better than those in the publicly supported poorhouses. Fifth, there was renewed consideration given the limited and usually inadequate public and private pensions already in operation for varying lengths of time.[3]

State old-age pension legislation

As early as 1915 states began to pass old-age assistance or pension laws. There were several instances where the constitutionality of these laws was tested in state courts. Several courts ruled against the laws in the form in which they were originally passed. By 1929 there were ten states and one territory, Alaska, which had old-age pension laws. In spite of the fact that these laws were dissimilar in many respects, they had certain characteristics in common. All of them were noncontributory plans and called for monthly payments to be made to the indigent aged who could meet certain residence and age requirements. Pensions were not to be granted to the aged if there were relatives who could support them. Essentially these early pensions were similar to poor relief. The amount of the pension, as with poor relief, was to be determined by need. Many of the state pension plans were administered by the same personnel who had administered the poor relief. In most instances, these

[3] *Ibid.*, pp. 360–66.

pension laws were little more than an attempt to improve the poor relief programs, rather than an effort to institute a plan of general pensions.[4]

During this period of the development of the state pension plans, one other aspect of local poor relief philosophy was apparent. When the states passed the new old-age pension laws, most of them were more or less in the form of enabling legislation. Counties of the states with this type of law could participate in the state program or refrain from doing so as they wished. The obvious weakness of such plans was apparent almost at once. Counties with low revenues usually elected not to join the state plan. This meant that aged citizens in some counties would benefit, whereas those in other (sometimes adjoining) counties would not. In the case of these early laws, only two states, Wisconsin and Minnesota, provided for state aid to the counties which elected to pay old-age pensions.[5]

After the stock-market crash in 1929 and as the Depression became more serious, other states began to pass old-age assistance laws. Most of those which did were the more highly industrialized states of the North and West. By 1934 Hawaii and Alaska and twenty-eight states had old-age pension acts. Most of the new laws made it mandatory for the counties to participate in the program. During this period several of the states which originally had optional laws changed to mandatory ones. As a result of the increased number of states with such programs and the mandatory provisions of the laws, the number of pensioners increased from about 70,000 in 1931 to approximately 235,000 by the end of 1934.[6] In the seven states which still had optional laws at the end of 1932, only 28 per cent of the population was covered as contrasted with 91 per cent coverage in the states with mandatory laws. However, it became increasingly difficult for some counties to continue their part of the

[4] *Ibid.*, pp. 378–79.

[5] Paul H. Douglas, *Social Security in the United States* (New York: McGraw-Hill Book Co., Inc., 1936), pp. 4–7.

[6] *Ibid.*, p. 7.

program and the state could not demand continued participation. As a consequence more and more states began to participate in the financial aspect of the programs. Where states did participate they assumed varying degrees of the cost. Delaware, in 1931, was the first state to assume the entire cost of the pension program.[7]

In spite of the increase in the number of states with pension laws and the increase in the number of persons receiving pension payments, there was an increasing number of problems being encountered. Part of the difficulty lay in the fact that thirteen of the twenty-eight states still depended upon the counties to supply all the funds, whereas in only six states were all the funds supplied by the state government. In many states the legislative bodies failed to appropriate enough money to maintain the program, or if taxes were levied from special sources, these sources failed to yield as much revenue as was needed for the program. Part of the difficulty in the financial realm grew out of the fact that more and more people became eligible for payments at the same time most states were being adversely affected by the Depression. North Dakota presented the extreme case where the average monthly amount paid to the 3,914 pensioners in 1934 was only $.69. Nebraska, with 926 pensioners, averaged only $1.22 per pensioner per month. Nevada had only seven pensioners who received a monthly average of $18.48. The average monthly pension payment in 1934 was $14.68; in 1933 the average monthly benefit had been $19.33. Due to decline in available revenues and to a substantial increase in the number of pensioners in 1934, the average payments had declined.

It became increasingly evident that the states with operative laws would be unable to continue to meet the problem of providing adequate benefits to more than a small fraction of eligible aged. Also it was evident that the poorer agricultural states would not voluntarily and without outside aid enact legislation for the purpose of providing pensions for the needy aged within their borders. As a consequence of

[7] Millis and Montgomery, *Labor's Risks and Social Insurance*, pp. 379–80.

these factors, there came to be more and more pressure exerted for the enactment of some type of legislation which would bring about more uniformity in the laws, the participation of all states in the program, and uniformity of pensions in the various states.

Background of federal legislation

Although improvements were being made in the state old-age pension laws, some of them were still inadequate in many respects. By the end of 1934 there were twenty states which either had no old-age pension law or had optional laws which were largely inoperative. The increasing financial difficulties which were encountered by the states with such laws, plus the increasing number of eligible pensioners made it increasingly difficult for the states to pay adequate pensions. As a result of these and other factors, pressure began to be exerted to have Congress encourage states to take action by giving them financial aid in the form of grants to carry out their programs. One of the most active groups involved was the American Association for Old Age Security under the leadership of Mr. Abraham Epstein.

A jointly sponsored bill was introduced into Congress in 1933–34 (the Seventy-third Congress). This bill did not have the support of the administration but was heartily approved by the majority of legislators. The bill was favorably reported out of committee in both branches of Congress but the inability to obtain the backing of the administration kept it from coming to the floor of either house for a vote. There seems to be evidence that it would probably have passed had it been voted on.[8] Failure of the administrative branch of the government to react favorably lay in its desire to present one all-inclusive Social Security Act rather than a patchwork of bills, each covering single phases of the problem of social security. Due to the complicated nature of the problem and to the exploratory nature of this legislation in this country, a great deal of time elapsed before the final form of the Social Security Act was prepared for

[8] Douglas, *Social Security in the United States*, pp. 9–11.

congressional action. In the meantime, because of the continued pressing need and the seemingly unnecessary congressional delays, the Townsend Plan came upon the scene. This plan came into national prominence in the latter part of 1934 and early in 1935. Briefly it was to provide $200 per month to every person over the age of 60, on two conditions. First, the person must retire from active employment and second, every person receiving this amount must agree to spend it within the month. There is little in the way of actual evidence that such a program was practical either from the administrative or financial point of view. One practical result of this movement was apparent when the Social Security Act came to a vote in Congress. Many members of Congress who did not approve or were not wholeheartedly behind the act voted for it in preference to seeing the Townsend Plan come up as the only alternative.

In January, 1935, the President's Committee on Economic Security presented its plan to Congress. Extended hearings were held before the House Committee on Ways and Means and the Committee on Finance in the Senate. The bill finally came to the floor of Congress for vote and was approved in August, 1935. The essence of Title I of the Social Security Act which provides grants to states for old-age assistance follows. Section 3 (a) of the act provided that the Treasury should pay to each state at the end of each quarter one-half of the amount expended by the state for old-age assistance during that quarter. The amount expended per month per individual was not to exceed $30. An individual had to be 65 years of age or older and could not be residing in a public institution if he was to become eligible for benefits. An additional 5 per cent of the sum appropriated to the states should be used to administer the program. The state plan had to be approved by the Social Security Board but states need not participate in the financial arrangement with the Treasury prior to July 1, 1937. This provision was made to allow all the states time to enact proper legislation, but at the same time allow them to receive some aid from the federal government.

Section 2 (a) of the act provided that, in order to be approved, it was necessary that all the political subdivisions of the state participate in the program, and if administered by them, be mandatory upon them, and, in addition, that the states participate financially in the program. One central state authority should be in charge of administering the act for that state. This body of administrators was to make the necessary reports to the federal administration and was to act as the board of appeals for claimants who were denied benefits by the local authorities. If the state or one of its political subdivisions collected any amount from the estate of a recipient of OAA, one-half of the amount collected was to be paid to the United States and be deposited in the Treasury to the credit of the appropriation of OAA.

Section 2 (b) provided that the board should approve any state plan which filled the above conditions, but that no plan should be approved which imposed the following as conditions of eligibility: an age requirement of more than 65 years, or an age requirement of 70 years effective until January 1, 1940. No resident of any state otherwise eligible should be excluded if he had resided in that state for five of the nine years immediately preceding his application, and continuously for one year immediately preceding his application. No citizenship requirements were to be imposed which would exclude any citizen of the United States from participating in the program if he were otherwise eligible.[9]

There were three important changes made between the final drafting of the act in committees and its passage in Congress. The power of the federal authorities to set minimum standards for the state administrative personnel was virtually eliminated. The board had no authority under the act as amended on the floor of Congress to lay down any provisions for the selection, tenure of office, or compensation of the state administrative personnel. One of the primary

[9] Adapted from Millis and Montgomery, *Labor's Risks and Social Insurance*, pp. 382–83, and Douglas, *Social Security*, pp. 87–88 and 151–55.

factors behind this amendment was the fear of domination of the state by federal bureaucracy. Further, it was contended that the state administrative appointees were more familiar with the local social situation than federally appointed personnel would be. It is true that the elimination of this particular curb may have left the way open for political favoritism on the state level. On the other hand, it was felt that the demands for personnel standards set by the board would be so high that the states would be unwilling to comply with them. Although many of the states had made remarkable progress in improving their standards, most of the standards were far below those which it was assumed the board would require.[10]

Another change made in the bill as presented in its final form had to do with the provision in the original bill which had stated that "old age assistance grants must be sufficient with other income, to provide 'a reasonable subsistence, compatible with decency and health.'" [11] By striking this phrase the several states escaped administrative scrutiny of their individual assistance cases. There would be no check by the board if the grants made by the states seemed to be unreasonably high or ridiculously low. As the bill stood on passage, and still stands, there can be no guarantee, beyond appeal by the recipients to the state administrative body, that they will receive enough to assure them an adequate income. There are two possible explanations for the elimination of this provision. First, there always has been and still is a general feeling that the amount granted recipients of public aid from public sources should ordinarily not exceed their former earned income. For to give assistance in amounts exceeding the possible earning capacity of the recipients would be to encourage the lower income groups to seek assistance rather than jobs. A second reason was the concern that the federal authorities not be able

[10] Cf. Douglas, *Social Security*, pp. 106–7, and Millis and Montgomery, *Labor's Risks and Social Insurance*, p. 384.

[11] Millis and Montgomery, *Labor's Risks and Social Insurance*, pp. 383–84.

to question the amount of assistance rendered to the indigent aged of minority groups such as Negroes in the South or Mexicans and Indians of the Southwest and West.

In its original form, the act also would have prohibited the states from making further restrictions as to eligibility on the grounds of age, residence, and citizenship. As it stood at passage, the residence requirements of some states had to be liberalized to conform with the act. Although the act finally specified that a citizen otherwise eligible (age, residence, and degree of indigence) should not be barred, it was believed there would be an effort on the part of some states to bar alien residents from consideration or to enact legislation which would bar members of minority groups from assistance under the law.

The bill in its final form was felt by some to be relatively weak. On the other hand it was strong enough to make it necessary for almost all of the states to change their assistance laws in such a manner as to improve their standards. Even though there is no question but that the average amount of assistance per individual in some of the poorer states is inadequate by almost any standards, there can be no question but that these amounts are far larger than they would be without federal aid. Furthermore, the administrative standards are higher and the eligibility requirements are less rigid than they would have been without federal participation in the program.

Amendments since passage of the original act

To the present time several minor amendments have been made in Title I of the Social Security Act. So far none of the more "vital" parts of this title have been changed by amendments. Each of the amendments, as will be shown below, has to do with an increased participation of the federal government in sharing the financial burden of the states in the assistance program.

The amendments of 1939 provided that, beginning on January 1, 1940, the federal government would pay one-half the amount the state expended up to $40 per month per individual.[12] In 1946 an amendment was passed calling for an increase in federal participation from $20 to $25 per month per individual. More important than the mere increase of federal contribution was a change in the formula determining this contribution. Instead of a straight fifty-fifty matching of state funds by the federal government, the new amendment increased the percentage of federal contribution. The amendment provided that the federal share would be an average of two-thirds of the first $15 of state expenditures and one-half of any additional state expenditures up to $45 per month per individual. This amendment was clearly aimed toward helping the poorer states either increase their contributions up to $15 or to increase the number of recipients on their rolls. States would have to contribute only $5 instead of $7.50 of the first $15 per individual recipient.[13]

The amendment of 1948 further increased federal participation to three-fourths of the first $20 expended by the state per individual recipient, and matched, on a fifty-fifty basis, the amount paid by the state above $20 up to a total of $50 per month per recipient.[14] The 1950 amendment provided that the federal government would match state expenditures for assistance to the aged who were in certain types of public medical institutions. If the state plan provided for assistance payments to the aged in either private or public institutions, federal matching funds would be made available to these states. This was to be done provided that the state meet the standards the federal government established for such institutions. The matching funds thus provided would be available for direct payment made by the states to

[12] "Social Security in Review," *Social Security Bulletin,* II (August, 1939), 3.
[13] "Social Security Legislation in 1947," *Social Security Bulletin,* X (September, 1947), 15.
[14] "Advisory Council on Social Security: Reports on Permanent and Total Disability Insurance and on Public Assistance," *Social Security Bulletin,* XI (July, 1948), 6–7.

the doctors, hospitals, or persons furnishing medical care to the aged of these institutions.[15]

In 1952 Title I was amended again. The object of this amendment was to allow the states to increase the amount of assistance to each recipient by the sum of $5 per month without causing them to increase their own outlay to the program. This was to be accomplished by having the federal share of the total matchable funds increased from $30 to $35 per month. This would simultaneously increase the maximum of matching funds from $50 to $55 per month per recipient. In other words, instead of the federal share being 60 per cent of the total maximum matching funds, as in 1950, it now became 64 per cent.[16]

In 1956 the maximum payments under old-age assistance were increased to $60. The federal share was raised to four-fifths of the first $30 plus one-half of the balance up to the maximum. This amendment did not provide for an automatic increase in the amount of payments to individual recipients. Whether recipients receive more depends upon the laws and administrative policies of the states. Each state can decide whether the additional federal funds will be used to give assistance to more people, to give larger amounts to current recipients, or to save state funds. Any state may decide to use any combination of the three choices.[17]

It should be noted in each of the amendments reviewed above, increases were made by Congress to enable the states to increase the amount of assistance given recipients. States might have retained the money and reduced the share paid from the state treasury. However, in general, the payments to recipients were increased in proportion, although not in the

[15] Wilbur J. Cohen and Robert J. Myers, "Social Security Act Amendments of 1950: A Summary and Legislative History," *Social Security Bulletin*, XIII (October, 1950), 5.

[16] Wilbur J. Cohen, "Social Security Act Amendments of 1952," *Social Security Bulletin*, XV (September, 1952), 8–9.

[17] Charles I. Schottland, "Social Security Amendments of 1956: A Summary and Legislative History," *Social Security Bulletin*, XIX (September, 1956), 10.

exact amount of the increase in federal funds. There were some cases where technical points in some state laws made it impossible for them to increase individual payments at once. In some cases where states were making payments at the higher levels, it was felt that payments were adequate and should not be increased.[18]

State differences in old-age assistance

It has been stated already that OAA is a noncontributory program. If an applicant meets the age, residence, and citizenship requirements which the state law imposes, he is given a "means" test. That is, his means of support are compared or contrasted with his needs. The representatives of the state agency administering the program then decide whether the applicant is eligible for assistance payments.

There are several crucial factors involved in making the decision as to whether the applicant will be granted assistance, and if so, in what amount. Most important, of course, is the availability of funds for assistance. In theory, if not in fact, in all states the amount of funds to be granted would be determined by the difference between the applicants' needs and their means. In order to determine the difference between the two it is necessary for the state agency to have a budget for an old person actually worked out, or to have some workable rule-of-thumb method of arriving at a relatively objectively determined figure as to the amount of assistance needed. If the state is unable to supply the full amount needed, it allots as much money as it feels able to. Since there are different standards of needs in the different states and since the amount of money available varies from state to state, an applicant in one state may be granted assistance whereas one in a similar economic condition living in another state might not be. Because of different administrative techniques it is even possible that of two applicants in similar circumstances in different political subdivisions

[18] United States Congress, House of Representatives, *Analysis of the Social Security System* (Washington, D.C.: 1953), Part III, 379–80.

within a given state, one might be given assistance, the other not.

In addition to differences in administrative practices, differences in budgets used to determine need, and differences in the amount of available money, there are other differences between the state laws. There are five areas where state laws differ from one another in administrative policy. First, provisions vary as to the amount and kind of property which a person is allowed to hold if he is eligible for assistance. A second difference is whether or not the state may seek to recover from the estate of a deceased recipient a portion of the assistance rendered by the state. Third, there is a difference in state laws as to whether relatives should be held responsible for the support or partial support of an old person. There is also a variation in definitions of who is a responsible relative, to what extent he should be held financially responsible, and what procedure should be used in making the relative accept the responsibility for support. Fourth, but of minor importance here, there is little uniformity as to the way the distribution of the burden of assistance is spread between county and state. Finally, the question as to whether records of assistance payments should be open to public inspection has been the subject of heated debate.

In analyzing ownership of property as a qualification for old-age assistance three types of property are taken into consideration: real property, homestead, and personal property. First, of course, the state law must decide whether ownership of these classes of property will be taken into consideration in determining the eligibility of a person for assistance. Ownership of assets not easily or profitably converted into cash is of little value in determining one's level of living. If, to be eligible for assistance, a person must first sell his property and spend the income from it, he may be more of a financial burden on the public treasury than he would have been had he kept his property. To be forced to sell one's house, homestead, or even private property in order to become eligible for assistance would be to penalize the person for having saved during the productive years. There is the distinct possibility that a person might deed or give property to relatives for the sole purpose of making himself eligible for public assistance. Most of the states foresaw this contingency and legislated against it.

Second, the state law must decide how much property will be allowed. Even after the amount of property allowable has been decided upon, someone has to appraise the property. It is in this area that a great deal of variability between subdivisions within a state, operating under the same law, occurs.

Many of the state laws relating to property qualifications were enacted early in the history of the federal-state assistance program. Since 1935 the value of property has increased appreciably; yet some of the state laws have remained unchanged in regard to property qualifications. Very broadly considered, the forty-eight states can be classified into five groups, depending upon the way they regard real property and the homestead of applicants for OAA. The gradations range from rather strict limitations to very lenient restrictions on ownership of property. However, within each of these five categories there is a great deal of difference in the amount of property which old people are allowed to keep before they are able to draw assistance.[19]

In addition to different policies of states regarding the ownership of property and the value set on this property there is the question of the disposal of property at the death of the recipient. The states have a choice of three procedures. First, they can enact a lien law against the real property owned by the recipient. This means that the recipient signs over all real property to the administrative body of the law. Second, states can enact laws providing that OAA shall be a claim against the estate of the deceased recipient. Finally, states need not make any provision for the recovery of OAA. There is a tendency for the states with the strictest

[19] Adapted from Wisconsin Legislative Council, *Problems of the Aged*, (Madison: 1953), Vol. I, Part II, 24.

property requirements to have no provision for the recovery of property on the death of the recipient of assistance.[20]

There are arguments both for and against lien laws. In support of such laws there are four arguments, the first two of which are related. First, there has been evidence that in some instances the recipients of assistance use the funds to help pay for or to maintain their real property. When the recipient dies the property is inherited by relatives who may have made no contribution to the support of their needy relatives. Second, lien laws act as a deterrent factor in keeping old people from applying for assistance. Responsible relatives would rather support their indigent aged than lose their share in the real property which they would inherit. But while it is true that the number of persons on assistance rolls has increased in states which have repealed their lien laws and decreased in states which have enacted them, it would be a mistake to attribute all of the increases or withdrawals to changes in the law. It is probable, however, that revisions in the law were responsible for much of the change in the numbers of applicants and cases. Third, the assistance program does not cost the taxpayer as much money when part of the payment can be recovered by enforcing the lien or claim laws. This saving would occur on both state and federal level. Fourth, lien laws allow a recipient to have his cake and eat it too. He is not forced to sell his property and consume the money from the sale before he becomes eligible for assistance. He can retain his property and draw assistance. Thus, it is alleged, it is only fair that his property be used after his death to repay the government at least partially for the money given him while he was on assistance.[21]

Those who oppose the retention or passage of lien laws say that such a law is a penalty imposed upon property owners which obviously cannot be imposed upon those who own no property. These opponents contend that applicants

[20] *Ibid.*, pp. 50–52.
[21] *Ibid.*, p. 54.

who are in need should be granted aid regardless of whether or not there is property. They also seem to attach more value to real than to personal property in that they generally agree that liquid assets have to be reduced to as little as $300 before the applicant becomes eligible for assistance.[22]

Another difference between state laws is based on the question of "relative responsibility." In 1952, only fifteen of the forty-eight states had enacted provisions concerning the responsibility of the relatives of aged persons. Three of these added their relative responsibility laws in 1951. Colorado's law was nullified by its state constitution. Since 1935 several of the states have changed their laws in this respect.[23]

It is possible that of all the problems regarding state OAA laws that of the responsibility of relatives is the most persistent. Pressure is constantly being brought to bear upon the state legislative bodies to pass such laws where they do not exist and to rescind them where they do. Some of the states have laws which provide that an applicant is not eligible for assistance if he has relatives who can support him. In a few states contributions from relatives are counted as a resource in determining the amount of assistance the state shall give.

There are several difficulties involved in the question of responsibility which must be resolved by the states which stipulate that relatives are to be held responsible for the support of their aged kin, namely, what relatives are to be held responsible; what criteria shall be used to determine if the relatives should contribute, and if it is determined they should, to what extent are they able to contribute financially; and finally, what means should be used to require relatives to support the aged for whom they are responsible.

After it is determined that an old person has a relative who can be held legally responsible for support, it is necessary to discover if the responsible relative can contribute, and if so, to what extent. In determining whether a relative can

[22] *Ibid.*, p. 54.
[23] *Ibid.*, pp. 35–45.

contribute, three things must be considered: his income, the number of dependents he has, and the fact that the relative himself should be preparing for economic security in his own old age. Twenty-three of the thirty-three states which have relative responsibility provisions have schedules or scales on which to determine contributions from relatives. Most of these scales take into consideration the prior obligations of the relative. When the net income after obligations has been determined, the states consider a certain percentage of the net income as the contribution such a relative could be expected to make. Difficulties are enountered in persuading responsible relatives actually to make the contributions which they are deemed able to make. In lieu of persuasion a strict interpretation of some of the state laws would result in the state withholding assistance from any indigent old person if he has relatives who could support him regardless of whether they do or not.

It is clear that where states have laws which require support of the aged by their relatives, the laws are only as effective as their potentiality for enforcement. Furthermore, even if the laws are potentially enforceable, administrative practice may largely negate them. Difficulties arise between the welfare agencies and the courts or the legal machinery which is devised to enforce the law. In some instances the welfare agency either does not or is not able to compile enough evidence to make a case upon which the court may act. In some instances where the welfare agency carries out its part of the procedure, the legal representatives of the county or state either delay action or take no action in the cases.

In states where the relative responsibility law provisions have been repealed, there has been a subsequent increase in the number of applicants for assistance. States which have enacted such legislation with penalty provisions after not having had such laws find that there is a decrease in the number of applicants as well as a withdrawal of some cases from the rolls. If it can be assumed that responsible relatives who are financially able, actually render the necessary amount of aid to their dependent needy, then the states would have more funds with which to provide assistance to the needy already on their rolls, or to include other needy old people on their rolls.

It is sometimes argued that to have relative responsibility provisions is to keep some needy old people from applying for assistance. It is said that they would rather do without assistance than have the financial condition of their children investigated by a public agency. Further, to require support by law is not humane, especially in cases where such requirements work a hardship on the children. Probably the strongest argument opposing such laws is that the monetary saving to the states may be more than offset by the hard feelings engendered by invoked or threatened legal action.[24]

What effect do lien or claims and relative responsibility laws have on state assistance loads? There are two sets of factors aside from state laws and their administration which influence the number of recipients on the state rolls: first, the general economic conditions; second, the relationship between the OAA and OASI programs. In states which are relatively more rural and agrarian, it can be expected that fewer of the aged will become eligible for OASI benefits, and of those who do, more will receive smaller benefits which may have to be supplemented by OAA. It is to be expected that the states which are less industrialized would have the least stringent laws and administrative practices regarding eligibility of persons for OAA.

It is apparent also that there are two factors involved in accounting for the fact that the number of recipients per 1,000 aged population has increased in fifteen states while the number has decreased in the remaining states between 1940 and 1953. In the first place, states in which the number of recipients per 1,000 population has increased are generally the rural states which started with a relatively small load in 1940. The second factor is the absence of restrictive laws on property recovery or relative responsibility. States which are largely agrarian and have neither lien or claim laws nor

[24] *Ibid.*, pp. 44–45.

relative responsibility clauses in their assistance laws are the ones which have generally shown increases in assistance loads (seven of ten states) in the thirteen years between June 1940 and 1953. The median number of recipients for these ten states was 303 per 1,000 aged population in 1953. Only six of the fourteen states with either claim or lien law or relative responsibility law have shown an increase in the number of recipients per 1,000 aged. In 1953 the median number of recipients per 1,000 aged population for these states was 267.

Finally, of the twenty-four states which had both a claim or lien law and a relative responsibility law, only two had more recipients in 1953 than in 1940, and the gain in these two was negligible. The median number of recipients for this category of states, per 1,000 aged was only 141 in 1953. Clearly there seems to be a negative relation between the presence of these restrictive laws and the number of recipients on the OAA rolls. There is considerable overlapping between the three categories presented here, part of which would have to be accounted for other than by the presence or absence of the laws themselves. These factors would include the enforcement and enforceability of the laws, the ability weighed against the willingness of the state to look after the aged, and other factors.

The final major difference between state laws which will be discussed here is the question of permitting public inspection of the assistance rolls. It is probable that no single question relating to OAA has caused as much publicity as this one. The original act provided that the rolls and pertinent information should be confidential and that if any state did not treat it thus the federal share of funds would be discontinued. In 1951 the legislature of Indiana passed a law requiring that the names and amounts of assistance should be open to public inspection with certain safeguards. Subsequently Congress amended the act to allow states to open the rolls for inspection. The amendment has been interpreted to mean that confidential information usually contained in case histories and records would not be available to the public.[25] Agitation on the part of a segment of the public brought this question to a showdown. Apparently in some quarters there has been the feeling that numbers of people were receiving assistance illegally. It was believed that if names and amounts were made public these people would have their names withdrawn from the assistance rolls. However, there is no evidence to indicate that there is an overwhelming desire on the part of the public to view these rolls or that any names have been withdrawn from the rolls because of the potential publicity.

Extent of old-age assistance

In December, 1956, there were 2,514,000 old-age assistance recipients. The average monthly payment was $57.99. A total of $145,810,238 was disbursed to recipients of old-age assistance during December, 1956. During the year ending December, 1956, the caseload of old-age recipients declined by 39,000 cases. Moreover, there has been relatively little increase in the caseload since 1950. Some of the recent decline in the number of people on old-age assistance is accounted for by an increase in both number and amount of payments of old-age insurance. Even though there are still some who receive income from both OAA and OASI this number has been reduced appreciably since recent changes in the OASI formula. The rate of old-age assistance recipients for the country is only 173 per 1,000 population aged 65 and over.[26]

Table 17 shows the rather startling difference between average amounts of old-age assistance payments for the five highest and five lowest states in 1941 and 1956. States with the lowest average monthly payments for these years were the poorer agricultural states. In 1956 the five states with the lowest average monthly payments were contributing nearly as much as the highest average payment states were contributing in 1941.

[25] *Ibid.*, pp. 81–82.
[26] "Social Security in Review: 1956 in Review," *Social Security Bulletin,* XX (March, 1957), 1–2.

TABLE 17

Average Payments for Old-Age Assistance in States with Highest and Lowest Payments, 1941 and 1956

December, 1941		December, 1956 [*]	
Lowest Average Payment per Recipient			
Arkansas	$7.95	Mississippi	$28.82
Georgia	8.56	West Virginia	31.97
Mississippi	8.94	Virginia	32.46
Alabama	9.03	Tennessee	34.56
Kentucky	9.26	North Carolina	34.72
Highest Average Payment per Recipient			
Massachusetts	$29.75	Massachusetts	$84.15
Colorado	29.91	New York	86.42
Washington	33.13	Washington	87.15
Arizona	34.14	Connecticut	90.66
California	36.51	Colorado	95.26

SOURCE: John J. Corson and John W. McConnell, *Economic Needs of Older People* (New York: The Twentieth Century Fund, 1956), p. 167; and "Current Operating Statistics," *Social Security Bulletin*, XX (April, 1957), 34.

[*] Includes vendor payments for medical care and cases receiving only such payments.

Summary

It has been indicated in this chapter that several factors are involved in determining both the number of OAA recipients and the payments to those who receive assistance. Most of the state differences in both caseload and payments to individuals are caused by differences in the state laws, different administrative standards in carrying out the laws, and a difference in the state's ability to provide an attitude toward providing assistance. On the federal level, differences in state loads are caused by amendments to the Social Security Act, primarily in the amount of funds available for federal matching, in changes in the OASI laws which have resulted in improving the income of recipients and making more old people eligible for OASI payments. On the negative side there has been a decrease in other public assistance programs such as public works programs, thus making it necessary for some people to fall back on old-age assistance for support.

On the nongovernmental or "impersonal" level, there are such factors as change in employment possibilities, changes in the cost of living, and increase in the total population from which recipients are drawn. In addition, it is well to note that where increases in both assistance load and cost are involved, the increase in cost is more than the sum of the two factors. For instance if a state starts with 100 cases, each getting $10 per month, the total state expenditure is $1,000 per month. If the average payment is increased to $15 the expenditure is increased to $1,500. If the state increases the load to 150 cases each receiving $10 the expenditure increases to $1,500. In both of these instances, the percentage of increase is 50 per cent. However, if in this instance both the caseload and the average payment increased at the same time, the amount of payment would be $2,250, or 125 per cent rather than only 100 per cent, as one might assume. Where both positive and negative factors are at work, such a simple illustration could not be used.

In conclusion, there is no doubt but that the average recipient in 1956 was being cared for better than was his counterpart in 1940. However, there is room to question whether the states with strict laws and strict enforcement of the laws are rendering assistance to as many people as might actually be in need. Two opposite stands might be taken in regard to assistance loads. First, in the case of a small load, a feeling of pride that the state has not allowed itself to be burdened by old-age "spongers" who take a "free ride" at public expense. Second, in the case of heavy loads, a feeling of pride that the state is doing all it can, even at the cost of payments to some "unworthy" cases, to help the indigent aged live out their lives in relative comfort. The ideal system would be one which would not allow any old person to suffer want but at the same time would not give assistance to anyone who, unaided, could maintain a level of living consistent with health and decency.

11

Old-Age Survivors Insurance Program

In addition to old-age assistance, the decade of the thirties demonstrated a need for some kind of government insurance program to help people meet the financial problems of old age. As originally conceived, old-age and survivors insurance was intended to encourage older workers to retire by furnishing retirement income. The labor market would be relieved of older workers, thus opening job opportunities for younger workers to earn their livings. At no time in the history of OASI was it contended that its benefits alone were presumed adequate to support old people in retirement; rather, the benefits were looked upon as supplements to retirement income, or a cushion to retirement. It is possible that this attitude was taken to help allay some of the criticisms of the program so that it would not appear to be a drastic departure from the American ideal that each individual should save for his retirement.

As first set up OASI benefits were not adequate enough to encourage older workers to retire. Its inadequacies in this area as well as its limited coverage were not sufficient to quiet the cry that such a program would kill individual initiative or that forced savings would discourage people from saving voluntarily. On the other hand, it was said the program was sufficiently attractive so that freedom of movement between covered and noncovered occupations would be practically eliminated and all migration of young workers into noncovered occupations would cease. One further purpose, on the part of those who accepted the philosophy of social security, was to expand the OASI program as it matured so that it would eventually make the old-age assistance program all but unnecessary. Payments of OASI benefits were to become more adequate and coverage was to be extended to include all gainfully employed people. OAA would still be necessary for retired workers with minimum OASI benefits and for indigent individuals who would not qualify under OASI.

As the program has matured some of the basic contradictions inherent in the original act have been eliminated. However, both friend and foe still find reasons to criticize the program. It is doubtful that there are many even among the most ardent opponents who would have the political, economic, or social temerity to advocate a complete elimination of the program. Rather, their efforts seem to be directed more toward crippling the program by trying to make amendments and changes which allegedly would strengthen it. There are still some who are opposed to the program for the same reason it has been opposed all along, which is that any social security program works in some mysterious way to undermine that which it attempts to do. Other critics, both friendly and unfriendly, have found fault with specific parts of the program rather than with the actual philosophy of social security. Some of these criticisms will be dealt with in more detail below. Both friendly and unfriendly critics have, however, done much to improve the entire program.

One of the first questions which had to be settled by President Roosevelt's Commission on Social and Economic Security in 1934 and 1935 was whether the Social Security Act should have a pension setup or an insurance setup for older people. There were several factors to be considered in making the decision. The final decision was to have two phases within the same broad program. Some of the arguments, pro and con, of contributory as opposed to noncontributory programs are to be found in the preceding chapter. For present purposes some of the reasons which were set forth to justify the dual program are considered here. It was said that a contributory system provides income for the aged as a right rather than as charity. Those who contribute to the system can benefit from it without regard to their need. Such a program can be made to support itself without having to fall back on public financing. An insurance program carries within itself a "built-in" protection against unjustified or unjustifiable "raids" on the funds. Those who benefit are those who have contributed. This offers a safeguard against undue demands for increasing benefits, as the contributors have to pay the bill.

Two of the principal arguments against contributory pensions are that they cannot cover everyone in the society and they are difficult to administer. Such a program cannot be set up to cover those who are 65 years of age or older at the time the program goes into operation. As long as such a program even roughly adheres to the principles of insurance, some people will receive maximum benefits, others minimum benefits, regardless of their needs. Separate accounts have to be kept for each employee and records kept of payments made to each account. Obviously this involves keeping records on all employees who have been issued social security cards. Without modern methods of record keeping, this would be virtually impossible.[1]

Legislative background

In its deliberation on the whole area of social security, the Commission on Social and Economic Security decided to recommend both a contributory and noncontributory system. Members of the commission were convinced that the ultimate cost of a noncontributory system would be too great for the federal government to bear. Further, the commission agreed that a contributory system would free the aged of having to submit to a means test to determine whether or not they needed the assistance. Finally, it was thought a contributory program would assure some relationship between the amount of pension received and the amount of money earned during productive years. Higher income pro-

[1] Harry A. Millis and Royal E. Montgomery, *Labor's Risks and Social Insurance* (New York: McGraw-Hill Book Co., Inc., 1938), pp. 393–98.

vides a higher level of living and those with higher levels of living would need more than a minimum income from pensions in retirement. The commission also became aware of the fact that a compulsory contributory pension plan would have to be federally administered. This was to be in contrast to the other phase of income provision for the aged, namely the old-age assistance program.[2]

Even after the commission had decided that two programs should be established to supplement each other there were several serious questions and problems to be considered. The United States was in the midst of a serious economic depression when the question of pensions was being discussed. There was no precedent here upon which to make conclusions, and, in light of the Depression, the commission had to be careful not to do anything that would threaten or weaken a very precarious economic balance.

Then there was the necessity of setting up a program which would be worthwhile as far as the participants were concerned. The problem was one of trying to arrive at a formula which would not overtax employees and employers to the extent of reducing current ability to buy goods. At the same time it should make possible a relatively adequate retirement fund without creating a reserve fund large enough to compose a major fraction of the total national wealth. Withholding a large sum from the potential purchase of consumer goods, with no surety that it would be invested immediately in capital goods, was too great a risk to be taken at that time.[3] As a consequence it was decided that although a 5 per cent payroll tax would be needed to provide an adequate retirement fund, this goal should be attained in gradual steps by a progressive increase in the tax rate during a twenty-year period. A reduction in the contemplated tax to only 1 per cent (divided equally between employer and employee) would mean older workers with relatively low incomes would receive annuities inadequate by any stand-

[2] Paul H. Douglas, *Social Security in the United States* (McGraw-Hill Book Co., Inc., 1936), pp. 35–36 and 55.
[3] Cf. *ibid.*, pp. 56–57.

ards. In order to bring these annuities up to a sum approximating adequacy, it was decided that those who contributed to the annuity for as long as five years would be eligible to receive as much as 15 per cent of what they had earned during the five-year period. This sum was to be increased by an increment of 1 per cent per year for each of the five following years. A person who contributed to the fund would thus receive up to 20 per cent of his earnings on retirement. The maximum annuity was to be set at 40 per cent of average wages.[4] The difference between what an older person paid in and what he was to receive would be advanced by contributions of younger workers. When the younger workers reached retirement age, if there was not enough reserve to pay their annuities, the federal government was to contribute as additional sums were needed.

The original act

Both the House Committee on Ways and Means and the Senate Finance Committee made several changes in the old-age insurance program as recommended by the President's commission. In addition, there were numerous points of conflict between the recommendations of these two congressional committees. However, the Social Security Act was finally approved by Congress to begin functioning in 1937 as far as the tax collecting aspect was concerned. The following paragraphs will give a summary of the essential features of the bill as it was originally enacted.

In the light of difficulties which had been encountered with the constitutionality of the Railroad Retirement Act in 1934, it was considered wise to separate the tax or contributions function of the bill from the disbursement function. Consequently Title II was designed to specify the annuities and benefit scale and Title VIII was designed to collect the required revenues to provide for the annuities called for in Title II. The taxes levied under Title VIII were on both employers and employees. The rate of the taxes

[4] Cf. *ibid.*, pp. 59–60.

began at 1 per cent on both parties and was to be increased by 0.5 per cent each two years until a maximum of 6 per cent was reached in 1949. It was to have remained at 6 per cent after that date. Neither employer nor employee was to pay this payroll tax on incomes exceeding $3,000 per year. Not all employees, however, were included in Title II to receive benefits; therefore these were also excluded from having to pay taxes under Title VIII. Those occupations excluded were as follows: agricultural labor; domestic service in a private home; casual labor not in the course of an employer's trade or business; maritime services within the territorial waters of the United States; employment in federal, state, or local governments; employment by nonprofit organizations in the field of education, religion, charities, science, or literature; and self-employment in farm and nonfarm occupations. No worker over the age of 65 was included. Employers were to pay their own tax and also to advance taxes levied upon their employees. The employee taxes thus advanced were "repaid" by withholding the sum from the employees' wages. Taxes under Title VIII were collected by the Bureau of Internal Revenue under the direction of the Secretary of the Treasury.[5]

Title II of the act provided that people in the occupations which were taxed under Title VIII, upon reaching the age of 65, would become eligible for monthly annuities as long as they lived, subject to two qualifications. These qualifications were that the person making a claim for annuities must have worked under covered employment during each of the last five years and must have received at least $2,000 in wages during that period. This provision automatically excluded all persons who had reached their sixtieth birthday before January 1, 1937. It also excluded those irregularly employed in occupations taxed under Title VIII if their employment was so irregular that they would not accumulate as much as $2,000 within any five-year period from 1937 to the time they reached the age of 65.[6]

[5] Douglas, *Social Security*, pp. 157–60.
[6] *Ibid.*, p. 160.

The formula used to determine monthly benefits for those who qualified was as follows. On the first $3,000 of total taxable income earned, the monthly benefit rate was 0.5 per cent. If an employee earned only $3,000 in taxable income during the five-year period before retirement, his monthly annuity was to be $15. If a person was taxed on as much as $45,000 in covered employment prior to retirement, his monthly annuity would be calculated on the basis of 0.5 per cent on the first $3,000 and $\frac{1}{12}$ of 1 per cent on the remaining $42,000.

The minimum annuity was to be based on a total earning of $2,000 and was to be $10 per month. The maximum annuity was to be $85 which would be almost the maximum amount obtainable even if there were no legal maximum. That is, an $85 annuity could be earned only by earning $3,000 per year for forty-three years. So, in effect, the potential minimum as well as the potential maximum annuity were both "built in" the bill in such a way that the minimum must be reached before any annuity was paid and to all practical purposes the maximum could not be exceeded. Regardless of the amount of money earned, the number of years of covered employment, or the size of the annuity, the annuities were to go only to the aged person who qualified and to no one else.[7]

It can be deduced from the above discussion that the formula of benefits was weighted to favor employees with low incomes and/or only a few years of earnings in covered occupations. For, as the total amount earned increased, the percentages used to calculate the annuity decreased. Provision was also made for those who did not qualify for annuity payments. Beginning in 1937 payroll taxes were levied on all employees in the occupations stated in Title VIII, regardless of whether they had reached the age of 60 prior to 1937, on those who might die before reaching retirement age, and on those who would not meet the $2,000 minimum requirements of the law. The law provided that a lump

[7] *Ibid.*, pp. 160–63.

sum of 3.5 per cent of the earnings be paid to those who would be over 60 when the act went into effect. The lump sum was to be paid to those whose incomes were less than $2,000 in five years, and to those who had not worked in covered occupations for five years prior to retirement. In addition, if an employee died before retirement his estate would be paid a lump sum of approximately the amount which he had contributed during the course of his lifetime under the provisions of Title VIII. This final feature was to furnish some protection for survivors and compensate them for the loss of the breadwinner.[8]

As it was envisioned at that time, there would be no annuities paid from 1937 to 1941 inclusive; however, the lump-sum payments referred to above would be paid. It was believed that the five-year period was necessary in order to build up enough monetary reserve to meet annuity payments when they started in 1942. It was calculated that contributions from younger workers would be sufficient to meet the annuity payments to older workers and, in addition, during the years up to 1980 a reserve fund of nearly $47 billion would be built up. It was calculated that from 1980 onward the amount of money coming into the fund and the amount being paid out would be equal. The law provided that the reserves were to be invested only in government bonds or obligations on which a 3 per cent rate of interest was to be paid.

The amendments of 1939

In the interval between passage of the original act in 1935 and the session of Congress in 1939 several circumstances arose which shed a new light on the original Social Security Act. Basically there were three reasons why the payment of monthly annuities was not to have been started before the first of 1942. One of these reasons was that time was needed to set up the bookkeeping involved in collecting, recording, and processing the expected 40 million individual

[8] *Ibid.*, p. 165.

accounts. Although the Social Security Board seemed to have been slow in registering the workers who were to come under Titles II and VIII, improved techniques were designed which facilitated this process. Use of business machines made bookkeeping relatively easy. Second, due to a series of circumstances the monetary reserves under Title VIII far exceeded the estimates which had been made. Finally, there was some confusion as to the meaning of certain parts of the law, for instance, whether money earned in any gainful employment automatically meant the withholding of monthly annuities from those who were otherwise eligible for them.

In the amendments of 1939 the social security system was expanded to include monthly survivor's benefits to widows and children and to dependent parents if there was no widow or child, in addition to the original provisions for benefits to retired workers or the lump-sum payment on the death of the employed person. Second, the benefits to be paid in the early years of the program were to be more liberal than originally contemplated. Benefit payments were to begin in 1940 instead of in 1942. Finally, both employer and employee contributions were frozen at 1 per cent of payroll instead of being increased to 1.5 per cent as originally planned.[9]

The benefit formula was to be changed to meet some of the problems which arose as a result of the shift in emphasis from individual benefits to the system of survivor benefits. The new formula was devised with the idea that there should be a closer relation between monthy wage level and retirement or survivor's benefits. As a consequence Congress forsook the formula based on total wage and substituted an average wage formula. At the same time it tried to retain the feature of the original bill which weighted the formula in favor of those who had a low income or those who had worked only a few years under the bill. Another feature was

[9] Wilham Haber and Wilbur J. Cohen, *Readings in Social Security* (Englewood Cliffs, N.J.: Prentice-Hall, Inc., 1948), p. 103.

added which was calculated to recognize the length of covered employment. The new formula was as follows:

Average monthly wage	Monthly benefits
$ 25	$10 plus 10 cents per year of coverage
50	20 plus 20 cents per year of coverage
100	25 plus 25 cents per year of coverage
250	40 plus 40 cents per year of coverage

Widow's benefits were to be three-fourths of the wage earner's; wife's, child's, and parent's, one-half of the wage earner's. In order to be eligible for benefits, a wife would have to be 65 years of age. A widow would receive benefits when she attained the age of 65, and orphans would receive benefits until they reached the age of 18 or married. If a widow under the age of 65 was left with minor children she would receive survivor's benefits until they reached the age of 18 or married. Between that time and the time she reached the age of 65, she would receive no benefits. Parents who had been dependent upon the wage earner for their support were to be given benefits if the deceased worker had no dependent wife or children. The new law introduced the following terms: "primary benefits," or the benefits to be received by the retired wage earner; "wife's benefits," "widow's benefits," "widow's current benefits" (for widows under 65 with dependent children), and "parent's benefits."

In order to meet the additional requirements of providing benefits for survivors and for those who would apply for benefits in 1940, the amendments provided that a wage earner with less than ten years of coverage prior to death or retirement must have spent at least one-half of his working lifetime since 1936 in covered employment. As a unit of measure the "calendar quarter" was adopted. A calendar quarter was considered a quarter of coverage if the employee received in that quarter $50 or more of wages in covered employment. As many as forty quarters of coverage, or half as many quarters of coverage as there were quarters elapsing between 1936 and either death or retirement, would give the worker an insured status. However, if a person had earned as much as $50 in wages in each of six of the last twelve quarters before he died, his widow and orphans would be eligible for survivors' benefits.[10] With some modifications these eligibility requirements have been retained in subsequent amendments.

There were three other facets of the problem which were not contended with at the time of the 1939 amendments and which continued as persistent problems during the years following. The problem of limited coverage made it possible for workers to shift into and out of covered employment. The number of persons involved in this shift was much larger than anyone had foreseen. Such shifts in employment made it possible for workers to contribute considerable sums to the retirement fund and yet not be eligible for retirement benefits. Other employees engaged in part-time covered employment might contribute only a minimum sum and be eligible for benefits. Shifting into and out of employment which was covered was detrimental to the welfare of the individual and to the program as well. Second, the question of restricting benefits to retired people who earned less than $15 per month in covered employment brought to the attention of the Social Security Board the fact that this work clause was keeping many people employed beyond retirement age even though they were otherwise eligible for benefits. Finally, in spite of the fact that the benefit formula was arranged to provide a maximum primary benefit of $85 per month, it was realized that it would take a long work life with earnings of $3,000 per year to attain this maximum. In other words, there was a rather wide gap during the early years of the program between the allowable maximum and the maximum which could be reasonably attained.

During the years in which the United States was engaged in the Second World War, there were few changes made in this phase of the Social Security Act. One area where lack of change was especially noticeable was under Title VIII. Although the tax formula originally was supposed to have

[10] *Ibid.*, pp. 241–43.

increased 0.5 per cent of payroll each three years, congressional action postponed this increase. At least in part, failure to increase payroll deductions was due to the financial soundness of the program. This healthy financial condition can be attributed largely to the fact that the total number of contributors and their individual contributions (on the average) increased during this period because of improved employment opportunities and higher pay. Also, due to these same conditions, a large number of persons eligible for retirement benefits failed to drop out of employment. Consequently, they continued to contribute to the fund rather than draw from it.

In both 1943 and 1946 there were a few relatively minor changes made in Title II of the act. In 1943 coverage was extended to seamen employed by or through the War Shipping Administration and in 1946 protection was extended to survivors of veterans for a limited period.

Limited coverage, 1936 to 1950

When the Social Security Act of 1935 was framed, this country had had no prior experience in the administration of old-age insurance. The history of similar laws in foreign lands was explored and many valuable ideas were incorporated into the American version. However, there is a difference between reading about how one law has worked in one place and actually putting a similar law into operation under another set of circumstances. It has been indicated above that between 1935 and 1937 there appeared to be some undue delay in setting up a workable program of keeping individual accounts under the program. The mechanics of handling millions of individual accounts was difficult but the problems connected with it soon were overcome. It was felt by some of those most directly concerned with the program that it would be unwise to include certain categories of employees until such a time as administrative details could be worked out. This led to the exclusion of three large categories of employees: the farm and nonfarm self-employed, agricultural workers, and domestic workers. One of the primary difficulties involved was in the area of collecting taxes for these people. Employers of domestic workers as an ordinary practice hire only a few people. The number of employers whose records would be handled would be increased beyond the ability of the Social Security Board to handle the accounts. Added to the large number of individual employers of domestic and agricultural workers would have been the large number of self-employed people. It was also believed that most of the employers of domestic servants and agricultural workers had little if any experience in bookkeeping.

Another difficulty in extending coverage to these categories was since the benefit formula was weighted in favor of the low-income worker, a large number of people in these categories might weaken and actually threaten the financial status of the entire system. Insofar as the self-employed farmers and nonfarmers were concerned, the problem of the numbers involved was one justification for their exclusion. Another argument was that both farmers and small independent businessmen were the embodiment of the American tradition of individualism and they might resent a compulsory insurance plan being forced upon them. Violent opposition to the act on the part of any large group of people might be harmful to the program.

In the case of both the agricultural and domestic workers and the self-employed farmers and businessmen, proponents of exclusion used two diametrically opposed arguments to justify exclusion. One of these arguments was that neither these people nor their employers (in the case of agricultural workers and domestics) could afford to pay the social security tax out of their low incomes. Any tax imposed on them would lower their take-home pay below the point of subsistence. Farmers and small businessmen would have to close down operations if they were saddled with additional taxes. At the same time, others were arguing that these categories did not need the protection of a social security program. The general idea was that farming had a built-in security system of its own as did self-employment. Domestic servants were secure financially since much of their income was in the form of food, clothing, and sometimes shelter furnished over and above monetary consideration. The personal relationship established between employer and employee was supposed to insure that the employer would look after the financial problems of the retired employee.

Three other large categories of employees were also excluded from coverage by the original act. First were the railroad employees who were covered by the provisions of the Railroad Retirement Act. Another group was state and local government employees. The primary reason given for the exclusion of the latter group was that the federal government did not have the constitutional right to tax individual states. In addition, various categories of employees within the state and local governmental divisions had their own retirement systems which were assumed to be superior to the OASI system. The third large category of employees excluded from coverage consisted of employees of nonprofit institutions and religious bodies. Representatives of the various organizations operating on a nonprofit basis believed that by joining the OASI program their organizations would somehow forfeit the tax-free status which they enjoyed. Religious bodies were afraid the traditional separation of church and state would be jeopardized. Further, many of the churches already had adequate retirement systems for the personnel engaged directly in religious activities. This argument, it may be noted, would not apply to janitors, secretaries, and other employees.

An analysis of specific criticisms

It should not be assumed that everyone who came under the provisions of the program was well-pleased with it. On the contrary, numerous categories of employers objected to the act for various reasons. Probably the basic reason for most of the objections was that the ideology of such a program was contrary to the values of the opponents of the plan. These may be classed as the categorical objectors or opponents of the system. Another of the objections seemed to come from the idea it was not the function of the federal government to inject itself into this area of activity. Many people expressed the idea that private enterprise was more capable of performing the task of assuring economic security than was the federal government. It could be done both more efficiently and at less cost. These opponents saw the program as an "invasion of their rights" by the federal government—a step away from traditional freedom of action toward some undesirable foreign "ism."

Some of the friends and foes criticized the Social Security Act on more specific grounds. For the sake of contrast it may be said these opponents disliked the program because of specific aspects and believed the only remedy was to scrap the plan. The proponents wanted to correct the flaws while keeping the plan. The difference in approach boiled down to whether the baby should be thrown out with the bath, or whether the water should be changed. The criticisms revolved around five problems: (1) limited coverage, (2) inadequacy of benefits, (3) earning restrictions placed on retired workers, (4) the "new start" provision, and (5) the reserve as opposed to the pay-as-you-go fund. These problems can now be examined in detail.

(1) Limited coverage: As was noted above, two reasons given for initial limited coverage were that there would be too great a problem involved in keeping records were coverage broadened, and that there was either positive opposition or indifference to coverage on the part of some of those who were excluded. It soon became apparent that there were problems involved in limited coverage itself. Apparently no one closely concerned with this phase of the act had more than a slight idea as to the amount of labor mobility in this country. It was generally assumed that there would be some movement into and out of covered employment but the actual extent of such mobility was greatly underestimated. For instance in January, 1940, there were 44.9 million people with wage credits, yet only 35.4 million of them had earned wage credits the previous year. In January, 1948, of the 76.9 million people with wage credits only

49.2 million had earned credits in 1947. Thus, in the two years cited, there were 9.5 and 27.7 million people with wage credits who had not added to those credits by working in covered employment during the preceding year.[11] The effect of this movement from covered status meant a large number of workers were contributing to a retirement system from which they might never benefit. Those who were covered for a while, then moved to noncovered employment for a period of time and later became covered again might lose a great deal in the way of benefits. This would be true as long as benefits were calculated on the basis of average monthly earnings and the months of noncovered employment were calculated in the total number of months worked.

Opponents of limited coverage argued that so long as certain jobs were covered and others were not, free labor mobility would be hindered. As has been indicated, this was probably not true to any appreciable extent during the early years of the program. Likewise, it was believed better workers would enter covered employment and leave the less efficient workers to fill the jobs not covered. This argument can hardly be proved or disproved. The truth rather might be that certain types of noncovered employment, because of unpleasant working conditions and low pay, habitually employ marginal workers. Some others of the noncovered occupations seem to offer more in the way of immediate gains than some types of employment which are covered. Employees or workers might believe they would be better off in the long run in the noncovered areas.

Another objection to limited coverage was that by omitting agricultural workers, farmers, and domestic workers, the more industrialized states would have a larger proportion of their working population protected than would rural states. In the final analysis this meant that those states less able to support an adequate old-age assistance program (i.e., the poorer rural states) would have fewer of their aged eventually receiving OASI benefits and that conversely, a

[11] Eveline M. Burns, *The American Social Security System* (Boston: Houghton Mifflin Co., 1949), pp. 70–71.

larger proportion of their aged population would be eligible for old-age assistance. People in the rural states entering retirement would have had less opportunity to save for their own retirement than those who were under the OASI program in the industrial states.

As the program has been in successful operation for nearly two decades and the benefits for both workers and survivors have increased, there has been an increased amount of active interest on the part of those who are not covered. Instead of active opposition or unconcern, the feeling of the excluded individuals and categories has changed to one of disappointment that they are not covered. As a result of an articulation of their feeling, plus the ability of the Social Security Administration to include them, more people have now been brought under the provisions of the act.

At present there are still several categories of wage earners who are not covered by the OASI program. First are those who are engaged in employment in which they do not earn enough to qualify for coverage, such as some agricultural and domestic workers. If their employment were better paid or more regular they would qualify. Second is a rather large group of workers, primarily railroad employees, civil servants, and local and state employees whose own retirement system either dovetails with the OASI program or whose employers (the individual states) have not cleared the legal barriers for participation in the program. Third are those whose participation is on a voluntary basis, such as employees of nonprofit organizations who have elected not to join the program for some reason. Many of these employees are not included because the required percentage did not vote for coverage. Fourth, there are those who, by their own request, have not been included, even on the permissive level. This category includes medical doctors, or religious workers who have taken a vow of poverty. Finally, parents employed by their children, and spouses or children under the age of 21 employed by their parents are not covered.

Under the present law it seems safe to say that the day when all wage earners in this country will be covered seems a long way off. Probably the last categories to be included will be those with minimum incomes and those who are convinced that the social security program is not in their interest and that they will be better off in other ways, if not financially, by remaining outside the scope of the program.

(2) Inadequacy of benefits: It is difficult to determine beyond a certain point whether any retirement program is adequate or not. One way is to fix retirement income as a certain percentage of average income during a period of the work life of the employee. In a previous chapter it was indicated that OASI payments, on the average, seem to be so low as to be inadequate in the light of estimated budget needs. Whether a retired worker and his wife or survivors can live on OASI benefits depends upon a host of variable factors such as cost of living, additional income, and standard of living.

Time has done a great deal to increase the average monthly benefits which are received by both retired persons and survivors. In addition, the change in method of determining benefits to calculating the formula on average instead of total wages generally increased the amount of benefit payments. The 1954 amendments allow a "drop-out"—some years of lower or no earnings are dropped when figuring average earnings upon which to calculate benefits. This technique is to some extent a duplication of some private pension plans which allows the selection of the years of highest pay on which to figure pension payments. In addition to more selectivity in choosing the base, the amount of the monthly benefit can be increased by changing the formula. This has been done by increasing the percentage and amount on which the percentage is figured in the first step of the formula. For instance, an increase in benefit would result if the formula called for 50 per cent of the first $100 of the average monthly wage rather than 40 per cent of the first $50 of average monthly wage. The benefit would be increased again by the second step being figured on the basis of 20 per cent rather than 10 per cent of the remaining average monthly wage.

(3) Retirement clause: There has been criticism of the program because of the limit placed on the amount of money a retired worker can earn while he draws retirement benefits, or on secondary benefits drawn by survivors. This was a particularly critical situation during the early years of the program. It has been noted that benefits during the early years were generally low due to the fact that workers had had few years in which to accumulate wage credits. At the same time, a retired person lost his benefits if he earned more than $15 in covered work in any month. The result of this ruling was two-edged. If a person had fairly adequate benefits and was able to earn more than the maximum allowable amount, he would be discouraged from seeking regular employment. On the other hand, if his benefits were low and his earning opportunities good, he would be discouraged from retiring. Initially the low amount of $15 was set to discourage retiring workers from re-entering employment. Later the Social Security Administration felt that the financial soundness of the program would be threatened if there was no limit on earnings of those who were receiving benefits. During the history of the program, this retirement clause has been changed considerably.

(4) "New starts": A technical question arises whenever coverage is extended to new categories not previously included, such as the large numbers who were brought under the provisions of the bill by both the 1950 and 1954 amendments. The problem involved is one of making it possible for older individuals in the newly covered groups to become eligible for benefit payments which bear some relation to their preretirement incomes. Some members of these newly covered groups contribute to the program for only a short time between entrance into the program and either death or retirement. It is possible for them to become currently insured after having worked for as short a period as six quarters. If the amount they earn during this period is used in

computing average monthly wages since 1937, their benefits would be very low. The "new start" provision, however, allows them to calculate average monthly income on the basis of the amount of time they were covered; that is, from the time of coverage until either death or retirement.

With "new start" provision it is possible for some people to receive larger benefits after only six quarters of coverage than others receive who have been contributing to the program, perhaps irregularly, since its inception. For the old-time contributor, the "new start" provision seems inequitable to say the least. It should be borne in mind, however, that the social security law was designed to replace wages lost due to death or retirement and not to establish a strict relationship between contributions and benefits.

At the present time it would be both impractical and virtually impossible to collect from newly covered employees or their employers taxes for the wages received and paid between the inception of the program and the date of coverage. The newly covered people, while apparently benefiting disproportionately from later inclusion by paying a smaller amount of taxes and receiving higher benefits, have not had the protection of the program which has been enjoyed by those first included. Such apparent inequalities will continue so long as new groups are brought in. Only when the only new persons being brought into the plan are young workers, will everyone be treated equitably.[12] The provisions in the 1954 amendments for "drop-out" of four (or five) years of low earnings or no earnings since 1936 help to eliminate some of the inequalities involved between the new start and old start individuals. (The fifth criticism of old-age insurance, the attack on the soundness of its use of reserve funds financing rather than pay-as-you-go funding, has been so persistent and is of such importance as to warrant a more complete treatment in the closing section of this chapter; see pp. 216 and 217.)

[12] Cf. United States Congress, House of Representatives, *Analysis of the Social Security System* (Washington, D.C.: 1953), Part IV, 648–69.

Recent amendments

It can be inferred from the above discussion that many changes have been made in the Social Security Act since 1948. It is possible to say that the law as amended in 1954 now contains most of the features which have been desired by its proponents since early in the life of the program. The changes have taken place gradually until at the present time it is believed that as many as nine out of every ten workers have social security coverage. Furthermore, with changes in the benefit formula, there is reason to feel that benefits, although not as high as some private pensions, are now or later will be much more adequate than they were during the first fifteen years of the plan. Most of the changes have occurred in the two areas of extension of coverage and changing the benefit formula and the base upon which the formula is calculated. In the section which follows, a brief analysis of the changes will be made.

First, the employer and employee tax rate which was to have been increased by 0.5 per cent every three years was successively frozen from 1939 to the beginning of 1951. In 1951 the rate was increased to 1.5 per cent for each employer and employee. Beginning in 1954 the rate was increased another 0.5 per cent. The self-employed tax rate was set, in the 1950 amendments, at one and one-half times the employee rate.

Second, the amount of wages on which taxes were levied was increased from $3,000 per year to $3,600 in the 1950 amendments and in the 1954 amendments to $4,200. If an employee earns as much as $50 per quarter in covered work, that quarter counts as a quarter of coverage. A self-employed person must earn as much as $400 per year to receive four quarters of coverage. By increasing both the tax and the base on which taxes are levied, the amount of money collected is increased appreciably. During the depression years only a relatively small proportion of those covered by OASI were earning as much as $3,000 annually. During the more prosperous war years and the years following the war, the proportion of wage earners being taxed on the maximum of $3,000 and later on $3,600 was increased.

Third, due to a change in the philosophy of the OASI program, the amount a person could earn in covered employment without having his monthly benefits suspended or reduced was increased from $15 to $50 in 1950. In 1952 this amount was increased to $75 per month. This limit was waived for all those who had reached their seventy-fifth birthday. The 1954 amendments further increased the amount which could be earned while continuing to receive benefits, but put it on an annual basis rather than a monthly basis. The annual earning permitted was increased to $1,200. This limit is more realistic in that it takes into consideration yearly income rather than monthly income. If a beneficiary (either retired worker, dependent or survivor) earns more than $1,200 per year he will lose one month of benefit payment for each $80 above $1,200 which he earns. Any beneficiary who has reached his seventy-second birthday has no limit imposed on the amount he can earn without having benefit payments suspended or withheld.

The 1954 amendments provide that the limit on earnings of those under 72 years of age applies to earnings from any source, whether or not the work is covered by the social security law. This does not, however, include "unearned" income from investments, pensions, property, and so forth.[13] This new limit, being extended to all earnings, might work a hardship on those who have retired from covered employment and have been supplementing their retirement benefits by working in employment which is not covered.

Even though this new provision may be difficult to enforce, it is probably more equitable in the long run than the former ruling that only covered earnings were considered. In the first place, many retired workers or their survivors are unable to obtain employment in noncovered work. Thus the old law put a premium on the ability to

[13] United States Department of Health, Education, and Welfare, *Your Social Security* (Washington, D.C.: 1954), pp. 20–21.

find employment in noncovered work and imposed a penalty on those who were employed in covered work. In the second place, before certain types of work such as self-employment and agricultural and domestic work were included under the provision of the law, a person might retire from his primary job and enter one of the noncovered areas. As the area of coverage expanded he would find he could no longer draw benefits and have no limit imposed on his earnings. Thus he would be forced either to reduce his earnings or give up some of his benefits. Under the 1954 law no distinction is made between wages earned in covered and noncovered work. If there is now any inequity, it is shared by all who are eligible for retirement benefits who need to and can supplement their benefits by doing additional work. That hardships occur because of the limit on earnings cannot be doubted.[14] However, the question should also be viewed in the light of the number of people whose rights were enhanced by the changes which have been made in the system since it was brought into being.

Fourth, it has been indicated above that the benefit formula has been changed on several occasions. The emphasis has always been in favor of the person with few years of coverage and those with low earnings. Until 1950 some consideration was given to the length of time a person had contributed to the program. This was done by adding to the basic amount of benefit 1 per cent of the basic amount for each year in which earnings were $200 or more. After 1950 this yearly increment was discontinued in calculating benefits. Until the 1950 amendments the benefits were figured by taking 40 per cent of the first $50 of average monthly wage since 1936. To this sum was added 10 per cent of the next $200 of average monthly wage. This total sum was increased by 1 per cent for each year in which the worker had earned more than $200 in covered employment. Under this formula the monthly benefits could not fall below $10 nor could they exceed the lowest of the following three:

[14] United States Congress, House of Representatives, *Analysis of the Social Security System* (Washington, D.C.: 1953), Part VI, 1000–7.

$85, twice the primary benefit, or 80 per cent of the insured worker's previous monthly wage. In figuring benefits in 1955 and subsequent years, only the first $3,000 of wages prior to 1951 and $3,600 between 1951 and 1954 can be used although the 1954 formula can be applied. The 1954 amendments also allow a "drop-out" of years of low or no earnings. Both the 1950 and 1954 amendments provide for a lump-sum death payment up to as much as three times the insured person's old age insurance amount, but not more than $225.[15]

By way of illustration, using the formulas for 1939, 1950, and 1954, and holding the number of years worked at ten (forty quarters of coverage), and the average monthly earnings constant at $200, it can be seen that the amount of primary benefit has been increased by merely changing the benefit formula.

Under the 1939 law

40 per cent of the first $50	$20.00
10 per cent of the next $150	15.00
	35.00
Plus 1 per cent increment for 10 years	3.50
Total primary benefit	$38.50

Under the 1950 law

55 per cent of the first $100	$55.00
15 per cent of the next $100	15.00
Total primary benefit	$70.00

Under the 1954 law

55 per cent of the first $110	$60.50
20 per cent of the next $90	18.00
Total primary benefit	$78.50

Based on the maximum earnings under each of the three formulas given above and holding the number of years worked at ten, the maximum primary benefits allowed under each would be $44.00, $85.00, and $108.50. These two sets of application of the three formulas illustrate how monthly benefits can be increased both by changing the formula and

[15] Cf. *Your Social Security*, pp. 12–16.

the average monthly earnings. Of course, if the 1939 formula had remained in force and the average monthly earnings had increased, there would have been an increase in benefits also. However, this increase would not have been as great as has occurred by using the new formulas.

The increased amount of average monthly benefits at the end of selected years is given in Table 18. It will be

TABLE 18

Average Monthly Benefits Under Old-Age and Survivors Insurance at End of Specified Years

Year	Average Benefit	Year	Average Benefit
1940	$22.60	1952	$49.25
1945	24.19	1953	51.10
1949	26.00	1954	59.14
1950	43.86	1955	61.90

SOURCE: *Annual Statistical Bulletin, Social Security Bulletin* (1955), p. 3.

noticed that the average benefits have increased nearly three times during this period. The most spectacular increases in average payments came during 1950, 1952, and 1954. These increases were primarily due to formula changes in the amendments which became operative in those years. It is well to remember that extremes are hidden by averages. There is a difference in average state payments due to differences in amounts of wages paid and due to the fact that individuals in the primarily agricultural states have had a shorter history of protection under this program than people in the more industrialized states have had. At the close of 1955 when the average monthly benefit for the nation was $61.90 the average payment in Connecticut was $68.69 and in Mississippi $49.27, almost $20 less.[16] In addition to a difference in average payments, the agricultural states generally have fewer insurance recipients than the industrial states have. In June, 1956, there were 454 beneficiaries per

[16] *Annual Statistical Bulletin, Social Security Bulletin* (Washington, D.C.: 1955), p. 40.

1,000 population age 65 and over for the country as a whole. In Rhode Island the number was 616 and in North Dakota only 232 per 1,000 aged population.[17]

Monthly benefits being paid at the end of 1956 totaled $482,600,000. This sum was received by 7,400,000 men age 65 and over and women age 62 and over. During the year 1956 the total amount of monthly and lump-sum benefits paid out by this program amounted to $5,715,000,000.[18]

During this period of expanding benefit payments to retired workers, benefits for eligible wives, widows or widowers, dependent children, and dependent parents have increased also. The formula for both eligible wife and survivor's benefits is based on a fraction of the primary benefit as follows:

Payment to	Fraction of primary amount
Wife	one-half
Child (when worker has retired)	one-half
Dependent husband	one-half
Widow (either 65 or with dependant children)	three-fourths
Child (after death of earner)	one-half (an additional one-fourth of primary benefit is divided equally among the children)
Dependent widower	three-fourths
Dependent parent	three-fourths

Fifth and last, as has been indicated above, amendments have greatly extended the area of coverage since 1936. Changes, both additions and deletions, were relatively slight prior to 1950. In 1951 (the 1950 amendments went into operation January 1, 1951) approximately 10 million additional persons were brought under the operation of the act. The 1954 (beginning January 1, 1955) amendments made it easier for some of the persons included in 1951 to acquire a covered status. The 1954 amendments further broadened the areas of coverage to include approximately nine out of

[17] "Current Operating Statistics," *Social Security Bulletin*, XIX (October, 1956), 29.
[18] "Social Security in Review: 1956 in Review," *Social Security Bulletin*, XX (March, 1957), 2.

every ten wage earners. For the sake of brevity the amendments of 1954 will be dealt with here, giving, where appropriate, the conditions which existed as a result of the 1950 law.[19]

Most people self-employed in a trade or business were brought under the law beginning in 1951. The 1954 amendments also included self-employed architects, professional engineers, accountants, and funeral directors. As is the case with other self-employed people, these are included if they have annual net earnings of $400 or more. Self-employed farmers must have a net income of $400 or more in a year.

Farm workers had been included under the 1950 amendments to the act. They were required to have one qualifying quarter of work in which they worked for one employer as many as sixty days and earned cash wages of $50 or more. The farm worker was then covered in the following quarter and any succeeding quarter as long as he worked for the same employer as many as sixty days and earned as much as $50. If he changed employers he had to work for one qualifying quarter as at first. Under the 1954 amendments if a farm worker earns wages of $100 or more in a calendar year from one employer, his earnings are covered. The 1954 amendments also were extended to cover workers in cotton gins who had been excluded by the 1939 redefinition of agricultural workers.

Domestic workers fall into somewhat the same category as far as the social security law is concerned. Household workers were excluded until the 1950 amendments. Between 1951 and 1955 if a household worker was employed by one employer for twenty-four days or more in a calendar quarter and earned a cash wage of $50 or more, he was covered. Since 1954 a domestic worker's wage from any employer, for work in a private household, is covered by the law if the amount earned is $50 or more in cash during a calendar quarter. Domestic work done on a farm which is operated for profit is considered farm work and the requirement for coverage is the same as for other farm workers.

[19] Adapted from *Your Social Security*, pp. 34–40.

The 1954 amendments also covered people who do industrial work at home. They are covered for the first time by the new law, regardless of whether their work is subject to licensing under state law.

The 1950 law provided that state and local government employees would be covered by OASI if the state and federal government entered into a voluntary agreement and further that no person employed in a position already covered by a state or local retirement system should be included. The 1954 law provides that state and local government employees in positions now covered by a local system can be covered by OASI if a majority of such employees vote for it. Policemen and firemen who are under a state or local system are specifically excluded. It is the policy of Congress not to impair the protection of members and beneficiaries under the local system if they vote for OASI coverage in addition to the system already in operation.

In 1950 social security coverage was extended to certain federal government employees. Some of the positions covered were national farm loan associations, federal credit unions, and federal reserve banks, and other groups which had no system of their own. Also included were most federal employees who have either temporary or indefinite appointments and who were not under the civil service retirement system.[20] Beginning in 1955 other federal employees who were not covered by another retirement system were covered by OASI.

The 1950 amendments extended coverage to nonprofit organizations if such organizations filed a certificate of waiver of their exemption from payment of social security taxes with the Director of Internal Revenue. Further, at least two-thirds of the employees of such organizations had to indicate their desire to be included under the law. If those two conditions were met, the employees signing the certificate were brought under OASI. Those who did not sign were not covered. Future employees would be covered.

[20] Cf. Federal Security Agency, *Your Social Security* (Washington, D.C.: 1952), pp. 42 ff.

The 1954 law provided that ministers of churches, members of religious orders, or Christian Science practitioners could secure coverage if they filed with the Internal Revenue Service a certificate indicating their desire to be covered. Coverage for this category of people is on the basis of self-employment, that is, they pay self-employed taxes and the church or order with which they are affiliated is not involved. This arrangement circumvents the question of separation of church and state.

The 1954 amendments provided that the OASI rights of people who have done a certain amount of work covered by social security but who have become totally disabled for work can have their wage credits "frozen." In order to qualify for the "freeze" of records, a person must have been working for five years out of the ten years before disability, and for one and one-half years out of the three years immediately preceding disability. This provision meant that as long as the person was disabled, the time he lost would not be counted in the total number of months used to compute his average monthly earnings. Obviously this "freeze" provision would increase the amount of monthly benefits due a disabled worker upon reaching the age of retirement. For instance, if a worker has ten years of insured earnings at the age of 50 and becomes disabled permanently, his benefit payments would be calculated on the basis of his average monthly earnings for ten years instead of twenty-five years as was the case prior to the 1954 amendments. This disability "freeze" is comparable to the waiver of premium in some private insurance contracts.

It was estimated in 1955 that there were 64,200,000 employed persons in this country. Of this number 51,700,000 were covered by OASI. Of the 11,200,000 workers not covered, 5,400,000 were local, state, or federal government employees. There were 1,300,000 self-employed or wage and salary workers engaged in agricultural activities who were not covered. Approximately 900,000 domestic servants and 1,400,000 upaid family workers were not covered. The remaining 2,300,000 "others" not covered by social insurance included categories who elected not to join or who are not eligible under the present law for any one of several reasons.[21]

The amendments passed in 1956 did not appreciably extend coverage under the act. The law was modified to include some farmers and farm laborers who had not been covered before. Other groups not previously covered included self-employed lawyers, dentists, veterinarians, naturopaths, osteopaths, and optometrists. These groups are to pay self-employed taxes for taxable years ending after 1955. The 1956 amendments also provided that members of the armed forces were to be covered beginning in 1957. Military service between 1940 and the end of 1955 would generally count toward benefits if it was not counted toward certain other federal benefits. Moreover, by the 1956 amendments employed women may now elect to retire at the age of 62 with reduced benefits. Wives of retired beneficiaries may become entitled to a wife's insurance benefits in reduced amounts at the age of 62 instead of 65. Widows of workers are entitled to survivors' benefits at the age of 62 without having benefits reduced.

The most important change in the 1956 amendments has to do with disability insurance payments. The 1954 changes provided for a "freeze" if a worker became totally disabled before reaching the age of 65. The 1956 amendments provide that after June, 1957, if a covered worker 50 years of age or older becomes permanently and totally disabled he is entitled to draw disability insurance provided he has had enough work under the social security law to qualify. Persons disabled before the age of 50 may have their earnings "frozen" between the time of disability and the age of 50. The disability insurance benefits are to equal the primary retirement benefits the person would have drawn had he become disabled at 65. Dependents of persons drawing disability insurance will not receive dependents' benefits until the disabled person reaches the age of 65 and applies for retirement benefits. If the disabled person dies before

[21] *Annual Statistical Bulletin, Social Security Bulletin* (1955), p. 16.

reaching the age of 65 his survivors may become eligible for survivors' benefits.[22]

A persisting criticism

A final criticism of the old age program has not been resolved by any of the changes in the law since 1935. This has to do with the question of reserve funds as opposed to the so-called "pay-as-you-go" plan. Under the system of reserves, contributions plus 3 per cent interest have been higher than the amount of benefits being disbursed. As a consequence, more than $20 billion in reserves has been amassed to the credit of the system. It is estimated that as the number of retiring persons increases, income into the fund and disbursements will be about equal, and that the program will be self-sustaining but with a much lower reserve. The pay-as-you-go plan would equate income and disbursements now instead of at some future date (*circa* 1980) by reducing the taxes or increasing the benefit payments.

Opponents of the reserve system criticize the present policy of the federal government in borrowing the reserve funds. Incidentally, the original act specified that the funds should be invested in government bonds. As the bonds mature the government has to redeem them. Money for this purpose comes from current government income as does the money to pay interest on the bonds. This procedure, it is claimed, is the equivalent of taxpayer support of the old-age and survivors insurance program. The entire implication seems to be that the federal government should not borrow money from one government activity to finance another. However, it should be noted that the government has been borrowing money from private insurance companies for some time. In other words, private insurance companies invest their reserves in government bonds. Yet, it

[22] Adapted from United States Department of Health, Education, and Welfare, "A Brief Report on the 1956 Amendments to the Social Security Law" (Washington, D.C.: 1956), pp. 1 ff.

is seldom claimed that the government is paying private insurance benefits when it redeems the bonds held by the insurance companies. Probably the chief advantages of the reserve fund are that the social security taxes can be kept relatively low and that they do not fluctuate when benefit payments are increased. Furthermore, it seems that the once contemplated financial participation of the government in the program is a long way off.

On the other hand, the proponents of the pay-as-you-go plan contend that their plan would better reflect the actual cost of social security. Further, the government could not use social security taxes to pay other government bills. The general idea is that the social security taxes could be adjusted up or down to meet the current benefits being paid out. If there were no large trust fund, there would be less chance that groups would bring pressure on Congress to increase benefit payments without regard to the future of the program. The advantage of a pay-as-you-go plan is that when pressure groups try to increase benefits to their own advantage, it would reflect in immediate higher taxes which would be necessary to pay the higher benefits.[23]

Summary

It was noted in the preceding chapter that under old-age assistance the number of recipients and the amount of money paid to them fluctuates with a change in any one of many conditions. On the other hand, there seem to be fewer variables to consider in the OASI program. Generally both the average monthly benefits and the number of beneficiaries, primary and secondary, increase from year to year. During the high employment and high income war years when benefits were still low, there was a decrease in the number of beneficiaries. With the postwar years and the marked expansion of coverage and increase in the number of eligible people over the age of 65, the number of beneficiaries has continued to increase. Average monthly benefits

[23] *Time,* LXII (December, 1953), p. 50.

have increased due to higher income and more years of covered employment, as well as to the series of amendments which liberalized the benefit formula.

With the passing of time since its enactment, the OASI program gradually has been changed so that at present it very nearly approaches what its long-time friends hoped it would be. First, there is almost universal coverage of wage and income earners. Family workers, certain professional categories, and those who have an option on coming into the program but who have either not yet voted or have voted not to come in, and very low-income people are still excluded from the plan. There are others who belong to other retirement plans who either have joint coverage (railroad employees with less than 120 months of credit under their retirement system), or have a retirement system of their own (civil service employees and state and local employees) who are not directly covered. Second, the minimum, average, and maximum benefits all have been increased enough to make it appear that in the future, benefits will come closer to bearing some relation to wages lost upon death or retirement. Third, the restrictions on earnings have been liberalized to the extent that a retired person or survivor can supplement his income up to $1,200 per year without losing his benefit rights. Furthermore, two provisions were made in the 1954 law which have been desired for a long time—the wage credit "freeze" and the "drop-out" of periods of low or no earnings. The provision for disability insurance benefits in the 1956 amendments and the lowering of the age of women's eligibility from 65 to 62 are two other changes which have long been sought.

By and large there seem to remain three categories of opponents of the OASI program. First are those who actually have or believe they have been given a "raw deal" under the program. Second are those who are categorically opposed to any kind of federal retirement system. Third are those who dislike some aspect of the program so deeply that they would like to see the whole program scrapped and substitute a new program. It is safe to assume that so long as our form of government remains the same as it is and as more and more people either directly or indirectly benefit by the program, it not only will remain strong but will assume a place of greater importance in the economic security of the people of this country.

12

Public Retirement Systems

Among the earliest pension systems to be found in this country were those established for public employees. The beginnings of these systems were in the form of mutual benefit societies organized for the employees by themselves for their own protection. Later the employing agencies joined in helping to administer and finance such plans and finally in instigating them. The rationale behind these early plans and also the later ones has been that since the salaries of public employees are generally relatively low when compared to those of industry, pensions would act as an additional incentive to attract and hold competent workers. Further, it is felt that some categories of public employees, especially uniformed employees, become more efficient with longer service, and yet reach the peak of their abilities some years before old age sets in. Therefore, public pensions will serve to hold employees in the services, yet allow them to retire before their abilities begin to decline to such an extent that they can no longer be effective.

Because of three related circumstances, there probably has been less uniformity in pensions for public employees than has been true with any other category of employees. First, there are employees on three levels of government, local, state, and federal. Second, each category of employees in each of the three levels feels itself to be unique. Problems faced by one set of employees may not be the same as those faced by another. Even within the local governmental units, firemen, school teachers, and office workers have little in common beside the fact that they are public employees and want some provision made for security in retirement. Civilian employees, or nonuniformed persons working with the police force and nonteaching school personnel, have little in common with uniformed police or with teaching personnel. Third is the traditional individuality and decentralization of governmental functions which prevailed during the latter part of the last century and early in the present century. The consequences of these last factors led to the establishment of separate pension plans for separate groups of employees on all three governmental levels. Each category has had the idea that what was good for some other group would not serve its own purposes. In all probability, members of each separate pension plan may also have felt they would receive better treatment if they entered into a contract alone with the employing agency than if they joined another group to achieve the same ends.

It will be noted in the discussion of private or industrial plans that different types of plans seem to fit different sized units of employees. Generally the same is true for government employees. Some of the employee groups number fewer than two dozen, others run into the thousands. It has seemed obvious to some employees as well as to some employing agencies that it is impossible and impractical to attempt to invent one workable plan which would satisfy the pension demands and desires of the heterogeneous categories of public employees. As a consequence of the above factors, one can point to a conglomeration of public pension plans in this country which would be difficult to duplicate.

Local and state pension systems

The three major categories of local employees for whom pension plans have been devised are teachers, policemen, and fire fighters. Most of the teachers' retirement systems began as local systems under the jurisdiction of the city employing agency. In the interval since the early days of mutual benefit societies teachers' retirement programs have undergone many changes. Some of the systems are supported solely by the municipality or state, others by joint contribution from teachers and employing agency. Both state and local programs cover all but about 20 per cent of the school employees in the country. Part of the number not covered by public retirement plans are state college and university personnel. Most of the retirement systems seem to be actuarially sound but sometimes state legislative bodies fail to have a continuing program of appropriation for them. In some instances the state or employing agency appropriates its share of the money only as it is needed to pay pensions to those already retired. This procedure means the employing agency may be faced with a large financial burden in later years when the number of persons in retirement increases. As is the case with other employees of local and state governments, eligibility for teachers' retirement is based on years of service rather than on age. Of the teachers already in retirement over one-half receive less than $100 per month in retirement benefits.

Both policemen and fire fighters traditionally have been favored groups under the pension system. There are several reasons given why police and fire fighters need a sound pension system which should be more attractive than other pension systems.[1] Probably the most important of these reasons is that it requires several years for policemen to reach the peak of their efficiency. If other pension systems were equal in value to that of the police system, there would not be the necessary incentive of a better retirement system to hold younger men in the police forces. Furthermore, adequate pension plans are necessary so that policemen will be encouraged to retire before their efficiency has been reduced appreciably by old age. In addition, adequate survivor provisions are virtually an all important adjunct in that policemen will pursue their duty, even to the point of endangering their lives, if they know their families will be well cared for in the event of an untimely death in line of duty.

Each of the above points is used as an argument against coverage of police either by a nationwide retirement plan

---

[1] Jack Dudek, "Pensions for the Uniformed Personnel in Public Employment," in *Report of 47th Annual Conference* (Chicago: Committee on Public Employment Retirement Administration of the Municipal Finance Officers of the United States and Canada, 1953), pp. 70–72.

such as social security or by a broad local plan which covers other local employees. Uniformity of retirement benefits, it is argued, would not offer an incentive for young policemen to remain in this occupation. Most policemen and fire fighters are hired under the local retirement rules. They think the local authorities are more concerned with changing conditions and so would be more capable of redefining the rules and regulations governing the retirement benefits of policemen.

As in the case of the policemen, representatives of the fire fighters voice opposition to any plan of integrating their pension systems with any other system, especially on the national level of social security. This is done on the grounds of special needs of the fire fighters for adequate protection. It is stated that the Social Security Act does not provide protection to fire fighters equal to the protection enjoyed under existing local plans. Uniformed personnel feel that their systems offer advantages which they would not be able to obtain under other systems. However, many of these systems are unsound actuarially, operating on a pay-as-you-go basis. Frequently pensions are paid from current appropriations and so are subject to the economic and political pressures of local government bodies.

There are several hundred state and local retirement systems, no two of which are alike. Within recent years there has been a trend toward consolidation of all systems within the state under one state system. At present there are those states with only one system which covers all employees; states with two systems, one of which covers teachers, the other all nonteaching personnel; and finally, states with a plan which covers all state employees and a system whereby all local governmental employees may be covered under state protection.

Under the impetus of growing concern and interest as well as knowledge in the field of pension plans, many changes and extensions have been made in the area of state and local governmental systems, especially in the past decade. Several factors have been at work to bring about consolidation and what is considered by some to be a strengthening of public systems. Among the factors are the larger number of people involved in government employment, the desire of the employees to have some kind of retirement system, and the feeling on the part of the employing agencies that a more efficient quantity and quality of personnel can be attracted and held if they have a retirement system. Changes and consolidations have been made because of demonstrated inadequacies of some of the systems originated earlier. It would not be amiss to state that the greatest sources of change in local and state pension plans have been the enactment of the Social Security Act and the 1950 amendments to the Social Security Act which made it permissive for those states with public employees not covered by retirement plans to enter into an agreement with the Federal Security Administration whereby the noncovered employees would be brought under the Social Security Act.

Two comprehensive nationwide studies have been conducted to determine the standing of state and local government retirement systems. Both studies were conducted jointly by the Bureau of the Census and the Social Security Board. The first of these was made in 1942, the second, ten years later. In 1952 there were approximately 4.5 million employees of state and local governments; of this number 3 million were covered by retirement systems. The 1942 census study showed that only 1.5 million such employees belonged to retirement systems. This number represented approximately half of the state and local government employees.[2] In addition to the fact that a higher proportion of such employees was covered by plans in 1952 than in 1942, some employees were covered jointly by local plans and old-age survivors insurance, others by OASI alone.

In 1942 there was a marked variation from state to state in the number of state and local employees who were protected by retirement systems. In Idaho there was no re-

[2] Dorothy McCammon, "Retirement Protection for State and Local Employees: Ten Years of Growth," *Social Security Bulletin*, XVI (May, 1953), 4 ff.

tirement system coverage, in twelve other states less than 10 per cent of the employees were covered. In about half of the states only about one-third of the employees were covered by any system. In only six states were two out of every three employees covered. This picture has changed materially since 1942. Part of the change has come about because of the extension of state-wide systems for local employees, part because of the extension of OASI to state and local employees. In 1952 in all but five states at least 66 per cent of the employment was covered by one system or another. There was no state in 1952 in which fewer than half of the state and local employees were covered.[3]

Coverage for nonschool employees is higher on the state than the local level in contrast to the conditions found among school employees. There is difficulty in organizing protection for a multiplicity of employee units with small numbers in each. Often the only thing these local nonschool employees have in common is their geographical location. In 1952 there were twenty-seven states in which nine-tenths or more of the state nonschool employees had retirement coverage. Most of this high proportion was attained through membership in state-administered systems. In this same year, in no state were as many as nine-tenths of the local nonschool employees under a retirement system.[4]

Some of the criteria for evaluating retirement systems for public employees are as follows. The retirement system should be established by a clearly and understandably worded law. There should be one retirement system in a legal jurisdiction, state or municipal. Large cities seem to be the chief offenders in this respect. There is a relationship between the size of the jurisdiction and the number of separate systems in operation. The movement toward consolidation has come a long way in recent years but it is not yet completed. The system should have enough members to make its administration practical. Some of the smaller communities have so few employees in each of the retire-

[3] Ibid., p. 7.
[4] Ibid., p. 10.

ment systems that they cannot be effective. Membership in the retirement system should be compulsory. Most systems as they start make participation compulsory for employees

TABLE 19

Estimated Number of State and Local Government Employees, by Type of Retirement Protection and Employment, October 1952 *

(In thousands)

Type of Employment	Total	Members of State and Local Systems	In Covered Positions but Not Covered	Covered OASI	No Coverage
State and Local Government Employees					
Total	4,510	3,021	304	438	746
School	1,853	1,374	123	90	265
Police and firemen	366	259	9	22	75
Others	2,291	1,387	173	325	406
State Employees					
Total	1,102	746	82	136	137
School	316	166	27	26	96
Others	786	580	55	109	41
Local Employees					
Total	3,409	2,276	222	302	609
School	1,537	1,208	96	64	169
Police and firemen	366	259	9	22	75
Others	1,505	808	117	216	365

SOURCE: Dorothy McCammon, "Retirement Protection for State and Local Employees: Ten Years of Growth," Social Security Bulletin, XVI (May, 1953), 4.

* Data are estimates and are subject to sampling errors. Figures comprising total have been rounded.

who are employed after the system goes into operation. Those who are employed at the time of enactment can usually elect whether or not they will join. Usually the current employees are given a period of time in which to decide one way or the other. In some systems the nontechnical personnel are excluded from the system which covers the technical personnel. The interested parties, employee and government, should provide funds by equal contribution. Systems should specify a voluntary retirement age beyond which the employee could be compelled to retire for medical reasons and a compulsory age when all employees must retire. A retirement system should provide adequately for the needs of the retirees. The conclusion is reached that this criterion is met only by a minority of the systems for which data are available. Where low retirement benefits are coupled with no compulsory retirement requirements, employees are virtually forced to remain at work after they have passed the peak of their efficiency.[5]

It appears that many of the local and state retirement systems fall far short of meeting these criteria as well as others which might be set up. Employees who expect to retire under most of these systems have been led to believe that their retirement income will be adequate for their retirement needs. As a matter of fact many of them will be disappointed.

Integration of local and state systems with OASI

The Social Security Act amendments of 1950 provided that local and state employees could be brought under the protection of OASI on agreements between the state and the Social Security Administration. (In 1946 the functions of the Social Security Board were transferred to the newly created Social Security Administration.) It has already been indicated that under provisions of this act there was an increased effort to provide both more adequate and broader retirement systems for state and local public employees. Table 19 above indicates some of the areas where advantage has been taken of the provisions of the 1950 amendment as well as some of the remaining inadequacies of a system which may be referred to as an imperfectly integrated state-

[5] Adapted from Arthur C. Meyers, Jr., "Criteria for Evaluating Retirement Systems for Public Employees," in *Report of 47th Annual Conference,* pp. 3–14.

federal system. The legislation of the amendment of 1950 enabling states to integrate their systems with the OASI was devised in such a manner as not to interfere with the existing state and local retirement systems. In spite of the wording of the amendment and in order to meet the qualifications of integration, some states dissolved their existing systems. States with no systems which approved integration could integrate any new system with the federal system. The state of Virginia was one state to act in this manner. They did have a system but dissolved it in order to qualify under the amendments. Other states and municipalities followed suit.

There seems to be some division on the part of local and state employees and their representatives as to the method in which the benefits of the OASI program should be extended to them or whether these benefits should be extended to them at all. Some of the employees with no local retirement coverage or those with inadequate coverage want social insurance coverage at almost any price. On the other hand, those who believe they are more adequately covered, especially teachers and the uniformed services, if they want OASI coverage at all, want it with certain qualifications. This latter group apparently wants to benefit by their present more favorable position while taking advantage of the supplementary nature of OASI.

There are several reasons why public employees are more willing to accept OASI now than they have been in the past.[6] Perhaps one of the best arguments in favor of being covered by OASI is that retirement credit can be taken from job to job by those who move between various governmental positions or to private industry. Second, a coordinated program would result in reduced cost of pensions to the taxpaying public. This is particularly applicable to employees who qualify under two or more public plans or under one public plan and under the civil service retirement program. Third,

[6] Charles R. Smith, "Is Social Security Coverage for All Public Employees Inevitable? Affirmative," in *Report of 47th Annual Conference*, pp. 73–77.

from the point of view of the pensioner and the survivors, a combination of public plan and OASI is more adequate than the provision of the public system alone. In addition to these and other points, prior to 1950 almost half of the state and local government employees were either without a retirement system or were not covered by a retirement system. Part of this latter condition was brought about by the fact that part-time workers and those hired for special types of work were not covered by the local system at all.

A great many of the arguments opposing extension of OASI to local and state government employees were arguments which had been used to oppose OASI in any form for anyone. Some local groups were opposed because they felt the local employing agency would not finance two plans or they would lose what money they had contributed to the local retirement system. There was also the question involving retirement age. Under OASI, retirement benefits begin at the age of 65 and under most local systems employees are allowed to retire after a specified number of years of employment.

By mid-1952 a majority of the states had made arrangements with the Social Security Administration whereby one or more groups of local or state employees were brought under OASI. In 1954 the Social Security Act was further amended to allow state and local employees already covered by a system to be brought under OASI if a majority of the employees voted for coverage. By their own request both policemen and fire fighters were excluded from this provision. Employees whose jobs are covered by a local system but who themselves are not eligible for local coverage may now vote to come under OASI protection. Any political subdivision within the state may be allowed to vote on coverage for its employees in public referendum as may employees of institutions of higher learning if the state government allows them to vote on the issue. State employees not covered by the federal system must depend upon the state for initial action.

The federal government as employer

The following sections of this chapter will be concerned with pension plans for employees of several categories of the federal government as well as with the railroad retirement system which operates under the federally legislated Railroad Retirement Act. The plans to be examined are similar in that they are involved either operationally or financially with the federal government or with some agency or department thereof. Aside from this similarity these systems seem to have little in common. The railroad retirement system, the civil service retirement system, and the retirement system of employees of the Tennessee Valley Authority are contributory systems to which the employee and employing agency contribute funds toward the retirement annuity. From the actuarial point of view they are financially sound. The retirement systems which come under the Department of Defense and the Veterans' Administration are all noncontributory. Payments to those eligible for pensions are made out of the current budget of the departments concerned. These systems are technically pay-as-you-go plans and under other circumstances would not be considered actuarially sound. These systems are as sound as the government is, as long as Congress appropriates enough money to finance them. In the case of the railroad retirement system the contributions of both employer and employee are held by the federal Treasury and benefits to retirees are paid by check from this department.

The civil service retirement system has been the focus of much congressional action. The size of the group involved and its conspicuous place in American society may account for its relative strength. This retirement system serves as an incentive to seek government employment, to remain in such employment until old age approaches and to retire before inefficiency sets in. The retirement plans under the Department of Defense are justified on grounds similar to those used to justify strong pension systems for fire fighters and policemen. Most embroiled in politics is the system of compensation and pensions for veterans and their survivors. Very strong pressure groups are involved in "fighting for veterans' 'rights.'" Even though it may be true that soldiers are forgotten in peacetime, veterans are not.

In 1956 a plan was approved to extend social insurance coverage to employees of the Tennessee Valley Authority, who, to that time had their own retirement system. The joint TVA-OASI plan provides for the coordination of benefits under OASI and the existing plan. This coordinated plan was made retroactive to January 1, 1956.[7] Federal employees not covered by the civil service or other federal systems are now brought under old-age and survivors insurance protection. This extension of social insurance also offers coverage to temporary and part-time employees of the government. Efforts to consolidate the civil service retirement system and OASI have met with resistance from spokesmen of the civil service system. Since their retirement income is usually more adequate than that of private industry and of OASI they fear that a joint system would work to their disadvantage. The one area where the civil service retirement system is weak when compared to OASI is in survivors' benefits. In 1953 figures indicated that there were more than 1,500,000 federal employees covered by the civil service retirement system, more than 500,000 covered by old-age insurance and approximately 20,000 covered by the other federal systems. In spite of the fact that the employing agency in these systems is the federal government the civil service retirement system suffers from lack of actuarial soundness. In both 1953 and 1954 Congress failed to appropriate the government's share of contributions to maintain the system on a sound basis. The possibility of failure to appropriate the government's share is always present, especially under an economy-minded administration.

[7] "Social Security in Review: 1956 in Review," *Social Security Bulletin,* XX (March, 1957), 2.

Civil service retirement system

Since its enactment in 1920 the Civil Service Retirement Act has been extended a number of times. At present it applies to "all officers and employees in or under the executive, judicial, and legislative branches of the United States Government." [8] Members of Congress may elect to join this retirement plan and heads of executive departments were included in 1946. Until social insurance was extended in 1953 and 1954 it was estimated that there were still some 500,000 federal workers outside of coverage of this system. Another weakness found in this system is that neither survivorship nor retirement protection is given federal employees with less than five years of service. Some of the same weaknesses are noted in this system which are found in any other system of limited coverage, for instance that neither temporary employees or part-time employees can belong.

Under the civil service retirement system if an employee remains at work for less than twenty years he may elect to withdraw his contributions rather than accept a deferred annuity. If this is done he loses all retirement protection under the act. Prewar figures indicate that as many as 20 per cent of the federal employees left their employment within the first year and an additional 10 per cent left during the second year. It was estimated that only one-third of all the civil servants remained until retirement age. Any service with the federal government which does not contribute to the retirement fund cuts down on the length of service and hence on the amount of credit which can be built up under any other system. Refunds are payable when an employee terminates employment with the civil service if he has not reached the age of 62 years and completed fifteen years of service. He may also receive a refund if he is transferred to a position under another federal retirement system even after twenty or more years of having contributed to the

[8] Helen Livingston, "Public Retirement Systems," *State Government*, XXV (February, 1952), 39–44.

civil service retirement fund. The refund which is received consists of all regular contributions as well as any service credit deposits made to the fund or any voluntary contributions, with interest.

Money is paid into the fund on an equal basis by a 6 per cent deduction from the basic salary of the members of the civil service retirement system. This is matched by appropriations made by Congress. Funds are invested by the Treasury in government securities and the interest is added to the total credited to the individual. If an employee elects to he may increase the amount of his future annuity in two ways. He may make deposits to cover prior service for which no deductions were taken from his salary or he may make additional payments or voluntary contributions.

Under this system an employee must serve at least five years before annuity benefits are paid. If an employee has served at least fifteen years he is automatically retired at the age of 70 unless he is retained by executive order. In the event that he does not meet the service requirement at the automatic retirement age he is retained in the service until he has completed fifteen years of service requirement. If he has thirty years' service at the age of 60, fifteen years at the age of 62, or thirty years' service completed between the ages of 55 and 60 he is eligible for optional retirement. The most lenient retirement provisions are those which pertain to employees whose duties are hazardous, primarily involving the investigation, apprehension, or detention of persons suspected or convicted of offenses against the federal criminal laws. Such employees may elect to retire at the age of 50 or after twenty years of service. Upon retirement an employee has a choice of three types of annuity. The choice is limited to some extent by the reason for retirement. The three types of annuity ordinarily allowed are the single life annuity which is payable as long as the person lives, the reduced annuity with benefit to the remaining spouse, or a reduced annuity with benefit to a person having an insurable interest in the annuitant. Lump-sum payments consisting of deductions taken from the employee's salary, including service credit deposits and redeposits plus interest, are made to survivors. If some annuity already has been paid to the retired person the lump sum to his survivors consists in the balance between what has been paid out to him and the amount he had deposited to his retirement, with interest.[9]

Armed forces and veterans' retirement systems

There are eight plans for retirement for different branches of federal service under the Department of Defense. For the purpose of this brief analysis these will be treated as one system. This conglomerate of pension plans is further complicated because of the hierarchal distinction between grades of enlisted personnel and ranks of officers as well as between active and reserve components of the various branches of the armed forces. These systems are noncontributory, the funds to pay current pensions being appropriated by Congress to the Department of Defense. There are no provisions made for survivors' benefits under these plans although lump-sum death payments are made to widows and orphans. Regular retirement can come after twenty years of active service and compulsory retirement after thirty years of service. Retirement pay is based on 2 per cent of basic pay of the last rank held multiplied by the number of years of service. If a person retires after twenty years of service his retirement pay would be 50 per cent of his basic pay. If he retires after thirty years' service, it would be 75 per cent of his basic pay. The minimum retirement benefit payable for disability retirement is equal to 30 per cent of basic pay or 50 per cent if and while the member is on a temporary disability retired list. It should be noted that it is possible for an enlisted man with twenty years of active service to retire at the age of 38 years with a pension amounting to 50 per cent of his basic pay. In the remaining years of his life he can build up wage credits under private pension plans, social security, or some other plan which would entitle him to pension payments upon reach-

[9] United States Civil Service Commission, *Your Retirement System*, Pamphlet 18 (Washington, D.C.: 1953), 1 ff.

ing the age of 65. In such cases the retiree would be entitled to dual payments which would be of considerable value to himself and a decided drain on the taxpaying public.

It is in the tradition of this country to provide for veterans of the armed services or for their dependents under certain stipulated circumstances. It should be noted that retirement of armed service personnel as dealt with in the preceding section might or might not conflict with or overlap with provisions made for veterans. By and large the persons who are covered by and who become eligible for retirement benefits are professional soldiers or sailors or career employees who are classified as employees of the Department of Defense. While these people in the armed services are veterans, they are distinguished from civilian nonprofessional personnel who volunteer or are drafted for service in the armed forces during times of national emergency only. These people may become eligible for veterans' compensation or pensions but would not have served sufficient time to become eligible for regular retirement under the Department of Defense retirement systems. It is possible under certain conditions for servicemen to be eligible for both retirement benefits and veterans' compensation or pensions. The law ordinarily takes care of such cases by allowing the individual involved to select the system under which he wishes to be protected.

A distinction is made between compensation and pensions for veterans and their survivors. Compensation is paid for service-connected disability to the veteran or to the widows, children, and dependent parents of deceased veterans. Pensions are paid for nonservice-connected disabilities to veterans or to their widows and orphans. As a rule the pension payments are not as high as the compensation payments, but both are based on the degree of disability. If the income of an unmarried veteran is $1,400 or more or the income of a married veteran and wife or widow and child is $2,500 or more, no pension is paid.

In 1950 there were approximately 2.5 million living veterans and dependents or dependents of deceased veterans of the eight major wars this country has been engaged in up to this time. Benefit payments amounted to nearly $2.5 billion dollars that year. It is clear from past history that the number of veterans and their dependents eligible for payments and the amount of benefits will continue to increase in the years to come. Merely because a person is a veteran, he is not automatically eligible for compensation or for pension; neither are his dependents or survivors automatically eligible. For some of those who are eligible, the amount of compensation or pension is inadequate to meet their needs. On the other hand, there is little doubt but that some who are eligible but not in financial need are drawing the full allowable amounts.

It is debatable whether restrictions on drawing compensations or pensions will be appreciably tightened or whether payments will be reduced in any great amount. Rather, it is safe to assume that as veterans' organizations become more powerful and veterans themselves become more numerous, there will be continuing pressure exerted to extend coverage to others who may not qualify under present laws and regulations. Probably also there will be pressure to increase the amount of compensation or pension granted both to veterans and to their dependents or survivors. It is clear that many of the people who qualify under these various laws are unable to support themselves and in the absence of the veterans' programs would have to be cared for under some other public program. However, it seems equally clear that some discretion should be exercised to insure that such individuals are not eligible for and benefiting under other publicly supported programs with no reference to their rights and benefits under the Veterans' Administration.

There is some indication that responsible lawmakers as well as the general public are becoming concerned with the ever-growing amount of money which is being paid to veterans and their dependents. As the veterans of World War I and later those of World War II reach retirement age, those who have worked in civilian occupations will be entitled to

OASI benefits or some other form of retirement benefit. The question arises as to the justice of paying these individuals two retirement benefits. The veteran who receives a pension for nonservice-connected disability is no different from any other disabled person. The solution to part of the problem is to broaden social security to such an extent that it would take care of all disabled persons and all retired persons or their survivors. Duplicate pension payments could be discontinued and thus no one category of citizens would draw double benefits.[10]

The railroad retirement system

It is fitting to include the railroad retirement system in this chapter on federal rather than private retirement plans. This system is not on the same level with the Social Security Act, neither is it on the same level with the civil service retirement plan. It represents, rather, a combination of the endeavors of private industry, labor, and the federal government. Its purpose is to set up a comprehensive retirement system to give adequate retirement incomes to one category of privately employed workers that represents a large segment of the American working force. At present the system is financed by joint contributions from employees and employers. The rules and regulations governing its operation are decided upon and passed by Congress, in the way of law. Congress acts upon recommendations of both employees and employers through the Railroad Retirement Board. The system has been referred to variously as the grossest example of class legislation in this country as well as the best example to be found of joint effort on the part of private industry and the national government in the realm of retirement plans.[11]

[10] Adapted from Committee on Veterans' Affairs, *Compensation or Pension to Veterans or Their Dependents* (Washington, D.C.: 1953), pp. 1 ff.; and John J. Corson and John W. McConnell, *Economic Needs of Older People* (New York: The Twentieth Century Fund, 1956), pp. 249–61.
[11] Joint Committee on Railroad Retirement Legislation, *Retirement Policies and the Railroad Retirement System* (Washington, D.C.: 1953), pp. 17 ff.

Private company pension plans in America originated in the railroad industry. The first such formal plan was started in 1874 by the Grand Trunk Railroad. Other companies soon followed the example set by this company. Four reasons are given for the early development of pension plans on the part of the operating railroad companies. First, the railroads represented the first large corporations to arise in this country. Second, due to the number of employees hired, there was a larger proportion of older workers on the payroll. Third, due to the hazardous nature of the work, private insurance companies were unwilling, or unable under the law, to underwrite many of the occupational risks of the railroads. Fourth, railroads, especially at the time in question, were much in the public eye and the firms in the industry had a feeling of public responsibility.[12]

A combination of factors in the early 1930's operated virtually to wreck the company-sponsored plans. First, and probably one of the most important reasons, was that current earnings, from which pension payments were made, nearly disappeared as the railroads felt the effects of the Depression. Second, both the amount of pension payments and the number of pensioners had been growing continuously and rapidly. These conditions came in part from the fact that life expectancy of the employees was increasing. This meant more employees lived beyond retirement age and collected more in pension payments. This trend was augmented by the system of seniority operating among railroad employees which called for laying-off of younger employees to allow older ones to remain on their jobs. The security of the pension plans was further damaged by lack of adequate actuarial soundness and improper legal safeguards in respect to both funds and the rights of the employees under the plans.

During the period of the development of company-sponsored plans, the railroad unions were attempting to set up their own pension systems. Five reasons are outlined which help to account for the interest of unions in providing their

[12] Adapted from *ibid.*, p. 24.

own systems. First, the company pension plans were considered inadequate. Annuities paid to the retirees were inadequate and disability payments were either insignificant or lacking altogether. Second, the number of the workers covered by companies with pension plans was small, often being reserved only for specified categories of employees. In addition, in the early beginnings only a small proportion of the railroads had any pension system of any kind. Third, company pensions, especially the early informal ones, were extended on the basis of charity which could be given or withheld at the will of the company. Fourth, the unions felt that company pensions could be used as a weapon to break strikes. Eligibility for pensions required continuous, uninterrupted service in order to qualify for full benefits. At that time, strikes were considered as an interruption of continuous service. Fifth, company-sponsored plans worked against the loyalty of workers to unions. During this period there was intense rivalry between unions and employers for the loyalty of the workers. Union-sponsored pension plans would do much to increase the workers' loyalty to their unions.[13]

The failure or threatened failure of both the company and union plans and the larger problem of mounting unemployment in the railroad industry during the Depression paved the way for seeking congressional action in the establishment of a financially sound contributory retirement system for the whole railroad industry. This system was to be designed to provide adequate benefits to retirees as well as pave the way for the orderly retirement of older workers, thus making room for the younger employees who had been laid off during the Depression.[14]

These, then, were the conditions which made the enactment of a retirement system seem the wise thing to do. Closely related was the general unsound financial position of the railroads in the total economy during the early years of the 1930 decade. With a curtailment of economic activity

[13] *Ibid.*, pp. 29–30.
[14] *Ibid.*, p. 49.

which followed the stock-market crash in 1929, the railroads suffered from lack of business. They had to meet heavy fixed costs and at the same time try to meet the competition of rapidly expanding modes of transportation which were competing with them. As a consequence of declining revenues, lines were abandoned and service was curtailed on the remaining lines. Due primarily to technological changes, the employment figure for railroads had decreased between 1926 and 1929. The effects of the Depression accelerated this trend in the four years following 1929. There was a loss of 600,000 job opportunities for railroad workers and many workers who were employed were faced with underemployment. The brunt of these conditions fell upon the younger employees who were "bumped" in conformity to the rules of seniority existing in the railroad unions. Consequently, the younger workers began to concern themselves with the establishment of an industry-wide retirement system which would rid the industry of its overload of older workers. Although some form of pension was already available to the older workers, such pensions were both uncertain and usually inadequate. Unsteady employment was chosen by older employees as the lesser of two evils; therefore as many of them as could continued working. Interest in the plight of the younger workers became the key to federal legislation in the area of a retirement system for railroad employees.

Public interest in a railroad retirement system traces its beginnings to public interest in legislation in the field of interstate commerce. Congress, since 1887, had intervened on behalf of railroad employees in providing regulations affecting the health, welfare, and security of the employees. It was a natural conclusion that employees should turn to Congress for help in the matter of old-age security and an adequate retirement system. The problem confronting Congress was the dual one of achieving safety in transportation by retiring superannuated workers and at the same time providing those people with adequate financial security in their old age. If it could be shown that such a system would encourage the replacement of older workers by younger ones, thus enhancing public safety, then a strong case could be made for federal intervention.

When the unions and the railroads agreed to a 10 per cent wage reduction in 1932, the agreement contained provision for a committee of representatives of the unions and the industry to study retirement insurance with possible federal legislation in view. In 1933 the first congressional hearings were held on the proposed bills. Representatives of railroad employees' pension associations and the Railway Labor Executives' Association expressed criticism of the existing private company pension plans. Representatives of the industry opposed the enactment of any federal legislation. They had specific criticisms to offer on the bills which were under discussion. There were three general criticisms. First, Congress had no constitutional power to impose compulsory legislation of this type on either the industry or its employees. Second, there was no precedent for a national pension plan of this kind—pensions should remain the concern of the individual companies and their employees. Third, the proposals were financially unsound.

In spite of these objections Congress passed the first Railroad Retirement Act in 1934. Before the act was two weeks old its constitutionality was challenged in the courts by a coalition of Class I railroads, the Pullman Company, and two express companies. When appeal was made to the Supreme Court in 1935, the decision was five to four that the act was unconstitutional.

In June, 1935, two separate bills were introduced into both the House and Senate. In both cases the first of the two bills forsook the commerce clause as justification for the act and relied upon the general welfare clause or on the right of Congress to levy taxes and spend for the general welfare. This bill provided for a railroad retirement system which was to pay benefits to retired railroad employees. The other bill was a tax bill which placed an excise tax on railroad employers and an income tax on the employees, in both cases on employee compensation not to exceed $300 per month. The tax receipts were assumed to be sufficient to meet the amounts appropriated under the retirement act.

The chief opposition to these two bills came from the carriers. They opposed the bills on the basis of their legality, cost, and lack of soundness as a pension system. The two bills, the Railroad Retirement Act and the Carriers Taxing Act of 1935, were passed by Congress and became law in August, 1935. The carriers challenged the constitutionality of the new acts of 1935 and by the middle of the following year a lower court ruled that the two acts were unconstitutional and that together they attempted to accomplish what the 1934 act had tried to do. It was obvious that the system could not continue for long without revenue to meet the cost of benefits which were already being paid out to retired workers. Representatives of the Association of American Railroads and of the Railway Labor Executives' Association agreed to appoint a committee to work out a system which was agreeable to both parties. The provisions of the agreement between these two parties led directly to the establishment of the 1937 Railroad Retirement Act as well as having a bearing on later amendments. Among other things the railroads agreed never to raise the issue of constitutionality of the act and the employees agreed never to propose any amendment which would depart from the equal taxation principle.

In the years between 1937 and 1945 several minor additions and revisions were made in the 1937 retirement and taxing acts. Most of the amendatory bills which were introduced into the House of Representatives emanated from employee groups. The first major amendments were made by the Crosser Bill in 1946. Two major changes introduced in this amendment were that survivors' benefits and temporary disability benefits were extended to railroad workers. In addition the new bill included a number of changes which were to clear up certain provisions in the old law, eliminate some inequities, and simplify administrative details. No sooner had the Crosser amendments become law than a concerted campaign was launched by the carriers to have them repealed. The Railway Labor Executives' Association countered with arguments favoring the continuation of the bill in the form in which it had been passed. The arguments which developed gave rise to another rash of proposed legislation during the early days of the first session of the Eightieth Congress.

The act was not amended until the Wolverton Amendments were passed by Congress in 1948. The primary change brought about in 1948 had to do with the retirement annuity formula, which had not been changed since the original bill in 1937. In this amendment the retiree's average monthly compensation was calculated on the basis of 2.4 per cent of the first $50 of taxable monthly salary, 1.8 per cent of the next $100, and 1.2 per cent of the remaining $150. The effect of this change was to provide an increase of 20 per cent on all retirement annuities except for those where the minimum formula was applied.

Legislative interest after 1948 stemmed from three principal sources. The cost of living had continued to rise and even though the retirees had received a 20 per cent increase in their annuities, the rising cost of living had just about nullified it. The amount of survivors' benefits had not been increased substantially since they had been put into operation in 1946. Second, wages for railroad workers had been increased on several occasions since 1937 but these increases had relatively little influence on increasing benefits under the retirement plan. This was the case because benefit payments were based on railroad service and earnings both before and after the initiation of the original act in 1937. Third, in 1950 Congress amended the Social Security Act, appreciably increasing the amount of benefits payable. In comparing the taxes paid under the Social Security Act and the Railroad Retirement Act, it was evident that the gap between the amount of benefits payable under the two acts was very much narrowed. The 1950 amendments to the Social Security Act increased survivor benefits to as much as one-third higher than those under the Railroad Retirement

Act. Prior to the 1950 amendments, survivor payments under the OASI had been as much as 25 per cent lower than those under the railroad system.

The amendments of 1951, known as the Douglas Amendments, called for eight major changes in the Railroad Retirement Act. They are as follows:

1. A 15 per cent increase in pensions and annuities.
2. A 33⅓ per cent increase in survivors' benefits.
3. A new benefit for a husband or wife aged 65 or over, amounting to 50 per cent of the employee's benefit, up to a maximum of $40.
4. A guaranty that the railroad retirement benefits would at least equal social security benefits.
5. Credit for service after age 65.
6. Unlimited right to revoke a joint-and-survivor annuity election.
7. Transfer to social security of workers who leave railroad work after less than 19 years' service.
8. A provision for a financial interchange between the Railroad Retirement Account and OASI so that the latter would neither gain nor lose from the separate existence of the Railroad Retirement System.[15]

Further changes in the Railroad Retirement Act were brought about by the 1952 amendments to the Social Security Act. In order to maintain the relationship between OASI and the railroad system, the Social Security Act amendments contained provisions which amended the Railroad Retirement Act also. First, the minimum benefits payable under the railroad act were increased to conform with the increases in OASI benefits. Second, the work clause was increased from $50 to $75 for both categories. Third, there was a clarification of military service credits where military service had not been credited under the railroad retirement system. Although these changes resulted in some increase in costs to the railroad retirement system, the increase in OASI benefits enabled it to reduce its over-all costs because of the financial interchange between the two systems.

[15] *Ibid.*, p. 134.

Because of further revision of the Social Security Act in 1954 the Railroad Retirement Act was changed again. Widows were allowed to claim survivors' benefits at the age of 60 instead of 65. Other liberalizing changes were also made. Under the railroad act, workers with less than twenty years' service would receive less in retirement benefits than OASI provides. Also OASI makes better provision for survivors than the railroad act does regardless of years of service or level of income. With the provision in the 1951 amendments to the Railroad Retirement Act, both primary beneficiaries and survivors cannot receive less under this act than they would under the OASI plan.

Summary

The numerous pension systems reviewed in this chapter offer illustration of the effect of postponing the adoption of a universal retirement program for the aged. As employee groups have felt the need for retirement systems they have begun programs which they believed offered better benefits than they could receive under a universal system. Many of these systems are perpetuated primarily because their spokesmen have a vested interest in maintaining a separate system or because those who will ultimately benefit do not want to lose their identity as a group. Indications are numerous that local and state government systems are inadequate in at least one and possibly in most areas where protection is sought. The several federal systems also suffer from one or more weaknesses, particularly their dependence upon Congress for the employer contribution to the system. Nonetheless, the railroad retirement system appears to be one of the strongest systems now in operation.

Since 1951 there has been a definite trend to relate many of these systems, in one way or another, to the OASI system. This has been done by using OASI to supplement the existing plan, by allowing uncovered employees to come under the protection of OASI, or allowing those with a short work history under any one of several systems to transfer wage credits to OASI. Finally, in the case of the Railroad Retirement Act there is a guarantee that benefit payments, regardless of the railroad formula, will not fall below OASI benefit payments.

Two questions remain unanswered. First, should the federal government continue to sponsor retirement systems which place any category of workers in a position which is more favorable than that of other employees? Second, should not some adjustment be made whereby no class of employees is given preferential treatment in the way of receiving duplicate retirement payments? It would appear that until there is a universal, compulsory retirement system which has adequate benefits for retired workers and their dependents and survivors, both of these questions will remain unanswered.

13

Private Pensions

Private pensions offer another way in which to meet the financial needs of older people in retirement. Private pensions have been referred to as constituting the third layer of retirement income. Individual savings, insurance, and investments are thought of as being the base of retirement income, and old-age and survivors insurance makes up the second layer. As a sort of third layer or icing private pensions are supposed to supply additional income over and above that required to sustain life in retirement. In a sense of the word these privately financed plans can be considered the "American way" of meeting financial needs because the plans are financed by employers with a minimum of interference from the federal government. Where the plans call for contributions from the employees they are considered "American" in that each employee is helping to finance his own retirement.

The history of private pensions in this country is a long one. Some of the plans now in operation have been in operation for many years. This is especially true of pensions for executives of industry and for employees who are in the upper echelons of industry. Many of the early plans which included workers were inadequately financed and did not weather the Depression years. Since the Depression the number of private plans has been increased. First, the Social Security Act helped to make Americans more aware of the problems of economic insecurity or helped make them security conscious. Second, private plans received an impetus from increased union activity. Third, the wage stabilization program during the Second World War and the Korean Conflict removed the emphasis from wage increases and placed it upon the so-called "fringe benefits." Pension plans were used by management as a method of attracting and holding employees in lieu of increased wages which were forbidden under the stabilization programs. As a consequence of these three factors the number of private plans has grown rapidly in the past decade and the number of individuals covered by these plans now is much greater than it was in the prewar and pre-Depression days.

Extent of private plans

For one reason or another, it is difficult to determine the exact number of private pension plans or persons covered by them at any given time. Table 20 is presented to give an ap-

TABLE 20

Number of Private Retirement Systems, United States, for Selected Years

Year	Estimated Number of Plans	Estimated Number of Workers Covered
1875	1	Figures not available
1900	12	" " "
1920	270	" " "
1930	720	2,400,000
1935	1,090	2,600,000
1940	1,965	3,700,000
1945	7,425	5,600,000
1950	12,330	8,600,000
1951	14,000	9,600,000
1954	21,000	12,500,000
1955	23,000	13,300,000

SOURCES: Thomas C. Desmond (chm.), *Birthdays Don't Count* (Albany: New York State Joint Legislative Committee on Problems of the Aging, 1951), p. 28; National Planning Association, *Pensions in the United States* (Washington, D.C.: 1952), p. 11; and Joseph Zisman, "Private Employee-Benefit Plans Today," *Social Security Bulletin*, XX (January, 1957), 9.

proximation of the number of plans in operation in selected years. It should be noted that there has been a marked increase in the number of plans over the years, especially during the 1940 decade. The future growth of private pension plans will depend upon several variables. One basic factor which will influence the growth in number as well as the continued existence of the plans already in force will be the economic condition of the country. All things being equal one can expect an increase in the number of plans when favorable conditions obtain. Conversely there will be some slowing down in the number of new plans added, or perhaps a curtailment of the existing plans if the country should face another era of depression.

The increase in the number of new plans will be determined partially by union demands for pension plans. When pensions are regarded as fringe benefits or bargaining points rather than primary issues, unions will probably not fight hard to get a plan. The attitude which management takes will also have an influence on the number of plans. More plans will be introduced when management believes pensions are desirable and needed. If management thinks they cannot afford to be without a pension plan and that more workers should be covered, they will try to get a plan; otherwise they will not. The cost of living and the level of the federal OASI program will also have an influence on the future of private plans. There will be less pressure and felt need for private plans if the cost of living is relatively low and the benefits under OASI relatively high. Management will feel less moral necessity for starting a pension and the workers will probably be more able to save for old age from current income if they believe that OASI benefits will be adequate for their retirement needs.

There may be a practical limit to the number of plans also. At present it appears that the elite industries and firms now have private systems. Under some plans it is financially impractical to cover small numbers of employees. Those firms which do not now have plans are those which have fought plans for one reason or another or those for which plans are financially impossible or undesirable.

Table 21 indicates the type of industry and commercial establishments which have private pension plans. It should be noted that these data pertain only to pension plans which are under collective bargaining. This accounts for some of the difference in the number of workers covered as presented here and in the previous table. Further, it should be noted that these data are for mid-1950. No doubt the number of workers and the range of industry groups have both been in-

TABLE 21

Workers Covered by Pension Plans Under Collective Bargaining Agreements by Major Industry Groups, Mid-1950
(in thousands)

| | Total Covered | |
Industry Group	Workers	Per Cent
Total	5,123	100.0
Food and tobacco	87	1.7
Textile, apparel, and leather	654	12.8
Lumber and furniture	14	.3
Paper and allied products	140	2.7
Printing and publishing	17	.3
Petroleum, chemicals, and rubber	361	7.0
Metal products *	2,011	39.3
Stone, clay, and glass	66	1.3
Mining and quarrying	466	9.1
Transportation, communication, and other public utilities (excluding railroads) ..	1,024	20.0
Trade, finance, insurance, and services ..	71	1.4
Unclassified	212	4.1

SOURCE: Bureau of Labor Statistics, *Employment and Economic Status of Older Men and Women* (May, 1952), Bulletin 1092, 49.

* Includes steel, automobiles, and machinery.

creased since that date. It can be seen that the industry groups with the most workers covered are those which employ large numbers of workers, such as steel and automobiles, as well as transportation and communication.

It is more or less a matter of conjecture as to how many people who are working under private pension systems will benefit from the pensions when they reach retirement age. Each person must serve a certain number of years with the company and under the pension plan before sufficient wage credits can be built up. The length of service with the company and/or under the plan, the age of the individual, and the level of income determine his benefits. Length of service has been waived under many of the plans now in operation in a fashion similar to waiving of length of service for older workers under the OASI plan both in 1937 and 1950. Employees approaching retirement age at the time of the instigation of the plan sometimes have been brought under the plan if they have been employed by the industry for a specific number of years and would not have enough work life remaining to serve the required time under the plan.

By way of illustration, if a newly organized company starts a retirement program soon after it begins operation, it may begin with an impressive looking retirement plan. It could have a plan set up to pay pension benefits at the rate of $150 per month at age 65, with a requirement of twenty-five or thirty years' service with the company. Any employee over the age of 41 would not be able to draw the maximum pension and no one would be able to draw any pension payments for twenty-five years. In this hypothetical case the company would have plenty of time to build up an ample reserve fund for pension payments. On the other hand, other companies which have been in operation for many years set up plans under which older employees may start receiving benefits in a year or two. Reserve funds must be built up quickly by these companies on the basis of past services of the employees. The pension benefits under the second set of circumstances would not be as great as those under the first set, and initial pension costs would be greater.

As a general rule, the amount of pension is figured on the basis of wages, either average wages during employment or a certain percentage of present wages. Length of service is also a factor which is used to determine the amount of pension benefit. People with longer service will draw greater pension benefits than those with short terms of service. Finally, age of retirement is involved here also. Employees who retire before the normal retirement age usually receive smaller benefits than those who continue working until the age of 65 or longer. Under some contracts additional credit may be acquired if the employee continues working beyond the normal retirement age.

One of the questions of greatest interest centering about pensions has to do with the proportion of employees who will remain with a single employer long enough to qualify for the maximum pension benefits. There is a widely held belief that the American labor force is a mobile one, and further, that mobility of labor is one of the advantages our economic system has over some others. With this in mind, it would seem that a mobile labor force might also be one where a relatively small proportion of workers would accrue enough service under one employer to qualify for the maximum pension payments. In January 1951, 13 million of the 59 million employed civilian workers had been with the same employer continuously since November, 1941 or earlier.[1] It should be recalled that this decade was one of great upheaval. There were great shifts in population during the Second World War, a shift from a wartime to peacetime economy after 1945, and a period of readjustment to a partial wartime level upon the outbreak of the Korean hostilities in 1950. Conditions during the decade being discussed were conducive to rapid labor turnover. Furthermore, it would have been impossible for large numbers of the working force in 1951 to have been employed for as long as ten years. This is due to the fact that many of them were in the armed services at least for a time during this period. Others of the 59 million, because of age, could not have entered the labor force until after 1941. A considerable number of those employed in 1951 may have entered the labor force during the labor shortage of either the Second World War or the Korean Conflict.

Table 22 shows that the larger proportion of the "longtime" employees consists of those who are older, those who were exempt from military service, and those old enough to have been in the labor force for as long as ten years. More

[1] Seymour L. Wolfbein, "Job Tenure of American Workers," *Monthly Labor Review*, LXXV (September, 1952), 257 ff.

than two-thirds of those who had long-term employment records were over 45 years of age. Of this category, the largest percentage were between the ages of 45 and 54 years. One-fourth of all these employees were between the ages of 55 and 64, and 11 per cent were 65 and over. The number of

TABLE 22

Number and Per Cent of Workers Employed in Jobs Acquired
Prior to World War II
(in millions)

Age	Number	Per Cent
All ages	13.0	100
Under 45	4.2	32
Over 45	8.8	68
45–54	4.2	32
55–64	3.2	25
65 and over	1.4	11

SOURCE: Seymour L. Wolfbein, "Job Tenure of American Workers," *Monthly Labor Review*, LXXV (September, 1952), 257.

those 65 and over was 1,400,000. In 1951 there were 3,020,-000 aged persons in the civilian labor force in this country. Roughly somewhat less than half of the older employees had been with the same employer for ten or more years.

Returning to the idea of pensions and the length of service required to qualify for pension benefits, it would appear that older employees are in a relatively favorable situation in this respect. On the other hand, it will be recalled that there were more than 11 million aged in this country in 1951. Of this number, approximately only one in four were in the labor force, and of those who were in the labor force one in four were either unemployed or were engaged in agricultural occupations. Only 2,242,000 of the more than 11 million old people in this country were in a position where it would have been vaguely possible for them to have become eligible for pensions. As was noted earlier, old people are involved in agriculture and self-employment more frequently than in employment where pension plans might be in force. On the other hand, older workers are also to be found in skilled jobs and as managers where many are covered by private pension plans.

It is difficult to ascertain how many of the retired aged are being benefited by private pensions. One estimate of the number drawing both OASI and private pensions, which together may be said to constitute adequate retirement income, places the figure at 350,000.[2] There is no question but that there are more than this number now and that the number would be even greater if one counted all those who were drawing pensions regardless of whether they were also receiving OASI benefits. This same source estimates that 5.5 million retired workers and their wives were receiving some kind of retirement benefits in 1952. Of this number an estimated 500,000 were receiving private pension payments. This amounts to approximately 10 per cent of the total number of aged who were receiving retirement benefits of one kind or another at that date.[3] Estimates in 1956 placed the number of retired persons who were receiving private pension payments between 800,000 and 1,000,000.

The function of pensions

Industrial pensions serve many different functions for industry, the workers, unions, and the over-all society. One employer may install a pension system for one reason, another for a different reason. So likewise, one union may press pension demands, the next may not. Individual employees have different ideas on the subject, influenced by the age of the individual, his concern for the future, and by what he thinks he can do to meet his future financial needs and the needs of his dependents.

From the point of view of the employer, private pensions can be counted upon to settle the following points. First, with a pension plan and a retirement system there can be a

[2] National Planning Association, *Pensions in the United States* (Washington, D.C.: 1952), p. 73.
[3] *Ibid.*, p. 12.

compulsory retirement age set for all employees. This plan can be enforced without having to turn the old employee out with no income. Second, private pensions may serve as the answer to the moral obligation felt by some of the employers to "look after" superannuated workers. A haphazard method of dealing with the retired workers may be costly from two points of view. Unless the employer is living in a land or age where all acknowledge that the employer-employee relationship is completely severed at retirement, there will be some feeling on the part of society that the employer should at least recognize some responsibility. Where financial help is given the retired worker with no plan back of the help, the cost may be very great. It is costly because of inefficiency and because ill will is engendered in the community and among the retired workers. There is too much chance of favoritism and too much chance that some needy cases may be overlooked if pensions are handled as gifts. Furthermore, gifts given over any period of time may come to be thought of as permanent, therefore if the employer has to stop payments, the recipients are unhappy. Such a method, regardless of other factors, would do little to encourage loyalty among the current work force.

A third function of pension plans is that of reducing labor turnover. It is a costly affair in some industries to train new men to replace those who have gone elsewhere for employment. Finally, granting a pension upon the demand of the workers or their union representatives diverts attention from what could be more costly demands. Negatively, pensions may serve as a factor in inducing some less efficient personnel to stay on the job. It is also possible that an ill-conceived and badly executed pension plan would cause more unfavorable reaction than no plan at all. In the event of inadequate financing or improper financing, employees and their families who had been led to expect much might receive little if anything from the plan.

Unions, as the representatives of individual employees, have demonstrated an interest in private pensions. There are several useful functions which pensions serve for the union. First, a pension, like any other granted demand, serves notice on the employer and the employees that the union is an organization which is serving its members. Second, and closely related to the preceding function, is the fact that pension plans stabilize union membership. It follows that if employee turnover is reduced, union membership turnover is also reduced. Third, pensions have served union negotiators as a sort of lever or trading point. Introducing suggestions for pensions is one way of convincing management that other concessions should be made. During periods when wages were stabilized by government edict, pensions served as one of the major areas of negotiation and acted as a substitute for increases in wages which could not be granted.

The function for the individual is related to that for the union and for society as well. Pensions serve as a promise of some economic security after retirement. The individual worker covered by a pension should be more content than one who is not covered. He knows that an established retirement plan does not play favorites and that he will receive his pension check with regularity. Private pensions serve the function of helping to relieve society of some of the burden of supporting its aged population. As long as there is a social consciousness and feeling of social responsibility, old people will be cared for. As long as private industry pays part of the cost of this support directly, less will have to be paid through federal, state, and local governments. There seems to be no question but that there is a living standard below which older citizens will not be allowed to fall. Private pension plans help to keep some individuals above this lower level of subsistence and so serve society as a whole.

The structure of pensions

The preceding section pointed out that there are four interested parties involved in pensions. The kind of pension each of the parties wants determines to some extent the kind he gets or at least the kind he will try to get. If any pension is wholly undesirable the plan will never be implemented in the first place. The structure of pensions varies enough in one way or another to satisfy a wide range of wishes on the subject. First, it can be assumed that the plan, no matter what its exact form, will conform to the law if the employer is to receive tax relief. The employer and union will be assured that it is such as to comply with the regulations of the Internal Revenue Service. There are certain limits to reason which will not be violated. The plan will not call for payments which are so small as to be meaningless or so large as to be impractical. Within the law and the bounds of reason there are still many choices as to the form pension plans will take. As a usual thing the choice of the exact form is left to the employer and his expert advisers. If the union is involved the choice lies with both union and employer. Following are several forms that pension plans may take.

First, how shall the plan be financed? In more technical language: shall the plan be funded or unfunded? If the plan is not funded it merely means that it is a pay-as-you-go plan. The pensions are paid out of current earnings and there is no reserve fund built up. Employers may set aside a certain amount each month or year from current earnings and earmark it for pensions. In such cases, there is no reason the firm cannot dip into these savings to meet current operating costs. Two difficulties are inherent in unfunded plans. First, in times of curtailed earnings or depressions, or if the industry is forced to close down, the pension payments cease. Second, these plans are seldom built on a sound actuarial basis, and so cannot "foresee" the number of retired workers who may eventually be dependent upon the plan for their income in retirement. It hardly need be pointed out that most unfunded plans could not be considered adequate. If pay for present work or pay for pensions must be sacrificed, the latter will go first. It is highly improbable that any company operating under the unfunded plan would seriously consider bankruptcy as a necessary step to keep up pension payments.

Closely akin to this problem is that of an increased pension load from year to year. Industry with a normal age distribution in its labor force will find that the number of pensioners increases every year for several years. That is, more workers retire than retired workers die within the first fifteen or so years after a plan has been started; consequently the amount of pension payments increases.

Funded plans are plans which are financed for each individual worker as a member of the group. The amount of money to be put aside is determined by the number of employees, their ages, length of service, their wages, the rate of labor turnover, and the amount of pension payments which has been promised. The employer sets aside a specified amount of money each month. He may keep this in a pension trust fund or he may turn the sum over to an insurance company or trustee to handle for him. When pension plans meet with the approval of the Internal Revenue Service, payments made into pension funds are deductible as a business expense. If there were no pension plan or if the plan did not meet federal requirements, a large part of the contribution made by the employer would be paid to the government in taxes. "Since March 1951, of every dollar paid to a pension fund by a corporation subject to surtaxes, 52 cents would have been paid to the federal Treasury in the absence of a pension plan." [4] In addition to this saving, the total amount which the employer pays into the fund can be reduced by the accrued interest on funds deposited and invested in bonds and stocks. Finally, when the plan is funded payments will be made to pensioners on schedule regardless of the financial condition of the company.

Another question which has to be answered is whether the plan shall be contributory or not. If it is contributory it must also be funded in some manner. If the plan is contributory it merely means that each covered employee contributes a certain percentage of his wage or salary to help pay for his retirement. The contribution is usually expressed in a ratio to that of the employer contribution, such as one to

[4] *Ibid.*, p. 18.

one or one to two. In few instances do the employees contribute the larger share.

Contributory plans are favored for any one of several reasons. As a rule they help keep the initial cost of the plan for the employer lower than it otherwise would be. It is a forced savings program for the employees who might otherwise not save for their retirement. Should the employee die or leave the company before the age of retirement, the contributions are returned to his beneficiary or to himself.[5] Periodic forced savings tend to make the employee more aware of and more concerned with the pension plan and the retirement system in general.

Some objections have been raised concerning contributory plans. Probably the most valid of these is that the employee should not be made to foot the bill for his own retirement. This is particularly pertinent if one adheres to the idea that pensions are deferred wages and are a part of the cost of production. Second, the pension fund receives a full dollar for less than a dollar contributed by the employer. Conversely, the fund receives less than a dollar for each dollar contributed by the employee. The employer is "forgiven" taxes on the part he contributes, but the part contributed by the employees is taxed. One of the arguments used in favor of contributory plans may also be turned against them. The employee's share may be withdrawn upon death or severance of employment. This would make for a less stable amount of money to be invested and would also mean more expense to the fund in the way of bookkeeping.

In theory it would seem that unions would not favor contributory plans because it would mean that employees contribute to their own income in retirement. They might, however, favor this type of plan because it would give them a right to have some voice in administering the pension or to have a reason to be allowed a representative on the pension board. As was indicated above, management would logically be in favor of a contributory plan since it helps reduce

[5] Arthur J. Menche, *Successful Pension Planning* (Englewood Cliffs, N.J.: Prentice-Hall, Inc., 1949), pp. 63–64.

the initial cost of the pension. On the other hand, management might not want the plan to be contributory because there would then be less reason for the unions to have a voice in administering the plan.

There is some disagreement as to the extent of contributory or noncontributory plans. It appears that the number of new plans with contributory provisions varies according to the general economic conditions of the country. The type of plan also varies according to the desires of the employees or their representatives as well as those of the employers. About half the plans adopted between 1943 and 1947 were contributory. Many plans established by management since the Second World War have been contributory. Most of the plans resulting from collective bargaining agreements have been noncontributory. More workers have always been covered by noncontributory than by contributory plans. Probably more than 75 per cent of the workers now covered by private plans do not contribute to them. There is some indication that plans set up for salaried workers and executives are more likely to be contributory than not.[6]

The amount of employee contributions, when they are called for, varies from plan to plan. Contributions are usually figured on the basis of a certain percentage of the annual wage or salary. Employee contributions are usually 2 or 3 per cent of the annual wage for the first $3,000 and somewhat more for wages above this amount. Employer contributions are usually calculated on the basis of the amount of contributions necessary to provide the promised pension benefits. In addition, the employer alone finances the benefits based on service prior to the enactment of the pension plan. If the employee does not contribute to the plan, the employer's contribution may take one of many forms. There may be an exact amount specified, or payments may be made on the basis of a specified amount per hour worked, or a

[6] Cf. *Management Record*, XI (November, 1949), 466; E. K. Rowe and T. H. Paine, "Pension Plans Under Collective Bargaining, Part I," *Monthly Labor Review*, LXXVI (March, 1953), 237 ff.; and National Planning Association, *Pensions in the United States*, p. 18.

specified amount or percentage of the monthly payroll. It is generally considered more realistic to have some adjustable sum rather than a flat rate of contribution so that the amount paid into the fund can vary with changing status of the fund.

Finally, another decision confronts the individuals drawing up a pension plan. Shall the fund be vested or not? That is, does the employee acquire a right to the pension before the age of 65 is reached, or does he forfeit all rights if he severs relations with the company before he reaches retirement age? It has already been noted that if the plan is contributory, the part paid in by the employee plus any interest on that part usually belongs to the employee and can be collected by him or his beneficiary if he severs relation with the company. This principle does not apply to the part the employer has contributed. If it is a noncontributory plan, unless specified otherwise, the employee would not be entitled to any payments from the fund prior to retirement.

Vesting is important and significant from several points of view. If an employee knows he will not lose any or all of his retirement benefits if he changes jobs, he will not be as hesitant to change. Full vesting, either immediate or deferred, does not discourage labor mobility. In the event of the death of the employee his beneficiary would receive the amount of money contributed to the fund by the employee plus interest thereon. From this approach it would seem that vesting would invariably be demanded by employees if they had a voice in the matter. However, vesting reduces the size of the pension payments, for vesting costs money and so increases the cost of pensions. Each vested dollar which is withdrawn would otherwise have gone to finance the payment of pensions of those who retire. From the view of the employee, nonvesting is desirable in the form of possible larger pension benefits only if one knows that he will be an employee who stays on the job and lives to enjoy a long period in retirement.

If one takes the view that pensions are deferred wages, then there should be vesting rights, because pensions should be collected by workers no matter how long they have worked. A plan which has vesting is said to be more attractive to young workers. This is due to the fact that the promise of a pension which cannot be realized for twenty-five or thirty years is not as attractive as one from which workers might collect something if they change employment early in life. More liberal provisions might attract good employees because they would know if they had to leave their jobs they would benefit nonetheless. If one takes the view that a pension is a reward for long and faithful service, it would not be consistent to have the pension vested.

Although it is probable that most plans have no vesting provisions, most of those that do provide that a specified time under the plan should have been served, or a specified age reached, before the employee becomes entitled to all the money accumulated to his pension account. The usual length of service required for vesting under a pension is about thirteen years and the usual age 45.[7] This type of vesting is known as deferred-full vesting. If the employee leaves the job before the specified time is served or the specified age is reached, he is not entitled to any of the sum. If he serves the required length of time he is entitled to all of his share, but often only after he reaches the age of 65 years.

It can be seen that employees under these plans have no vested rights in the pension until after they have reached an age where they are relatively stable in employment. Yet one of the purposes in vesting is to protect the pension equity of those who leave their jobs before they become eligible for retirement benefits. Since at least ten years' service is usually required it can be seen that the value of vesting, to the individual employee, is severely limited. Even when plans are contributory it is generally considered to be unwise to give the employee his share of the pension in cash when he leaves the employment of the company. In the event he is rehired later, the question will arise as to the state of his pension. Will he have to refund the part he took?

[7] Rowe and Paine, "Pension Plans Under Collective Bargaining, Part I," p. 239.

Will the employer have to make it up? Will he have to start out again building up a retirement fund for himself? Closely akin to this is the fact that if the employees receive a cash sum, high labor turnover might be encouraged. It is believed that some employees would leave their jobs whenever they wanted to get their hands on a sum of cash. If funds are vested and the employee has served the required time and then leaves his job, the sum accumulated to his account may be held in trust for him until he reaches retirement age or dies. Sometimes the sum is used by the employer to purchase a paid-up insurance policy for the employee. It may be used to reduce the premiums on an insurance policy, the employee paying the balance of each premium.

The way plans are financed

There are four generally accepted ways in which pensions are financed.[8] One of these is called the trust fund plan. Under this type, the company hires an actuary who determines the amount of the contributions needed to provide pension benefits. Funds are deposited in trust under an agreement between the industry and trustees. These funds are then invested in securities to yield an interest return. Usually the funds are administered by a bank or trust company. Pension benefits are paid out of reserve funds when they fall due, or if the plan calls for it, the trustee may purchase single premium immediate annuity policies when the workers retire. The services of an actuary are necessary to be sure the assumptions on which the plan is based are correct. If the assumptions are not correct, contributions have to be adjusted to meet the new conditions. Usually a large number of workers is required under a plan of this kind so that the law of averages will work. One advantage in the trust fund plan is that the employer can gear his contributions to business conditions. Most of the plans of this de-

---

[8] Beatrice F. Browder, "Funding a Pension Plan," *Management Record,* XI (November, 1949), 466–68 and 502–3. See also Dan M. McGill, *Fundamentals of Private Pensions* (Philadelphia: University of Pennsylvania Press, 1955), pp. 69–125 for a detailed analysis of financing private pensions.

scription are noncontributory. Benefits are paid to the extent that there are funds available in the trust. Neither the employer nor the trustees can guarantee that all benefits provided for under the plan will be paid when due.

Group annuity plans are underwritten and administered by insurance companies. Contributions are in the form of premiums which are paid by the employer in accord with the contract made between the employer and the insurance company. As a rule a minimum of fifty employees is required for this type of plan. Retirement benefits consist of a series of paid-up deferred annuities purchased on the basis of one each year to cover retirement benefits for that year. Each year's transaction is a full purchase of one unit. Income at retirement is the total of all units purchased during membership in the plan. The premium charge for each successive year increases until it reaches a high point just before the employee retires. Unless younger employees are kept coming in, the plan tends to be very costly because it is more expensive for older workers nearing retirement age.

Many of these group annuity plans provide for contributions from the employees. No death benefits are paid other than the contributions which have been made by the employee, plus interest on these contributions. The employer does not receive any return for death of covered employees since the contributions are discounted for death. Contributions are suspended if the employee is temporarily laid off. If the employee leaves the employment of the company, a credit of 96 per cent of the employer's contribution in his behalf is allowed the employer.

The deposit administration plan is another form of insured pension plan which is growing in popularity. It is a combination of the pension trust fund and group annuity plan. The employer deposits contributions with the insurance company. The funds are accumulated to purchase annuities as the employees retire. The insurance company acts as the trustee of the funds and guarantees the rate of interest to be earned by the fund as well as the annuity premium rates for specified periods of time. The insurance company furnishes advice as to the amount of funds needed to pay specified benefits. This plan has more flexibility than group annuity plans. The contributions made by the employer may be discontinued for severance of employment or for any other reason. Benefits paid to employees may be based on final wages, whereas under the group annuity plan benefits are based on average wages. In the former case, premium costs are higher.

Individual policy plans are those in which an insurance policy is purchased for each employee who enters the plan. Policies are issued in the name of the participating member for the amount of the retirement benefit provided under the plan. The policies are held by trustees. Although any number of employees can be included under this type plan, it has the disadvantage of being somewhat inflexible. It is difficult to adjust retirement income to earnings unless the employee is able to and allowed to purchase additional units. This type of plan is very similar to ordinary insurance policies. Contributions are on a level-premium basis. If this plan calls for employee contributions and the employee is unable to meet the premiums as they fall due, he ceases to belong to the plan. The cash-surrender value of these policies is low in the early years but at the end of ten years the value may possibly exceed the amount of the premiums paid. The difficulty with this type of plan is that it is not adjustable to fluctuations in wages or to lay-offs. For these reasons, it is usually used only by salaried people. In order to assume permanency of employment a rather long waiting period is required before employees will be brought under a plan of this sort.

Other plans which are now in operation generally include features from one or more of the plans described above. In addition to these plans another plan which is popular among some employers and employees is that of profit-sharing. A portion of the companies' earnings are deposited in trust and the funds are used to provide retirement benefits. Perhaps the best known of these plans is that of Sears, Roebuck and Company. Some pensions under the Sears plan are said to reach as high as $80,000 for some of the higher paid, long-time employees.

Some pension defects and suggested remedies

It should be remembered that the area of private pensions, as well as widespread government pensions, is a relatively new field of endeavor. As the growth of the number of private plans has been rapid in recent years, so changes are being made to adjust them more adequately to perform the basic functions for which they were designed. There has never been any serious contention that private plans should entirely replace the governmental plan of OASI, nor that either of these two plans should make it unnecessary for workers to save for old age. Further, there is little indication of any serious effort to make the income from federal or private plans equal to the amount of monthly income which a person earns during his lifetime of work.

But certain criticisms of private pensions merit serious attention. A few of these are considered in the following paragraphs.[9]

A common criticism today is that pensions are not designed to meet fluctuations in the cost of living. Most pensions are based on prior earnings of the employee and are paid in monthly checks of stipulated amounts, regardless of the cost of living. This criticism would be invalid, of course, if our economy were a more stable one less given to fluctuations and wide discrepancies between the cost of living and incomes. It should be noted that all employers are not insensible to the inadequacies of pensions in times of inflation. Regardless of the adequacy or universality of the practice, certain employers have made attempts, with no outside compulsion, to meet some of the needs of some of their pensioners by making supplementary payments to them.[10] Under the present method of funding and acquiring a fund from which

[9] Cf. John J. Corson and John W. McConnell, *Economic Needs of Older People* (New York: The Twentieth Century Fund, 1956), pp. 356–403 for an appraisal of private plans.

[10] W. J. Couper, "Present-Day Pension Problems," *Management Record*, XI (January, 1949), 4–6.

payments are later made, it seems highly improbable that any system can be devised whereby pension payments will be tied in with the cost of living as are wages in certain industries.

There has been one plan devised that is an attempt to move in the direction of relating pension benefits to the cost of living.[11] The Teachers Insurance and Annuity Association has an alternate plan whereby up to one-half of the periodic contributions can be invested in common stock. These contributions purchase units in the fund at a price based on the market value of the stocks purchased. The annuity is not paid in a fixed number of dollars per month but is based on a fixed number of units per month which fluctuate with the market value of the stocks in which the contributions are invested. The retired teacher receives his annuity in two parts, one-half of the annuity in terms of a fixed number of dollars and the other half in an amount of dollars which have a reasonable relation to the current purchasing power of the dollar. If nothing else, the above indicates an awareness that pension payments which may be relatively adequate when they are first set up may prove to be inadequate at some later date. Congress, by various revisions in the Social Security Act, has made an effort to adjust benefits to the changing economic conditions of the country.

A second criticism of pension plans is that the present plans operate to bar older job-seekers from employment. This seems to be true, especially where the monthly premiums are based on the age of the employee or where the pension promises to pay a stipulated sum per month rather than a sum based upon length of service under the plan. Probably the easiest answer to this criticism is that no private pension plan is required to (and few probably ever do) cover 100 per cent of the employees. There would be some strenuous objections by some, but the employer might stipulate that all newly hired employees who had passed their fiftieth year would not be eligible for pensions. Further,

[11] Cf. W. B. Dunckel, "Investment Problems in an Inflationary Period," *Management Record*, XIV (May, 1952), 176 and 205–7.

it might be stipulated that all employees hired between the ages of 40 and 50 would not receive the full retirement benefit, but a pro rata share of it. Perhaps some would-be employees would not accept employment under those conditions, but most men over 40 or 45 who are jobless would prefer a job with no pension rather than no job at all.

As a matter of fact, it seems that the pension excuse is not very valid because there are employers who have no pension plans who refuse to hire older workers. If pensions serve the function of stabilizing the work force, employers might do well to hire older people to begin with rather than trying to hire younger people who are not as steady as older ones are. Under some plans it would be possible and acceptable to have proportionately reduced pensions for people who are hired at an older age. The retirement age of such persons might be set back so they could be employed for the number of years deemed necessary for them to acquire full pension credits. Under some plans the pension cost is not increased unless an unduly large number of older workers is hired. The age of employees at entrance into some plans has little effect on the cost. Under any system of hiring which is generally acceptable, over a long period the number of persons to retire will be the same whether they are hired early or late. In any event, inconsistencies appear when the employers use added cost of pensions as the sole reason for refusing to hire older workers. One suggested alternative to pensions for employees who are hired late in life is that they be given severance pay at retirement. Severance pay may be calculated on the basis of a certain number of weekly wages for each year served with the company.

A third criticism of present-day private pension plans is that they encourage the establishment of a compulsory retirement age, usually 65. There are some plans which are set up in such a way that as workers reach the age of 65 their share of the pension payment is ready for them. It then becomes an administrative problem as to what to do with their annuities if they continue to work. Questions usually raised here are these: Shall the employee continue to draw the same wage and his retirement benefit also? Shall his wage be reduced and supplemented to the old level by contributions from his pension? If he draws no pension payments, will more money be paid into his pension account after he has passed the retirement age?

One way to deal with the question is to have all employees automatically retire at the age of 65. After that time they can be rehired on a new status, with no pension payments and without seniority standing in the organization. They will negotiate a new contract with the employer as though they had never worked for him. However, pension payments would not be made to them until they had severed all relation with the company. Another method which conforms to the marginality theory of labor is to have the employee continue work after the age of 65. His wage after that time will be reduced in accordance with his productivity in the job. His total income, however, will not be reduced because the wage he receives will be supplemented by retirement benefits. Theoretically, when his productivity reaches such a low point that he is no longer earning wages but receiving only pension payments, his relation with the company is severed and he lives on his pension without working. In one study it was found that approximately 200 of the 300 plans examined permit workers to continue accumulating credit toward their pensions after normal retirement age is reached. Ninety per cent of these plans allowed all of the work to be credited to the pension account. Plans with no compulsory retirement age were more lenient in this respect than those with compulsory retirement ages.[12]

There are two important questions to be considered: just how many private plans have compulsory retirement age limits, and to what extent are employees forced to retire at the compulsory age? The age of compulsory retirement is defined as that age at which a worker can be retired by reason of age alone. This is not the same as mandatory age

---

[12] E. K. Rowe and T. H. Paine, "Pension Plans Under Collective Bargaining, Part II," *Monthly Labor Review*, LXXVI (May, 1953), 487.

of retirement in that the employer can waive the rule. As a general practice the normal retirement age of 65 is also the compulsory retirement age. If no provision is made for employees working beyond the compulsory retirement age or any specified later date, then retirement at the compulsory age is known as automatic retirement. The employer's waiving of the compulsory rules and the employee's electing to continue work are consistent with the full utilization of manpower. The entire field of compulsory retirement is fairly responsive to the socioeconomic demands of the economy. Most of the argument regarding compulsory retirement age is not concerned with the cost of pension or the administration of pensions, but with who has the right to say when the employee is to be retired.[13]

Finally, it is said that pension plans restrict the mobility of workers. From a more objective position it is correct to say that pension plans restrict the mobility of some workers. First, only about one-sixth of the workers are covered by private pension plans. If pension plans restrict the mobility of others, it is only in a very indirect way. It may be remembered that one criticism leveled at OASI in its early days was that it would restrict the mobility of workers. It was found, however, that one of the weaknesses of this phase of social security was that there were large numbers of individuals who had acquired wage credits under OASI and then had migrated to jobs which were not covered. This was one of the main points used as an argument for the extension of OASI coverage. As far as private plans are concerned, information presented above shows that a majority of American workers do not stay continuously with the same employer for as long as ten years. Further, the younger the employee the more mobile he is. Under some plans an employee must serve with the company for as long as five years before he is brought under the pension plan. This qualification means that many workers must be relatively stable in employment before they can join a pension plan,

[13] *Ibid.*, p. 489.

not that they are stabilized because they have been brought under the provisions of the plan.

The nature of the industries which have private retirement plans should also be examined in this connection. It has been indicated already that most of the industries with adequate plans are the so-called elite of industry. These are the industries with high incomes which pay high wages and have relatively few work stoppages. Due to high wages and many fringe benefits other than pensions, they tend to have a more stable work force than the lower paying industries which do not operate continuously. In other words, the industries which, because of their very nature, tend to have little labor turnover are the ones which have pension plans. So the criticism should be modified to read: pension plans may be one factor in reducing labor mobility for a small portion of the American labor force. It is then granted that a certain degree of labor mobility is desirable and if private plans tend to reduce mobility below the desirable level, then steps should be taken to minimize the stabilizing effects of private pensions.

It has been noted already that stability of labor is said to be desired by management. So, it is from the over-all view that this must be considered. Several ways are suggested in which the stabilizing influence of private pensions may be mitigated.[14] First, more liberal vesting rights could be granted. Instead of having to serve long periods (ten or more years) before the employee is eligible for vesting privileges, any pension credit accrued during shorter periods could be credited to him. No matter how many plans the employee participated in during his work life, at the age of 65 or on retirement, he would receive pension checks from each of his former employers who had pension plans. The pension income would be made up of many small amounts rather than one large amount. Second, at present there are several multi-employer plans in effect. The best

[14] Rowe and Paine, "Pension Plans Under Collective Bargaining, Part I," pp. 242 ff.

known of these multi-employer plans is that of the United Mine Workers Welfare and Retirement program. Money for the fund is collected from a royalty on each ton of coal mined. Other similar plans include all firms which manufacture similar products in a given geographic area. Still others include all firms which have in common only the fact that all employees are members of the same union. Under this arrangement, the pension fund is contributed to by all the firms involved. Employees are at liberty to move from one employer to another without losing their pension rights. It would be a safe assumption that this type of multi-employer plan will increase in popularity with unions and that they will grow in numbers as industry-wide or area-wide collective bargaining agreements become more widespread.

Still another way to encourage mobility is to have provision for early retirement of workers. These provisions would allow workers before retirement age to leave their employment with a pension if they had served a specified number of years under the retirement plan. They would, theoretically, be able to take up employment elsewhere or start into business for themselves with a longer work-life expectancy than if they had retired at the normal age. Still another method which is being used by some firms is that of severance pay to those who leave their jobs. In addition there are a few instances of reciprocal agreements between industries which have retirement plans. After some years under one plan, an employee can have his pension credits transferred to another plan when he changes jobs. Thus he does not lose his credit nor does he have to start out all over again on his retirement program. More widespread use of reciprocal agreements between industries would facilitate mobility of the labor force.

In addition to these proposals reviewed above, there are others. Each of these other suggestions is similar in that each proposes a common pool or trust for pension contributions, or that all pensions be handled from a common source. At present these proposals do not hold much promise in the face of the individuality in American industry and labor, and the diversity of such plans. There is no indication that a uniform pension plan will be devised in the foreseeable future, or if it were, that it would be universally acceptable. Another suggestion is that pension contributions be used to purchase government annuities in the name of the individual employee. The annuities thus purchased would belong to the individual no matter for whom he worked nor how many times he changed jobs.

Still another way, also calling for centralization, would be to have private pension funds paid into the OASI program. These payments would be in addition to the OASI taxes now being paid. The employees would receive credits to their accounts in addition to their OASI credits. The additional credits would be invested in the same manner OASI funds are now invested. If employees changed jobs or changed to employers with no pension plans, their credits would not be affected. Upon retirement, the benefits received would consist of a check made up of OASI benefits plus benefits from the private plan and interest on the latter. This plan has the advantage of shifting the administration of the pension to a bureau of the government which is already operating in this area. It would be less costly to the industry therefore. Further, it would be more advantageous to survivors who now, under certain types of private plans, do not receive any benefits from the pensions after the employee dies, whether it be before or during retirement. The beneficiary, not the pension fund, would profit by such a plan. It seems highly improbable that any such proposal will be followed in the immediate future even if it could be demonstrated that a saving to the employer and greater benefits to the employee or his survivors would accrue. For some, the question of practicality is outweighed by other considerations.

Adequacy of private pension benefits

Nothing has been said thus far as to the adequacy of pension payments. It has been suggested, however, that private pension plans are designed to supplement personal savings and old-age insurance. Since this is the case one could not expect the ordinary pension to be very large. This does not apply to pensions for high-ranking executives of large corporations, nor does it necessarily apply to the more fortunate employees of long standing who participate in the liberal share-the-profits programs. It is usual to have pension benefits based on average salary or wages which have been earned over a period of years in a fashion somewhat similar to the manner in which OASI benefits are calculated. In such cases, the amount of pension benefits would reach the maximum after one had served under a plan for thirty years with a maximum average monthly income of $400 on which pension benefits would be figured. In some cases the maximum time and average monthly wage might be less than the figures just mentioned. Any time short of the maximum or any average wage below the maximum would consequently result in lower pension benefits.

Another popular method which has been used widely is that of combining maximum private pensions and OASI benefits so that the sum of the two will equal a specified amount, usually $100 or $125 per month. When the benefits under OASI were increased in 1952 and in subsequent years some organizations did not reduce their share of the total sum in order to keep the total at the stipulated amount but rather they allowed the employee to profit by the increase in OASI benefits. If, for instance, the combined programs were to equal $100 and the benefits from OASI were increased for a given employee by $5 per month, his total pension income would be $105 rather than the amount formerly agreed upon. Table 23 shows the relation between selected private plans, figured on the basis of $350 average monthly wage, after thirty years' service at the age of 65 and OASI benefits figured on the same basis. It will be noted that there is a wide difference in both the total amounts and the percentage relation of private pension payments to the OASI benefits. From these data it would seem that pension benefits, calculated on the basis of thirty years' service and an average monthly wage of $350, from both sources—the private plan and OASI—approach adequacy. However, it should be noted that OASI benefits in these examples amount to $107.50 which is a near maximum for a single man under

TABLE 23

Examples of Monthly Benefits Payable at Age 65 after 30 Years' Service, Based on a $350 Average Monthly Wage for a Single Man

Private Pension Plan	Private	OASI and Private	Private Plan as Per Cent of Combined Amount
U.S. Steel Corporation	$ 55.00	$163.50	33.6
Ford Motor Company	67.50	176.00	38.4
Goodyear Tire and Rubber Co. ...	54.00	162.50	33.2
U.M.W. Welfare and Retirement Fund	100.00	208.50	48.0
Amalgamated Clothing Workers of America	50.00	158.50	31.5
International Ladies Garment Workers Union	65.00	173.50	37.5
Westinghouse Electric	67.50	176.00	38.4
Aluminum Company of America ..	55.00	163.50	33.6
Du Pont (E.I.) de Nemours & Co.	116.00	224.50	51.7
Consolidated Edison Co. of N.Y. ...	146.00	254.50	57.4
General Electric Co.	84.00	192.50	43.6
Cities Service Co.	96.25	204.75	47.0
Johnson and Johnson	94.50	203.00	46.6

SOURCE: Joseph Zisman, "Private Employee-Benefit Plans Today," *Social Security Bulletin,* XX (January, 1957), 16.

the 1956 program. In December 1956 the average monthly benefits under OASI were only $63.09. It seems improbable that many pensioners are drawing from private plans anything that approximates the maximum payments.

One final question which will be considered here has to do with the ability of American industry to support pension plans. In the final analysis the answer to this question can be found only if one can answer the question of the ability of American industry to continue to function. The answer to the first question might be as simple as asking whether American industry can afford not to continue private pension plans. Certainly old people are going to be helped financially by some representative of society. It has been said that stockholders of the larger pension-paying industries will not sit idly by and watch their dividends be divided among the retired employees in the form of pension payments. It is questionable if dividends have been reduced much if at all to finance pensions. At any rate, two things can be remembered: the cost to the employer and stockholders can be reduced by making the plan a contributory one; there is an oft repeated statement that business never pays a tax—it is always the consumer who pays. Presumably the same maxim applies to pension payments also.

Summary

During World War II the number of private pension plans grew from an estimated 1,965 in 1940 to approximately 15,700 in 1952. Most of this growth resulted from favorable tax concessions made to corporations by the Internal Revenue Service upon the approval of their pension plans, and from the fact that, during the war, pensions were used in lieu of wage increases to attract and hold employees. Since the close of the war, unions have demonstrated a growing interest in pension plans, and have, in some cases, taken them out of the category of the so-called fringe benefits.

In deciding upon a pension program for employees, management has a wide variety of possible plans to choose from. Apparently no one plan can be devised to suit all companies. Within a general pattern, plans are more or less tailor-made to suit each employer. There is no evidence to show that the perfect plan has yet been invented, but more adequate plans as well as more plans with wider coverage will be made as more knowledge is acquired in this relatively new area of endeavor. Bearing in mind that fewer than one-fourth of all employees are covered by pension plans and only approximately 800,000 pensioners are now on private pension rolls, one of the functions of pensions is beginning to be manifest. This is, of course, to act as a supplement to individual savings and OASI benefits as the base of income in old age. The private pension setup is closely related to the OASI program, and will continue to expand as the latter gains in experience and popularity.

Part IV

CHARACTERISTICS OF THE AGING

14

Physiosomatic Characteristics
of the Aged

It is not the purpose of this and the following chapter to explore all of the characteristics that are usually associated with older people. Rather a cursory examination will be made of some of these characteristics. This chapter should help make clearer some of the many differences that exist among older people and help to account for some of the characteristics found in old people which are generally considered unpleasant or undesirable by younger people. It has been indicated in other chapters that no two old people are alike and also that a person may age more rapidly in one aspect of life than in another. It has been said that if a curve of the aging process could be drawn for different parts of the body in all probability no two curves would perfectly coincide.[1] The same, no doubt, is true for different people and for different psychophysical aspects of the individual. This is not to imply that there is no relation between the different aspects of the body. Rather the individual should be viewed as a functioning whole, his personality at any given moment being influenced by his own feeling as well as by his attitude toward how others feel and react to him.

Some physical characteristics of older people

No doubt anyone who has been observant carries in his mind a stereotype of the physical characteristics of older

[1] Robert H. Felix, "Mental Health in an Aging Population," in Wilma Donahue and Clark Tibbitts (eds.), *Growing in the Older Years* (Ann Arbor: University of Michigan Press, 1951), p. 26.

men and women. If any serious thought is given the subject, it is realized that, as with all other stereotypes, the picture is a blurred "average" or applies to one specific individual, but that it rarely if ever fits more than one person. Be that as it may, certain physical characteristics are noticed in both men and women, and when these characteristics appear or are poorly camouflaged, it is said of the individuals that they are getting old or that they look old. Some of these physical characteristics which are most obvious are listed here. As men grow old their hair begins to turn grey and then white, or it thins out and finally baldness occurs. Few women become bald but their hair thins and becomes grey or white as they grow older. Both men and women begin to lose their hearing, and their eyesight dims as they grow older. Depending upon circumstances, most of them lose their teeth in later life. When this occurs it is often accompanied by a sagging of the jaw and a look of old age about the mouth and chin. Facial skin as well as the skin on the rest of the body loses its elasticity as one grows older. Wrinkles appear in the skin around the eyes, mouth and forehead.

Another characteristic which is generally more apparent in older than in younger people is a slowing down in walking. Often older people develop some difficulty in walking; either their joints or their feet hurt. If there is no actual pain involved in walking, their pace becomes slower and more careful. Frequently this is because of the knowledge that older people seem more prone to falling and that old bones do not knit as rapidly or as thoroughly as young ones do.

Also related to this slowing down is a shortness of breath associated with the poorer functioning of some internal organs. This malfunctioning of the internal organs sometimes is associated also with the external characteristics of stooping that can be observed in many older people. Stooped shoulders and a poor physical posture frequently cause the malfunction of internal organs because of undue cramping of the organs within the body. Although the internal organs cannot be seen, the effects of aging can be inferred by outward signs or by the way in which a person handles himself. Some of the characteristics usually associated with aging are a weak heart, hardening of the arteries, poor digestion, sluggishness in the digestive system, constipation, and a deterioration of the kidneys and liver.

It is generally believed by younger people that there is a sharp decline in the sexual urges of both men and women as they approach old age. The menopause in women very definitely is the close of the child-bearing period. However, there is no indication that sexual activity in women or the desire for sexual activity need decline sharply immediately after the menopause. There is no decided dividing line in the sexual or reproductive life of men. There is evidence that for men, the ability to reproduce lasts long into what is called old age. There seems little doubt that the sexual desire of both men and women declines as they become older, but to what extent it declines is not known. There is some evidence that as some men and some women begin to feel a weakening of the sex desire they react by a more active sex life. Where this occurs, it is probably a psychological condition brought about by the fear of loss of sexual appetite. It is in this phase of aging that the cultural norms of society play an important role. The sex mores of this country have been influenced and colored by the Puritan tradition of sexual morality. Many people as they grow older may be torn between their natural sexual desires and a desire to conform to the mores. To generalize, overt sexual experience is taboo, and older people are supposed to repress these desires if they are present.

Is old age natural?

At present it is a truism that aging is a natural condition. Both plants and animals begin the aging process as soon as life begins. Cells die and are replaced by other cells so the process of life continues until such a time that cells, for one reason or another, fail to replace those which have died. A slowing down of the process of cell reproduction marks the beginning of what is called middle age and old age.

The aging process can be hastened or retarded in both plants and animals by withholding or introducing certain chemicals and food elements into the body. There are some clinical cases on record of people in their early years who have all of the physical characteristics usually associated with old age. There are cases on record also of people who have lived well beyond the age of 100 years and have, during their lifetime, continued to function as well or better than others not half their age. It is a matter of common knowledge and observation that some people in our society who are well past the age of 65 show few of the characteristics associated with old age. Others of similar age may be impaired in some ways but may be "remarkably young" in others. Some people in the seventh decade of life may retain their eyesight and hearing; others may be physically strong and active and able to do a good day's work. Still others turn grey very slowly or lose little hair.

These cases raise the question as to the naturalness of old age as a physical phenomenon. If some people live such long and active lives, why is the average and the usual span of life so much shorter? Why do some people become old so much earlier in life than others do? An "off-the-cuff" medical answer to these questions is that those who live long "take care of themselves." There is also a common belief, backed by some scientific evidence, that longevity runs in families. If this is true then there is little need to try consciously to prolong the lives of individuals whose ancestors have had short lives. If the first proposition is taken seriously, then a definition of taking care of oneself should be spelled out. It seems to be the practice for newsmen to interview people who have lived well into the ninth decade or beyond and to ask the stock question, "To what do you attribute your long life?" It should be noted parenthetically that this is a polite way of asking how the person has managed to keep from dying. There are probably as many answers to this question as there are people who have answered it. Some of these answers contradict each other. One person may say he has lived long because he has never used tobacco or drunk alcoholic beverages. The next person may say he has used these things in moderation, while the third may attribute his long life to the fact that he has always followed his appetites. Some older people say their life has been long because they do not worry; still others have other explanations.

If we return to a statement made earlier in this chapter, one of the basic reasons for long life seems to be that bodily cells continue to replace themselves at a fairly constant rate. If this is the real answer to long life, then another question needs to be asked. Why is it that cells in some people continue to replace themselves while this does not occur in others? There is a corollary question to this. Is it "natural" for cells to replace themselves, or is it natural for them not to do so? This question can be answered only when medical science understands cells better than it does now. If it is assumed that it is natural for them to replace themselves and that they should continue to do so at only a slightly reduced rate, so postponing old age and death, what can be done to slow down the process of aging or cell deterioration and the reduced rate of replacement? [2]

The answer to this question is not known by medical science yet, but there is no reason to believe that it will not be known at a later date. There seems to be some evidence at hand which points to two possible partial answers from the point of view of medicine. First, there is good reason to believe that a proper diet throughout infancy, childhood, and youth, and on into adulthood slows down the aging process. Second, there is some evidence that if people can remain healthy and free of the so-called "common" diseases of childhood and maturity that their later life, if not ap-

---

[2] Albert I. Lansing, "Some Dynamic Aspects of Aging," in John M. Maclachlan (ed.), *Health in the Later Years* (Gainesville: University of Florida Press, 1953), p. 64.

preciably prolonged, will at least be healthier than would have been the case if they had had numerous illnesses.

Advances in medical science to reduce the incidence of childhood diseases, higher incomes with which to purchase better (not necessarily more) food, advanced knowledge regarding proper diets, better sanitation, and better living and working conditions may, together with additional elements, make for longer and healthier lives in the years to come. It has been indicated in earlier chapters that the life expectancy of people in this country has been extended appreciably since the turn of the century. It is true that most of this increase has been the result of saving and prolonging the lives of infants, children, and young people. In the period between 1900 and 1954 only two and one-half years have been added to the life expectancy of those over 65 years of age. If one views this in a positive rather than a negative way, it might be concluded that this is a remarkable accomplishment. If one were to speculate, it could be concluded that at least part of the prolongation of life of those 65 and over is due to a healthier period of childhood. It remains to be seen whether the children born in the decades of 1940 and 1950 will live longer than those born during the 1920's and 1930's. In the later two decades the level of living has been much higher than it was in the preceding decades and the knowledge of child care has been expanded.

At the present the question as to whether old age and death are natural phenomena is an academic one. We have not yet reached the point, in the development of science, where human life can be prolonged indefinitely. It is doubtful whether society would be prepared to cope with such a situation were it to confront us now. Until such time as life is so prolonged, the human race will continue to try to adjust itself to the present span of life and to eventual death of its members.

In this discussion it should be remembered that the physical is only one aspect to be considered and that long life and physical health are dependent upon the total personality of the individual. There are cases where older people have been in apparent good health but have died or become ill because they have had no reason to continue living. Some people become ill to attract attention to themselves, to try to retain their status positions, or for other psychological reasons. The total person is involved to some extent in the business of a healthy and long life.

Chronic diseases in later life

Aging may or may not be a natural process, but it is a normal one in that sooner or later all living organisms experience it. This section will deal very briefly with some of the diseases which are most commonly associated with the later years of life. Some of these diseases are also to be found in younger people, but regardless of the age of the individual, these pathological conditions may be viewed as a disruption in the normal aging process.[3] Disabling conditions of this kind are generally associated with one specific part of the body, such as the heart, arteries, kidneys, or respiratory system; they may, however, also cause damage to other parts of the body not directly involved. In all probability an illness of any considerable length or severity hastens the aging process which is occurring and results in a more rapid deterioration of the other organs than would have occurred in the absence of the disease. In effect an illness in later life may result in the speeding up of a process already under way. Thus it is often difficult to draw the line between normal and abnormal aging.

Chronic illness and other disabling conditions are not necessarily a characteristic of old age. Rather, some disorders or illnesses are at least in part the result of mistreatments which the body has been subject to during the prior years.[4] Poor diet, overwork, unhealthy living conditions, overindulgence in smoking, eating, or drinking, too strenuous recreation, and inadequate rest and sleep may all play a

[3] Cf. Jeanne Gilbert, *Understanding Old Age* (New York: The Ronald Press Co., 1952), p. 181.
[4] *Ibid.*, pp. 181–82.

part in setting the stage for disease to attack the body. Disease and disability are not found in otherwise healthy bodies, but bodies weakened by mistreatment are ready hosts of disability and illness. As people grow older there seems to be a cumulative effect of the mistreatments the body has received. Ordinarily the incidence of disability due to chronic disease is higher among older than among younger people.

Some of the more prevalent diseases of later life, those which occur more frequently in older than in younger persons, are the degenerative ones, respiratory diseases (including pneumonia), rheumatism, digestive diseases, orthopedic impairments, nervous and mental diseases, and cancer. Accidents as a cause of disability are also more prevalent proportionately among the old than the young.[5] Late data gathered by the National Health Survey indicate that chronic disease or gross physical impairment was found in approximately 58 per cent of all persons 65 years of age and over.[6] It is of importance to note that chronic illness and senescence are not the same phenomenon. It is of equal importance to note that some diseases of old age are characteristic of the general population while other diseases which are the direct result of physiological aging of the bodily tissues are primarily diseases of old age. In addition to physiological aging brought about by cellular and tissue deterioration, physiological aging is associated with decreased strength of the skeletal muscles and reduced muscular reaction.[7]

At the present time little has been done to avert those changes brought about by physiological aging. Apparently this process may be slowed down but cannot be completely halted. However, the knowledge gained by the science of geriatrics and gerontology can be used to help adjust the older person to physiological changes which will be encountered. As is the case with any other medical problem,

[5] This list adapted from Federal Security Agency, *Illness and Health Services in an Aging Population* (Washington, D.C.: 1952), No. 170, 1 ff.

[6] Michael M. Dacso, "Physical Restoration and the Older Person," in *Growing in the Older Years*, p. 100.

[7] *Ibid.*, p. 101.

preventing or retarding the onset of physiological deterioration is more desirable than seeking to cure or alleviate the condition after it has begun.

Retarding the aging process

The first stage in rehabilitation of the aged lies in the prevention and retardation of the aging process insofar as it is possible. Thorough medical examinations given periodically are of great aid in detecting the processes of aging before they have gone far. Although the detection of these factors is not a cure-all for aging, some remedial action is practical and therefore worthwhile. In the final analysis much depends upon the individual. If he gives up or succumbs to old age there is little that can be done medically to slow down the process of deterioration. If one develops neglected physical potentialities, the rate of physical decline will be slowed, and retarding decline will also help to develop neglected areas.[8] There is no magic drug which can indefinitely postpone decline and death, but much can be done to postpone the obvious onset of old age and so prolong life.[9]

The action of the individual himself to postpone the process of aging can be divided into two phases.[10] It will be noted that these suggested ways of retarding physical decline involve only a part of the total process. Since the total personality is composed of many characteristics, the physical is only one aspect to be considered. Some of the methods used to combat decline or to retard the onset of old age will be dealt with here.

One of the first steps which can be taken by individuals as they enter middle life is to try to improve their general appearance. The onset of the well-known and publicized "middle-age spread" sets people to exercising in an effort to reduce their weight and to strengthen and restore the abdominal muscles. Another corrective measure is to improve

[8] Gilbert, *Understanding Old Age*, p. 311.
[9] Cf. *ibid.*, p. 311.
[10] Adapted from *ibid.*, pp. 311–40.

the general posture by holding the stomach in either artificially or by what may amount to sheer will power. Shoulders can be held back, chest out, and an effort made to "stand
tall." This procedure improves the appearance and makes
the person feel better since the various organs of the body
are not unduly and unnaturally crowded. A correct posture
also takes pressure off the nerves. Good posture should not
be a strain, for good posture is a natural condition; it is poor
posture which produces strain and poor health. Closely
associated with good posture is a proper gait. As they grow
older, some people assume a shuffling gait. This may be
because they fear falling and believe that if they shuffle the
danger of falling is reduced. Shuffling may be caused by
stiffness of hip or knee joints or by foot trouble of some kind.
When faulty posture is corrected one is more likely to walk
correctly, and conversely, correct walking habits may help
improve posture.

One of the very important things for an older person to
watch, both from the point of view of general good appearance and good health, is weight. It is known that people who
are overweight generally have a shorter life span than those
who are normal in weight. Gilbert states that some people
past middle life begin to overeat because they feel "this is
the only thing left for them in life." [11] The more they eat the
fatter they become and the fatter they become the less there
is to live for. The answer to the problem of overweight here
is one of curing the "cause" which has brought on the feeling
of insecurity, rather than curing the symptom of overweight.
It is not uncommon for very old people to become too thin.
This is frequently the result of improper eating habits and is
possibly found more frequently in women than in men.
Improper eating habits may develop when the older woman
has become widowed and has no one to prepare meals for
except herself. There seems to be little incentive for cooking adequate meals for oneself. If older men become widowed and attempt to cook for themselves, they probably do

[11] *Ibid.*, p. 317.

not feed themselves even as well as older women feed themselves.

Overweight is brought about by an excessive intake of calories. After a person has satisfied his hunger drive with bread and potatoes he may think he is well-fed. However, proper diet consists in more than satisfying the hunger drive. In this sense overweight may be an indication of improperly balanced diet. There is no indication that a diet which is good for younger people is not adequate for older ones, nor is there any reason to believe that healthy older people should have a special diet.[12] A well-balanced diet during the younger years and into old age will help postpone the onset of declining physical ability and an unattractive physical appearance. If the older person is still engaged in active work or if he is undergoing conditioning or therapeutic exercises, a properly balanced diet is called for.[13] Only a proper diet can supply the energy which is consumed by work and/or exercise, thus it is as important for an active older person to be properly fed as it is for a younger person. The properly balanced diet calls for the basic food elements of proteins, fats, and carbohydrates as well as an adequate supply of vitamins and minerals.[14] An undersupply of either vitamins or minerals, even where there is a sufficient quantity of the basic foods, will result in dietary deficiencies with a consequent decline in the physical capacity of the individual.

In addition to this action which can be taken by the individual himself to retard declining physical ability, the individual can present himself to his doctor for periodic medical examinations. In all probability most doctors would recommend at least one examination a year for those who have reached their fortieth birthday. Parents in middle-class American society today are careful to have their young

[12] Dacso, "Physical Restoration and the Older Person," in *Growing in the Older Years*, p. 108.

[13] *Ibid.*, pp. 108–9.

[14] *Ibid.*, p. 109.

children examined periodically. This practice has, no doubt, saved lives or uncovered physical difficulties which later would have caused serious illness. The same principle holds true for older people. The primary aim of the physical examination for older people is to discover and treat physical difficulties before they become chronic disabilities. There are cases on record where an older person has refused to have these examinations. When the person has become acutely ill or has suffered a fracture, routine examinations have uncovered chronic conditions of long duration. It is possible that these conditions could have been retarded or eliminated altogether if the person had been more careful and had submitted to regular physical check-ups.

Routine physical examination would include eye tests and the prescription of corrective devices where called for. An examination of the digestive system would include a check on the amount of stomach acid, which is an important aid to digestion. This phase of the examination would also indicate whether the diet being followed was a proper one and whether the individual could continue some of the dietary habits which he had acquired at a younger age. The heart, blood stream, and glands, as well as the respiratory system, should be examined. Special attention should be given to the various areas of the body which are most prone to cancerous growths.[15]

Extent of chronic illness among the aged

It is possible that not many older people observe the precautions that medical doctors would prescribe when they pass the age of 40 years. Taking a positive view, it is remarkable that so many older people live as long as they do and enjoy as good health as many appear to enjoy. In spite of this, as time passes and people begin to enter the seventh decade of life, a larger percentage of them are overtaken by chronic diseases or long-term disabilities. It is not inevitable that all old people, as they approach the end of their span

[15] Cf. Gilbert, *Understanding Old Age*, pp. 319–22.

of life, will spend a period of time in a hospital or that they will be bedridden at home for any appreciable length of time. Some older people apparently enjoy good health until the day they die or at least they are well enough to remain ambulatory and so are not recorded in hospital statistics. Still others may die as the result of accidents instead of spending their last days in what is known as "terminal" illness.

Chronic illness and long-term physical disabilities among the aged account for much physical and mental suffering. Some of the unfortunate results of disabilities are strained family relations, economic hardships, and a curtailment of employment or employability. In 1950 it was estimated by the Public Health Service that more than 2 million (or 17 per cent) of the 12 million people over 65 had a long-term disability. For purposes of this survey, long-term disability was defined as a disability which lasted for three months or more. The total number of persons estimated to have long-term disabilities on this date was 5,289,060. Those 65 and over constituted nearly 40 per cent of all those so classified.[16] These figures show that a sizable proportion of the aged are disabled for long periods of time. Although the aged constitute less than 10 per cent of the total population, they contribute four times more heavily to the total disabled category than they do to the total population.

In 1953 a survey was made of patients in 6,539 hospitals in the United States. At the time of the survey there were 1,207,000 patients in the hospitals in the United States. Twenty and four-tenths per cent or 246,436 of the total number of patients were 65 years of age and over. The types of hospitals with 50 per cent or more patients over 65 were convalescent and rest homes which registered by the American Medical Association as hospitals; institutions such as homes for the aged and infirm, and soldiers homes; and "all

[16] Adapted from The Council of State Governments, *The States and Their Older Citizens* (Chicago: The Council of State Governments, 1955), p. 154.

others" including chronic disease, physical medicine, cardiac, incurable, and skin and cancer hospitals.[17]

A survey was made of long-term patients in institutions in the state of Maryland in 1954. The type of institutions given were proprietary and nonprofit nursing homes, homes for the aged, chronic disease hospitals, and almshouses; long-term patients in general hospitals were included. The percentages of patients 65 and over in Maryland at this date were 87 per cent for proprietary and 81 per cent for nonprofit nursing homes, and 98 per cent for homes for the aged. The percentages of older patients were 65.6, 34.7, and 74 respectively for chronic disease hospitals, long-term patients in general hospitals, and almshouses. A breakdown of those 65 and over in this study shows that, in the last three categories of hospitals, those between 65 and 74 years of age constituted the largest proportion of aged patients. Those between 75 and 84 years of age constituted the largest proportion of aged in nursing homes and homes for the aged.[18]

Several conclusions can be drawn from these data. First, those 65 and over suffer from long-term disabilities proportionately more than younger people do. Second, after spending some time in general hospitals or hospitals for particular disabilities, older patients are more often transferred to nursing homes or homes for the aged where they spend their last years. Third, the percentage of patients over 85 in the total patient load declines because the death rate is very high at that age. If a person becomes chronically ill in his later years, any one of three things may occur. He may recover from his illness and resume his place in society. He may die in a relatively short time, or he may continue to be ill for an indefinitely long period of time. In the first instance he would probably return to his home; in the last instance he could remain as a patient in the hospital or be transferred to a nursing or convalescent home or to his own home, where he might remain as a patient until recovery or death.

[17] *Ibid.*, p. 149.
[18] *Ibid.*, p. 154.

Rehabilitation of the long-term patient

This section will be concerned with the rehabilitation of the chronically ill or long-term patients who ordinarily would remain ill either in the hospital, a nursing home, or their own home, and terminate their lives without having regained their health, or at least without having resumed their place in society as useful, functioning individuals. It is estimated that there are approximately five to six million disabled people in this country. Each year nearly half a million individuals are added to this number. At the same time perhaps less than one-quarter million of the total number are rehabilitated each year.[19] Of the total number who are disabled, perhaps as many as two-thirds are 40 years of age and over.[20] It is probable that most of the effort made to rehabilitate the handicapped is focused on those who are relatively young, those who presumbly would benefit by the treatment to a greater degree. It is also true that it is easier to work with patients who have been disabled for a short period of time.

Briefly there seem to be four reasons the rehabilitation program has moved slowly in this country.[21] First, there is generally not enough money set aside to carry on any more activity than is being undertaken. Second, there is a lack of trained personnel to work with rehabilitation programs. Such programs call for trained personnel, either those who are regularly employed or those who volunteer their services. Third, the general public, members of the medical profession, and social workers are often unaware of the existence of facilities for rehabilitation even when they are available. As a consequence of this lack of information, some patients are pushed back into seclusion either in nursing homes, hos-

[19] Albert J. Abrams and Clark Tibbitts, "Summary and Challenge," in Wilma Donahue (ed.), *Rehabilitation of the Older Worker* (Ann Arbor: University of Michigan Press, 1953), pp. 167–68.

[20] John L. Thurston, "All Are Needed," in *Rehabilitation of the Older Worker,* p. 9.

[21] Abrams and Tibbitts, "Summary and Challenge," in *Rehabilitation of the Older Worker,* pp. 167–70.

pitals, or private homes instead of being given rehabilitative treatment. Fourth, ignorance on the part of the public as to the desirability and feasibility of rehabilitation has been an unfortunate factor. If the general taxpaying public could be made aware of the potentialities of the rehabilitation program and could be shown how much money would be saved by such a program, they would perhaps be willing to undergo higher initial expense in order to save money in the long run. Constant or almost constant nursing care, hospital or nursing home bills, or public support of the dependents is expensive. From the point of productivity, a person who is incapacitated is a drain upon the national economy in that he is a consumer but does not produce.[22]

In the past, rehabilitation has carried with it the idea that the sole purpose was to fit the individual for employment. This is a very important part of the program, but it is wider in scope than mere re-employability. The term now carries with it the idea that the individual should receive treatment and physical retraining so that he can carry out the demands of everyday living, putting as little dependence upon others as is possible. In some instances individuals are so thoroughly disabled that it takes great will power on their part and great determination by them and the trained personnel before they can relearn the most simple forms of self-care. Some people have to learn again how to feed themselves, turn themselves in bed, comb their hair, shave or do any of the other daily tasks which most people do as a matter of habit. Learning how to walk again unassisted or learning to balance oneself on braces or crutches or how to manipulate a wheelchair is often the result of weeks or months of intensive neuromuscular training. Patients who are paralyzed or those who have advanced cases of arthritis require long periods of intensive retraining before they can care for themselves.

It is important that retraining begin as soon as possible after the disability has occurred. Frequently one disability

[22] The Conference Board, "Conference Board Hearing on Medical Aspects of Rehabilitation," in *Rehabilitation of the Older Worker*, p. 38.

may bring on another and the longer a patient is disabled and completely dependent upon others, the more he becomes accustomed to his condition and depends upon others for the satisfaction of his daily needs. Those who become blind can learn how to live relatively normal lives and with the help of seeing-eye dogs have been able to take their places in the industrial, professional, and business world. Records are replete with cases where those who have lost their limbs or the use of limbs through disease or injury have found employment in competition with those who have full use of their extremities. It has been said that very few people are physically fit for all types of employment; that is, almost all of us are physically disabled for some types of work. On the other hand, almost no one is disabled for all kinds of work.[23]

One of the major hurdles to be overcome after the patient has been rehabilitated and retrained for work is to educate employers to hire the rehabilitated worker. Part of the difficulty encountered here is the attitude the employer holds toward handicapped workers, especially those who come into contact with the public. In special reference to the disabled older workers there is a double hurdle to overcome. It was seen in Chapter 6 that many employers do not want to hire older workers. If an older person is also one who has a physical handicap it is much more difficult for him to find employment.

The type of employment which a rehabilitated and retrained person should seek depends upon a great many factors.[24] Questions pertaining to his interests and abilities should be answered. Also it is of no avail that a person is trained to take a particular type of work if the employer will not hire him or if there are no jobs available. The whole problem boils down to one of preparing the man for the job and at the same time making jobs available for those who have been retrained.

[23] Thurston, "All Are Needed," in *Rehabilitation of the Older Worker,* p. 9.
[24] The Conference Board, "Conference Board Hearing on Employment and Placement," in *Rehabilitation of the Older Worker,* pp. 80–103.

One approach is to have community-sponsored sheltered workshops. These shops, where they are found, are so organized that the rehabilitated person can start working under favorable physical surroundings. Special seats, special attachments on machines, special tools, longer rest periods, and shorter work days are provided so that the worker can gradually build up tolerance for work. If the workshops are sponsored by the community, as many are, it is not necessary that they show a financial profit at the end of the month. Their primary purpose is not to make money but to fit people to return to gainful competitive employment as well as to offer employment to those for whom there is no hope of ever re-entering competitive employment. Sheltered workshops should serve as "dead-end" enterprises for those who are incapable of competitive work and as way-steps for those who can return to regular employment.

When the worker in a sheltered shop has built up tolerance to work he can return to the "open market." There are several alternatives open to him. First, he can seek employment in industry on the same terms that other workers do. Here, of course, there is opposition from the employer. In addition, many placement services do not have staff members who are adept at placing handicapped workers. It has been suggested that legislation can be enacted to require employers to hire a certain percentage of their laborers from those over 65 years of age or from those who are rehabilitated.

Whether it is a practical approach to have an anti-discriminatory law for the benefit of the rehabilitated is a question which deserves further consideration. In some instances rehabilitated workers have gone on a split shift; that is, two rehabilitated workers each take four hours of an eight-hour shift. Generally arrangements for split shifts are made informally between management and labor. A second course open to the rehabilitated person is self-employment. As a matter of fact this might seem to be the best solution to the problem. Small business concerns need capital to begin operation and generally competition is keen. Where the local, state, or federal government offers semi-monopolies for the rehabilitated, the business might be more likely to succeed. Such semi-monopolies include newsstands, snack bars, or soft-drink stands in local, state or federal buildings and other government-controlled property. Otherwise self-employment may turn out to be a snare and delusion with the handicapped person not having adequate income to support himself. Self-employment has been used in frequent instances as a rather poor "out" for the handicapped simply because they were either inadequately trained for industrial jobs or because they were unable to find employers who would hire them.

Finally, there are those who will never be rehabilitated to the extent that they can seek employment outside the sheltered workshop or their own homes. The workshop can serve as an end in itself for these people. At the present, laws of most states discourage work for the homebound. These laws were passed largely to curtail the "sweat shop" aspect of home employment of an earlier time. There is some indication that these laws should be reviewed and revised so as to enable the homebound to do some kind of work in their own homes under conditions that do not smack of exploitation. Any revision of such restrictive laws would have to be carefully drawn to safeguard the health of the worker and at the same time make home employment economically feasible for him.

The whole question of rehabilitation and re-employment of older, physically disabled persons is one calling for the cooperation of the individual, the employers, and the entire community. Without the cooperation of any one of these parties involved, little progress can be made. In the meanwhile some general hospitals and the Veterans Administration hospitals have met with marked success with a limited number of long-term patients. Patients classified as hopeless, bedfast, and helpless have been trained to care for themselves at least partially. Where these people could return home and not be a constant burden on their families, the financial strain has been somewhat reduced. Where the patients have learned to live relatively normal lives, resume family living, and obtain work, much hardship has been eliminated. Any person who is rehabilitated more than pays for the cost of his rehabilitation in taxes he later pays as an employed member of society. How much money is saved and how much society benefits from the rehabilitation of one worker, no one can calculate.

Summary

As people grow older they develop certain physical characteristics that mark them as being "old." The process of aging apparently can be slowed down by the effort of the individual to maintain a youthful appearance and a youthful attitude. Proper diet in old age helps to prolong life and make for a healthier life. In spite of all that has been done to improve the health of people as they enter old age and to prevent chronic illness, there is a great amount of chronic illness or long-term disability among the aged. Many of the aged who suffer from chronic diseases can be rehabilitated to some extent. Two of the primary reasons rehabilitation has not proceeded further than it has are the lack of adequate funds to expand the program and lack of trained personnel to do the work of rehabilitating. Part of the difficulty springs from ignorance on the part of the public, for the public is generally unaware that there is such a thing as a rehabilitation program. Taxpayers ordinarily do not want their money to go for something they do not know about or do not understand. Yet if more money were available, more workers could be found to carry out the program.

Some of the people who have been rehabilitated can do no more than learn how to care for their own physical needs; others who have been classified as permanently and totally disabled have been restored to useful lives as employees and as members of their own homes and society. Only the future will tell to what extent our society will improve the program of rehabilitation to refit the chronically ill and those with long-term disabilities to resume a functioning place in society.

15

Psychosocial Characteristics
of the Aged

For the sake of analysis it is necessary that these chapters relating to the characteristics of aging deal with each aspect separately. At the risk of overemphasis it should be made clear that the individual, regardless of his age, is a functioning whole, not a series of compartmentalized characteristics. In dealing with some of the physical characteristics in preceding chapters it was noted that the physical condition of the person might influence his emotional, intellectual, and social attitude and characteristics. Likewise, these characteristics influence each other as well as the physical characteristics.

Because of this complexity it is difficult or virtually impossible to analyze a person's behavior in terms of any one aspect of his total personality. When an older person scores low on an intelligence test, it is hard to know to what factors the low score can be attributed. The easiest answer would be that he has a low level of intelligence. That, however, would not answer the question as to whether his score at the age of 65 was lower than it would have been at 45 or 25. Was the low score due to an inadequate motivation while taking the test? to unfamiliarity with the testing device? to the fact that he believed he was not capable of scoring high and hence did not think there was any use in exerting himself? Social adjustment enters the picture when it is remembered that the common belief on the part of both young and old is that older people do not learn well, that they forget soon, and that they are not as intelligent as they once were.

The idea is sometimes expressed that older people should "take a back seat" and let the younger generation "have a go at it." Where this is the accepted belief, older people might intentionally not do well. The physical condition of the person may well influence his score on intelligence tests as well as his score as far as emotional adjustment is concerned.

Mental ability of the aged

Various tests have been devised by psychologists to test the intelligence of the population. It is conceded that there is no way known at the present time to test the innate or in-born ability of a person. The tests which are in current use attempt as nearly as possible to eliminate the environmental factors. Some tests succeed more nearly than others along this line. Older people have been given these tests in an attempt to find out whether their level of intelligence has changed over the years. More often, however, the tests have tried to determine whether the level of intelligence is higher among the young than among the old.

The only way to find out whether an individual's test intelligence (that which is tested by intelligence tests) has increased or decreased is to test the same person over a period of years with comparable tests, then compare the score results of the tests.[1] This type of "longitudinal test" has not been given often because of the relatively short time people have been interested in this particular aspect of test results. It would be rather difficult to carry out successive tests because of the difficulties involved in finding subjects for them. Several such attempts have been made, but the subjects, at the time of the second tests, were not "old" in the sense that they had passed into later maturity. Many of the tests given have been administered to captive populations. Inmates of hospitals, rest homes, nursing

---

[1] Cf. Nathan W. Shock, "The Contribution of Psychology," in Milton Derber (ed.), *The Aged and Society* (Champaign, Ill.: Industrial Relations Research Association, 1950), p. 171; and Wilma T. Donahue, "Psychological Aspects of Aging," in T. Lynn Smith (ed.), *Problems of America's Aging Population* (Gainesville: University of Florida Press, 1951), pp. 55 ff.

homes, and homes for the aged quite conceivably are not a representative group of old people.

Testing and comparing the scores of younger and older people, in "cross-sectional tests," has been done more frequently than longitudinal testing. In these cross-sectional tests, if younger people score higher than the older ones, it is inferred that the intelligence level of the older people declines as they reach old age.

Drawing inferences from such test results is hazardous for several reasons. In the first place, the tester is dealing with different individuals, no two of whom are coming to the test experience in the same physical or emotional condition. No two people are ever reared in identical environments or subject to identical cultural or social conditions. Although it may be assumed that the mental outlook of younger people is, on the average, better than that of older people, it must also be kept in mind that older people, on the average, have not had the opportunity to receive as much formal or recent education as younger ones have had. Admittedly many of the intelligence tests are based to some extent on classroom learning. Many older people have never had to take tests constructed like these intelligence tests; that is, true-false, multiple-choice, and completion questions. This objective type, as contrasted to subjective or essay tests, is a relatively new testing device. Many of the intelligence tests have a time limit on them. The score of the person being tested is influenced by the amount of time it takes to complete the test. If a person has difficulty in seeing the questions, if his hand shakes as he attempts to mark the right answer, or if he is unable to hear the instructions, he is at a disadvantage. People in their advanced years are much more likely to suffer such handicaps than are younger people.

Since many of these tests are classroom oriented, the longer a person has been away from the classroom, the poorer he would score on the tests. This being the case, the younger persons could be expected to score higher (everything else being equal) than the older ones. Closely related to this factor is that of the sustained interest of the subjects in keeping up with the world of formal book-learning. People who have actively engaged in mental activities—reading, writing, and thinking—ordinarily rank higher on tests than those who have not. A college professor at the age of 65 might make a higher score than his 20-year-old student. On the other hand, the 20-year-old student would probably rank higher than a 65-year-old unskilled laborer who finished only six grades of school and confined his reading to the comic strips in the newspaper.

In addition to the variables listed here, there are quite possibly others of equal weight which would influence the result of tests given to large aggregates of people whose age and other characteristics vary to any appreciable degree. In essence, the one variable which is sought seems to be one which is most evasive. Does the innate intelligence of people decline as they reach old age, and if so, to what extent?

What the tests show

In addition to the simple intelligence tests discussed above, there is a variety of other tests designed to inquire into the learning ability of people at different age levels. Tests have been devised to test speed of learning and retention of learned items. It was indicated that many tests have been given to inquire into the question of intelligence of older as compared to younger people, but seldom have the same tests been given by different testers, and certainly no two tests have been administered under exactly the same circumstances. Almost all of the simple tests, the results of which have been described widely, show an increase in the test scores up until about the twentieth year, a gradual decline to the ages between 45 and 50, then a more rapid decline up to the eighth decade. Some results show a more gradual decline between the ages of 20 and 45 than others do; some show that beyond the age of 60 or 65 the decline is less than it has been up to that time.[2]

[2] Jeanne Gilbert, *Understanding Old Age* (New York: The Ronald Press Co., 1952), pp. 110–24.

It should be kept in mind that the results just referred to are in terms of average scores for people in the various age categories. It is an oft-repeated fact that averages hide extremes. It is not surprising to find that some of the individuals in the younger age groups rank higher than some individuals in the older age levels. The reverse is true also. On some of the tests the curve of average scores for those close to the age of 60 years is about the same as the average for those in their middle teens. In one test two groups of academic men were compared. One group of 45 men varied in age between 60 and 80 years, and the other of like number between the ages of 25 and 35. The tests given were diversified and the findings on the several tests did not prove conclusively that there were signs of psychological decline in the older group. As a matter of fact, there were more noticeable individual differences than there were differences which could be attributed to age alone. The conclusion was drawn that where the older group did decline, it was the result of disuse of the mental faculties and the construction of the test, not a psychological decline in the ability of the older persons. Age was believed to reduce the rate rather than the quality or accuracy of mental operation.[3]

In another test given to 100 "normal" people between the ages of 60 and 90 years, there was no significant difference indicated in intellectual deterioration between men and women. This study also concludes that the mental deterioration index is independent of educational influences and the original level of intelligence. This test does not indicate that there are no original differences but that there is no difference in the rate of deterioration between the classes of people tested.[4] Gilbert suggests that some older people who score high on intelligence tests may do so even though their mental ability may have deteriorated below the level which they had once attained. For instance, if a person 75 years of age has a score of 115 on any standard test there is no way of

[3] *Ibid.*, pp. 115–16.
[4] Robert J. Howell, "Sex Differences and Educational Influences on a Mental Deterioration Scale," *Journal of Gerontology*, X (April, 1955), 190–93.

knowing how much higher he would have scored if he had taken a similar test in earlier life.[5]

There are tests other than the more or less standardized intelligence tests which have been treated in the foregoing paragraphs. In the discussion of the physical conditions of the aged it was indicated that all parts of the body do not deteriorate at the same rate of speed. It is not unreasonable to assume then that the mental ability of people does not decline at the same rate in the various facets of intellectual capacity. This view is generally validated in considering the results of tests given to people of various ages. Tests have been administered to determine the amount of decline in ability to memorize and retain memorized materials, in comprehension of materials read, in vocabulary, and in judgment, reasoning, and related areas.[6] The results of these tests show a decline in ability as the individuals become older. There appears to be more rapid decline in some areas than in vocabulary and in judgment and reasoning. As far as memorization and retention of memorized material is concerned, it is a matter of common as well as scientific observation that older people have more difficulty remembering new material than they have in recalling prior experiences. Part of the inability to memorize stems from the fact that memory tests have a time limit. Inability in this area may, in part, result from slowness to grasp the new rather than from lack of ability to do so. It may be due to a lack of practice or lack of use of the power to memorize. Part of this apparent inability to learn may stem from lack of motivation. Older people may not want to learn just for the sake of learning. When older people know they are being compared with younger ones in a test situation, they may feel inferior and not try to compete, or they may be overcautious and spend more time than necessary to master the material.

[5] Cf. Gilbert, *Understanding Old Age*, pp. 122–23.
[6] Cf. Gilbert, *Understanding Old Age*, pp. 124–36; and Donahue, "Psychological Aspects of Aging," in *Problems of America's Aging Population*, pp. 57–60.

On vocabulary tests older people do not differ appreciably from younger ones. The vocabulary is one area which is used constantly throughout life. In a study of gifted adults, it was found that many intellectual functions do not decline with age and such abilities as information and word knowledge in the group tested show continuous improvement well into the later years.[7] These studies indicate that a person, regardless of his age, does not lose his ability to do the things he has always done as rapidly as he loses his ability in areas which are used infrequently.

It must be concluded that there is some slowing down of the mental processes as individuals become older. Whether this slowing down continues throughout the entire period of senescence or stops at some time in later life is not known. The speed of deterioration revealed in testing varies from individual to individual as well as with the type of test being used.

Pathological mental conditions among the aged

Toward the end of the lives of some older individuals there is a rapid acceleration in the normal physiological aging process. There seems to be the same condition present as far as the psychological is concerned. When the "normal" decline or deterioration of mental abilities is speeded up appreciably, it is classifiable as an abnormal condition. Rapid deterioration is not the only symptom of mental disease, however.

The only reliable statistics concerning the number of mentally diseased persons are those gathered by the various hospitals in this country. Naturally these figures do not include persons who are not admitted as patients to hospitals. These figures indicate the extent of mental illness in the age groups over 65 as well as the mental illness rate of the general population. Statistics show that the number and percentage of the aged admitted to hospitals for the mentally ill have increased very rapidly during the last half-

[7] Nancy Bagley and Melita Oden, "The Maintenance of Intellectual Ability in Gifted Adults," *Journal of Gerontology*, X (January, 1955), 91 ff.

century. A great deal of this increase may reflect social-cultural conditions. In the first place, at the present time there are many more hospitals and larger hospitals for the mentally ill than was the case at the turn of the century. At earlier dates the number of admissions was low because of partial lack of facilities; now more facilities are available. Because adult children know about the facilities and because there is less social stigma attached to mental illness now than in the past, they are less hesitant to commit an aged parent or relative to an institution. Some adult children have relatives committed on a slight pretext simply because a mental hospital is the "best way out" of an unpleasant situation. Another reason for the increase in number of older people in institutions for the mentally ill is that there are more old people now than ever before.[8]

In addition to these reasons for a higher commitment rate, there are sociocultural factors which make for a higher incidence of mental disturbance now than was found earlier. People who feel secure and happy do not become mentally ill with as great frequency as those who feel insecure and unhappy. Much in the current life of older people in this country leads to unhappiness and insecurity, hence to worry and perhaps eventually to mental illness. Many of these conditions have been mentioned in different connections in earlier chapters. These conditions include lack of economic security, lack of a feeling of usefulness or of a defined role, a home situation which lacks mutual love and affection, and a feeling of lack of independence and self-respect. Poor physical health is another factor which has some influence on the mental health of those approaching old age.

The following statistics indicate something of the magnitude of the problem of mental illness among those approaching old age.[9] In 1950 when persons 65 years of age and over

[8] Robert H. Felix, "Mental Health in an Aging Population," in Wilma Donahue and Clark Tibbitts (eds.), *Growing in the Older Years* (Ann Arbor: University of Michigan Press, 1951), p. 27.

[9] The Council of State Governments, *The States and Their Older Citizens* (Chicago: The Council of State Governments, 1955), pp. 75–80.

constituted 8 per cent of the total population, they constituted 25 per cent of the patients in mental hospitals. The percentage of older people admitted to hospitals varies from state to state. In Colorado one in every two patients admitted is 65 or over, while in Louisiana only one in every nine patients admitted has attained this age. A survey of 5,443 hospitals in 1953 by the American Medical Association reported 129,488 mental patients 65 and over. The total number of mental patients reported was 583,826. Thus 22.2 per cent of all patients in mental hospitals at that time were 65 years of age and over.[10] In the period between 1904 and 1950 the number of first admissions of persons 65 and over to mental hospitals increased ninefold. During this same period the number of persons of this age in the population increased only fourfold.[11] These statistics bear out the statement that those 65 and over contribute more than their proportionate share of commitments to mental hospitals.

Detailed statistics show that the rate of commitment varies a great deal from state to state. Part of this difference may be explained by faulty reporting, part by the lack of hospital facilities in some states, and part by the fact that because of differences in subcultures between states, there may be less mental illness in some than other states. In addition to these and possibly other reasons, the standards of admission may be stricter in some states than in others. Three states, California, Maine, and Missouri, have legislation which restricts admission of persons to mental hospitals. In these three states an effort is made to limit admissions to older patients who need psychiatric care. Respectively, these states set severe limitations on admitting those with "harmless mental unsoundness," those requiring only "infirmary care," and those needing "senile custodial care" only. The admission rate for each of these states is low compared to that of other states.[12]

[10] Adapted from *ibid.*, p. 151.
[11] *Ibid.*, p. 75.
[12] *Ibid.*, p. 77.

Mental hygiene and rehabilitation

Probably the best answer to the problem of mental illness, as with physical illness, is one of prevention rather than cure. If mental health of the aged is to improve, the conditions causing mental illness must also be improved. If the sociocultural environment which is unfavorable to good mental health could be altered, the incidence of mental illness would be reduced. It is likewise necessary that the physical health of those over 65 be improved to help reduce the rate of mental illness. In some instances a measure of mental health has been attained merely by providing a balanced diet or one which is fortified by vitamins.

In addition to these factors the individual, as he grows older, can by his own efforts retard the decline in mental ability by continuing to make use of the faculties he has, rather than letting them lie fallow. He can continue to learn new things even though it may take more time than formerly. Within recent years there have been a number of grandmothers and grandfathers who have gone back to college as well as older parents who have gone to college with their children. No doubt some of these people feel self-conscious sitting in a classroom full of students young enough to be their grandchildren. Without a doubt some of these older people have a hard time keeping up with the younger members of the class, although some of them have done above-average work.

Formal college education is one way to keep the mind healthy, but one need not go back to high school or college to accomplish this. Reading and studying subjects which are of interest both in one's own field and in nonrelated fields can be rewarding. This helps broaden one's perspective and from this new vantage point interesting conversations and questions can be used to learn even more. Reading to keep up with current events furnishes conversational material and is a much more stimulating subject than aches and pains. The ability to talk with some knowledge on interesting subjects instead of only on the past or oneself will help make life worthwhile for an older person. Instead of losing friends he will be much more likely to keep those he has and to gain new ones. His presence will be enjoyed and welcomed rather than shunned. This in itself will be one source of mental health. If the mind is occupied in a healthy manner good mental health is very likely to be one result. The process of remaining mentally healthy should begin early in life, long before mental deterioration sets in. Anyone who has not read anything more stimulating than the sports page for thirty years will probably find it rather difficult to accomplish much in the way of serious reading after he has entered the later years.

It has been stated that when some older people become senile their relatives use this as an excuse to have them committed to an institution for the mentally ill. To some extent this procedure is understandable. Overcrowding of three generations in small urban dwellings calls for understanding and patience on the part of all involved. If the older person is only slightly unsound mentally or is in need of senile custodial care, it is an easy way out for relatives to have the person sent to an institution. If all the older persons having only slight disorders became patients in mental institutions, the demand for such care would far exceed the number of beds available. The problem then is to attempt to balance the welfare and happiness of the home and the ability of the various levels of government to care for the aged who suffer from varying degrees of mental illness.

It would, of course, be ideal if the socioeconomic environment were to improve to the point where adult children were financially able to care for their aging parents or the parents could afford a home of their own. Further, if all environmental conditions which foster mental illness were removed and everyone was schooled in mental hygiene, fewer aged would become ill. At present this situation is far from being realized, and mental hospitals continue to be overcrowded. Part of the overcrowding is due to committing people who could get along well under custodial care. Overcrowding is also caused by the fact that overworked staff members cannot devote sufficient time and energy to rehabilitating patients who could be restored to at least a degree of mental health and normal living outside institution walls.

It was indicated that three states, California, Maine, and Missouri, are meeting the problem in part by refusing to admit as patients those who obviously do not need hospital care. Some of the programs in operation in the other states include the following.[13] New York State plans to construct a building to house 200 female seniles and to carry out experimental and specialized treatment of these patients with an eye to rehabilitating them. North Carolina has adopted a plan whereby in a period of three years nearly 500 patients are released from the mental hospitals. These patients go to live with relatives or in boarding homes which are supervised by county welfare departments. Plans for placement of the patients are made jointly by patients and social workers after consultation with members of the hospital staff and relatives or friends of the patients. A high degree of successful placement is reported. Kansas has a plan whereby older patients who do not need further care are released either to relatives or to nursing homes. If the patient needs further psychiatric treatment he can be returned to the hospital with a minimum of difficulty. Hospitals in both Kentucky and Washington report that after treatment by new drugs and electro-shock has been given, the rate of dismissal of older patients has speeded up. Some of the discharged patients in Kentucky were able to obtain full-time work after release. Group psychotherapy has been tried with some success on older patients in Norristown (Pennsylvania) State Hospital.

New York State is starting a project to establish mental hygiene clinics for treatment, rehabilitation, and prevention of mental illness among the aged. "These programs include psychiatric clinics, consultant services by psychiatric specialists, in-patient psychiatric services in general hospitals, rehabilitation services for those who have been mentally ill, and other community mental health activities." [14]

[13] *Ibid.*, pp. 77–78.
[14] *Ibid.*, p. 78.

There is encouraging evidence that membership in clubs for older adults has helped prevent mental deterioration. For instance, during a period of four years there has been no commitment to mental institutions from more than 6,000 older adult members of clubs in Minneapolis.

The following are some of the recommendations made by state study groups.[15] Aged persons who need special care, but are not mentally ill, should be cared for in private homes or foster and nursing homes under the supervision of a hospital staff. Cases should be screened carefully to determine whether the patient would be better off in an institution or in a noninstitutional setting. Rehabilitation units should be established in all mental hospitals for the purpose of returning to community life as many patients as possible. "Half-way houses" should be established to care for aged mental patients who are not ill enough to be in hospitals, yet not ready to be returned to community life. Other suggestions are for mental hygiene programs and psychiatric services which would be available outside mental hospitals. These and other services would be designed primarily for prevention of the onset of mental illnesses.

Not all mental illness can be prevented or cured. There is an indication, however, that although much has been done, still more remains to be done along the line of prevention and cure. It is encouraging that the authorities in some states see the need for an expansion of preventive and rehabilitative services for the aged who may later or have already become mentally ill.

Emotional characteristics of aging

Throughout life there are emotional needs which have to be met in order for the individual to remain well-adjusted. These needs are a combination and synthesis of biological needs (known as biological drives) and sociological needs (called secondary or derived drives). As an illustration, the biological drive to satisfy physical hunger is present in all men. However, they are not hungry for just anything which

[15] *Ibid.*, p. 80.

will satisfy that need. They are hungry specifically for food prepared and served in a particular manner. They are hungry for a rare steak or a fried egg. As individuals grow older and their roles and status positions are modified, their needs or drives are modified. A boy of seven may think his happiness depends upon receiving an electric train for Christmas. A college graduate may believe his life is not complete until he has a new automobile. On the other hand, a person of 75 may feel the need of being wanted more than he feels the need for anything else. There is always some one need or several needs, and in all cases the needs differ. They may be either on the physical, material level or on the emotional, nonmaterial level. The intensity of a drive or need and the different amounts of emphasis vary from individual to individual and within any individual from time to time. The needs of different age groups vary in degree, and probably to a much lesser extent in kind. The classic sociological breakdown of needs is that of the "four wishes" given originally by W. I. Thomas. These are the wishes for security, for recognition, for response, and for new experience.

When we think of security for older people it is usually in terms of economic security. Economic security for the aging is best obtained by maintaining income at a level commensurate with the level of living they have previously enjoyed. This is attained by keeping their jobs. It has been indicated in Chapter 5, however, that only about 40 per cent of the men over 65 are gainfully employed, and that only about 7 per cent of the women over this age are. Those who are not working must rely upon savings, pensions, social security, old-age assistance, or gifts. The average pension, or unearned income in retirement, is often not sufficiently large to enable a person to live in any degree of economic security. The knowledge that this condition exists for large numbers of older people, and the fear that it will be true for themselves, makes the approach of old age for many people a time of worry and fear. In addition to the economic security which older people need, there is a need for security within the family circle. The person must feel that he is secure as an individual member of the family group and that he is secure in having a place to live. When the feeling of security is lacking, he becomes emotionally upset and as a consequence is more subject to mental, emotional, and physical disability. These conditions in turn further rob him of whatever feeling of security may have remained to him.

All men have a desire for recognition; that is, everyone wants to be thought of as a distinct individual with a distinctive personality. Older people desire this as much as anyone else. They want to be recognized for what they are, not for what they have been. If they are deprived by the society of their worthwhile status positions they must rely for recognition on some of their past achievements. This is one explanation why so many older people tell and retell the experiences of their youth. It leads younger people to refer to older ones as "has-beens." Losing one's sense of importance as a functioning individual also causes emotional distress.

The need or wish for response is also stated as the need for love and affection. The need for love which infants and young children have has been studied rather extensively. It is concluded that if an infant is deprived of love and affection he frequently becomes a maladjusted individual. Several of the obstacles to the satisfying of their need for love which older people encounter are that their lifelong mates die, their children leave home or become primarily interested in their own families, and their long-time friends either die or move away. It becomes difficult for older people to retain their friendships and difficult to form new and abiding ones. Part of the difficulty in forming new friendships stems from the fact that there is a lack of communication between the generations. Frequently younger people hesitate to form friendships with older people for various reasons. Some older nonmarried people have attempted to satisfy their need for love or response by remarrying a person of their own age, or in the case of some men, a younger person. Our society generally frowns on these marriages or ridicules those who marry well after the prime of life has been passed. For some reason sex activity or the thought of it in older people seems repulsive or "indecent" to many younger persons.

Finally, for this analysis, there is the wish or need for new experience. It may be questioned whether older people need this as much as younger ones do. There is certainly less of the explorer in an older person than in a pre-teenage boy. To some extent younger people help to stifle this need by believing and insisting that older relatives should stay at home, that they should not travel, that they should not engage in any activities other than sedentary ones. Some of the things which older people might enjoy doing would be classified as "undignified" at their age. This is a form of social pressure which keeps older people from seeking new experiences. Another possible explanation for older people's failure to seek new experiences may be that it is the result of a stagnation beginning in some people by middle age. They are not intellectually curious and when they become older the desire to seek new experiences mentally or emotionally may have been starved to such an extent that it cannot be revived.

Attitudes of older people

Perhaps one of the most strongly held stereotypes younger people have of older ones is that older people are more conservative than younger ones. This usually implies that older people are extremely conservative in all matters and that younger ones are liberal in all matters. Common sense should belie the truth of these stereotypes. A more reasonable statement is that in some areas some older people are more conservative than some young people or that some people are more conservative in some areas than others are. In the first place, attitudes are the products of past experiences. They are influenced by what has been encountered and the persons with whom an individual has had contact. One important thing to remember concerning the conservatism of older people is that most of them have not received as much formal education as most younger people have. Generally less well-educated persons tend to be more conservative along certain lines than the better educated ones.

One should also ask a further question: conservative in what respect? There are innumerable areas in which a person may be conservative. Some of these areas are physical activity, clothing and personal appearance, personal behavior in public, and economic, political, religious and moral attitudes. In the first place, physical activities are governed to a great extent by one's physical condition plus the knowledge of consequences of certain acts. A seven-year-old boy may jump off the roof with an umbrella to see what would happen. An older person does not have to experience the jump (or perhaps he did as a child) to be able to imagine the consequences of such action. In this area we may well assume that most older people are conservative. However, some older men have been known to be anything but conservative in shoveling snow from driveways, patching roofs, or climbing unsteady ladders.

The matter of conservatism in attire is not solely one of selecting subdued colors or styles. This may be determined in part by the style of clothing which is available and comfortable. In this area there are some customs or social pressure at work, for older people are sometimes criticized for dressing as young people do. Personal behavior is the product of past experiences. As they grow older most people try to keep from attracting unfavorable attention to themselves. Children have this impressed upon them beginning early in life, primarily because their parents do not want attention drawn to themselves via their misbehaving children.

There is a vast array of possible attitudes which may be held toward any one or all of the many areas of the economic, political, religious, and moral institutions. It is possible for one individual to be outspokenly in favor of a free world market and equally opposed to farm price supports. It is possible for the same person to have very liberal ideas concerning the rehabilitation of juvenile delinquents and to be very conservative in the area of intergroup relations. A man of 65 may think it is perfectly proper for him to take a drink of whiskey but believe it is morally wrong for his adolescent daughter or the preacher to do the same thing. A person may claim not to believe in the existence of a heaven or hell, yet object when women fail to wear hats in church.

It becomes apparent that it is a hazardous practice to classify older people as conservative. Conservatism is a relative matter, what may be liberal in a Southern senator may be considered conservative in a Northern senator. What is liberal in a Democrat may be conservative in a Socialist. Indeed, the further the subject is pursued the more complex it becomes. The essence of the concept of conservatism is to conserve. Those who seek to maintain the status quo are conservatives and their position is one of seeking to conserve or hold what they have. People who are satisfied with what they have and with the social, moral, political and economic order wish to keep these things as they are. If they feel they have lost money, power, or prestige as the cultural situation has been modified, they may seek to re-establish things as they once were. That is, they want to re-establish the old order. Those who would return to a former order are sometimes known as reactionaries. A third group may feel neither the past nor the present yields as much to them in money, power, or prestige as some new untried conditions would yield. These people would like to modify or replace the present system with something new. These people are called either liberals or radicals according to the amount and extent of change they advocate.

As long as older people are relatively content with what they have and with the positions they occupy in society they will tend to be conservative. Those who believe they have lost by changing conditions will be reactionaries and want to return to the "good old days" in one way or another. Those who believe they will profit by change in one area or another will be liberal or radical. The Townsend Plan, which called for $200 per month in pensions for older people, attracted many followers. Older people with little or no economic security were led to believe the plan offered something which no other plan offered. To a lesser degree the Social Security Act which received the approval of older people is still considered "radical" by some. In the final analysis this program was enacted and has been revised because of real or imagined pressure by older people or at the very least with the interest of the older citizens in mind. Certainly, at its enactment the Social Security Act passed with little congressional opposition.

Politically, socially, economically, and morally, older people, like others, resist change if they feel they will lose by it. Perhaps the older people become the more they feel change per se is "bad" because they fear that loss will be incurred. Perhaps they resist change because they have suffered and lost to some extent by changes which have occurred.

One fear which some people in this country express is that those over 60 or 65 will at some later time constitute a powerful political "party," one strong bloc to hold the balance of power. They fear either that this "party" of older voters would be so conservative that needed legislation and social action plans would fail to pass or that new and radical and therefore impractical legislation would be introduced by this "party." There is no way of looking into the future to see whether either of these things will come to pass. It is possible, however, to make some assumptions on the subject.

First, if the analysis of conservatism and liberalism presented is accurate, it can be assumed that older people who are happy with their lot will hesitate to accept any rapid change, much less formulate any radical departure from the status quo. If they feel that change would benefit them, they can be moved to change. Second, and probably most important, old people are not alike. Each older person is an individual in his own right, each has a mind of his own, and by and large older people, like others, will vote and act according to the way they interpret the situation. All old people will vote for one person or one act only when they are all convinced they will get the most for themselves and their own interests. It would be a rather unusual situation which would elicit this type of mass response. If society wanted to forestall the possibility of bloc voting by the aged, it could do so by a continuing educational program for the aged and by taking any other steps necessary to assure older people of economic, physical, and social security in their declining years.

Personal adjustment of the aging

The factors which have been discussed in both this and the preceding chapter, plus other factors, help or hinder the adjustment older people make to their own old age and to the social environment. Personal adjustment is a subjective situation and the estimate of good or poor adjustment varies a great deal from one individual to another. Perhaps the best measure and the easiest method of testing is to have the person himself take a test and answer questions which are designed to determine whether he thinks he is well adjusted or not. A questionnaire "Your Activities and Attitudes" prepared by the University of Chicago is such a test.[16] It has been used widely both by the University of Chicago personnel and by others in testing self-attitudes of adjustment of older people. These inventories have been prepared in pamphlet form. Included are questions relating to early life, health, family, friends, clubs and organizations, past employment, economic security, religion, and similar topics. The questions dealing with attitudes, feelings, and beliefs are set up on a scale of agree-disagree or a scale eliciting the answers much, some, little, or none.

These personal adjustment tests show many facets of a person's life, both past and present, which make for a good or poor adjustment in old age. They show that the adjustment of an individual is the function of many variables and that for a person one factor may be of much greater significance than another. For example, it has been revealed that there is a difference in adjustment levels between those who

[16] Ruth S. Cavan, et al., Personal Adjustment in Old Age (Chicago: Social Research Associates, 1941), Appendices A and G.

are working and those who are not; between those who rate themselves high in health and those who rate themselves low; between those who are engaged in several as opposed to few activities; between those who read the Bible and attend church and those who do not; between those who believe their early life was a happy, well-adjusted one and those who believe otherwise; and between those who feel that they are still useful and those who do not. The first item in each of the above series receives a higher personal adjustment score than the second. It is possible for a person to rate high in some areas and low in others or for him to fall at almost any point along the continuum from good to poor adjustment.

In a study of 100 subjects representing a cross section of older people it was concluded that good family relationships in youth almost guarantee happiness in old age.[17] Active social participation in the younger years was also found to be an important factor in the happiness of the subjects. In another study of workers and nonworkers in the Moosehaven community in Florida, it is concluded that workers attained a higher adjustment score than did nonworkers.[18] When self-ratings on health were standardized into three categories, good, fair, and poor, for workers and nonworkers, both workers and nonworkers reporting good health scored higher on the adjustment attitude inventory than those who rated themselves as having poor health. The workers scored higher on the subclasses of the inventory dealing with health, feeling of usefulness, and happiness. The author concludes that work is an important factor in the personal adjustment of the older individual. A study of retired school teachers in Chicago showed that family, friendships, and club activities were more important in the adjustment of retired women than men and that some type of work activity was the most important factor in the adjustment of retired male teachers.[19]

[17] Ruth Albrecht, "The Social Roles of Old People," *Journal of Gerontology*, VI (April, 1951), 138–45.

[18] Robert W. Kleemeier, "The Effect of a Work Program on Adjustment Attitudes in an Aged Population," *Journal of Gerontology*, VI (October, 1951), 372–79.

[19] Joseph H. Britton, "The Personal Adjustment of Retired School Teachers," *Journal of Gerontology*, VIII (July, 1953), 333–38.

In a personal adjustment inventory of institutionalized (nursing home residents) and noninstitutionalized older people in Austin, Texas, noninstitutionalized older people had a higher adjustment level than the institutionalized ones.[20] The feeling of usefulness was the most important factor in both groups, with the control group rating higher. The next most important factor found in this survey was that of past adjustment in life. This factor was significant not only between the two samples but within each sample. The adjustment level was higher for the control group than for the nursing home sample in frequency of contacts with friends and young people; for those having more activities than for those having few; and for those who read the Bible frequently and attended church than for those who did not. The author believes people who have a poor adjustment level become nursing home patients rather than that living in a nursing home lowers the personal adjustment level.

A somewhat different approach is employed by another author in measuring the factor of church membership and personal adjustment in old age.[21] The factors of age, nativity, place of residence, years of schooling, marital and family status, self-rating in health, and participation in social organizations and self-ratings on happiness were held constant, with the factor of church membership or nonmembership as the variable. This test showed no significant difference in the adjustment in old age between members and nonmembers. Although similar studies show that there is a significant difference in the personal adjustment level of members and nonmembers, it was the author's opinion that if other variables were held constant no difference would appear. He believed that nominal church members are not influenced in their personal lives to a greater degree than nonmembers are because so many of the nonmembers have at one time been members. His study revealed no significant differences in

[20] F. G. Scott, "Factors in the Personal Adjustment of Institutionalized and Noninstitutionalized Aged," *American Sociological Review*, XX (October, 1955), 538–46.

[21] D. O. Mobery, "Church Membership and Personal Adjustment in Old Age," *Journal of Gerontology*, VIII (April, 1953), 207–11.

the level of adjustment between long-time members and those who had never held church membership.

Perhaps this last study points up the technique which could be used to determine just how much each one of the variables influences the personal adjustment level of older people. This procedure was followed in the above-mentioned study by pairing individuals who were similar in all but one category and measuring the influence of that category on their adjustment scale. If enough cases are tested so there will be a sufficient number of pairs in each category, they can be tested in this manner. One pitfall should be guarded against. Although there may be a high correlation between one subscore and the total adjustment score, a cause-effect relationship cannot be assumed to be present. If a person rates himself high on health and receives a high adjustment score, the latter may not necessarily be a result of the former. As a matter of fact, it may be the other way around. If a person is well adjusted he may rate himself high in health, whereas the clinical record of health, which is more objective, may be very low. This points up the idea that it is how a person feels, his inner organization, and his total orientation which make the difference between a high and low level of adjustment. If this line of reasoning is valid, a person's adjustment level depends more on his past life experiences than on any immediate factor or even on any combination of factors. As was mentioned above some studies on the subject bear out this contention.

Summary

This chapter has reviewed briefly some of the results of intelligence tests given to older people. In studying the validity of intelligence tests, both those of a general nature and those designed to test memory and retention, many variables have to be considered. Results differ when the tests are not administered in the same way, and the score made by an individual may vary depending upon how he feels physically and emotionally and upon the extent to which he is motivated. The general conclusions to be drawn are that a person ranks higher in areas with which he is familiar and in areas which he uses frequently than he does in other areas. These test results are usually given in terms of averages which hide the range of individual scores. Generally older people make lower scores than younger ones do, and scores seem to become lower gradually up to middle age and then drop off more rapidly.

Mental illness is much more prevalent among people over 65 than among the rest of the population. Various states are starting programs of prevention of mental illness and rehabilitation of aged who are mentally ill. As is the case with physical illness, prevention seems to be more desirable than cure.

Every person has a need for security, recognition, response, and new experience. These needs vary in intensity according to a person's age, but if they are not satisfied in some measure, the person becomes maladjusted emotionally. A person's attitudes are conservative or not, depending upon how well satisfied he is with his environment and upon his values and early life. Perhaps the attitudes of older persons are even more varied than those of younger people because older people have had more contacts from which attitudes are formed.

The level of personal adjustment has been the subject of numerous tests. Although there are many factors which make for or against good personal adjustment in old age, these tests generally conclude that good adjustment in old age is the result of good adjustment throughout life. A sense of usefulness, worthwhile activities, and good health are also positive factors which help insure good social adjustment in the later years. By and large, findings of tests discussed in this chapter bear out the conclusion that what a person is in old age is largely the result of what his life before the onset of old age has been. No one undergoes a complete transformation on his sixty-fifth birthday, but he continues to be what he has always been—a product of his past experiences.

Part V

SOCIETY AND ITS AGING
POPULATION

16

Homes for the Aged

One of the deep-seated traditions in this country is that adult children will care for their aged parents when necessary. Part of this care includes housing. With the change from rural to urban living and the greater emphasis on a higher level of living, two pertinent changes have taken place. First, there is a higher proportion of home ownership among the older age categories which makes it increasingly less necessary for old people to have to reside with their relatives. Second, because of the desire of younger people to maintain a high level of living, it is less desirable for them to have to house and help support a parent or parents. Even though there are many homes with four and five bedrooms, there has been a definite trend, especially in the middle price range of housing, toward smaller houses with two or three bedrooms. Bringing another adult into such relatively cramped living quarters imposes a hardship on all three generations. Both parent and grandparent generations seem to recognize some of the unhappy consequences of this type of arrangement.

There is some difference of opinion on the part of those who deal with the problem of housing the aged. The first question is whether or not a special type of house or apartment is needed for older people. The second is concerned with the ecological location of houses or apartments for the aged; whether the aged should be segregated or not. Finally, there is a general question which enters into the discussion of housing. How should new housing units be financed, or who should be responsible for the construction of new units or the renovation of old ones? The general impression is that private industry can furnish housing for certain income categories;

yet many people, especially the aged, cannot afford to pay the purchase or rent price asked by private industry. As will be indicated below, the inability on the one hand of private enterprise to furnish low rent dwellings, and the inability on the other of many older people to pay the price asked for privately constructed dwellings poses a dilemma. Any discussion of housing for the aged might well be approached from the point of view of how the housing is to be financed—by private industry, by churches or philanthropic organizations, by direct governmental subsidy to private builders, or by actual governmental construction. Another approach to the question is that of viewing the dwelling through the financial, physical, and emotional needs of the older person involved.

Household relationships of the aged

Most of the aged in this country live in households; that is, in single dwelling units or apartments. In 1950, 94 per cent of all men and 95 per cent of all women over 65 lived in households.[1] Of this category, 77 per cent of the men and 62 per cent of the women lived in their own households, either with their spouses, with a relative other than spouse, with a nonrelative, or alone. Six per cent of the men and 5 per cent of the women lived in quasi-households, that is, in institutions, transient hotels, rooming houses, or similar dwellings. In other words, 80 per cent of the men and 71 per cent of the women lived in families with one or more relatives present, while 20 per cent of the men and 29 per cent of the women did not live in families. In 1952 the Bureau of the Census interviewed persons aged 65 and over in 15,000 households in forty-two states. Findings of this survey are presented in Table 24. This information indicates that nonmarried men and women have to rely on their children for housing more often than married couples do. Nonmarried women are more dependent upon their children than are nonmarried men. The above information does not in-

[1] Adapted from Joint Committee on Railroad Retirement Legislation, *Retirement Policies and the Railroad Retirement System,* Part II (Washington, D.C.: 1953), pp. 30–32.

dicate what proportion of either the couples or nonmarried elders have to live in institutions or boarding homes.

Information on housing conditions of the aged indicates that they are in a relatively good situation in contrast to the general population. The aged have lower housing costs,

TABLE 24

Living Arrangements of Older People, 1952
Percentage Distribution

Living or Not Living with Children	Couples	Widowed, Single, Divorced, and Separated	
		Males	Females
Not living with children	74.1%	69.3%	54.7%
Living with children	25.9%	30.7%	45.3%
Older person head	22.6%	11.0%	15.9%
Adult child head	3.3%	19.7%	29.4%

SOURCE: Adapted from: Peter O. Steiner and Robert Dorfman, *The Economic Status of the Aged* (Berkeley: University of California Press, 1957), p. 22.

because at least 68 per cent of the nonfarm aged own their own homes. A smaller percentage of the aged owners have mortgages to be paid off than has the nonfarm population of all ages. Relatively few of the aged are in the process of buying a home or contemplating such a step. Those who pay rent usually pay less than other nonfarm families pay. In addition to these factors, there is less overcrowding in the homes of older people than in the homes of the general nonfarm population. This is so because as parents grow older their children leave home. Older heads who rent homes and apartments find it unnecessary to rent large units. Generally small units cost less to buy or to rent than large ones. Another factor in lower rent expenditures is that many older people who rent cannot afford to pay higher rent than they do. There is often no alternative as far as they are concerned—a low rent unit or none at all. These apparently favorable housing circumstances can be accounted for when one considers that home ownership increases with age. The older a person becomes the more chance he has had to save money to buy a home of his own and to own it mortgage free.

On the negative side of the picture, neither home ownership nor low rent inevitably means adequate housing. Statistics show that housing for the aged in nonfarm areas is somewhat worse than for the rest of the population. A slightly larger percentage of the aged than of the general nonfarm population is living in units which are either dilapidated or in need of major repairs. Because of lower income and smaller families more older people are living in old homes in old neighborhoods. A larger percentage of the homes of the older people lack proper sanitary facilities as well.

Individual housing units

Basically there are two aspects of the problem of housing older people. The first is to make available to the aged who are financially and physically able to provide for themselves housing which conforms to modern standards of decency and comfort. This, it is thought, should be done within a social environment where the inhabitants will continue to be a functioning part of the larger community. The second is to provide housing for those who are financially and physically incapable of providing for themselves. Housing for this category of the aged should also conform to generally accepted standards of comfort, decency, and adequacy. It is with these problems and criteria that the remainder of the chapter will be concerned. Some evaluation will be made of past and present efforts as well as projected plans which seek to meet the needs of the aged in this important area of their lives.

Living with Relatives. The few studies which have been made on the subject indicate that older people who live with relatives ordinarily would prefer not to. There seem to be two primary reasons why either single individuals or aged couples live in the same household with relatives. The first of these is related to economic considerations; that is, the older person is not financially able to have a home or rent a place in which to live. Second is the matter of poor health. Even if the older person could afford a separate unit he would not be able to take care of himself or the property. In the final analysis the matter of money is also involved here, for if there were enough money available he could afford a nurse, housekeeper, or companion.

In an unpublished report quoted by Donahue[2] it was found that older people in Los Angeles County, California, gave the following reasons for not wanting to live with other members of their families. They were unhappy because of overcrowding, annoyances with small children in the home, and unpleasant interpersonal relations with others in the same home. Whether because of the actual facts of the matter or merely through the subjective belief on the part of the older people, they felt they were not wanted in the home, that they were in the way, or that either physically or financially they were a burden on the family.

One possibility has been suggested to improve the situation of older people living with relatives. This is the addition, where financially possible, of either an attached or detached subunit. The matter of happiness and contentment of the aged as far as housing is concerned is not so much a matter of the quality of the physical surroundings as of the psychological atmosphere.[3] If it were possible either in the light of zoning laws or from a financial standpoint to build a free-standing subunit or an attached room and bath to the existing house, many of the problems involved in having three generations under the same roof would be removed. The new unit could be attached by a covered walkway for easy access and be provided with a house telephone for easy communication. The older person would be largely independent to do as he pleased, yet both the older person and the younger family would know that assistance was readily

[2] Quoted in Wilma Donahue, "Where and How Older People Wish to Live," in Wilma Donahue (ed.), *Housing the Aging* (Ann Arbor: University of Michigan Press, 1954), p. 29.

[3] E. Everett Ashley III, "Where and How Older People Live Today," in *Housing the Aging*, p. 18.

available if necessary.[4] Where such an arrangement is possible, certain facilities such as a common living room, dining room, and kitchen might work out to the satisfaction of all concerned. In instances where the sub-dwelling is too far from the main house the older person might feel he had been relegated to the "dog house" and might be unhappy with the arrangement. Experiments in England with subunits for older people seem to have worked well.

Single-Dwelling Units for the Aged. There are as many as 1.4 million single individuals in urban areas over the age of 65 who maintain their own separate households. The assumption can be made that most of these older people as well as aged husband-wife families prefer adequate, comfortable quarters suited to their needs. On the basis of this assumption there are three categories of older people for whom new individual houses are needed. First are those who live in their own homes which are either too large or are inconvenient or dilapidated. Second are those who live in rented homes or apartments which are unsuited to their needs. Third are those who live with relatives. There are three considerations that make the ideal of universal individual ownership or tenancy for the aged difficult to attain. These are financial inability to purchase their own homes, physical or mental inability to live alone or with another aged person, and the individual desire to live with relatives or in a congregate housing situation.

No doubt there is a large number of older people who could sell their own uncomfortable or overlarge homes and buy smaller, more comfortable ones. Often, however, this entails leaving the home and neighborhood where they have lived for many years and to which they have sentimental attachments. On the other hand, probably many of those who are willing to move are financially unable to do so. It has been indicated that the income of most of the aged in this country is very low. In 1954, 66.6 per cent of those aged 65 and over had incomes of less than $1,000 per year, while 81.9

[4] Cf. Robert T. Monroe, "Needs and Problems," in *Housing the Aging*, pp. 107–15.

per cent had less than $2,000 per year. Only 3.6 per cent of those 65 years of age and older had incomes of $5,000 or more during 1954.[5]

As a rule private industry has not been able to construct housing within the reach of people with such low incomes. Probably private industry does not discriminate against old people as such. Rather the discrimination—if it can be called that—is directed against poor people, and a large number of the aged are poor. Much of the money ordinarily used to finance private housing is obtained from banks and building and loan corporations. People who handle and invest this money want to be sure they are not investing it in doubtful projects. A good deal of the investment money held in trust by these banks and corporations represents a substantial part of the savings of people who make such investments. About 70 per cent of all the home mortgage lending "is conducted with funds of people other than those making the loans."[6] Hence one of the policies of the lending organization is to be conservative. Lending institutions do not want to make loans which would work a hardship on borrowers. That is, they do not want to lend money which cannot be repaid or on terms which would involve too great a sacrifice on the part of the borrowers.[7]

In a survey made concerning the policies of mortgage lending institutions, three generalizations were reached.[8] First, the institution will make the loan if it can see the possibility that it will be repaid. It can be paid either by regular payments from the income of the borrower or his family, by the pledge of life insurance written on the borrower, or by another person, preferably a relative, who is willing to cosign the note with the borrower. Second, as a general rule these institutions require a larger proportion of the total cost of the home to be made in the down payment

[5] Lenore A. Epstein, "Money Income Position of the Aged, 1948 to 1955," *Social Security Bulletin*, XIX (April, 1956), 9.

[6] Norman Strunk, "Financing Homes for Owner Occupancy," in *Housing the Aging*, p. 159.

[7] *Ibid.*, pp. 159–60.

[8] *Ibid.*, pp. 161–62.

so that monthly payments are smaller and the balance can be paid off in a relatively short time. An effort is made to keep monthly payments on the loans to as small a proportion of income as is possible. This is done because of the greater probability of illness and because there is little likelihood of an increase in the income of the older borrower. Third, most loan companies like to have the loan payment schedule arranged so that the loan will be paid off by the time the borrower reaches his seventieth or, at the latest, his seventy-fifth birthday. If such a schedule cannot be arranged, the lenders look for some other source of money to retire the loan, either a cosigner or the pledge of life insurance.

In the survey it was found that only about 5 per cent of the current lending volume goes to people who are 60 years of age or over. Between 2 and 3 per cent of the loans were made to people over the age of 65. On the other hand, about 16 per cent of current lending is to borrowers 50 years of age or over.[9] This information indicates that many of the older people who would like to borrow money to buy their own homes have difficulty doing so. This is true because of their inability to meet either the down payment or the amount of the monthly payments. Financial difficulties faced by older would-be borrowers indicate that if a person wants to become a home owner it is easier for him to accomplish this goal if he sets out to do so before he reaches the age of 60.

Ryderwood, A Special Community. One project which might set the stage for home ownership by the aging is a village of single dwelling units to be occupied and serviced by the aging. This is a private project and, it should be noted, does not embody the idea of integrating older people into a community composed of families of all ages. Rather this community tends to follow the concept of voluntary segregation. In this connection it should be recalled that the aging have many and diverse tastes and desires. It is quite possible to find many aged in two-person families who prefer to live in communities composed only of older persons.

[9] *Ibid.,* p. 160.

The town of Ryderwood, Washington, was built as a lumber town during the 1920's. As the timber was cut out the town ceased to serve its purpose and was sold to a group of businessmen for $90,000. In April, 1953, these men organized Senior Estates, Inc., as a business venture to sell individual homes to retired men. The businessmen have renovated and reconditioned 183 of the 400 houses and have put them up for sale. Sales of the houses are limited to those who have a legitimate retirement income of between $135 and $200 per month. It was felt that individuals in this retirement income bracket would be in need of housing of this type. Anyone with an income of less than $135 could not afford the price of a house, and those with an income of more than $200 were considered too well off to qualify. In mid-October 1953, 44 homes had been sold and 35 were occupied. The homes are sold on the following basis: four-room homes at $2,500 with a $200 down payment and $20 per month installment; five-room homes for $3,000 with a $250 down payment and $25 per month installment; and six-room homes for $3,500 with a $300 down payment and $30 per month installment. The homes are sold on nonassignable contracts and the monthly payments are figured to include 6 per cent interest. The character of the town is to be preserved by not giving purchasers unlimited resale rights. In the event a purchaser dies or moves, Senior Estates, Inc., will buy back the property. It may be sold directly to a new purchaser if he meets the age and financial requirements of the corporation.

The heavy work of renovating was done by the corporation; the lighter work such as interior decorating was left to the individual purchasers to do. It was felt that individual tastes in matters such as colors would be more nearly suited than if the work were done on a wholesale basis. Community businesses are to be operated by the retired residents. In October, 1953, these citizens had in operation a grocery store, garage, filling station, appliance shop, and barbershop. Another resident has set up a furniture shop in which he makes furniture to order. Still another has started making and marketing small toy ducks. Senior Estates, Inc., believes that there is plenty of opportunity for other retired residents to set up small business enterprises in the town. Outsiders are discouraged from coming in to do so. The nearest doctor is thirteen miles away, but he is planning to open a clinic staffed by a registered nurse. He would spend one day each week in the community and make calls to people at any time they were required. There is a community building which contains meeting rooms and a theatre with a seating capacity of 150. So far, community singing and games have been organized. If this project is a success from the point of view of the financial backers and the individual inhabitants, it may well set the pace for similar ventures elsewhere.[10]

Trailer Park Living. Probably the least expensive way of maintaining one's private residence is by buying a trailer and parking it in a well-organized trailer park. The total cash outlay for such housing is much less than for the average home. One retains at least a semblance of mobility. Utilities and park rent are at near minimum amounts. The value of trailers does not depreciate as rapidly as that of automobiles and it is relatively easy to sell or buy a second-hand trailer. One has a wide choice as to where he will locate and if he does not like his surroundings he can move with little difficulty. In the more permanent camps in mild climates, some of these trailer villages are reserved for older retired people. Many of the trailerites build sun porches or sheds (called cabanas by the residents) onto the trailers for additional closed-in living quarters. Small yards can be planted in shrubs or flowers for purposes of beautification. Although this solution to the housing shortage would not have equal appeal to all of the older citizens, there is reason to believe that the number of oldsters who will spend their retirement years in such "homes" will continue to increase in the years to come.[11] Some of these trailer camps have recreation

---

[10] Cf. "Ryderwood, Wash., A Thriving Community for Retired Workers," *Aging* No. 9 (January, 1954), 2–3.

[11] R. M. Beall, "Trailer-Living," in T. Lynn Smith (ed.), *Living in the Later Years* (Gainesville: University of Florida Press, 1952), pp. 53–55.

halls or similar places where the residents can gather en masse in inclement weather or at night for fun and games.

In one study of trailer living it was found that in general the inhabitants liked living in retirement trailer parks.[12] The first reason given by the respondents was that such living allowed for more association or sociability. The trailerites tend to have the feeling of homogeneity of social class; they are thrown into contact with each other in the recreation center, bath house, and laundry. As much of their living is out of doors, they see a great deal of each other and become better acquainted than if they stayed indoors, as is often the case in conventional homes. A second reason advanced, which was almost as important, was that there was a high degree of mutuality. The presence of other older retired persons made them feel "at home." Mutual aid also played a part in this feeling. Finally and of less importance was the feeling that there was less disturbance in a park reserved for retired people than in a park open to people of all ages. Other reasons given for liking trailer park living in general were its economy and mobility and the smaller amount of work and worry involved.

On the average, parks charge between $15 and $30 rent per month for space and utilities. Some of the parks have a recreational program which is directed by the park manager. The incomes of trailer inhabitants vary between $1,000 and $20,000 annually. Some of the inhabitants are only semi-retired, living in the parks for half a year and returning to their permanent homes for work during the remainder of the year. Others live in the same park for many years, or move from park to park, perhaps in search of more congenial neighbors or perhaps merely to assert their freedom of movement.[13]

Foster Home Living. A few communities have recently instituted a foster home program for older people. Younger

[12] Cf. G. C. Hoyt, "The Life of the Retired in a Trailer Park," *American Journal of Sociology*, LIX (January, 1954), 361–70.

[13] Cf. L. C. Michelon, "The New Leisure Class," *American Journal of Sociology*, LIX (January, 1954), 371–78.

families "adopt" an elderly person who comes to live in the home with them. In the better planned programs an effort is made to match the younger couple and the older person in somewhat the same fashion that young children and foster parents are matched before adoption is allowed. In the case of the older person, when it can be managed, at least a nominal amount of rent is paid to the adopting couple. If care is exercised in matching the parties concerned there will be few interpersonal difficulties in the procedure. A distinction should be made between the practice of "adoption" and conventional boarding house care. In the latter case several older people may have rooms, and there is little in the way of personal relations between the boarder and the landlady. In "adoption" cases there is an effort made to put the affair on a personal, noncommercial basis. How successful such a program is depends upon the several variables present in each situation.

Apartment housing for the aging

One solution to the problem of housing for the aged is for them to rent rather than buy. However, if there are no available apartments the problem remains. New York has hit on a plan whereby 5 per cent of the publicly financed housing is to be set aside for older people. These units are to have special features which make them more comfortable for their inhabitants without making them more expensive. One requirement is that they be first floor apartments which are easily accessible. They need not be as large as apartments which are to be occupied by families with several members. Depending upon whether there are two or three rooms, the apartments are constructed to rent for $30 per month or slightly less. Another possible move is to allocate 5 per cent of the vacated public housing to older people also. As long as public housing is available to people with a limited income, there is a turnover of tenants as the income level of some of them exceeds the maximum allowed to continue living in the project. If 5 per cent of the vacated apartments are earmarked for older people and 5 per cent of all new housing units are reserved for older people, an approach would be made toward a solution to the housing problem for older people whose incomes allow them to take advantage of public housing.

So far privately owned housing projects have made few if any concessions to older people. Older people, in theory, have the same opportunities for renting as anyone else has. However, generally no special consideration is given them in the way of reserving first-floor or easily accessible apartments. There are, however, a growing number of exceptions. For instance, a private housing company in New York has agreed to build special apartments for the aged according to the specifications of the New York State Division of Housing.[14] The total number of such apartments will be 200 or at least 5 per cent of the apartments. The rentals for these apartments is expected to be about $75 to $92.50 per month.

Some authorities believe there is a need for housing units for the aged who have incomes above the maximum set for public housing but below that needed to rent apartments from private concerns which charge as much as the above-mentioned project. There is a feeling that federal action is needed in this area. It has been proposed that, in return for FHA insured loans to private builders, the federal government require these builders to set aside at least 5 per cent of their units for older people.

There are two schools of thought on the subject of special concessions to the aged. One school contends that special features should be incorporated into the units so that life would be more comfortable and less hazardous for older occupants. The other school is represented by two points of view. The first is that there should be no special concessions. It is believed that whenever a unit or project is earmarked for a single purpose it is more expensive to build and at the same time it loses much of its value because it cannot be easily reconverted to other uses. The second

[14] Herman T. Stichman, "The Aged and Public Housing," in Thomas C. Desmond (chm.), *Enriching the Years* (Albany: New York State Joint Legislative Committee on Problems of the Aging, 1953), pp. 105–7.

approach is that if all points of comfort and convenience were incorporated in all housing units, there would be no need for further consideration of the needs of older people. If housing were made comfortable and convenient for one age group, it would be comfortable and convenient for all. One exception would be in the amount of space and the number of rooms required by young couples with a growing family and older couples with no children. Young childless couples, however, do not require any more space than older couples.

The New York State Housing Commission as well as other authorities on the subject have set forth certain criteria for housing for the aging.[15] First, there are to be two types of apartments. The first type is designed for couples 63 or 65 years of age. These apartments consist of a double bedroom, a separate living room combined with dining and kitchen facilities, and a bathroom. The second type, somewhat smaller, is designed for older couples and is not inconveniently large should one of the couple want to remain after the other has died. This type apartment has a combination living-bedroom, a separate dining-room–kitchen and a separate bath. This second type has been criticized because of the combination living-bedroom. If either one or both of the people are sick there would not be the desired amount of privacy.

Both types have adequate window space and ample closet space. Thresholds are eliminated so as to lessen the danger of tripping. Electric stoves replace gas ranges. This is done to eliminate dangers which result from carelessness or forgetfulness in the use of gas. All shelves are placed at easy-to-reach levels, and fixtures in both bathroom and kitchen are at levels that reduce bending, stooping, and reaching to a minimum. Windows are mechanically operated to eliminate the straining to lower or raise which sometimes occurs with the traditional type window. The apartments for the elderly are equipped with labor-saving devices such as refrigerators, mechanical incinerators, and, if they are not on the ground floor, elevators. Flooring

[15] Cf. *ibid.*, p. 106.

in the apartments is of nonslippery material. Bathtubs or showers are equipped with both handrails or handgrips and seats. The apartments are away from the entrance of the building and are located in a southerly direction to allow a maximum of sunshine. Other criteria such as proper lighting, central heating, and cross-ventilation are basic requirements to all present-day housing.

It is generally felt now that there should be no separate apartment buildings reserved for aging people only. Rather, the elderly should take their place in apartment buildings which accommodate all other age categories. Cleveland, Ohio, has taken a step in this direction in its public housing program.[16] This new project is an extension of an already existing housing project. There are two unique features to be found in the new development. First, of the 156 new apartment suites, 100 are especially designed for older people. The second feature is that the first floor of the new development is set aside for an old-age center. This center is financed by voluntary contributions and is operated by a citizen board of trustees. The project is thus made possible by the joint effort of the public housing authority and the voluntarily financed old-age center.

The Cleveland Housing Authority recognized that there were several things to be considered in planning the housing project. Even though the suites for older people are on the second floor, they are serviced with elevators, thus eliminating stair-climbing. An effort is made to cluster together the older people who have a community of interests but at the same time to arrange their living quarters so that they are not isolated from younger families. By administrative control one-third of the 156 units are two-bedroom units to be occupied by couples having an aged parent living with them or by couples with babies.

A number of one-bedroom units are reserved for older couples. These units are designed so that they can be converted into twin living-bedroom combinations by installing

[16] Leona Bevis, "Cleveland Combines Housing with an Old-Age Center," *Aging*, XI (May, 1954), 2–3.

a closet in the living room. The object is to make it possible to deal with the problem created when one member of a two-person family dies. Heretofore the Housing Authority has had to evict the remaining spouse. Under the new plan it is possible for the remaining spouse to continue living in the same suite and be joined by another aged person of the same sex. Two such aged one-person "families" can share the converted twin living-bedroom combination and continue to enjoy privacy by installing movable screens in the room. The two persons will share the other rooms—the bath, closet, and kitchen. These apartments have the safety and comfort features which were listed above. The aging residents can make use of the social, recreational, and counseling services of the old-age center located on the ground floor. This center serves a noon meal at cost to any old person who wishes to eat there. This meal includes one-half the nutritional needs of an individual for one day.

Institutional or congregate housing for the aged

Under this heading can be grouped the various "homes," and institutions for the aged. This over-all classification covers housing which is provided by some agency to take care of the housing needs of older people who are not financially able to buy or rent a house or apartment, and/or of those who are not physically or mentally able to maintain themselves and their residence without outside assistance of some kind. These people, then, are the ones who either have to or want to live where such care is given. In addition to these categories is a third one composed of older people who either of their own accord or because of family pressure seek congregate housing or institutional housing in preference to individual units in order to be with other people in their age category. Obviously these three groups of older people represent many diverse individuals. They include the sick and the able, the rich and the poor. Briefly, the older people who occupy or are looking for housing in institutions have in common that they either do not want to or cannot continue to maintain a separate abode by their own physical or financial efforts.

Roughly there are three methods by which congregate housing for these older people is financed and maintained. These are public ownership, quasi-public ownership (churches, lodges, unions, etc.), and private ownership. There are many types of homes known by a variety of names. These include facilities which offer special services and are known as homes for the aged, convalescent homes, nursing homes, rest homes, boarding homes, and homes which were once known as "poorhouses" or "poor farms." No matter by what name they are known, their task is to furnish special services to older people which they could not have in their own homes. These types of homes are financed either in whole or in part by one or a combination of the following methods: first, by appropriations from local and perhaps state governments; second, by gifts, donations, or assessments on individuals or members of the organization which is responsible for the home; and finally, by the fees which are paid by the occupants or their families.

These institutions or homes vary in size from those housing only three or four persons to those with as many as several hundred occupants. They may be composed of one or two rooms in a home which houses a younger family, or they may be built in dormitory or barracks style with common sleeping quarters. They may have separate private or semiprivate rooms or apartments either in large buildings or in a series of smaller cottages.

In some of the larger institutions in recent years there has been a trend toward having a central or "parent" cottage for recreation, dining, and community activities in general and smaller cottages for sleeping. This type of arrangement is also found in apartment-type buildings in which part of the basement or ground floor is reserved for such activities. The present emphasis upon creative activities and homelike qualities has altered the character of the institutional living or reception room. In some instances this room served as a reception room to impress visitors with the neatness and homelike qualities of the institution but was strictly off-limits to the people who lived there. This characteristic of the older homes was not the only one which tended to mar the atmosphere of many of the homes and set them apart from some of the better homes of the present time.

Homes for the Indigent: "Poor Farms." Prior to 1935 when the Social Security Act was passed it was the tradition in this country that the indigent aged should be cared for by the counties in which they resided. These "poorhouses," or "county farms" as they were called, were a carry-over from past centuries. They represented one of the cultural survivals of the late Middle Ages in philosophy if not in actuality.[17] One of the principal purposes of these homes was to get the indigent aged out of sight. The result, almost universally, was to commit the indigent to these homes and forget about them. Often the inmates included not only the aged but any other class of indigents whom the county decided to place in these so-called homes. The populations of these places, often housed indiscriminately, included the aged, the feeble-minded, the mentally ill, drug addicts, alcoholics, and "ne'er-do-wells" of all ages and both sexes. If any of these people were married and living with their spouses, then the family might be committed. These poor farms acted as a catch-all and housed those unfortunates for whom no other adequate provisions were made.

There was little if any uniformity in the administration of these farms. Frequently the only qualifications needed to become the "keeper" or superintendent was the proper political connection. It was probably more the exception than the rule, especially in the predominantly rural states, that the keeper had training which fitted him for work of this nature. More frequently his qualifications for the job depended upon his ability to farm. The superintendent would look after the farm, using inmate labor to assist him.

---

[17] Adapted from William E. Cole and Russell R. Dynes, *Homes for the Homeless of Tennessee* (Knoxville: The University of Tennessee Press, 1951), pp. 25 ff.

Produce from the farm was used to help feed the inhabitants and what was left would be sold to supplement the income of the superintendent. The duty of the keeper's wife was to cook or help inmates prepare the food, to keep the living quarters in habitable condition, and to look after the health and welfare of the sick people under her care. More frequently than not, the only qualifications she had for her job was that she was a woman and fortunately or otherwise was the wife of the keeper.

Until recently it was the practice in some counties to pay the keeper in relation to the number of inmates in the poorhouses. Other keepers were paid a straight salary plus car or truck and his home with a few other items such as a telephone. The rule, in running the county homes or almshouses, was to operate on as small a budget as possible. This in turn led to inhumane treatment of the inhabitants in many of the homes. The limited number of staff members, generally untrained, added to the deplorable conditions found in such places. Overcrowding in old buildings which were not originally designed to serve as homes for the aged, indiscriminate mixing of various categories of indigents regardless of their physical or mental difficulties, and finally, improper care or no care at all for the social-environmental needs of the inmates were characteristics of many of these homes.

Although these poorhouses were not universally to be condemned, there were enough substandard ones to justify an over-all change. This type of thinking was reflected in Congress by the framers of the Social Security Act. In brief, their idea was to get rid of the deficiencies by getting rid of the poor farms. Title I of the original Social Security Act provided that to be eligible for the federal matching funds in the old-age assistance program, residents of institutions for the aged would have to take up residence elsewhere. The implication was that these people could obtain enough in the way of assistance to support themselves outside the poorhouses. There were several unforeseen consequences of this action. Individuals who qualified for OAA were given a choice between remaining in institutions where care was often inadequate or drawing public assistance which might be equally inadequate. They had to fend for themselves to find available housing facilities for the rent they could afford to pay. Those who left the poorhouses to go on the assistance rolls frequently made the change from the public slums of the poorhouses to the private slums of rooming houses. This provision of the Social Security Act merely subsidized the slums of the cities by making it financially possible for the recipients of OAA to rent only the substandard walk-up, cold-water flats or rooms, thus prolonging the life of these places which were unfit for human habitation.

It soon became apparent that the population of the poorhouses would not be wiped out merely by refusing them public assistance. Many of the inhabitants, for one reason or another, were not eligible for assistance and others who were ill could not subsist outside the poorhouses on OAA alone. In order to get around the dilemma thus created, some state funds were granted to the people who otherwise were eligible but who wanted to or had to remain in the homes. These funds were not matched by federal funds. When it became apparent that withholding federal matching funds from the inmates of poor farms did not solve the problem, the Social Security Act was amended in 1950 to allow recipients to remain in these and similar institutions provided the states set up an authority to establish standards for the institutions in which the aged were to reside. The provisions of this amendment went into operation in 1953.

Congregate Housing for the Handicapped Aged. There is no evidence to indicate that all of the traditional type county poorhouses will be done away with in the near future. However, there is some reason to believe that local government owned and controlled institutions for the aged are beginning to assume a new role. With more and better pensions eventually there will be less actual need for outright poor homes. With greater medical control of acute medical cases among the older population there will be a concomitant increase in the number of the aged who need, at the least, some constant medical supervision. As time goes on there will be a shift in emphasis on the part of local authorities from homes for the aged who are well but indigent to an emphasis on the care of those who have some financial resources but who need medical supervision. Insofar as this is a correct analysis, the trend will be toward county infirmaries or nursing homes for those who need medical care but cannot afford care offered by private agencies.

Private Care in Nursing Homes and Homes for the Aged Who Are Well. The idea is expressed that a good many of the congregate, institutional, and noninstitutional "homes" for the able-bodied aged should examine their policies more closely. In the first place, very few people, regardless of age, are physically perfect. If congregate homes for the aged admit only the ambulatory aged or those claiming to be well, possibly they are admitting old people who have some chronic disability but who are well enough at the time of admittance to be up and about. If these people do not receive medical attention, their disabilities will be aggravated to an acute stage. If such a home has no medical facilities the ill person will have to be transferred to a hospital and if, at a later date, the hospital dismisses him, he will have to seek nursing care in another place. There should be no homes for the aged which are completely without regular medical supervision for those who live in them. Some kind of nursing unit is needed for those who are either temporarily acutely ill or who have been dismissed as convalescent from a hospital. Too frequent shifts from one institution to another, according to the state of health of the older person, can be a trying emotional experience. The older person feels most secure in his own home. If he is forced to leave his home and take up residence in a home for the aging he has to make rather radical adjustments in his pattern of living. This is a time of insecurity for him. If he becomes ill and is forced to leave his second "home" for a hospital, infirmary, or nursing home, his readjustments have to be repeated at a time when he is physically weak and consequently less able to meet the emotional strain of such an adjustment.[18]

A great many of the institutional homes for the well aged, by whatever name they are known, do not meet all the needs of their clients. By the use of different names some of these institutionalized "homes" avoid fulfilling part of their responsibilities toward those who live in them. In other words, if a home attaches to its name a word which implies that it accepts only those who have no physical disability, then this home assumes no responsibility for its residents who become ill. Some homes assume no responsibility for the emotional, recreational, social, or personality needs of those who live there. Some of these places are homes for the aged in name only and serve as temporary shelters during the interval between having to give up one's own home and death.

All homes, no matter what they are called, should provide some kind of nursing care for all those for whose care the home accepts responsibility. Since this is the goal, the same set of requirements should be applied to all homes in the same categories, regardless of their names. To attain this goal two classes of homes are needed: first, homes for the aged who are well, to provide standardized infirmary service for its members who become ill and need supervisory care; and second, nursing homes which would be set up to receive and keep only those who are chronically ill. More supervision and attention by doctors and trained nurses would have to be given to the people in these homes than to those in the first class mentioned. The standards of performance for medical attention would be higher in the second class of home than in the first. There is little to justify the applying of different sets of standards and licensing procedures to homes which offer similar services but which operate under different names. Nicholson points out that:

[18] Edna Nicholson, "Nursing and Convalescent Homes," *Housing the Aging*, pp. 116–19.

At the present time, blind, crippled, disoriented, and sick old people are often huddled in so-called boarding homes, where no pretense is made to meet their needs for medical attention and nursing care, and where they have no protection from licensing authorities or standard-setting bodies, and this because the name of the place in which they are living is assumed to indicate that no protection is needed. Even government institutions and voluntary philanthropic homes are guilty of this offense.[19]

Sheltered care for the aged

There is no way at present to ascertain the number of "homes" which offer sheltered care for the aged. This term carries with it the idea that the "guest" is unable to care for himself and that this need is met by the personnel of the home. The number of homes purporting to offer such care has grown rapidly within the past twenty years. Rough estimates place the number of inhabitants of these homes at about 200,000 older people.[20] A nationwide survey was conducted by the National Committee on Aging of the National Social Welfare Assembly. In four consecutive issues of *Parade*, findings of this committee were publicized. While some of the homes studied met all of the high standards for care of the aged, there were many which either met only the minimum standards or no standards at all. Some of the reasons given for this deficiency were lack of licensing on the part of the government on any level, lack of a system of inspection, and failure to require homes to come up to the standards which had been set. Failure to insist on adhering to a set of standards can be traced to public apathy reflected in a too meager allocation of funds to carry on the work such inspections would entail.

Some of the substandard conditions brought to light by these surveys include the following. In some of the homes patients were actually mistreated by the home staff. There

[19] Edna Nicholson, "Nursing and Convalescent Homes," *Housing the Aging*, pp. 116–19. By permission of the University of Michigan Press.
[20] Robert P. Goldman and Sid Ross, "How We're Kicking Our Old Folks Around," *Parade* (February 14, 1954), p. 9.

were instances of physical violence against some of the older persons, sometimes the "guests" were tied in bed, locked in their rooms, or had their crutches hidden from them. Drugs were given in some homes to keep semi-invalids in such condition they would not cause trouble by demanding service. Sanitary conditions were reported to be beyond belief; vermin, body filth, unwashed bed clothes, and trash in the rooms were the rule rather than the exception in many homes. The homes of the poorer type were usually overcrowded. Originally built to house one family, some of these places housed as many as two dozen old people. Many of them were of frame construction, two or three stories high, with narrow, dark, crooked stairways and halls. In recent years homes of this type have been the cause of old people losing their lives in fires. Underlying these substandard conditions is the fact that often these homes are operated by untrained staffs. Some of the proprietors operate the homes purely as a money-making project, with no regard for the clients. In other cases proprietors, though well-intentioned, are not professionally trained and have untrained staffs.

General Standards. In the course of time, standards have been established to protect children, the mentally and physically ill, and other categories of citizens from exploitation by those who are charged with their care. Both voluntary and governmental agencies have accepted standards which are used to guide them in their responsibility to those who are dependent upon them.[21] The rapid growth in the number of homes offering sheltered care for the aged has led to certain abuses. As unfavorable conditions have come to light through surveys, it has become increasingly obvious to those concerned that the aged in institutions should be protected by a system of licensing and inspection. The 1950 amendments to the Social Security Act provided that if a state plan for old-age assistance (with other categories)

[21] Edith Alt, *Standards of Care for Older People in Institutions* (New York: The National Committee on the Aging of the National Social Welfare Assembly, 1953), Part I, 18–46.

included payment to individuals in private or public institutions, the state must establish or designate an authority to establish and maintain standards for the institutions. This provision became operative on July 1, 1953.

Both governmental and voluntary organizations have felt the necessity for establishing uniform standards for the institutions offering sheltered care. In order to be effective the standards must be adequate, they must be enforced, and a regular, rigid inspection must be provided. The following list indicates some of the standards which are set by these agencies. Homes for ambulatory aged should provide more active recreation than nursing homes. Nursing homes or homes for convalescent people should provide more trained medical supervision and more in the way of programs for rehabilitation than homes which have no patients needing rehabilitation. No matter what services the homes purport to render, the physical plant should conform to accepted standards of decency and health. Overcrowding and hazardous conditions should not be allowed to exist. Adequate living, dining, and recreational rooms should be available and readily accessible. The food should be planned by a trained dietitian and be prepared by an efficient staff. Meals should be served and eaten in a homelike atmosphere. There should be an adequate staff of registered and practical nurses, physical therapists, social workers, and recreational directors in relation to the type of guests in the home and the number to be served. It is estimated that in homes where persons require relatively little personal care and nursing services, the ratio of staff to patient should be about one to two. In homes which have patients requiring continuous care, the ratio should run as high as 1.5 to 1.8 staff members per patient.[22] There is one basic requirement for the person in charge of running such a home: he must be trained in this type of work and have an interest in it. Adequate salaries and widespread community interest are both important adjuncts to a good home. It is generally agreed

[22] Nicholson, "Nursing and Convalescent Homes," in *Housing the Aging*, pp. 129–32.

that the homes, no matter what their primary function, should have ample grounds and be close enough to the main stream of life so that patients can take advantage of community recreational, economic, and religious facilities. Easy access to the homes encourages people to visit those who live in them.

In some places, especially in England, services have been devised whereby the chronically ill or convalescent older person can remain in his own home. He receives calls from doctors designated by the hospitals for such duties. In addition community volunteers offer cleaning services, help prepare meals, or bring meals into the homes of those who can take only partial care of themselves. One advantage of the home services is that the older person does not have to leave his own home, yet he has almost all of the care he needs. By remaining at home he does not occupy hospital space which is expensive and may be needed for other more seriously ill persons.

Private and quasi-public congregate homes for the well aged

There are some elderly people who are in relatively good health who have enough money to afford to live in private or quasi-public homes for the aged. These people may like to live in such places; they may not want to live with relatives or maintain their own homes. They apply for admittance to a congregate type of home for the aged. Several of these homes are widely known and have a favorable reputation. Their waiting lists are usually very long. Some church homes are in this class. Perhaps Moosehaven, Penny Farms (Memorial Home Community), and certain Jewish homes are among the most widely known. Through the efforts of labor unions and industries, or their combined efforts, more of these homes are being established all the time. Many homes restrict admittance to those who belong to the denomination or religion owning the home or to members of a lodge or union or to one race or nationality. This policy makes for a homogeneous population, a condition which may or may not be desirable, depending upon one's point of view.

On admission the elderly person either has to pay a monthly or yearly fee or sign over to the organization his or her property, which reverts to the organization at the death of the guest. If the guest remains for only a short time, the property rights, minus a fixed charge for room and board, are usually restored. Some of the homes charge a fixed amount for lifetime residence, a fee which may be as high as $5,000 or more, depending on the number of rooms occupied and the location of the rooms. Others depend on a fixed monthly rent, while still others, as Moosehaven, require that all insurance and the estate be transferred to the organization. In such cases no other charges are made.

A brief description of some of the "old stand-bys" can be given to acquaint the reader with the best known of these homes.[23] The section of Penny Farms reserved for the aging is known as Memorial Home Community. Upon being recommended by their churches an older person or couple will be admitted. A charge of $3,500 is made and the person is assured a home for life, but he is responsible for his other living expenses. River Garden Hebrew Home for the Aged is restricted to older persons of the Hebrew faith who have resided in Florida for thirteen years prior to application. There are three categories of guests and three wings in this establishment. The guests are placed in wings according to the degree of nursing care they require. Moosehaven admits those who are 65 years of age or older who have been members in good standing in the lodge (or wives of lodge members) for at least ten years prior to applying. The person must place his estate and insurances with the supreme lodge. After admittance of the member and his wife, all expenses incident to care and keeping are carried by the lodge. If the guests do any of

[23] Cf. Henry S. Churchill and Panel Contributions, "Housing for Aged and Retired Persons," in *Living in the Later Years*, pp. 37–70; and Wilma Donahue, "Programs in Action," in *Housing the Aging*, pp. 243 ff.

the necessary work around the home they have more expense money than those who are "on sunshine," that is, not working.

There is a well-known home called the Home for the Aged and Infirm Hebrews in New York. This home is supported by a subsidy from the Federation of Jewish Philanthropies of New York, contributions by relatives and friends of the residents, and funds administered by the New York City Department of Welfare. In addition to the care of resident members, there is a home care program which serves about sixty people in their own homes. Pilgrim Place in Claremont, California, is sponsored by the Congregational Church. The community is composed of residence halls and of small homes which are owned either by the residents or by Pilgrim Place. Both the Methodist and Presbyterian churches have some homes whose standards are as high as those found in other homes. There are in addition to these listed here, many other homes sponsored by churches, labor organizations, and other groups.

There are several characteristics that most of these homes have in common. First, there is some other restriction on admittance besides age, such as membership in the sponsoring organization. Second, even though they vary greatly in size, an attempt is made to give the "home" a homelike atmosphere. Both the physical and recreational needs of the residents are cared for adequately; an infirmary or hospital unit and a recreational space and program are provided. Third, although the cost of entering or remaining in most of these better homes is prohibitive as far as many older people are concerned, such places generally have a long waiting list and are therefore concerned with the necessity of enlarging their facilities. Finally, most of these homes now make provision for accepting persons of all marital conditions, single, widowed, or married. Furthermore, those which generally have accepted only married couples now allow the remaining spouse to continue living in the home.

Summary

There are several conclusions to be drawn from this chapter. The vast majority of the aged live in households either alone or with spouse or other relatives. In addition to the fact that they do so, there is evidence to indicate that most older people prefer this type of housing arrangement. Although there is a higher proportion of aged home ownership in urban areas than there is in the general urban population, many of the aged have to live in boarding homes or in homes of nonrelatives. Difficulty is encountered by the aged in financing new homes or in renting apartments which would be better suited to their needs than are the places in which they live. Most of this difficulty exists only indirectly because of age, more directly because of their poverty. Both public and private housing authorities are becoming more aware that some provision should be made to care for the housing needs of this segment of the population.

Modern versions of the old-fashioned county farm or poorhouse are to be found in both inadequate and substandard housing for the indigent and ill older citizens. Efforts are being made to establish and enforce standards in all the so-called "sheltered-care" homes. Some of the nursing homes, convalescent homes, and rest homes, as well as homes catering to the well, are meeting high standards of care. On the other hand, there are innumerable places which fall as far short of furnishing decent housing and care as did the county poorhouses in earlier years. The most favorably known homes are those which have been established by philanthropic organizations, lodges, unions, and religious bodies. Admission requirements, however, tend to be strict and the amount of monthly rent or down payment would be prohibitive for most of the older people in this country.

17

Recreation and Education

Often when speaking of either recreation or education, a distinctive adjective, "adult," is used to prefix these words. The implication is that both recreation and education are activities normally indulged in only by relatively young people. It has only been fairly recently that a distinction has been drawn between recreation for young adults and older people as has long been made between education for youth and adults. This may be due to an increasing awareness in these two fields, as in so many others, that the problems faced by younger and older adults are not similar. The action programs designed to satisfy the needs of the one group might fall short of meeting those of the other.

On the surface this conclusion is more valid for recreation than for education, but as a matter of fact, it would probably be as true for one as for the other. As far as recreation is concerned, one has to consider that a difference in age also means a difference in physical ability to engage in certain activities, or a difference in desire, even though the necessary physical ability may be present. By recreation is meant the expression of interests and the seeking to satisfy needs during leisure. Leisure is the surplus time remaining after the practical necessities of life have been attended to.

An immediate difference can be noted between recreation, or use of leisure time, for younger and older people. Traditionally in primitive and even in modern societies almost all time for children is leisure time, but it is during this time and through leisure time activities that children learn to live and interact with others in their own age groups and in general learn activities which will fit them for adult participation. Leisure time for adults, from the time they start gainful employment until they cease working, is composed of weekends, vacations, holidays, and after-work hours. Leisure time for this age group comprises the surplus time not used in gainful employment or the fringe of time left over from the more serious duties of earning a livelihood or homemaking and rearing a family. For a person who has retired, work comprises the fringe of time and leisure the major portion of time available to the individual. Leisure is thought of as a way to break the oft-hard routine of the employed person. It may be viewed by the unemployed or retired older person as something far less attractive and desirable because it is present, so to speak, in so much larger quantities. A two-week vacation for an employed person presents him with all kinds of possible recreational opportunities. A similar period later in the life of the same person who is retired means only another two-week period of doing nothing, or another two weeks to live through. As has been noted, this excess or so-called leisure time comes during the period in a person's life when he has fewer contemporaries with whom to enjoy his time, less money to spend in a different and entertaining manner, and frequently less physical energy to engage in any out-of-the-ordinary activity.

Insofar as education is concerned, there are two phases which will be treated in this chapter. One of these which is of significance for the older person is education of the individual for his own old age. This education includes such things as education for retirement, education on health matters involving topics concerned with physical aging, diet, personal care and related matters, and finally education of the individual for continued active participation in community activities and interests after he has become older. A second phase of adult education involves formal education, or a continuation or re-entrance into formal education —the "book learning" which so many of our senior citizens did not have an opportunity to receive. Our public educational program was in its early stages of development when those who are now in, or approaching, old age were of school age. Many of our aged were born and reared in other countries where they had less opportunity to obtain formal education than they would have had here. As a consequence there are many among the older citizens who would like to study English, American history, current affairs, some foreign language, politics, or other subjects in which they have an interest. Some want to prepare themselves for a second career, while others merely wish to round out their knowledge of subjects in which they have had a lifelong interest.

Recreational leadership and program planning

Any successful formal recreation program requires leadership.[1] At the present time in this country there are people who are professionally trained recreation leaders. Many of these people are receiving special training in recreation for the aging. In the final analysis there is a similarity of qualities required for one who would lead recreation for both younger and older people. Qualities that would fit a person to be a recreation leader for one age group would also fit him to lead other groups. However, the good leader must constantly keep in mind the ages and capabilities of those with whom he is working.

The following list of qualifications for leaders of recreational programs for the aging points up what some experts on the subject have said.[2] Skillful leadership is the key to a successful recreational program for the aging. The leader must be well-trained, enthusiastic and imaginative. To be a good leader one must enjoy satisfaction in working with older people. First the leader must recognize that the habits and past experiences of older people make their tastes in recreation different from those of younger people. He must be able to recognize that age itself places certain limitations on what the participants can accomplish. He must take

[1] Adapted from Gail Clay, "Recreation Programs for the Aging" (Graduate Research Paper, University of Tennessee, 1955).

[2] Cf. James H. Woods, *Helping Older People Enjoy Life* (New York: Harper & Bros., 1953), pp. 35–38; and Harold D. Meyer and Charles K. Brightbill, *Community Recreation* (Boston: D. C. Heath and Co., 1948), pp. 374–80.

into consideration the personal likes and dislikes of the participants and organize his program to fit individual tastes. He must combat, both within himself and the people with whom he is working, the common negative attitudes toward older people. He must, through his skills, be able to discover and exploit the interests and capabilities of the individuals with whom he deals. Finally, the leader must believe in and have a sincere liking for recreational leadership for the aging.

In addition to the trained professional leader, there is a place for volunteer and part-time workers in the recreational program. The volunteer workers can assist the leaders in planning and conducting recreational activities. They can also stimulate interest and understanding of the program within the larger community. Obviously, the role of volunteer workers should be more than that of sympathetic well-wishers; they should be interested in the betterment of the community as a whole. Any training program for volunteer workers should emphasize the need for understanding older people and the value of working with them rather than for them and of being patient yet firm with them. An understanding of older people in general should be supplemented by a knowledge of the social and economic background of the older people within the community and particularly of the people whom the program is designed to serve. Part-time workers need not receive as extensive training as full-time volunteers, although they may be utilized in numerous ways. These part-time workers may serve as teachers in specific areas such as drama, arts, music, crafts, dancing, and similar activities. They may serve by furnishing transportation to and from program activities, aiding in publicizing program activities for the aged, and presenting lectures and leading discussion programs on topics of interest.

Any sound recreational program should be based on the needs and interests of the people whom it is designed to serve. Activities that are merely time-consuming do not constitute such a program. Rather, a sound program is one which balances opportunities for self-expression, service, and pure enjoyment of life. Planning the program and selecting the activities are the first responsibility of the trained leader, volunteers, and the individuals for whom the program is designed. Such cooperative planning should insure that the goals of the program will be reached. Without sound leadership, the program might deteriorate into projects for special interest groups. Without assistance from the participants, the program might not meet the real interests and needs of the participants themselves. Some of the common pitfalls to be avoided are the following:

1. Allowing trained leadership to dominate.
2. Failing to recognize that these people are apt to reflect experiences which are not consistent with present thinking.
3. Failing to consider the limitations of old age.
4. Overlooking the sensitivity and the personal likes and dislikes of each individual.
5. Permitting leadership by the more aggressive members of the group to dominate.
6. Condoning the volunteer help of "do-gooders" who make the members of the group feel like charity cases.
7. Using undesirable physical facilities for meetings.
8. Placing financial restrictions on membership through dues and assessments.[3]

The National Recreation Association [4] asked a number of sponsors of successful programs for the aging which policies and practices they found most effective and what notes of warning should be given groups planning to undertake such programs. A composite picture of the findings of the survey is given in the following paragraphs.

Programs for the aging should stress informality, fun, and a social atmosphere conducive to the formation of friendship. The schedule should allow ample time for unorgan-

---

[3] Wilma Clizbe, "Why Recreation Programs for the Aging?" *Recreation,* XLVIII (February, 1955), 59–60.

[4] James W. Gilman, "Recreation's Public Relations," *Recreation,* XLIII (December, 1949), 429–32.

ized activities and informal talking and visiting. Sociability is the key to success, no matter what the formal program stresses. Any semblance of charity or paternalism should be avoided in presenting the program. Although parties and entertainment with free refreshments are good ways to institute the program, they should be dispensed with at an early date because such activities increase the feeling of dependency among the participants. Practically all leaders believe that responsibility for the program and the cost of the program should be shared by the members of the group for whom the program is designed. Programs which require the participation of all members should be stressed. This procedure guards against the tendency of some of the less socially and physically active people merely to sit and watch others perform. One point stressed is that there should be a proper balance between club activities, such as singing and dancing, and small group activities, such as playing cards and checkers. A balanced program would check the undue development of small cliques within the club. There should be as few regulations and restrictions as is consistent with common sense. Participants come to enjoy themselves, not to be tied down with restrictions which detract from a feeling of freedom and a good time.

Broad community interest and cooperation are necessary. Both trained and volunteer leaders should publicize club activities through the use of channels such as newspapers and radio. A feeling of participation can be attained by having individual members write news notices of the meetings. Where possible, mention should be made of individual members who have contributed to the success of a previous program, of those who have had birthdays, or of those who have been elected to offices in the club.

As a general rule, subjects for discussion should be carefully chosen to avoid any issue which is controversial to the extent that it might cause a rift in the club. In no event should discussion programs be allowed to deteriorate into private arguments. In order to avoid controversial issues, a knowledge of the background of the club members is necessary. This is not to mean that no debatable issues should be discussed but it does mean that certain aspects of some subjects should not be touched upon. For instance, if the membership of the club is part Protestant and part Catholic, a debate or discussion on which of the two was "right" about certain theological matters could easily split the club into two hostile groups. Subjects which evoke violent emotions should have no place in such a club. Such topics as national or international affairs are often of interest to older people, however. Properly directed discussions can be both constructive and helpful.

Sponsoring organizations

For many years there has been a tendency to emphasize recreational programs for young people. Only within recent years have communities and various organizations recognized the need for a recreational program for older people. Leadership in initiating such recreational programs has come from public recreation departments, councils of social agencies, community centers, and other similar agencies. Although older people seem to be anxious to participate in leisure-time activities, they have not, except in a few instances, taken the initiative in asking agencies to establish such services for them. Many groups such as churches, civic groups, private clubs, and others have been instrumental in carrying out successful programs for the aging after they have been organized.

Large urban communities have established community-wide committees on the aging often under the sponsorship of councils of social agencies. These committees assume responsibility for surveying the recreational needs of older people and eliciting community support. They serve as centers for cooperative planning and as clearing houses for the exchange of thinking and experience. Some communities directly sponsor one or more of the services.[5]

[5] Arthur Williams, *Recreation for the Aging* (New York: Association Press, 1953), p. 28.

Clubs

In organizing a recreation program for the aging, it seems necessary to stress club work. Clubs provide an opportunity for older people to have a sense of belonging and a feeling they can continue their social relationships. Clubs serve as referral centers to other community agencies which then supplement the offerings of the clubs. Clubs for the aging were organized early in this century when it was found that in spite of social services rendered the aging, older people still had a sense of loneliness and idleness and a feeling of being useless and unwanted. It was not until the mid-forties, however, that clubs for the aging attained widespread popularity.

In the actual organization of a club, the first meeting is of great importance. The leader must know who the older citizens are, where they live, and how they can be reached. Sources of this information are lists of individuals receiving old-age assistance and lists of names of those who have been retired from business or industrial firms. Churches, fraternal organizations, and labor unions should be able and willing to furnish the names of older retired people who have been or are active members. Plans for the first meeting should be flexible enough so as to take care of any size group that shows up. The program should be interesting and stimulating so that those who attend will enjoy themselves enough to want to come again and bring a guest. Personal recruiting by the charter members is one of the biggest factors in membership growth. Standards for membership should be set at the first meeting. As a general rule the only restriction on membership should be age. Some clubs set 60 as the minimum age, while others go as low as 55, and still others set 65 as the minimum. The usefulness of the club may be hampered unduly if other requirements relative to marital status, the nature of prior jobs, or religious affiliations are set up. It is quite possible for members to be drawn from diverse social, economic, and educational backgrounds and still find much in common upon which to base a strong club organization.

The meeting place for the club should be as centrally located as possible to encourage attendance. If it is easily accessible by public transportation, automobile, and walking, attendance will remain higher than if it is relatively inaccessible. The club rooms should be located on the ground floor or in a building which has elevator service. It is desirable to have the club rooms attractively furnished with bright walls and draperies. Some clubs encourage the members to select the color the room is to be painted and have members, or a committee of members, make draperies. It is important that the room be furnished with comfortable furniture—chairs, tables, divans, lamps, and rugs. Some of the furniture can be donated by members or by interested nonmembers. No furniture or furnishings should be accepted simply because they are offered; only attractive, comfortable, and useful things should be accepted.

It is necessary for the club to have one large room and several smaller ones. One small room is often reserved as an office in which committees meet. Other small rooms are used by older members who want to read or play sedentary games. One room may be reserved for radio or television viewers. The main room is used by more active members for dancing, playing nonsedentary games, singing, playing musical instruments, or listening to speeches or discussion programs. Where space and other considerations warrant it, some of the rooms are used by members actively engaged in pursuing hobbies or as classrooms where hobbies are taught. It is necessary to have kitchen space so that snacks can be prepared for parties. Toilet facilities should be conveniently located. It is important that the club room or rooms be well lighted and cheerful in appearance.

From one point of view it is better for the old people to use space which is also used by other groups. Sharing a room or meeting place gives the feeling of being a part of the larger community. On the other hand, if the room or meeting place is not shared with other groups, the older people have a feeling of ownership and can exercise more flexibility in their programs.

As a general rule, once a week is about as often as most clubs meet. Some clubs are open every afternoon so that members may drop in to see each other and to play games. Such an arrangement gives those who live in boarding houses a place to go where they can be with friends. Some clubs in larger cities sponsored by fraternal organizations or unions remain open all day and serve as gathering places for members. Some clubs require dues from their members. Dues are usually small and in no case should they be prohibitive. The object is to give the members a feeling of helping to support the club. The object of the clubs is to get the members together, not to discourage new members. If the membership is composed of poorer people, they are given an opportunity to contribute but no record is made of the contributions. Often a box is kept in a convenient location so that members can put money in as they see fit.

The cost of making recreational facilities available to older citizens is normally low. The two major items in the budget are salaries for the professional leader and rent for the club room. If the club can use facilities which are used by other organizations, such as YM or YWCA's, churches, veterans' clubs, settlement houses, or fraternal clubs, the cost of operating the club will be low. Clubs have sometimes been housed in buildings donated by public-minded citizens or philanthropic organizations. The need for a large center usually develops after the program has been in operation long enough to build active community interest and support. The sponsoring organization usually pays the rent on the building where the meetings are held, provides some of the basic furnishings and equipment, and pays for the professional leader as well as for other items which make up a large part of the budget. The expense of food, transportation, and other minor items is usually met by the members after the program has started. The money for these expenses may be raised through dues or donations from the members or through club sales and shows.

There are two aspects of recreational programs for the aging which need publicity. The first is that recognition should be given by the club to individual members. Recognition should be given within the club to those who have birthdays or anniversaries. Special "birthday" parties should be scheduled once a month to honor those who have birthdays falling within the month. If members have received publicity through handicraft shows, note should be made of it. Each person should be given an opportunity to participate in club activities. If there are any members who are bashful, a special effort should be made to draw them into games, dancing, or group singing, or to have them take part in producing or acting in shows. Special notice should be taken of any success which is achieved by these people. In addition to these types of recognition, there should be a committee composed of less active members whose responsibility it is to send cards and flowers to members who are sick or to those who have not attended meetings within recent weeks. One advantage of a smaller club is that individual members are likely to be missed when they are absent and those present can mention it when the member returns.

Second, general publicity is good for the club. In addition to new members who may be brought in through publicity efforts, citizens in the community are made aware of the physical needs of the organization. The community can become aware of the necessity for supporting such recreational activities. Publicity of the nature referred to here concerns such things as public announcements regarding time and place of meetings and announcements concerning speakers for special programs. If the club has classes in hobbies and/or handicrafts, publicity is given to the displays and to the sale of such items. There are many other similar ways in which the attention of the public may be drawn to clubs for the aging. Such publicity will help make the members feel they have something to contribute to the community and will help the community realize something of its responsibility to its aging members.

Some brief mention has already been made of some of the activities which club members may engage in. The central emphasis of any recreational program and club organization is to offer an opportunity to the members to relax and enjoy themselves, to forget their anxieties and worries. An adequate recreational program provides enough activities to attract and hold members and has something for everyone to enjoy. Areas of activities include social programs, outdoor activities, arts and crafts, hobbies, music and drama, as well as service and educational activities. Informal parties are the outstanding social activity of most groups. If these parties are well-planned, they can provide fun for everyone. In instigating a recreational program for the aging, it is well to have a party for the first meeting. It is through parties that a skillful leader can encourage everyone to participate in the program. In making plans for social activities, the tempo of the games should be slow enough to satisfy the participants. Some games should be slow; others not so slow. A well-balanced program includes such things as get-acquainted games, mixers, quiet games, dances, and entertainment. Care should be exercised in selecting games so that those who are physically handicapped will not be excluded from joining the fun. Activities with easy-to-follow directions will go a long way in building up confidence and the ability to progress to new games.

Dancing is a popular activity in any program for the aging. It is usually a part of each program and can be included as a special event. It is wise to mix dancing with quieter activities; in this way, no one will be left out for long and over-enthusiastic members will not become too tired. There are several types of dances which are popular. Smoothness of style and grace should be stressed rather than speed or endurance. Standard procedures can be used to teach new steps and dances.

Day centers

Some of the larger municipalities are establishing day centers for their senior citizens. These centers perform a variety of functions, but their primary one is to provide a place for older people to find fun and companionship. One well-known center is located in the housing project for older people in Cleveland. This center is located on the first floor of the apartment building which has one hundred suites designed especially for older people. (See Chapter 16.) It is open to occupants of the apartment building, neighbors, and all older persons in the city. Qualified workers direct the program which includes social activities, crafts, and hobbies. A cafeteria is located in the center and is open to serve the noon meal to those who attend the center.[6] Another such organization is San Francisco Senior Center, which began its activities with only a few members in 1950. It has expanded since that time to include five satellite centers, each of which has a full program of activities for older people. These centers are sponsored jointly by public and voluntary agencies within the city.[7] Other California cities are following the example of San Francisco.

Somewhat similar to these centers are service centers for older people. As a rule the service centers, in addition to establishing a place for older people to meet and engage in recreational activities, offer a variety of services for them. Two such centers are those in Boston and Los Angeles County. The center in Boston helps its clients find out more about themselves. It helps them adjust to retirement, find jobs, and get the proper medical care if it is needed. This center is gathering extensive data on many aspects of aging.[8] The Los Angeles County Service Center acts as a coordinating agency for the older people of that locality. Information regarding governmental services is made available to those who want it. Part of this program is designed to stimulate community action in behalf of older adults.[9]

[6] Leona Bevis, "Cleveland Combines Housing with an Old-Age Center," *Aging*, XI (May, 1954), 3.

[7] Louis Kuplan, "California Moves Ahead," *Aging*, XVII (May, 1955), 2.

[8] *Business Week* (April 2, 1955), pp. 66–69.

[9] Catherine L. Wahlstrom, "Los Angeles County Presents Its Senior Citizens Service Center," *Aging*, XXII (March, 1956), 1.

Camping and picnicking

Camping is becoming increasingly popular with older people. The type of camping is adjusted to their needs, interests, and physical capacities. The first problem in planning a camping trip for older people is finding a place to camp. Cooperation with other local groups is desirable in getting good camp sites. In selecting a camping place consideration must be given to the physical needs and comforts of the older campers. Often it is possible for older people to use camp grounds which other groups use. The older people can use these camps either before or after the regular camping time or during periods when no other group is using the facilities. Cabins should accommodate from two to four persons and should be warm and well-lighted. Paths around the area should be free from stones and roots if possible. Where steps are necessary they should be provided with railings. Toilet facilities should be conveniently located if it is not possible to have toilets inside the cabins. No attempt should be made to stress camping as an adventure in primitive living, but rather an adventure in outdoor living and a break in the routine of life. The dining hall should be centrally located. It can be used for an assembly hall, if there is no other hall available. Camp grounds should be well-lighted at night to eliminate the danger of falling in the dark or running into trees, rocks, and other obstacles.

Usually camping trips last for one week, although some organizations make provision for longer periods. Eligibility for camping is generally based on a minimum age. Some camps may be for men only, others for women only, while still others may include men and women or only married couples. Usually a nominal fee is charged to cover the cost of some of the essentials such as food and recreational equipment. Prior to being accepted as campers, each person must undergo a simple physical examination and receive a statement from the doctor that there will be no danger involved for the person. Usually most older people who want to go on camping trips and feel they are physically able, have little trouble in passing the physical examination.

In addition to the regular run of activities engaged in at club meetings, in a camp situation there is an opportunity for swimming or wading, leisurely walks, nature study, or similar activities. It has been found that a leisurely program which begins with breakfast at about 7:30 A.M., has a rest period after lunch, and closes with a fireside program of hymn singing and Bible reading at about 9:30 P.M. fits the desires and physical capabilities of most campers. Older people are good campers and are less prone to accidents, snake-bite, and poison ivy than younger campers are.

Day camps can provide camping experiences for older people in communities where there are no facilities for regular camps. Usually fees for day camp include transportation and food. Day camps offer opportunities to those who either do not care to or cannot afford the regular camping experience. If neither type of camping seems to be practical, the summer months provide an opportunity for picnics. Older people enjoy a change of scenery and a few hours in the country together. Care should be exercised in choosing a picnic ground not too far from home and one which is not overcrowded with picnickers of other ages.

Arts, crafts and hobbies, music and drama

These leisure-time activities can serve the dual purpose of giving older people something useful and, at the same time, entertaining to do with their leisure time. They can provide an activity which is shared with other like-minded individuals, and in some instances, products of these activities are turned into an interest which brings either material or nonmaterial rewards. It is doubtful whether merely making something or doing something with no other goal in mind except that of keeping busy is really worthwhile. Rather, one or all of the purposes listed above should be kept in mind. Friendly competition in a group activity or a hobby show with prizes and other interest-centered goals should be set up. Publicity for the club and individual recognition in the way of prizes, rewards, or publicity for achievement make hobbies and allied activities worth something to those who participate.

Music plays a large part in recreational programs for the aged. Older people enjoy listening to music as well as performing it. Musical activities include singing in choral clubs and singing old-time favorites as well as performing instrumental music. Older people in some communities have organized orchestras and have given concerts during the summer months. Informal drama is also popular with older people. Skits, pageants, and similar dramatics are preferred to longer formal plays. This informal type eliminates long rehearsals, perfection of performance, and excessive memorization. Such dramatic presentation is valuable in that it involves group participation and helps to stimulate interest in the recreational program. In addition to the actors, other members of the club may write the play while still others prepare the costumes and scenery when needed.

Education

There is a relationship between education and certain phases of the recreational program for the aged. This relationship is especially obvious when such things as hobbies and similar activities are discussed. However, education for adults involves much more than education for recreational activities. In truth, education for adults involves education of the adults themselves and education of the larger community to the needs of the older citizens. Part of the difficulty in preparing an educational program for the aging stems from the fact that formal education as it has developed here is education for young people. This education is specifically designed to help the person find his place in society as a functioning adult. Part of the problem is related to the general concept of education as the domain of young people; that is, we have come to believe that people past "school age" are not as educable as those of younger years. Concerning the educating of the community to older people's needs, there seems to be the general impression that there is no useful purpose to be served. After all, we know how to get along with old people, and really there is no problem involved anyway. Why make a mountain out of a molehill? The true situation here is shown by statistics relative to the rapidly growing number and percentage of older people in the population. When older people were the responsibility of their families and when there were relatively few of them, there were relatively few problems involved; consequently, there was not so much necessity for community education. At the present, because of various changes in our national and community life, there is a growing need to educate the younger population and the community as a whole for a society which contains a higher percentage of older people.

From the point of view of society, the problem of educating the aging is the responsibility of the larger community. First, there should be education to make the public aware that the aging are an important part of the larger community. Second, society has the task of developing in its citizens the habit of continual learning so that citizens can continue to grow and change to meet the changing circumstances which confront them. This latter point is important, for as our population continues to age the average age of our professional, political, and business leaders will increase. If the national leaders in these areas of life begin to stagnate by middle age, our national life will tend to stagnate also. On the contrary, if these leaders continue to grow and continually learn to readjust themselves to changing times, the nation will continue to grow with and through them.

A successful educational program for adults is designed to reach and hold the aging rather than the aged. There is less practical value in educating a retired person than in educating a working person for retirement. The same holds true for medical education. It is of much greater practical value to teach a person how to take care of his physical body as he ages than it is to teach him how to live with the infirmities of old age. This is especially true when proper, continuing education might have forestalled or entirely prevented the advent of some of the disabilities. Similarly, it is more worthwhile to educate a person to supplement his income by a secondary occupation than it is to teach him to live on a drastically reduced budget after he has retired. In the final analysis, education of adults is a matter in great part of educating for prevention of certain physical, social, or economic disadvantages rather than teaching them to live with these disadvantages.

As a practical matter any program of education for the aging should begin with the educational institution and agencies, that is, the educational system or more specifically, the schools and colleges. The responsibility of these agencies to the community should not be discharged merely with the graduation of seniors. The schools could take the initiative in instigating community-wide planning for the aging. They could help in coordinating activities and actions along educational lines. Schools and other agencies could co-sponsor activities looking toward education for the aging. These other agencies, such as associations of doctors, social agencies, employment bureaus, and housing authorities, assisting the schools, could then build a program on a sound knowledge of what is taking place. Such a procedure will be inexpensive and worthwhile to all concerned. The primary consideration is that services for older people be a community responsibility. Educational planning with and for older people should be a community attempt to meet and satisfy the needs of an aging population.[10]

Special programs for older years

In general there are several approaches to education for the older years. Schools, in cooperation with other agencies and organizations, could use as the basis for adult education the special programs outlined below. These programs are

[10] United States Department of Health, Education and Welfare, *Education for a Long and Useful Life,* Bulletin No. VI (Washington, D.C.: 1950), 9.

designed to reach the middle-aged as well as those further advanced in years, for the middle-aged of today will be the older persons of tomorrow.[11]

(1) General cultural orientation. The primary purpose of this program is to build the proper attitudes toward aging in the general public as well as in those who are nearing old age. Desirable attitudes include the following: that old age normally should be as happy a period as any other period in life; that preparation for a later maturity should begin early; that plans and preparation for retirement should begin early and should be just as important as plans for work; that adults should continue to adjust during middle age as changing circumstances demand.

(2) Health education. This phase of education attempts to impress the aging with the changes that occur in their biological makeup as they become older. It is also important that these individuals become aware of the progress which medical science has made in the care, prevention, and cure of some of the degenerative diseases within recent decades. Such education includes instruction in mental hygiene, accident prevention, and dietary and exercise requirements for aging people.

(3) Family life education. This phase of education seems to be overlooked in many instances. It is just as important to study the adjustment of the family to aging and aging to the family as it is to study child care and development or adjustments in marriage relations. Older persons can be taught to become parents of adult children as well as how to assume the role of grandparents. Older people find value in learning how to return to the "empty-nest" phase of the family cycle as well as how to make a satisfactory adjustment to widowhood.

(4) Use of leisure time and vocational education. People should be taught early in life the importance of a hobby or secondary occupation. Work beyond retirement can be of value to society because the individual involved is not

[11] Adapted from *ibid.*, pp. 14–29.

a parasite but is continuing to make a positive contribution. Such activity is of value to the individual in that he feels he is a contributing member of the community; he has something worthwhile to contribute and he may help support himself, thus relieving society of at least part of that burden.

(5) Citizenship education. In general it seems that older people take a more active part in community activities than younger adults do. It is important that their experiences in leadership be transmitted to those who will take their places. It is of importance that older people be aware of changes which have occurred in the community, nation, and world. Discussion programs, forums, and public lectures by politicians or political science teachers make older people aware of changes which have occurred. Often a person's knowledge of a subject has not advanced beyond where it was when he left school. If an older person is to be a responsible citizen, it is imperative that society help train him for that role.

Guidance services

It is generally assumed that young people need guidance in vocational, educational, and personal matters.[12] Such guidance programs are believed necessary to prepare these people to take their proper place as functioning members of society. They are about to enter adult status positions for which they have had only theoretical training and in which they have had no practical experience. Society recognizes the necessity for such training and generally has made adequate provision for it. To the contrary, however, little thought has been given to this kind of training for older people as they approach old age. It should be recognized that older people have spent a large part of their lives working and living as functioning members of society, and that they, in old age, are entering another status position which calls for a reorientation of their lives to the facts of old age. Many older adults are unable by themselves to approach

[12] *Ibid.,* pp. 27–29.

their changing situations with objectivity and to make rational plans for themselves. They are entering an experience for which they have not been trained.

A great deal can be done with older adults through group situations to prepare them for changes which they will have to meet. Every person, however, must be able to translate general theory into an action program which is his own. Many of these older persons will need personal help with this process. It is important that counselors for older people be thoroughly aware of the needs and capabilities of the aged and that they are made aware of some of the possibilities for older people.

Counseling the aging has a number of specific aspects. These include counseling on occupational changes, dealing with fixed attitudes of older workers, and meeting the prejudices of employers. Experiences in counseling older people have shown that if there is to be any significant reorientation, several sessions are necessary. It is important to learn as much as possible about the background of the person being aided, about his interests, family situation, formal education, psychological abilities, job interests, hobbies, budgetary habits, and social relationships. If it is not possible to set up a complete guidance and rehabilitation center, it is possible in most urban communities to send the person to the specialized services in the community. These special agencies include vocational rehabilitation services, psychiatric clinics, educational agencies, and group work agencies. Advice to the older person should be based upon knowledge of the individual as well as knowledge of available opportunities for him.

Most of the facilities for taking care of the needs of older persons will have to come from both private and public agencies within the community. Primary responsibility for seeing that the agencies provide the required services, as well as responsibility for proper use of these services, rests with the individuals in the community. Individuals who are directly involved are the ones who should take a lead in using the services which are available. By using and developing the facilities which are offered or which can be offered, older people will be better fitted to fill a useful position in society. As a consequence, both the individual and society will benefit. The individual will benefit by having a richer, fuller life, and society will benefit by having older citizens who are good citizens making a positive contribution to the welfare of society.

Summary

It would seem that the primary purpose of both recreation and education of older adults is similar. This purpose is to prepare the older person for continued functioning in society. Basically the idea seems to be to impress upon the individual and upon society that a person does not cease to function when he reaches retirement age. Many years of useful life remain for most people after that time. The problem is to determine how the use may be made of that time so that society can continue to enjoy the fruits of a useful life and how the individual himself can continue to be both useful to society and an asset to himself and his associates. Obviously, this cannot be accomplished by hit-and-miss efforts on the part of either the individual or society. Society must be set up to take care of its older citizens just as it is to take care of the needs of its youth and younger adults. The individual older person must stand ready to make use of the facilities which are offered and to benefit by them just as young people entering adulthood are. Without cooperation in this program of training, both parties involved stand to lose. With cooperation, society will be amply rewarded.

18

American Society and the Aged

This chapter will inquire into some of the stereotypes of the aged which are held by the general population as well as by the elders themselves. It will also be the purpose of this concluding chapter to analyze the relation of the society to the aged in the framework of majority-minority relationships. The final section will explore briefly some of the efforts being made on the part of communities, states, and the federal government to cope with the emerging problems involving the older people of this country. This section will seek to interpret the research, legislative, and action programs in the framework of majority-minority relations.

The aged as a minority

One of the well-known principles of sociology is that if an individual believes a situation to be real, he will react to it as though it were real. That is to say, a person reacts to the subjective reality, or what he believes to be true, in the same way he reacts to the objective reality, or what is actually true. Hence, in the area of the sociology of the aged if there is belief on the part of a substantial proportion of younger people and adults that older citizens, as a social category, possess certain characteristics, these people will react to older people as though they in fact did possess these characteristics, regardless of the truth of the matter. If older people themselves believe that older people in general possess these characteristics they will react as though it were true. As is true of all stereotyped ideas, those regarding older people may be divided into four general classes.

First, there are those stereotypes which are generally true for all older people. For instance, there is the widely held idea that almost all older people are not as active physically as most people in their early adult years are. Second, there are those stereotypes which may be true for some older people but are not true for a majority of them. An illustration of this class of stereotype is the commonly held idea that all older people are hard of hearing. Third, there are those stereotypes which are generally adhered to but for which there is insufficient evidence or no evidence to prove the truth or falseness of the idea. An example here is the commonly held belief that older employees resent having to work under younger supervisors. Fourth and finally for the purposes of this analysis are the stereotypes generally held by the population which are factually untrue. In this class fall the stereotyped beliefs which have widespread adherence because generalizations are made from limited and faulty observations. Here is found the stereotype that the rate of illness and absenteeism of the older worker is higher than it is for young employees.

The above analysis leads to the conclusion that people generally see what they expect to see and want to see. We have an idea about how older people will act; we see the action which we expect to see and either fail to see or discount as atypical the acts which do not confirm our already formed opinions. Closely related to this behavior is the fact that people will often act as they think other people expect them to act. In part this phenomenon is the result of not wanting to be conspicuous or of not wanting to attract unpleasant attention. For instance a young couple may debate whether to take an elderly relative to a late picture show. One of them may argue that there is no use asking the older relative because "old people do not like to stay out late at night." The relative in question may not accept the invitation for any one of several reasons, but not necessarily because she does not like to stay out late. So, when the invitation is refused, the young people believe more firmly than before the stereotype which they already held.

Another point which deserves some attention is that people who have passed their sixty-fifth birthday carry with them into old age personality characteristics and behavior patterns they acquired long before they reached chronological old age. If this characteristic or behavior pattern is an unpleasant one or is merely thought of as being "queer" or undesirable, a younger person may say it is a behavior pattern characteristic of all old people. To be correct in his analysis, the young person must say that this is a characteristic of a particular person who happens to be over the age of 65. What usually occurs, however, is that there is another stereotype of the aged in the making. When a similar unfortunate behavior pattern is observed in another older person it is well on the way to becoming a trait expected of all older people.

A series of studies has been conducted to determine the extent to which people of different ages subscribe to erroneous and stereotyped ideas concerning older people. Two different questionnaires have been devised for this study. One of these is designed to test the extent of stereotyping of the aged in general; the other to test the attitude of younger people toward the older worker. A majority of the statements on these questionnaires are negative or derogatory, presenting ideas which seem to be widely held by people about older people. Some of the statements such as "older people like to associate with young people" do not, on the surface, appear to be negative. In a context of other negative statements like "old people are grouchy" it would be interpreted as a "bad" thing for older people to want to associate with younger ones, or there would be a connotation of "pushiness" applied to the behavior of the older person.

The statements given in the questionnaires for the series of studies are derived from three categories of ideas. There are ideas which have valid basis in fact, those ideas for which there is sketchy or inconclusive evidence, and, in the majority of statements, ideas for which experimental evidence is completely lacking.[1] The assumption is that with the emphasis on youth and speed, older people are expected to play less active roles in both the social and economic life of this country. These circumstances encourage the formation of misconceptions and stereotypes about old age. In broad categories the questions regarding old people in general include statements under the heading of physical changes with age, family relationships, personality traits, conservatism, and others. Questions dealing with older workers include those on the subject of physical and mental decline, reaction to criticism, and attitudes toward the job.[2]

The series of questionnaires has been given to public school pupils, undergraduate and graduate college students, parents of college students, and aged residents in the community and in nursing homes. Some of the statements were agreed to by a large majority of those answering, others to a lesser extent, while some statements were seldom agreed to.

Most of the respondents believe that on the job older workers need more time to learn new plant operations and require more time to recover from injury and illness. Only about half of the respondents believe older people are slow and are more interested in security than in advancement. Less than 10 per cent of the respondents subscribe to the idea that older workers cannot win the confidence and loyalty of co-workers, that they have no ambition, that they are paid too much, and that they quit their jobs frequently. In general this study showed that respondents do not have very favorable ideas concerning the learning ability of older people. However the respondents indicate a favorable attitude toward the aged concerning personal relations in work.

[1] Jacob Tuckman and Irving Lorge, "Attitudes Toward Older People," *Journal of Social Psychology*, XXXVII (May, 1953), 249 ff.

[2] Cf. Jacob Tuckman and Irving Lorge, " 'When Aging Begins' and Stereotypes About Aging," *Journal of Gerontology*, VIII (October, 1953), 489–492; and Tuckman and Lorge, "Attitudes Toward Older Workers," *Journal of Applied Psychology*, XXXVI (June, 1952), 149–153.

In a survey involving the attitudes of different age groups toward older people in general, the authors found a great deal of variation in the acceptance of specific statements by each of the age categories.[3] There was also a variation in the acceptance of the statements between the categories of respondents. In general women tend to subscribe to erroneous or stereotyped statements more than men do and younger people tend to agree with the erroneous or stereotyped statements more than older ones do. In another study the questionnaire was given to three groups of elders between the ages of 60 and 88.[4] The findings of this study upheld the hypothesis that as individuals become less able to function in society they subscribe more to beliefs and erroneous ideas about older workers. Older people who are in closer contact with society and are still able to function do not hold to negative ideas to the same degree as do the aged who are institutionalized.

In these studies the authors conclude that older people and those less able to function subscribe to erroneous and stereotyped statements because it is indicative of the concepts these people have about themselves and their adjustments. Older people have more intimate acquaintance with old age and so are more inclined to accept the cultural expectations of decreasingly active roles of old people in the social-economic life. The tendency for most of the respondents seems to be to think of old age in terms of physical disability. There seems to be substantial acceptance of misconceptions and stereotypes about old people and older workers. Responses from students and university undergraduates indicate that they look upon old age as a

[3] Jacob Tuckman and Irving Lorge, "The Effect of Family Environment on Attitudes Toward Older People and the Older Worker," *Journal of Social Psychology*, XXXVIII (November, 1953), 207 ff.; and Irving Lorge and Jacob Tuckman, "Attitudes of Junior and Senior High School Students Toward Aging," in Thomas C. Desmond (chm.), *Growing with the Years* (Albany: New York State Joint Legislative Committee on Problems of the Aging, 1954), pp. 59–61.

[4] Jacob Tuckman and Irving Lorge, "The Attitudes of the Aged Toward the Older Worker: for Institutionalized and Non-Institutionalized Adults," *Journal of Gerontology*, VII (October, 1952), 559–64.

period of life characterized by economic insecurity, poor health, loneliness, resistance to change, and failing mental and physical powers. The responses seem to reflect the cultural expectations regarding the activities, personality characteristics, and adjustments of older people. It is concluded that older people are living in a social climate which is not conducive to a feeling of adequacy, usefulness, security, and good adjustment to old age.[5]

In another study a shorter list of erroneous and stereotyped statements was used to determine whether the attitudes which college students hold toward older people were influenced by frequency of contact, physical closeness of contact, and intimacy of contact between themselves and older people.[6] Closeness of contact was determined on the basis of whether the respondent had lived in the home with an old person in the past, was now in the home with an old person, or never had lived in the home with an old person. Frequency of close contact was scaled in terms of frequent, fairly frequent, or seldom. The degree of intimacy of contact was arrived at in terms of intimate, fairly intimate, and casual or impersonal contact. On the basis of the information gathered by this study it was concluded that, in terms of living arrangements, intimacy, and frequency of close contact of the sample of college students tested, the opinions held toward older people did not vary to any statistically significant degree.

What roles should elders play?

An extensive study has been made regarding the attitudes of young people as to the roles they believed older people should play.[7] The questionnaire included a long list of activities which people over the age of 65 might engage in. Some of the things listed are generally con-

[5] Jacob Tuckman and Irving Lorge, "Attitudes Toward Older People," *Journal of Social Psychology*, XXXVII (May, 1953), 260.

[6] Joseph T. Drake, "Some Factors Influencing Students' Attitudes Toward Older People," *Social Forces*, XXXV (March, 1957), 266–71.

[7] Robert J. Havighurst and Ruth Albrecht, *Older People* (New York: Longmans, Green & Co., Inc., 1953), pp. 350 ff.

sidered "good" things for older people to do, others are not. Some of the items listed might be "good" for women to do but not for men, or vice versa. The respondents were of all ages. The respondents were asked to assume that the older person was in reasonably good health. They were asked to signify approval or disapproval of old people's engaging in the activities listed by checking one of the following statements for each item. The statements were: A, this is all right, I approve of it; B, neither good nor bad; and C, this is a bad or foolish thing to do. Items or activities listed in the questionnaire included the following groups: civic activities, clubs and neighborhood participation, recreation; church, family, work, and financial matters.

In analyzing the results of the study and to determine the various types of activities that were approved or disapproved, the scores were grouped into four levels. Forty-one activities were strongly approved; 24 activities were mildly approved; 26 activities were reacted to with indifference or mild disapproval; and 37 activities were strongly disapproved. The activities which were strongly approved included the continuation of life as in middle age with "reasonable tapering off" or the playing of specific "old peoples' roles." The respondents mildly approved the playing of specific "old peoples' roles" regarded as permissive but not highly favored. Activities viewed with indifference or mild disapproval included overactivity or prolonging activities of middle age beyond reason, carrying on in a slightly improvident or irresponsible manner, heavy involvement in the everyday life of adult children, or activity on a level below that which is regarded as desirable for good citizenship or good social behavior. The activities which rated strong disapproval were complete inactivity and social isolation, acting much younger than one's age, and behaving immorally.[8]

Several conclusions can be drawn from this survey. As a whole the public tends to favor greater activity for older men than for older women. This is particularly true in the

[8] *Ibid.*, pp. 352 ff.

areas of public life. Generally men favor more active participation for older men than they do for older women. Women favor more active participation for older women than men do, although women at the same time favor more active participation for older men than they do for older women.[9]

As far as difference in age of respondents was concerned, there was no appreciable change in approval level of activities except on a few items. Some items showed an increase in approval as the ages of the respondents increased. Younger people withdraw approval of older people engaging in certain classes of activities which are thought to require physical, mental, and social characteristics no longer found in people who are classified as "old."[10] Older people generally hold more erroneous and stereotyped ideas about old people than young people hold toward them. They also disapprove for themselves more activities than young people disapprove for them.

These conclusions seem to fit into the general framework of dominant-minority relations. Members of the dominant groups ordinarily hold strongly to stereotyped and erroneous ideas concerning characteristics of the minority groups. Minorities conscious of their minority status within the society often hold the same attitudes toward themselves as are held toward them. Often, because of certain factors, minority members may be even less generous toward themselves than the majority or dominant members are. This idea is expressed in the dominant-minority concept of "self-hatred." Older people generally agree with the statements that older people are grouchy and are slow to catch new ideas more often than younger people agree to the same statements. An element of self-pity or persecution, another well-known aspect of minority groups, is indicated when older people believe more than younger ones that old people receive no sympathy from their relatives and that old people are not useful to themselves or to others.

[9] *Ibid.*, p. 358.
[10] *Ibid.*, pp. 359–62.

Are the aged a minority?

Perhaps the question needs to be asked whether the aged really constitute a social minority in this country. At least one writer believes that, as a category, they possess some of the characteristics of a social minority just as women, as a category, do.[11] However, there are some salient differences between the aged and women on the one hand and racial, ethnic, or religious minorities, on the other. It is probably more valid to use the concept "quasi-minority" when referring to the aged. In one crucial respect the aged are not a true minority, because they are not members of an independently functioning subgroup as are those who constitute the traditional minority groups. Another way of stating this is to say that the aged participate in the same culture the rest of the society participates in, and the rest of the society, to a large extent, participates in the same culture which the aged participate in. Some of the more important areas of cultural life in which there is joint participation are the values, the traditions, the religious beliefs, and the language. There is no history of the aged as there is a history of the racial, ethnic, and religious minorities in this country. The aged participate in the family life of the larger groups to which they belong and are members of families in these groups in a sense that the ethnic minorities cannot be. In other words, the aged have at one time been accepted members of their own particular social groups and it is only as they reach old age that they begin to lose their status positions, not as a group of affiliated individuals, but as distinct individuals. Members of ethnic minorities are either born into or marry into the minority groups.

The aged are not a minority in the traditional sense in that they have free access to residential areas; there are no restrictive covenants which prohibit them from living where

[11] Milton L. Barron, "Attacking Prejudices Against the Aged," in *Growing with the Years*, pp. 56–58; and Milton L. Barron, "Minority Characteristics of the Aged in American Society," *Journal of Gerontology*, VIII (October, 1953), 477–82.

they can afford to live. They are not excluded by law or practice from public places nor are they forced to ride in segregated sections in public conveyances. No local laws have been enacted to prohibit their participation in public life and no signs have been erected to prohibit them from entering stores or other public places as has been done with other minorities. If there is any "gentlemen's agreement" among store owners or hotel people to exclude the aged, most people do not know of it.

On the other side of the question there are numerous conditions which indicate that the aged as a category do occupy a minority status in American society. It has been mentioned above that there are widespread stereotypes of the aged held by other age groups. This is true of majority-minority situations also. Some of the stereotypes of the aged are no more complementary to them than are some of the stereotypes of the ethnic minorities. There is a great deal of evidence to indicate discrimination by employers against the aged as a category. A form of discrimination, with its basis in stereotypes, can also be found in areas of life other than employment. The chronologically aged are often not accepted in official positions within organizations because it is felt that they talk too much, that they are too forgetful of details, or that younger people object to working with them on committees and other action bodies.

There are very few official ways in which the aged in this country benefit by their minority status. "Glorified" minorities may benefit by their status both officially and unofficially. Unofficially the aged benefit by having a certain amount of deference shown them by their associates. Porters are probably more prone to help an elderly lady with her bag than they are to help a young healthy looking man with his. In the family situation it is often the case that the choicest or tenderest cuts are saved for the older person. They are allowed to have a certain amount of personal freedom that would not be admitted to a younger person. Unofficially society allows them to indulge in certain personal habits which would be frowned upon if practiced by younger people.

As a general rule it is assumed that members of dominant social groups do not like members of religious or ethnic minorities. Also as a general rule it can be assumed that the chronologically young do not dislike old people as such. In a questionnaire distributed to approximately 400 college students, among other items the students were asked whether they liked old people.[12] No student in the sample checked the statement "I dislike old people very much." Only three of the sample stated that they had a mild dislike for old people and only ten checked the statement "I don't care much one way or the other about old people." The vast majority of the respondents were divided about equally between liking old people very much or liking them fairly well. The study found no relation between the answers to the question of liking or disliking and the acceptance or rejection of stereotyped and erroneous statements about old people. Perhaps the most obvious conclusion to be drawn would be that younger people, while professing to like old people, continue to hold erroneous and stereotyped ideas about them. It could be a case of liking a person but disliking some of his actions and characteristics. It is not socially acceptable to admit disliking the aged, whereas, in some localities and some social groups, it is in the folkways to dislike members of ethnic minorities as well as the minority group as a whole.

In some respects the aged react to their status position as a category in ways which are similar to the reaction of ethnic minority groups. "Classical" minority reaction to their status includes some of the following. Self-hatred is one of the reactions. The aged show self-hatred by denying that they are chronologically old. Traditionally this has been true of women more than of men in this country. Older men seeking employment probably deny their age also. Almost universally older people seek to camouflage their true age by the use of cosmetics, false hair, false teeth, the use of contact lenses and of small hearing aids which, in the words of the advertisers, are "inconspicuous." In addition,

[12] Unpublished findings, University of Tennessee, 1956.

some older people become very critical of other older people, apparently trying to give the impression that they themselves are not old. A second minority reaction, self-pity or the persecution complex, has been mentioned earlier. Low morale as a minority reaction is closely akin to the persecution complex. This involves "giving up" and not trying any more because of the rebuffs which one is afraid he will meet if he does try.

Another minority reaction sometimes manifested by older people is that of withdrawal or voluntary isolation. This technique is often resorted to so that the person will be able to avoid as much as possible any contact with majority group members. Experience has taught minority members that contacts have been or are potentially the source of unpleasant experiences. They desire to be rid of unpleasant occurrences and apparently the easiest way to do so is to keep contact with majority members to a minimum. This technique is rather widespread among the aged in this country. One study shows that more than half of a sample of 1,200 people 60 years of age and over do not belong to any club or other organization.[13] Nearly 40 per cent of the respondents claim they are hardly ever asked to give advice to the members of their families. Slightly more than one-third claim to have no really close friends. This study also indicates that the unemployed are more isolated socially than the employed are.

From the foregoing analysis it must be concluded that the aged in our society partake of some of the characteristics of a social and economic minority even though there does not appear to be any organized or categorical discrimination against them. The following section indicates that there is both an organized and categorical attempt on the part of official representatives of the three levels of government to "do something" about old people as a social and economic group. It is possible that efforts along this line may have the unforeseen consequence of setting the stage for

[13] Milton L. Barron, "Attacking Prejudices Against the Aged," in *Growing with the Years*, p. 57.

categorical discrimination against the aged on the part of the rest of society.

Research and action programs

One of the first criteria of a social problem is an awareness on the part of society that a social situation exists which is defined, or thought of, as being undesirable. A second criterion is that this undesirable situation is capable of being "solved." The history of social action in this country is replete with illustrations of attempted solutions to situations which have been defined by society, or segments of it, as constituting social problems. In general the first stage of the process is that a small number of socially alert individuals take some public notice of the situation. Their ideas are formulated, and either in public forums or in writing they speak in broad generalities about the problem as they see it. They advocate some kind of action program for the solution of the problem.

As more and more general interest in the subject is aroused, more people step forward to join the movement and add their voices to those already speaking and writing on the subject. Before much longer there is a realization by some of these people that intelligent social action cannot be taken until some factual information is gathered. Statistics have to be gathered and analyzed, the extent of the problem has to be determined, broad lines of demarcation have to be drawn, and some effort has to be made to define the problem in workable terms. Terms have to be defined and frequently there is an effort made to substitute a new word or phrase for the word or phrase originally used to designate the problem. Frequently the original word has taken on unpleasant or derogatory connotations, and it is apparently believed that a change in terms will elevate the status of the problem and even perhaps of the individuals who are involved in it. Illustrations are referring to illegitimate children as children of illegitimate parents, using the term "mentally ill" instead of the legal term "insane," or the word "alcoholics" instead of the popular expression "drunks," [14] and using various euphemisms to describe old people. Some of these in professional usage now are "the aging," "senior citizens," "the elderly" and other similar words or phrases.

After some time spent in preliminary preparation, committees are formed and conferences are held on a national or state level. Early conferences on the subject attempt to attract a few well-known people who may or may not have an interest in the particular problem. These are "prestige people." Less well-known "resource persons" are invited to attend to give the conference an air of scientific respectability. These early conferences usually have two results. First, they arouse public interest in the subject, and second, they point out some of the areas for further study, study which is designed to give the subject more scientific validity.

In broad outline this procedure seems to have been followed in many of the so-called "problem areas" of American life: intergroup or race relations, delinquency, crime, and physical and mental disability. The same is generally true as far as the study of gerontology is concerned. There seems to be a parallel growth of interest in older people and in child welfare and intergroup relations. One might infer that those who have studied, investigated, and begun action programs see the study of older citizens in somewhat the same light as some others have viewed the study of other problem areas; that is, as a special social category or as a minority group. In effect, such programs are an attempt to better the position of those under study, both economically and socially, by bringing them into the mainstream of American life and raising them to the same level with the dominant, adult, white-Protestant group.

The remaining sections of this chapter will offer a classification of some of the activities which have taken place in gerontology within the past decade. All such developments cannot be dealt with here; this discussion is intended to indicate some activity in some areas of the country, what

[14] There are many other instances of this phenomenon in the history of human relations in this country.

has been done, and perhaps indirectly, what can be done. The selection of illustrations—conferences, commissions and societies, and local action groups—is strictly arbitrary. To mention every conference in detail, the exact function of each commission, and every action of all of the local groups would be an endless task because this is an on-going process where "snow-balling" is the order of the day. Especially on the local scene, success with one project leads to the formulation of other projects. When one community meets with success, another community is encouraged to attempt the formulation of a program of its own.

Conferences

In August of 1950 the first National Conference on Aging was held in Washington, D.C. This conference was sponsored by the Federal Security Agency at the direction of President Truman. Briefly stated the objectives of the conference were: (1) to provide a forum for persons concerned with aging; (2) to re-evaluate the potentialities of older people; (3) to stimulate the exchange of ideas among interested people with a view to solving problems of the aging; (4) to define the nature and extent of the problems; (5) to promote research in the various phases of aging; and (6) to transmit the findings to interested groups as guidelines for the development of policies with regard to older people.[15] Oscar Ewing, then Federal Security Administrator, stated at the beginning of the conference that its underlying purpose was to focus attention on the problems and needs of the aging. From the information thus presented he hoped community action would work to change the pattern of behavior toward older people.[16]

In September, 1952, a joint conference of state commissions on aging and interested federal agencies met in Washington. This conference was called at the suggestion of

---

[15] John L. Thurston, "The Conference," in Federal Security Agency, *Man and His Years* (Raleigh: Health Publications Institute, Inc., 1951), p. 10.

[16] "Man and His Years," *Aging*, August 6, 1951, p. 1.

several of the state commission chairmen. In addition to members of the established state commissions on aging, delegates were present from eighteen states which had no official commissions. The general purpose of the conference was to enable the official state commissions and delegates to exchange ideas, information, and techniques as well as to learn about the resources of the federal government which are available for the development of state and community programs for the aged.[17]

In 1956 President Eisenhower established the Federal Council on Aging. The purpose of this council was to coordinate interdepartmental policies and programs in the field of aging, to renew existing activities, and to make recommendations to meet the pressing needs of older people. In the summer of 1956 this council met with the Council of State Governments. This latter organization is an agency established and supported by the various states to promote research and consultative services, to serve as a medium for improving legislative and administrative practices, and to improve interstate and state-federal relations.[18] These two organizations held a Federal-State Conference on Aging. The conference proposed the following goal: "A society, in which people, regardless of age, may walk with dignity and have the opportunity for a full and satisfying life."[19] The conference studied six broad areas of aging which were: employment, vocational rehabilitation, and retirement; income maintenance, including welfare services; physical and mental health; housing and living arrangements; education and recreation; and organization and functions in the states.[20] At the close of the meeting the various groups or committees which had studied each of the main topics submitted a list of recommendations to the conference as a whole.

[17] "The Conference of State Commissions on Aging and Federal Agencies," *Aging*, III (January, 1953), 1.
[18] Dorothy McCammon, "Federal-State Conference on Aging," *Social Security Bulletin*, XIX (August, 1956), 3–7 and 31.
[19] *Ibid.*, p. 3.
[20] *Ibid.*, p. 3.

One of the primary purposes these and other similar conferences serve is to stimulate wider interest in the field of gerontology. Those who attend the conferences go back to their respective communities and agencies with new ideas and, perhaps, with new interest and vision. Thus the influence of conferences on the federal level filters down to the states and eventually to communities.

State commissions

Either as a direct or indirect result of the First National Conference on Aging, several states took action to form commissions to study the problem of aging within their states. In some instances these commissions were appointed by the governors, in others they were formed by legislative action. As a direct result of the National Conference, the North Carolina delegates met with their State Commissioner of Public Welfare. The Governor's Conference on Aging resulted from this meeting. The conference which met in Raleigh was organized around six discussion sections which inquired into research, employment, education and recreation, health and rehabilitation, family life, and professional personnel. The conference recommended that the governor appoint a special committee on aging to follow up the work of the conference.[21]

A different approach, on a somewhat more limited basis, was used in Florida in 1949. The governor of Florida made use of an existing agency to inquire into a problem relative to older people which is more peculiarly a Florida problem. The Florida State Improvement Commission was directed to study the migration of retired persons into the state and the social and economic implications of the migration. At the same time, to work in conjunction with this commission which was an on-going enterprise, the governor created a Citizens Commission on Retirement. The goals of this retirement research commission are to stimulate interest in both the problem and opportunities which retired persons

[21] Annie M. Pemberton, "Mobilization in North Carolina," *Aging*, August 6, 1951, pp. 2–3.

meet; to stimulate institutions of higher learning to conduct research in this area; to further cooperation with other state agencies in research into problems of retirement; to encourage the building of suitable retirement housing; and to provide reliable information for retired people who wish to live in Florida.[22]

Governors of other states followed the example of the pace-setting states. They either appointed, or asked their legislatures to appoint commissions to study the problem of the aged in their respective states. Some of the commissions were appointed on a temporary basis, others on a permanent basis. The purposes of some were restricted to information gathering; others had a broader scope covering virtually all phases of the problem. As time has passed, these commissions have been followed by the formation of commissions in other states. Studies in the form of factual information concerning general problems of population distribution of the aged, income needs and sources of income, problems of employment and rehabilitation, and other related questions have been investigated. The results have been reproduced for distribution to interested persons and agencies. Among the more prominent, in terms of either length of duration or ends achieved, are the Commissions of New York, California, Connecticut, Massachusetts, Minnesota, Rhode Island, Michigan, Maine, Oregon, New Mexico, and Indiana.

Conferences and societies

In addition to the conferences held by the state commissions, there are several widely known conferences of a continuing nature. Some of these are well on the way to attaining national prominence among people who are interested in and concerned with the subject of gerontology. These conferences attract speakers from every part of the nation. Individuals and official representatives from most of the interested agencies of the federal government as

[22] Irving L. Webber, "Fact Finding in Florida," *Aging*, August 6, 1951, p. 5.

well as representatives and officials from many local and state agencies attend these conferences. Probably the oldest and best known is the Annual Conference on Aging which is held at Ann Arbor each year. The Division of Gerontology, Institute of Human Adjustment of the University of Michigan, and the United States Department of Health, Education and Welfare and the Department of Labor usually sponsor these conferences jointly. Dr. Wilma Donahue, who is the moving spirit and director of the conference, edits the reports of these conferences. The theme of the conference changes from year to year but deals with problems relating to old age. The programs at these meetings are divided between general sessions and discussion groups or workshops.

The University of Florida Institute of Gerontology holds its Annual Southern Conference in Gainesville in mid-winter. The reports of these conferences are published in book form under the editorship of persons connected with the university. Here, as in Michigan, various topics are chosen as themes of the conferences and nationally known persons contribute to the programs.

An annual meeting, sponsored by the New York State Joint Legislative Committee on Problems of the Aging, is held in Albany. Technically, these meetings can be classified as "hearings" before the committee where the various speakers "testify." Ostensibly this testimony is for the purpose of bringing before the committee expert information which might lead to the enactment of legislation by the government of the state. The series of published speeches is, in a sense, somewhat similar to the reports of the two conferences mentioned above. No other conference thus far seems to be as widely and regularly attended or to attract consistently so many figures of national prominence as these three.

There are some less well-known conferences which may later become prominent in their own right. Some of these have not yet attained the status of regular annual meetings, while others are well on the way toward such a goal. Many of the states have held such conferences, which are usually sponsored by the governors' commissions. Some of the conferences are sponsored by state university institutes, extension divisions, or committees on gerontology, such as the one at the University of Washington and at Florida. The first nonsectarian Church Conference on Aging was held in Dallas in April, 1955. The University of North Carolina is host for the Southern Regional Conference on Recreation for the Aging. In 1955, the Inland Empire Conference in Spokane, Washington drew participants from Washington, Idaho, and Montana. This should serve to give some indication of the growing interest which is being shown by states and regions in this field.

Another type of conference is that sponsored by societies. For the purpose of this discussion these societies can be classified on three levels. First are the societies which have been established because of interest in geriatrics and gerontology; second are the welfare societies which consider geriatrics and gerontology only one of several subjects of interest to themselves. Societies of this nature may devote one entire meeting to the subject of gerontology or may have one or more sessions of a general conference set aside for the discussion of problems of the aged. Third, there are the academically oriented societies which, in their annual meetings, have one or more sessions dealing with various phases of the subject.

Under the first head would fall the International Gerontological Congress, the Gerontological Society, the American Geriatrics Society, the American Society for the Aged, and the Gerontological Society of Connecticut. The Florida Council on Aging and the Western Gerontological Society are recent comers to the field. Closely akin to these, but falling under the second heading, are the National Committee on Aging of the National Social Welfare Assembly and the Division on Later Maturity and Old Age of the American Psychological Association. Both these organizations are branches of larger societies with broad purposes. Under the third heading are the American Sociological Society and the

Southern Sociological Society. In the annual meetings of the first of these, several entire sessions have been set aside for papers dealing with sociological research in gerontology. Only one or two papers on this subject have been read at recent Southern meetings.

Local action

Action on the local level is, as a general rule, inspired originally by commissions, conferences, and societies such as those mentioned above. After the instigation of an action program on the local level, representatives of these groups may report on their activities to such conferences. Reports of successful local action often serve as an added incentive to other individuals who are present. These people, on returning to their respective agencies, are inspired to attempt action in their own localities. Aside from federal and state legislation on the subject, most of the actual, practical programs begin on the community level. Within recent years and with a growing impetus, one locality after another has started programs of various types. The most popular types seem to be in the areas of education, recreation, housing, hobbies, and employment opportunities. Cities in all parts of the country have already developed such programs under the auspices of either public or private agencies and organizations.

Experts advise that community programs should have the following broad, basic objectives. In the realm of the economic, the community should provide equal opportunities for the aging and prevent indigency of the aging. In the realm of the social, the community should attempt to prevent loss of status, and to promote useful, creative, social participation by the aging. Communities which are engaged in local programs usually find it necessary to attack stereotyped ideas about the aged which may act to retard the fulfillment of community action.[23]

[23] Albert J. Abrams, "Community Programs for the Aging," in Thomas C. Desmond (chm.), *New Channels for the Golden Years* (Albany: New York State Joint Legislative Committee on Problems of the Aging, 1956), pp. 109–17.

The best way to judge the success of any local program is to determine how well it is meeting its objectives. Certain criteria have been suggested as norms by which to measure success.[24] To be successful any program must reach a large and representative number of the aging. No program can be called successful if its activities are limited to only one area of action such as recreation. Services should be rendered according to need, not according to the ease of rendering the service. To be successful the program has to be financed adequately and must have the backing and involvement of professional, political, and civic leaders. Finally, both the community and the elderly themselves must accept the program and understand its objectives.

Two of the most important principles to be observed in the formation of community organizations for the aging are: (1) facts should be gathered and (2) all agencies and organizations which are concerned with the aging should become involved in the program. Blindly striking out to "get something done" with no information available is a waste of time. Unless all of the interested agencies and organizations are enlisted in the projects, there will be duplication of effort and a consequent waste of time, money, and talent. Any unnecessary duplication will almost invariably lead to professional or organizational jealousy which frequently means constructive effort is diverted from the avowed objectives and channeled into intra-agency squabbles and discords.

Summary

Although it cannot be stated categorically that the aged constitute a social minority, it is clear that they do possess some of the characteristics of racial and ethnic minorities. It is also clear that some segments of the society view them as members of a minority in that they are denied full social and economic opportunities in the life of the society. One indication of the minority status of the aged, in the eyes of the rest of the society, is the fact that society, through

[24] *Ibid.*, p. 112.

its agencies and organizations, has organized itself to "do something" about the aged. If this, in and by itself, is not conclusive proof of the minority status, it is proof that the aged are at least viewed as a social problem. The criteria of a social problem are that society is aware of the so-called undesirable situation, that there is a general conviction that something can be done to remedy it, and that steps are being taken to do so.

The past six years particularly have seen the birth and rapid growth of state commissions, conferences, institutes, and societies whose primary objective is to study and make recommendations concerning various phases of the total problem of the aged. Interest in the subject has been shown on all three governmental levels, in civic clubs, by churches on the various hierarchal levels, by institutions of higher learning, and by philanthropic organizations and foundations. It is not surprising to find that some states and localities have shown no interest or only a passing interest in the matter while others have gone a long way in preparing on-going, permanent organizations which are designed to instigate and coordinate action programs in areas where they are believed to be needed. It is not unreasonable to believe that, as time passes and the number and percentage of the aged increase, more and better organizations will be formed to carry out the programs which the earlier formed organizations have begun.

Bibliography

Multi-author works

ARMSTRONG, DONALD B. (chm.). *The Social and Biological Challenge of Our Aging Population.* (Proceedings of the Eastern States Health Education Conference, March 31–April 1, 1949). New York: Columbia University Press, 1950.

> Allen, Edward B. "Psychological Factors That Have a Bearing on the Aging Process."
> Davis, Kingsley, and Combs, J. W., Jr. "The Sociology of an Aging Population."
> Hochman, Julius. "The Retirement Myth."
> Kiser, Clyde V. "The Demographic Background of Our Aging Population."
> Seegal, David. "On Longevity and the Control of Chronic Disease."

CALDWELL, MORRIS G., and FOSTER, LAURENCE. *Analysis of Social Problems.* Harrisburg, Pa.: The Stackpole Company, 1953.

> Drake, Joseph T. "The Aged."

COMMITTEE ON PUBLIC EMPLOYMENT RETIREMENT ADMINISTRATION OF THE MUNICIPAL FINANCE OFFICERS OF THE UNITED STATES AND CANADA. *Forty-seventh Annual Conference, Miami, Florida* (May 31–June 4, 1953). Chicago: 1953.

> Dudek, Jack. "Pensions for Uniformed Personnel in Public Employment."
> Meyers, Arthur C., Jr. "Criteria for Evaluating Retirement Systems for Public Employees."
> Smith, Charles R. "Is Social Security Coverage for All Public Employees Inevitable? Affirmative."

COWDRY, E. V. (ed.). *Problems of Ageing.* Baltimore: The Williams and Wilkins Co., 1939.

> Dublin, Louis I. "Longevity in Retrospect and in Prospect."
> Miles, Walter R. "Psychological Aspects of Aging."
> Shock, Nathan W. "Biology of Aging."
> Wissler, Clark. "Human Cultural Levels."

DERBER, MILTON (ed.). *The Aged and Society.* Champaign, Ill.: Industrial Relations Research Association, 1950.

> Barkin, Samuel. "Union Policies and the Older Worker."
> Brown, J. Douglas. "The Role of Industry in Relation to the Older Worker."
> Burgess, Ernest W. "Personal and Social Adjustment in Old Age."
> Kaplan, Oscar J. "The Mental Health of Older Workers."

401

Moore, Elon H. "Self-Provision for the Aged."

Moore, Wilbert J. "The Aged in Industrial Societies."

Sheldon, J. H. "Medical-Social Aspects of the Aging Process."

Shock, Nathan W. "The Contribution of Psychology."

Shryock, Henry S., Jr. "The Changing Age Profile of the Population."

Slichter, Sumner H. "Retirement Age and Social Policy."

Smith, T. Lynn. "The Aged in Rural Society."

Welford, A. T., and Speakman, D. "The Employability of Older People."

Witte, Edwin E. "Social Provisions for the Aged."

DESMOND, THOMAS C. (chm.). *Age is No Barrier.* Albany: New York State Joint Legislative Committee on Problems of the Aging, 1952.

Abrams, Albert J. "Discrimination in Employment of Older Workers in Various Countries of the World."

Barkin, Solomon. "Redesigning Jobs in Industry for a Maturing Population."

Berger, Graenum. "Vacation Services for Older Persons."

Bohlin, G. S. "Rehabilitation of Older Persons."

Coleman, Marguerite H. "Next Steps in Placement of the Elderly."

Hochhauser, Edward. "Sheltered Work for Older Persons."

Lorge, Irving. "Psychology and Our Older People."

Murray, Clyde E. "Group Work and the Aged."

Robbins, Ira S. "Housing Our Aging."

Stickman, Herman T. "Public Housing for the Aged in New York State."

Taylor, Eugene J. "Rehabilitation in Community Programs for the Aged."

Warren, Ronald L. "Old Age in a Rural Township."

DESMOND, THOMAS C. (chm.). *Birthdays Don't Count.* Albany: New York State Joint Legislative Committee on Problems of the Aging, 1951.

DESMOND, THOMAS C. (chm.). *Enriching the Years.* Albany: New York State Joint Legislative Committee on Problems of the Aging, 1953.

Abrams, Albert J. "Should There Be a Fixed Retirement Age?"

———. "Training of Older Persons Through Correspondence and Private Trade Schools."

Barshop, Irving, *et al.* "Employment in the Later Years."

Brown, E. Blanchard. "The Older Person and the New Handicraft Program for Older Persons."

Desmond, Thomas C. "Beware the Farm Fantasy."

———. "Schooldays for Grandpa and Grandma."

———. "Upgrade Your Hobby."

Kuplan, Louis. "California's New Program for the Aging."

Stevenson, George S. "Mental Hygiene and the Aged."

Stichman, Herman T. "The Aging and Public Housing."

Warren, Dorothy. "A Pilot Project in Vocational Training of the Older Worker."

DESMOND, THOMAS C. (chm.). *Growing with the Years.* Albany: New York State Joint Legislative Committee on Problems of the Aging, 1954.

Abrams, Albert J. "Job Engineering and Job Reassignment for the Older Worker in American Industry."

Barron, Milton L. "Attacking Prejudices Against the Aged."

Boas, Ernest P. "Financing Medical Care in the Later Years of Life."

Bortz, Edward L. "Medicine and the Older Patient."

Hobbs, G. Warfield. "Private Enterprise and the Older Worker."

Kilpatrick, William H. "Education for the Years of Retirement."

Kutash, Samuel B. "Personality Patterns of Old Age."

Lorge, Irving, and Tuckman, Jacob. "Attitudes of Junior and Senior High School Students toward Aging."

McCloskey, Mark A. "Education for Senior Citizens in New York City."

Pressey, Sidney L. "Employment Potentialities in Age, and Means for their Possible Increase."

Randall, Ollie A. "The Older Person in the Modern Family Structure."

Sargent, Dwight S. "An Employer Views the Older Worker."

DESMOND, THOMAS C. (chm.). *Making the Years Count.* Albany: New York State Joint Legislative Committee on Problems of the Aging, 1955.

Charnas, Theodore. "Care of the Senile."

Clague, Ewan. "The United States Department of Labor Moves Forward to Help the Older Worker."

Corsi, Edward. "How the Employment Service Can Help the 40-Plus Obtain Jobs."

Curran, Jean A. "The State University of New York and Our Older People."

Desmond, Thomas C. "Recreation in the Later Years."

Fuller, Carleton S. "Maine Committee on Aging."

Goldberg, Roshelle. "Wanted: More Facts, Fewer Opinions on Absenteeism."

Hart, Walter R. "Certification of Our Seniles."

McCarthy, Henry L. "Do Children Support Their Aged Parents?"

Mayo, Leonard W. "Chronic Disease and Our Aged."

Mulvey, Mrs. Gordon F. "Old Age in Rhode Island."

The Personnel Club of New York. "The Employer and the Older Worker."

Rausenbush, Carl, and Berman, A. J. "Occupational Patterns of Older Workers, 1940 and 1950."

Schottland, Charles I. "Have We Reached Our Goals in Social Security?"

Switzer, Mary E. "Issues in Vocational Rehabilitation."

Thresher, Irene K. "Massachusetts Takes Steps to Meet the Problems of Aging."

DESMOND, THOMAS C. (chm.). *New Channels for the Golden Years.* Albany: New York State Joint Legislative Committee on Problems of the Aging, 1956.

Abrams, Albert J. "Community Programs for the Aging."

Cohart, Edward M. "The Health of the Aged in New York City."

Gilbreth, Lillian N. "Employment of Older Workers."

Goodhart, Robert S. "Nutrition and the Aging."

Gorman, Mike. "The Major Need—Psychological Research on Senility."

Grauman, John V. "The Aged in the World: A Demographic Point of View."

Hoch, Paul H. "The Mentally Ill Aged."

Hollander, Louis. "Labor and the Forty-Plus."
Kaplan, H. Eliot. "Civil Service and the Older Worker."
Linden, Maurice E. "Public Policy and Mental Problems of the Aging."
Roosevelt, Eleanor. "Aging in the Modern World."
Tryon, Arthur H. "New Services for the Aging in Los Angeles."
DESMOND, THOMAS C. (chm.). *No Time to Grow Old.* Albany: New York State Joint Legislative Committee on Problems of the Aging, 1951.
Abrams, Albert J. "The States and the Aged."
————. "Unions and the Older Worker."
Hohaus, Reinhard A. "Group Life Insurance and the Employment of Older Workers."
Kelley, Kenneth J. "Massachusetts Law Against Age Discrimination in Employment."
Mead, Margaret. "Cultural Contexts of Aging."
Miller, Frieda S. "Older Workers and Older Women."
Moore, John H. "Action by the National Committee on Aging."
New York State Employment Service. "The Public Employment Service Views the Older Job Seeker."
DONAHUE, WILMA (ed.). *Housing the Aging.* Ann Arbor: University of Michigan Press, 1954.
Ashley, E. Everett, III. "Where and How Older People Live Today."
Donahue, Wilma. "Programs in Action."
————. "Where and How Older People Wish to Live."
Monroe, Robert T. "Needs and Problems."
Nicholson, Edna. "Nursing and Convalescent Homes."
Strunk, Norman. "Financing Homes for Owner Occupancy."
DONAHUE, WILMA (ed.). *Planning the Older Years.* Ann Arbor: University of Michigan Press, 1950.
Becker, Harry. "Labor's Stake in Employment and Retirement."
Convery, John M. "How Industry Looks at the Employment of Older People."
Curtis, Henry S. "Almshouses, Poorhouses, or Infirmaries."
Randall, Ollie A. "Living Arrangements to Meet the Needs of Older People."
Shock, Nathan W. "Broadening Horizons in Gerontology."
Woodbury, Coleman. "Current Housing Developments for Older People."
DONAHUE, WILMA (ed.). *Rehabilitation of the Older Worker.* Ann Arbor: University of Michigan Press, 1953.
Abrams, Albert J., and Tibbitts, Clark. "Summary and Challenge."
The Conference Board. "Conference Board Hearings on Employment and Placement."
The Conference Board. "Conference Board Hearings on Medical Aspects of Rehabilitation."
Thurston, John L. "All Are Needed."
DONAHUE, WILMA, and TIBBITTS, CLARK. (eds.). *Growing in the Older Years.* Ann Arbor: University of Michigan Press, 1951.
Dacso, Michael M. "Physical Restoration and the Older Person."
Felix, Robert H. "Mental Health in an Aging Population."
Frohlich, Moses M. "Changes in Emotional Needs with Aging."

Heyns, Roger W. "Group Development and the Education of Older People."

Mountin, Joseph W. "Community Health Services for Older People."

Soop, Everett J. "Proposed Programs in Education for an Aging Population."

Tibbitts, Clark. "National Aspects of an Aging Population."

Van Sant, Thomas A. "Responsibility of Education to the Older Adult."

FEDERAL SECURITY AGENCY. *Man and His Years.* Raleigh: Health Publications Institute, Inc., 1951.

Federal Security Agency. "Employment, Employability, and Rehabilitation."

Thurston, John L. "The Conference."

HURFF, GEORGE B. (ed.). *Economic Problems of Retirement.* Gainesville: University of Florida Press, 1954.

Clague, Ewan. "Do American Workers Save for Retirement?"

Cohen, Wilbur J. "Government Policy Concerning Private and Public Retirement Plans."

Hewitt, Edwin S. "Industrial Retirement Plans as Viewed by Management."

Hobbs, G. Warfield. "Investment Management for Pensioners and Pension Funds."

Kimball, Comer J. "Business Enterprises: Pitfalls as Well as Opportunities."

Kulp, C. Arthur. "Industrial Pensions: Strength and Limitations."

JONES, HAROLD E. (ed.). *Research on Aging.* (Pacific Coast Committee on Old Age Research.) New York: Social Science Research Council, 1950.

Bateson, Gregory. "Cultural Ideas About Aging."

Living in the Later Years. Proceedings of a Conference on Old Age. Huntington, W. Va.: Marshall College, 1950.

Tibbitts, Clark. "Social Implications of the Aged."

MACLACHLAN, JOHN M. (ed.). *Health in the Later Years.* Gainesville: University of Florida Press, 1953.

Ball, Robert M. "The Economic Situation of the Aged."

Burgess, Ernest W. "The Role of Sociology."

Lansing, Albert I. "Some Dynamic Aspects of Aging."

MEAD, MARGARET, and CALAS, NICHOLAS (eds.). *Primitive Heritage.* New York: Random House, Inc., 1953.

Freuchen, Peter. "Burying the Mother Alive in a Snow House."

Lejeune, Father Paul. "Killing the Old Mother."

NAFTALIN, ARTHUR, *et al.* *An Introduction to Social Science.* New York: J. B. Lippincott Co., 1953.

The Pilgrim Trust. "Men Without Work."

SMITH, T. LYNN (ed.). *Living in the Later Years.* Gainesville: University of Florida Press, 1952.

Alleger, D. E. "Retirement Farming in Duval County, Florida."

Beall, R. M. "Trailer Living."

Blodgett, Ralph H. "Finances for Living in the Later Years."

Churchill, Henry S., and Panel Contributions. "Some Random Thoughts on Housing the Aged."

Ferderber, Murray. "Physical Restoration of the Aged to Industry."

Hitt, Homer L. "America's Aged at Mid-Century."

Meredith, W. V. "Religious Activities of the Older Adult Group."

Reed, Charles E. "America Alerts Her Senior Citizens."

Tibbitts, Clark. "Cultural Activities in the Later Years."

SMITH, T. LYNN (ed.). *Problems of America's Aging Population.* Gainesville: University of Florida Press, 1951.

Dickinson, Frank G. "Economic Aspects of the Aging of Our Population."

Donahue, Wilma. "Psychological Aspects of Aging."

Smith, T. Lynn. "The Migration of the Aged."

Thompson, Warren. "Our Old People."

Webber, Irving L. "The Retired Population of a Florida Community."

Wolff, R. P. "Comments."

Other books

ALT, EDITH. *Standards of Care for Older People in Institutions.* 2 Parts. New York: The National Committee on the Aging of the National Social Welfare Assembly, 1953.

BOND, FLOYD A., *et al. Our Needy Aged.* New York: Henry Holt & Co., Inc., 1954.

BRECKINRIDGE, ELIZABETH. *Community Service for Older People.* Chicago: Wilcox and Follett Co., 1952.

———. *Effective Use of Older Workers.* Chicago: Follett Publishing Co., 1953.

BURGESS, ERNEST W., and LOCKE, HARVEY J. *The Family, from Institution to Companionship.* 2d ed. New York: American Book Co., 1953.

BURNS, EVELINE M. *The American Social Security System.* Boston: Houghton Mifflin Company, 1949.

CAVAN, RUTH S. *The Family.* New York: The Thomas Crowell Co., 1942.

———, *et al. Personal Adjustment in Old Age.* Chicago: Social Research Associates, 1941.

COLE, WILLIAM E., and DYNES, RUSSELL R. *Homes for the Homeless in Tennessee.* Knoxville: University of Tennessee Press, 1951.

CORSON, JOHN J., and McCONNELL, JOHN W. *Economic Needs of Older People.* New York: Twentieth Century Fund, 1956.

DOUGLAS, PAUL H. *Social Security in the United States.* New York: McGraw-Hill Book Co., Inc., 1936.

GAGLIARDO, DOMENICO. *American Social Insurance,* rev. ed. New York: Harper & Bros., 1955.

GILBERT, JEANNE. *Understanding Old Age.* New York: The Ronald Press Co., 1952.

HABER, WILLIAM, and COHEN, WILBUR J. *Readings in Social Security.* Englewood Cliffs, N.J.: Prentice-Hall, Inc., 1948.

HAVIGHURST, ROBERT J., and ALBRECHT, RUTH. *Older People.* New York: Longmans, Green & Co., Inc., 1953.

HOLT, JOHN B. *Under the Swastika.* Chapel Hill: University of North Carolina Press, 1936.

LANDIS, PAUL H. *Social Policies in the Making,* rev. ed. Boston: D. C. Heath & Co., 1952.

McGILL, DAN M. *Fundamentals of Private Pensions.* (Pension Research Council of the University of Pennsylvania.) Homewood, Illinois: Richard D. Irwin, Inc., 1955.

MEYER, HAROLD D. *Recreation for the Aging in North Carolina.* Chapel Hill: Institute for Research in Social Science, University of North Carolina, 1956.

———, and BRIGHTBILL, CHARLES K. *Community Recreation.* Boston: D. C. Heath & Co., 1948.

MENCHE, ARTHUR J. *Successful Pension Planning.* Englewood Cliffs, N.J.: Prentice-Hall, Inc., 1949.

MILLIS, HARRY A., and MONTGOMERY, ROYAL E. *Labor's Risk and Social Insurance.* New York: McGraw-Hill Book Co., Inc., 1938.

POLLAK, OTTO. *Social Adjustment in Old Age.* (Social Science Research Council, Bulletin 59.) New York: 1948.

SIMMONS, LEO W. *The Role of the Aged in Primitive Societies.* New Haven: Yale University Press, 1945.

STEINER, PETER O., and DORFMAN, ROBERT. *The Economic Status of the Aged.* Berkeley: University of California Press, 1957.

STERN, BERNARD J. *The Family, Past and Present.* New York: Appleton-Century-Crofts, Inc., 1938.

TUCKMAN, JACOB, and LORGE, IRVING. *Retirement and the Industrial Worker.* New York: Columbia University Press, 1953.

WILLIAMS, ARTHUR. *Recreation for the Aging.* New York: Association Press, 1953.

WOODS, JAMES H. *Helping Older People Enjoy Life.* New York: Harper & Bros., 1953.

Periodicals

ABRAMS, ALBERT J. "Barriers to Employment of Older Workers," *The Annals of The American Academy of Political and Social Science*, CCLXXIX (January, 1952), 62–71.

———. "Advisory Council on Social Security: Reports on Permanent and Total Disability Insurance and on Public Assistance," *Social Security Bulletin*, XI (July, 1948), 5–14.

ALBRECHT, RUTH. "The Social Roles of Old People," *Journal of Gerontology*, VI (April, 1951), 138–45.

BAGLEY, NANCY, and ODEN, MELITA. "The Maintenance of Intellectual Ability in Gifted Adults," *Journal of Gerontology*, X (January, 1955), 91–107.

BALL, ROBERT M. "What Contribution Rate for Old-Age and Survivors Insurance?" *Social Security Bulletin*, XII (July, 1949), 3–9.

BANCROFT, GERTRUDE. "Older Persons in the Labor Force," *The Annals of The American Academy of Political and Social Science*, CCLXXIX (January, 1952), 52–61.

BARKIN, SAMUEL. "Organized Labor Says No," *The Annals of The American Academy of Political and Social Science*, CCLXXIX (January, 1952), 77–80.

BARRON, MILTON L. "Minority Group Characteristics of the Aged in American Society," *Journal of Gerontology*, VIII (October, 1953), 477–82.

BEARD, BELLE B. "Are the Aged Ex-Family?" *Social Forces*, XXVII (March, 1949), 274–79.

BEVIS, LEONA. "Cleveland Combines Housing with an Old-Age Center," *Aging, XI* (May, 1954), 2–3.

BRITTON, JOSEPH H. "The Personal Adjustment of Retired School Teachers," *Journal of Gerontology, VIII* (July, 1953), 333–38.

BROWDER, F. BEATRICE. "Brief on Pensions and Other Benefits," *Management Record, XV* (January, 1953), 16–17.

———. "Funding a Pension Plan," *ibid.*, XI (November, 1949), 466–68 and 502–3.

BURGESS, ERNEST W. "Family Living in the Later Decades," *The Annals of The American Academy of Political and Social Science, CCLXXIX* (January, 1952), 106–14.

BURNS, ROBERT K. "Economic Aspects of Aging and Retirement," *American Journal of Sociology, LIX* (January, 1954), 384–90.

CARLSON, ANTON J., and STEIGLITZ, EDWARD J. "Psychological Changes in Aging," *The Annals of The American Academy of Political and Social Science, CCLXXIX* (January, 1952), 18–31.

CAVAN, RUTH S. "Family Life and Family Substitutes in Old Age," *American Sociological Review, XIV* (February, 1949), 71–83.

CHANDRASEKHAR, S. "The Hindu Joint Family," *Social Forces, XXI* (March, 1943), 327–33.

CHEN, CH'ENG K'UN. "Familism, the Foundation of Chinese Social Organization," *Social Forces, XXIII* (October, 1944), 50–59.

CLIZBE, WILMA. "Why Recreation Programs for the Aging?" *Recreation, XLVIII* (February, 1955), 59–60.

COCHRANE, CRAIG P. "Some Managements Prefer Flexibility," *The Annals of The American Academy of Political and Social Science, CCLXXIX* (January, 1952), 74–77.

COHANY, HARRY P. "Employment and Age in Union Contracts," *Monthly Labor Review, LXXIX* (December, 1956), 1403–07.

COHEN, WILBUR J. "Income Maintenance of the Aged," *The Annals of The American Academy of Political and Social Science, CCLXXIX* (January, 1952), 154–63.

———. "Social Security Act Amendments of 1952," *Social Security Bulletin, XV* (September, 1952), 3–9.

———, and CALHOON, JAMES L. "Social Security Legislation, January–June 1948: Legislative History and Background," *Social Security Bulletin, XI* (July, 1948), 3–14.

———, and MYERS, ROBERT J. "Social Security Act Amendments of 1950: A Summary and Legislative History," *Social Security Bulletin, XIII* (October, 1950), 3–14.

COUPER, W. J. "Present-Day Pension Problems," *Management Record, XI* (January, 1949), 4–6.

"Current Operating Statistics," *Social Security Bulletin, XIX* (October, 1956), 29.

"Current Operating Statistics," *Social Security Bulletin, XX* (April, 1957), 34.

DINKEL, ROBERT M. "Attitudes of Children Toward Supporting Aged Parents," *American Sociological Review, IX* (August, 1944), 370–79.

DONAHUE, WILMA. "Education's Role in Maintaining the Individual's Status," *The Annals of The American Academy of Political and Social Science, CCLXXIX* (January, 1952), 115–25.

DRAKE, JOSEPH T. "Some Factors Influencing Students' Attitudes toward Older People," *Social Forces*, XXXV (March, 1957), 266–71.

DUNCKEL, W. B. "Investment Problems in an Inflationary Period," *Management Record*, XIV (May, 1952), 176 and 205–7.

EPSTEIN, LENORE A. "Money Income Position of the Aged, 1948 to 1955," *Social Security Bulletin*, XIX (April, 1956), 7–14.

FARIS, ROBERT E. L. "Interaction of Generations and Family Stability," *American Sociological Review*, XII (April, 1947), 159–64.

GALLAGHER, O. R. "Looseness and Rigidity in Family Structure," *Social Forces*, XXXI (May, 1953), 332–39.

GILMAN, JAMES W. "Recreation's Public Relations," *Recreation*, XLIII (December, 1949), 429–33.

GLICK, PAUL C. "The Family Cycle," *American Sociological Review*, XII (April, 1947), 164–74.

———. "The Life Cycle of the Family," *Marriage and Family Living*, XVII (February, 1955), 3–9.

GOLDMAN, ROBERT P., and ROSS, SID. "How We Treat the Aged," Part I, *Parade* (February 14, 1954), 8–12.

———. Ibid., Part II (February 21, 1954), 8–10.

———. Ibid., Part III (February 28, 1954), 12–15.

———. Ibid., Part IV (March 7, 1954), 8–9.

HARLAN, WILLIAM H. "Community Adaptation to the Presence of Aged Persons: St. Petersburg, Florida," *American Journal of Sociology*, LIX (January, 1954), 332–46

HAUSER, PHILIP M. "Changes in the Labor-Force Participation of the Older Worker," *American Journal of Sociology*, LIX (January, 1954), 312–23.

HAVIGHURST, ROBERT J. "Flexibility and the Social Roles of the Retired," *American Journal of Sociology*, LIX (January, 1954), 309–11.

———. "Social and Psychological Needs of the Aging," *The Annals of The American Academy of Political and Social Science*, CCLXXIX (January, 1952), 11–17.

HOPE, STANLEY C. "Some Managements Say Yes," *The Annals of The American Academy of Political and Social Science*, CCLXXIX (January, 1952), 72–74.

"How to Ease Into Retirement," *Business Week*, No. 1335 (April 2, 1955), 66–69.

HOWELL, ROBERT J. "Sex Differences and Educational Influences on a Mental Deterioration Scale," *Journal of Gerontology*, X (April, 1955), 190–93.

HOYT, G. C. "The Life of the Retired in a Trailer Park," *American Journal of Sociology*, LIX (January, 1954), 361–70.

KAPLAN, OSCAR J. "Psychological Aspects of Aging," *The Annals of The American Academy of Political and Social Science*, CCLXXIX (January, 1952), 32–42.

KLEEMEIER, ROBERT W. "The Effect of a Work Program on Adjustment Attitudes in an Aged Population," *Journal of Gerontology*, VI (October, 1951), 372–79.

KRAUS, HERTA. "Housing Our Older Citizens," *The Annals of The American Academy of Political and Social Science*, CCLXXIX (January, 1952), 126–38.

KUPLAN, LOUIS. "California Moves Ahead," *Aging*, XVII (May, 1955), 1–3.

LEE, CHU-CHING. "China's Traditional Family," *American Sociological Review*, XVIII (June, 1953), 272–80.

LEVINE, HARRY A. "Community Programs for the Elderly," *The Annals of The American Academy of Political and Social Science*, CCLXXIX (January, 1952), 164–70.

LIVINGSTON, HELEN. "Public Retirement Systems," *State Government*, XXV (February, 1952), 39–44.

LOCKE, HARVEY J. "Mobility and Family Disorganization," *American Sociological Review*, V (August, 1940), 489–94.

MCCAMMON, DOROTHY. "Federal-State Conference on Aging," *Social Security Bulletin*, XIX (August, 1956), 3–7 and 31.

———. "Retirement Protection for State and Local Employees: Ten Years of Growth," *Social Security Bulletin*, XVI (May, 1953), 3–10 and 24.

"Man and His Years," *Aging*, August 6, 1951, p. 1.

MANLEY, CHARLES R., JR. "Migration of Older People," *American Journal of Sociology*, LIX (January, 1954), 324–31.

MICHELON, L. C. "The New Leisure Class," *American Journal of Sociology*, LIX (January, 1954), 371–78.

MITCHELL, JAMES P. "An Introductory Note," *Monthly Labor Review*, LXXIX (December, 1956), 1402.

MOBERY, D. O. "Church Membership and Personal Adjustment in Old Age," *Journal of Gerontology*, VIII (April, 1953), 207–11.

"Money Income Sources for Persons Aged 65 and Over, June, 1955," *Social Security Bulletin*, XVII (December, 1955), 22–23.

O'DELL, CHARLES R. "Employment Services for Older Workers," *The Annals of The American Academy of Political and Social Science*, CCLXXIX (January, 1952), 171–79.

OGDEN, JEAN, and OGDEN, JESS. "Sharing Community Responsibility," *The Annals of The American Academy of Political and Social Science*, CCLXXIX (January, 1952), 98–115.

"Old Hands Snub Pensions," *Business Week*, No. 1107 (November 18, 1950), 124–26.

PAYNE, STANLEY L. "The Cleveland Survey of Retired Men," *Personnel Psychology*, VI (Spring, 1953), 81–110.

PEMBERTON, ANNIE M. "Mobilization in North Carolina," *Aging*, August 6, 1951, 2–3.

RIESMAN, DAVID. "Some Clinical and Cultural Aspects of Aging," *American Journal of Sociology*, LIX (January, 1954), 379–83.

ROBINSON, RONALD I. "Beyond Retirement," *American Association of University Professors Bulletin*, XLI (Summer, 1955), 328–35.

ROWE, E. K., and PAYNE, T. H. "Pension Plans Under Collective Bargaining," Part I, *Monthly Labor Review*, LXXVI (March, 1953), 237–48.

———. *Ibid.*, Part II (May, 1953), 484–89.

"Ryderwood, Wash., A Thriving Community for Retired Workers," *Aging*, IX (January, 1954), 2–3.

SAKS, JOHN I. "Status in the Labor Market," *Monthly Labor Review*, LXXX (January, 1957), 15–21.

SCHOTTLAND, CHARLES I. "Social Security Amendments of 1956: A Summary and Legislative History," *Social Security Bulletin*, XIX (September, 1956), 5–15 and 31.

SCOTT, F. G. "Factors in the Personal Adjustment of Institutionalized and Non-institutionalized Aged," *American Sociological Review*, XX (October, 1955), 538–46.

SHOCK, NATHAN. "Older People and Their Potentialities for Gainful Employment," *Journal of Gerontology*, II (April, 1947), 95–100.

SIMMONS, LEO W. "Social Participation of the Aged in Different Cultures," *The Annals of The American Academy of Political and Social Science*, CCLXXIX (January, 1952), 43–51.

"Social Security in Review," *Social Security Bulletin*, II (August, 1939), 1–6.

"Social Security in Review: 1956 in Review," *Social Security Bulletin*, XX (March, 1957), 1–4.

"Social Security Legislation in 1947," *Social Security Bulletin*, X (September, 1947), 13–15.

"Social Security: The Why of the Tax Increase," *Time Magazine*, LXII, (December 28, 1953), 50.

STAHLER, ABRAHAM. "Job Problems and Their Solution," *Monthly Labor Review*, LXXX (January, 1957), 22–28.

STEAD, W. H. "Trends of Employment in Relation to the Problem of Aging," *Journal of Gerontology*, IV (October, 1949), 290–97.

STECKER, MARGARET L. "Beneficiaries Prefer to Work," *Social Security Bulletin*, XIV (January, 1951), 15–17.

STEVENS, DAVID H., and SPRINGER, VANCE G. "Maine Reviews Responsibility of Relatives," *Public Welfare*, VI (July, 1947), 122–25.

SWITZER, MARY E., and RUSK, HOWARD A. "Keeping Older People Fit for Participation," *The Annals of The American Academy of Political and Social Science*, CCLXXIX (January, 1952), 146–53.

"The Conference of State Commissions on Aging and Federal Agencies," *Aging*, III (January, 1953), 1–2.

TIBBITTS, CLARK. "Retirement Problems in American Society," *American Journal of Sociology*, LIX (January, 1954), 301–8.

———. "The Conference on Aging," *Social Security Bulletin*, XIII (October, 1950), 15–19.

TUCKMAN, JACOB, and LORGE, IRVING. "Attitudes Toward Older People," *Journal of Social Psychology*, XXXVII (May, 1953), 249–60.

———. "Attitudes Toward Older Workers," *Journal of Applied Psychology*, XXXVI (June, 1952), 149–53.

———. "The Attitudes of the Aged Toward Older Workers: for Institutionalized and Non-Institutionalized Adults," *Journal of Gerontology*, VII (October, 1952), 559–64.

———. "The Effect of Family Environment on Attitudes Toward Old People and the Older Worker," *Journal of Social Psychology*, XXXVIII (November, 1953), 207–18.

———. "The Effect of Institutionalization on Attitudes Toward Older People," *Journal of Abnormal and Social Psychology*, XLVII (April, 1952), 337–44.

———. " 'When Aging Begins' and Stereotypes About Aging," *Journal of Gerontology*, VIII (October, 1953), 489–92.

VANCE, RUPERT B. "The Ecology of Our Aging Population," *Social Forces*, XXXII (May, 1954), 330–35.

WAHLSTROM, CATHERINE L. "Los Angeles County Presents Its Senior Citizens Service Center," *Aging*, XXII (March, 1956), 1–2.

WEBBER, IRVING L. "Fact Finding in Florida," *Aging*, August 6, 1951, 5.

WENTWORTH, EDNA C. "Why Beneficiaries Retire," *Social Security Bulletin*, VIII (January, 1945), 16–20.

WOLFBEIN, SEYMOUR L. "Job Tenure of American Workers," *Monthly Labor Review*, LXXV (September, 1952), 257–62.

ZISMAN, JOSEPH. "Private Employee-Benefit Plans Today," *Social Security Bulletin*, XX (January, 1957), 8–12.

Government publications

COMMITTEE ON VETERANS' AFFAIRS. *Compensation or Pensions to Veterans or Their Dependents*, House Committee Print No. 173 (83d Cong., 1st sess.). Washington, D.C., 1953.

FEDERAL SECURITY AGENCY. *Illness and Health Services in an Aging Population*, Public Health Service Publication No. 170. Washington, D.C., 1952.

————. *Fact Book on Aging*. Washington, D.C., 1953.

————. *Your Social Security*. Washington, D.C., 1952.

Pensions in the United States, Report of the National Planning Association, Joint Committee Print (82d Cong., 2d sess.) Washington, D.C., 1952.

RAILROAD RETIREMENT BOARD. *Annual Report, 1950*. Washington, D.C., 1951.

Retirement Policies and the Railroad Retirement System, Report of the Joint Committee on Railroad Retirement, 2 Parts (83d Cong., 1st sess.) Washington, D.C., 1953.

UNITED STATES BUREAU OF THE CENSUS. *1950 Census of the Population, Characteristics of the Population*, II, Part I. Washington, D.C., 1953.

————. *Current Population Reports, Consumer Income*, Series P-60, No. 11, May, 1953.

————. *Ibid.*, Series P-60, No. 20, December, 1955.

————. *Ibid.*, Series P-60, No. 23, November, 1956.

————. *Current Population Reports, The Labor Force*, Series P-50, No. 34, September, 1951.

————. *Ibid.*, "Annual Report," Series P-58, No. 59. Washington, D.C., 1955.

————. *Current Population Reports, Marital Status and Family Status; 1956*, Series P-20, No. 72. December, 1956.

————. *Current Population Reports, Mobility of the Population of the United States: March 1955 to March 1956*, Series P-20, No. 73. March, 1957.

————. *Current Population Reports, Population Estimates*, Series P-25, No. 123. Washington, D.C., 1955.

UNITED STATES CIVIL SERVICE COMMISSION. *Your Retirement System*, Pamphlet 18. Washington, D.C., 1953.

UNITED STATES BUREAU OF LABOR STATISTICS. *Employment and Economic Status of Older Men and Women*, Bulletin No. 1092. Washington, D.C., 1952.

UNITED STATES CONGRESS, HOUSE OF REPRESENTATIVES. *Analysis of the Social Security System*, 6 Parts (Hearings Before a Sub-committee of the

Committee on Ways and Means, 83d Cong., 1st sess.). Washington, D.C., 1953–1954.
————. *The Historical Development of Veterans' Benefits in the United States* (The President's Commission on Veterans' Pensions, 84th Cong., 2d sess.). Washington, D.C., 1956.
UNITED STATES DEPARTMENT OF HEALTH, EDUCATION AND WELFARE. *Abridged Life Tables, 1954,* LXIV, No. 2. Washington, D.C., 1956.
————. *A Brief Report on the 1956 Amendments to the Social Security Law.* Washington, D.C., 1956.
————. *Annual Statistical Bulletin, 1955: Social Security Bulletin.* Washington, D.C., 1956.
————. *Education for a Long and Useful Life,* Publication of the Federal Security Agency, Bulletin No. 6. Washington, D.C., 1954.
————. *Your Social Security.* Washington, D.C., 1954.
UNITED STATES DEPARTMENT OF LABOR. *Pension Plans Under Collective Bargaining,* Bulletin No. 1147. Washington, D.C., 1953.
————. Bureau of Employment Security. *Pension Costs in Relation to the Hiring of Older Workers,* Bulletin No. E150. Washington, D.C., 1956.

Miscellaneous

CLOSE, KATHERINE. *Getting Ready to Retire,* Public Affairs Series, No. 182. New York: Public Affairs Committee, Inc., 1952.
COUNCIL OF STATE GOVERNMENTS. *The States and Their Older Citizens,* Chicago, 1955.
ESSO STANDARD OIL COMPANY. *Preparation for Retirement: A Study of Post-Employment Adjustment.*
INDUSTRIAL RELATIONS CENTER. *Making the Most of Maturity.* Chicago: The University of Chicago Press.
Pertinent Facts on 'Earning Opportunities for Mature Workers.' Ann Arbor: The University of Michigan Press, 1953.
SONQUIST, DAVID E. (ex. dir.). *Senior Achievement, Inc.* (Chicago).
WISCONSIN LEGISLATIVE COUNCIL. *Problems of the Aged,* Legislative Research Report, 2 vols. Madison, 1953.

Unpublished papers and speeches

CLAY, GAIL. "A Recreation Program for the Aging." Graduate Research Paper, University of Tennessee, 1955.
DRAKE, JOSEPH T. "The Retirement of Aged Farm Owners." Unpublished Ph.D. dissertation, University of North Carolina, 1950.
————. Unpublished Findings from "Some Factors Influencing Students' Attitudes Toward Older People." University of Tennessee, 1956.
HOFFMAN, OSCAR F. "Culture of the Centerville-Mosel Germans in Monitowoc and Sheboygan Counties, Wisconsin." Unpublished Ph.D. dissertation, University of North Carolina, 1942.
RHEA, B. BUFORD. "Central Tendencies in Age Categories." Unpublished Master's thesis, University of Tennessee, 1955.
SONQUIST, DAVID E. "The Effect of Work Activities on Health." Address delivered at the Ninth Annual Conference on Aging. Ann Arbor, July, 1956.

Name Index

415

Subject Index

Abandonment, 17, 18
Academic men, 305
Accidents
as cause of disability, 288; rates, 93
Action
criteria for local, 399–400; local, 398–99; local programs, 390; principles of local, 399–400; social, 390–91
Adjustment
factors in old-age, 321–24; level of, 323–24; product of past experience, 324; score, total, 323
Adoption, 338
Adult education; *see* Education, adult
Age
balance of employees, 88; chronological, 10, 46; denial of, 388; intellectual, 10; lower limits of, 47; prejudice in employment, 90–94; psychological, 10; relation to occupation, 46; sociological, 10
Aged
conservors of tradition, 12; discrimination against, 387, *see also* Barriers to employment and reemployment; dislike for, 388; employment of, 63–64, *see also* Employment; farmers, 68–69; geographic distribution of, 58–59; immobility of, 56–57; internal organs of, 282–83; level of intelligence of, 302; life expectancy in rural setting, 13, *see also* Life expectancy; living arrangements, 328–29, *see also* Homes; mental ability of, 302–7; migration of, 56–59, *see also* Migration, Mobility; migration as function of

economy, 59; minority, 378–83; new occupations, 71; nonproducers, 52; participators in culture, 386–87; physical characteristics of, 281–86; religious function of, 19; responsibility of relatives for, *see* Relative responsibility; self-attitudes, 10, 11, 381–82; skilled, 69–70; social category, 378; social participation, 389; unskilled labor, 69; ways of treating, 8
Aging
emotional characteristics of, 313–19; natural phenomenon, 286–87; normal process, 287; process of, 284–85; retardation of, 289–92; status modification, 314, *see also* Roles, Status position
Agricultural workers, 197, 201, 202, 212
Almshouses; *see* Poorhouses
Ancestor worship, 20
Annuities, 155; *see also* Private pension plans
Antagonism between generations, 94
Antidiscrimination laws, 116–17
Apartment housing, 338–42; *see also* Homes
characteristics of, 338–40; design of, 339–41
Apprenticeship, 86
Armed forces retirement
benefits under, 234–35; weakness of, 235
Assets, 154–55
ownership of as qualification, 176–77, *see also* Old-Age Assistance
Assistance; *see also* Old-Age Assistance
amount needed, 175; eligibility

421